Women's Rights and Religious Law

AF695027

The three Abrahamic faiths have dominated religious conversations for millennia but the relations between state and religion are in a constant state of flux. This relationship may be configured in a number of ways. Religious norms may be enforced by the state as part of a regime of personal law or, conversely, religious norms may be formally relegated to the private sphere but can be brought into the legal realm through the private acts of individuals. Enhanced recognition of religious tribunals or religious doctrines by civil courts may create a hybrid of these two models.

One of the major issues in the reconciliation of changing civic ideals with religious tenets is gender equality, and this is an ongoing challenge in both domestic and international affairs. Examining this conflict within the context of a range of issues including marriage and divorce, violence against women and children, and women's political participation, this collection brings together a discussion of the Abrahamic religions to examine the role of religion in the struggle for women's equality around the world. The book encompasses both theory and practical examples of how law can be used to negotiate between claims for gender equality and the right to religion. It engages with international and regional human rights norms and also national considerations within countries.

This book will be of great relevance to scholars and policy makers with an interest in law and religion, gender studies and human rights law.

Fareda Banda is a Law Professor at SOAS, UK where she teaches courses on Women's Rights, Family Law and Law and Society in Africa.

Lisa Fishbayn Joffe founded and directs the Project on Gender, Culture, Religion and the Law at the Hadassah-Brandeis Institute of Brandeis University, USA.

Law and Religion

The practice of religion by individuals and groups, the rise of religious diversity, and the fear of religious extremism, raise profound questions for the interaction between law and religion in society. The regulatory systems involved, the religious laws of secular government (national and international) and the religious laws of faith communities, are valuable tools for our understanding of the dynamics of mutual accommodation and the analysis and resolution of issues in such areas as: religious freedom; discrimination; the autonomy of religious organisations; doctrine, worship and religious symbols; the property and finances of religion; religion, education and public institutions; and religion, marriage and children. In this series, scholars at the forefront of law and religion contribute to the debates in this area. The books in the series are analytical with a key target audience of scholars and practitioners, including lawyers, religious leaders, and others with an interest in this rapidly developing discipline.

Series Editor: Professor Norman Doe, Director of the Centre for Law and Religion, Cardiff University, UK

Series Board:
Carmen Asiaín, Professor, University of Montevideo
Paul Babie, Associate Professor and Associate Dean, Adelaide Law School
Pieter Coertzen, Chairperson, Unit for the Study of Law and Religion, University of Stellenbosch
Alison Mawhinney, Reader, Bangor University
Michael John Perry, Senior Fellow, Center for the Study of Law and Religion, Emory University

Titles in this series include:

Religious Expression in the Workplace and the Contested Role of Law
Andrew Hambler

Religion in the British Constitution
Liberty and Limitation
Javier Oliva and Helen Hall

Forthcoming titles in this series include:

Constitutionalism, Democracy and Religious Freedom
To be Fully Human
Hans-Martien ten Napel

Women's Rights and Religious Law

Domestic and International Perspectives

Edited by
Fareda Banda and Lisa Fishbayn Joffe

Routledge
Taylor & Francis Group
LONDON AND NEW YORK

First published 2016 by Routledge

2 Park Square, Milton Park, Abingdon, Oxfordshire OX14 4RN
52 Vanderbilt Avenue, New York, NY 10017

Routledge is an imprint of the Taylor & Francis Group, an informa business

First issued in paperback 2020

Copyright © 2016 selection and editorial matter, Fareda Banda and Lisa Fishbayn Joffe; individual chapters, the contributors

The right of Fareda Banda and Lisa Fishbayn Joffe to be identified as the author of the editorial material, and of the authors for their individual chapters, has been asserted in accordance with sections 77 and 78 of the Copyright, Designs and Patents Act 1988.

All rights reserved. No part of this book may be reprinted or reproduced or utilised in any form or by any electronic, mechanical, or other means, now known or hereafter invented, including photocopying and recording, or in any information storage or retrieval system, without permission in writing from the publishers.

Notice:
Product or corporate names may be trademarks or registered trademarks, and are used only for identification and explanation without intent to infringe.

British Library Cataloguing in Publication Data
A catalogue record for this book is available from the British Library

Library of Congress Cataloguing in Publication Data
Women's rights and religious law : domestic and international perspectives / Edited by Fareda Banda and Lisa Fishbayn Joffe.
pages cm. – (Law and religion)
Includes bibliographical references and index.
ISBN 978-1-138-85597-7 (hbk) – ISBN 978-1-315-72000-5 (ebk)
1. Women–Legal status, laws, etc. 2. Women and religion. 3. Religious law and legislation. 4. Women's rights. I. Banda, Fareda, editor. II. Joffe, Lisa Fishbayn, editor.
K644.W67 2016
342.08'78–dc23 2015030060

ISBN: 978-1-138-85597-7 (hbk)
ISBN: 978-0-367-59707-8 (pbk)

Typeset in Galliard
by Out of House Publishing

Contents

List of contributors vii
Acknowledgements x

Introduction 1
FAREDA BANDA AND LISA FISHBAYN JOFFE

PART I
Gendered rites: gendered rights? 11

1 Culture, religion and women's international human rights 13
FRANCES RADAY

2 Marriage, religion and gender equality 32
JOHN EEKELAAR

3 Gender, religion and human rights in Africa 45
FAREDA BANDA

4 Implications of the Vatican commitment to complementarity for the equality of the sexes in public life 68
MARY ANNE CASE

PART II
Negotiating gender and religion in state law 89

5 Between strict constructionist sharī'ah and protecting young girls in contemporary Northern Nigeria: the case of child marriage (ijbār) 91
SARAH ELTANTAWI

6 Family law reform, spousal relations, and the "intentions of Islamic law" 108
CELENE IBRAHIM

7 The woes of WoW: the Women of the Wall as a religious social movement and as a metaphor 123
PNINA LAHAV

8 Religious coercion and violence against women: the case of Beit Shemesh 152
SIMA ZALCBERG BLOCK

PART III
Religious divorce in civil courts 177

9 The impact of "foreign law" bans on the struggle for women's equality under Jewish law in the United States of America 179
LISA FISHBAYN JOFFE

10 Systemic misunderstanding between rabbinical courts and civil courts: the perspective of an American rabbinical court judge 202
RABBI ARYEH KLAPPER

11 Socio-legal gendered remedies to *get* refusal: top down, bottom up 223
YAEL MACHTINGER

12 Challenging stereotypes: gender-sensitive imams and the resolution of family disputes in Montreal 255
ANNE SARIS

Select bibliography 278
Index 307

List of contributors

Fareda Banda was born and educated in Zimbabwe. She has two law degrees from the University of Zimbabwe and a doctorate from the University of Oxford. She is a Professor of Law at SOAS, University of London where she teaches family law, human rights of women and law and society in Africa. Her publications include *Women, Law and Human Rights: An African Perspective* (Hart, 2005) and a major report for the UN OHCHR entitled *Project on a Mechanism to Address Laws that Discriminate against Women* (2008). Her favourite activity is reading children's books with her two daughters, Azera and Shamiso.

Mary Anne Case is the Arnold I. Shure Professor of Law at the University of Chicago Law School. Her scholarship to date has concentrated on the regulation of sex, gender, and sexuality, and on the early history of feminism. Among her previous positions are Class of 1966 Research Professor at the University of Virginia, Visiting Professor at New York University, Bosch Public Policy Fellow at the American Academy in Berlin for the spring of 2004, Crane Fellow in Law and Public Affairs at Princeton University for the 2006–7 academic year, and Samuel Rubin Visiting Professor at Columbia Law School for the spring of 2013.

John Eekelaar taught family law at Pembroke College, Oxford from 1965 to 2005. He was a founder member of the International Society of Family Law, of which he was President from 1985–8, and founding co-editor of the *International Journal of Law, Policy and the Family.* He has written and researched widely in family law. He was elected a Fellow of the British Academy in 2001 and Distinguished Visiting Fellow by the New Zealand Law Foundation in 2005. His books include *Family Security and Family Breakdown* (1971), *Family Law and Social Policy* (1978, 1984), *Regulating Divorce* (1991) and *Family Law and Personal Life* (2006, 2007). He edited, with Rob George, the *Routledge Handbook of Family Law and Policy* (2014).

Sarah Eltantawi is a scholar of Islam who focuses on the social meaning of political transitions in Egypt and Nigeria. She is currently Assistant Professor of Comparative Religion at The Evergreen State College. Her book on *Sharīʻah Re-Implementation and the Stoning Punishment in*

Contemporary Northern Nigeria is under review with the University of California Press. She holds a PhD (2012) in the Study of Religion from Harvard University and has held postdoctoral fellowships at Brandeis University (2013), UC Berkeley (2013), and the Forum Transregionelle (EUME) at the Wissenschaftskolleg in Berlin (2013–2014).

Lisa Fishbayn Joffe directs the Project on Gender, Culture, Religion and the Law at the Hadassah-Brandeis Institute of Brandeis University. The mission of the GCRL Project is to produce scholarship that explores the tension between women's equality claims and religious laws. She is an expert on women's rights under Jewish family law and African customary law and on the intersection between secular and religious law. She has co-edited several anthologies, including *Gender, Religion and Family Law: Theorizing Conflicts Between Women's Rights and Cultural Traditions* (Brandeis University Press, 2012), and *The Polygamy Question* (Colorado University Press, 2015). Her next project, on women's rights and Jewish divorce, is entitled *Gender, Justice and Dialogue in Jewish Law*. She is editor of the Brandeis University Press Series on Gender, Culture, Religion and the Law and is co-founder of the Boston Agunah Taskforce, devoted to research, education and advocacy for women under Jewish family law.

Celene Ibrahim holds a joint appointment between Hebrew College and Andover Newton Theological School as Islamic Studies Scholar-in-Residence. She co-directs the Center for Inter-Religious and Communal Leadership Education, a premiere global hub for interreligious studies, and publishes widely on themes ranging from Muslim feminist theology and Qur'anic studies to Islamic leadership in North America.

Rabbi Aryeh Klapper is Dean of the Center for Modern Torah Leadership, Rosh Beit Midrash of its Summer Beit Midrash Program and a member of the Boston Beit Din. He previously served as Orthodox Adviser and Associate Director for Education at Harvard Hillel, as Talmud Curriculum Chair at Maimonides High School and as Instructor of Rabbinics and Medical Ethics at Gann Academy. Rabbi Klapper has published in *Tradition*, *Meorot*, *Dinei Yisrael*, *Beit Yitzchak* and other journals and has presented at numerous academic and community conferences. He is a popular lecturer who is consulted internationally on issues of Jewish law and whose work is cited regularly by both academic and traditional scholars.

Pnina Lahav is a Professor of Law at Boston University. She is a graduate of the Hebrew University in Jerusalem, Yale Law School and Boston University. She earned several prestigious fellowships including a Rockefeller Fellowship, a fellowship at the Center for Advanced Studies in the Behavioral Sciences at Stanford, CA and a fellowship at the Center for Advanced Studies at the Hebrew University in Jerusalem. She also served as a Religion Fellow at Boston University's School of Theology. Professor Lahav has published numerous articles on constitutional law, freedom of expression and women's rights. Most recently she has been working on the issue of women's prayers in Judaism and Islam. She is the author of the acclaimed biography *Judgment in Jerusalem: Chief Justice Simon Agranat and the Zionist Century* (University of California Press, 1997) and is the editor of several other volumes. Presently she is working on a biography of Golda Meir through the gender lens.

Yael Machtinger is a PhD Candidate in Socio-Legal Studies, at York University. Machtinger's Doctoral Dissertation, supported by the Social Sciences and Humanities Research Council Doctoral Fellowship, Ontario Graduate Scholarship, and Religion and Diversity Project Fellowship, explores overlapping Jewish and secular legal norms relying on socio-legal literatures on religion, identity and culture, as well as gender and storytelling. Applying social theory, religious feminism and legal pluralism, Machtinger examines women's narratives of being "chained" to a marriage. Machtinger is also an award-winning teaching assistant in the Law and Society Program.

Frances Raday, Professor of Law, is Director of the Concord Research Center for Integration of International Law in Israel at the Haim Striks Law School, COLMAN. She is a Special Rapporteur of the UN Human Rights Council, in the Expert Working Group on Discrimination Against Women, and previous Expert Member of the Committee for the Elimination of Discrimination Against Women. Raday is Professor Emerita, Hebrew University, Lieberman Chair for Labour Law; Honorary Professor, University College London; and Doctor Honoris, University of Copenhagen. She is the author of numerous academic books and articles on labour law, international human rights law and feminist legal theory.

Anne Saris is a law professor at UQAM (Lld). Her research focuses on the phenomenon of internormativity (overlapping of different norms such as religious norms, ethical norms and legal norms) and the analysis of state law and its agents from both an insider and outsider perspective. Her areas of expertise include women's human rights, civil law (legal personhood, legal status of the body faced with the advances in biotechnology, family law), and law and religion. Her research combines a theoretical (overlapping of normative orders) and ethnographic approach (empirical research on the different modes of alternative dispute resolution and conflict prevention used by Canadian Muslim women in family matters in Montreal for instance).

Sima Zalcberg Block holds a PhD from the Department of Sociology and Anthropology, Bar-Ilan University, and an MSc from the Faculty of Industrial and Management Engineering at the Technion – Israel Institute of Technology. She has been a researcher of social and policy issues at The Myers-JDC-Brookdale Institute in Jerusalem, for more than a decade. In recent years she has been writing and teaching on issues related to gender, religion, modern-Orthodox society and ultra-Orthodox society in Israel and the United States. Her most important publications deal with the hasidic women of the Toldot Aharon extremist sect.

Acknowledgements

The genesis of this book was a year-long collaboration between SOAS, University of London and the Hadassah-Brandeis Institute Project on Gender, Culture, Religion and the Law at Brandeis University on the theme of *Gender, Religion and Public Life*. It was funded by the British Council trans-Atlantic "Bridging Voices" programme through the auspices of the Henry Luce Foundation. The project explores the role of religion in the struggle for women's equality around the world. The Project on Gender, Culture, Religion and the Law was founded and is supported by a generous gift from the Sylvia Neil and Dan Fischel Philanthropic Fund.

Our thanks go to our colleague Lynn Welchman who worked with us to conceptualize the project. We owe an enormous debt of gratitude to John Eekelaar who has helped in every conceivable way. He read many versions of the book proposal and has been key in the editorial process of this book. Thank you John. We are also grateful for research and editorial assistance from Rachel Putterman, Zanefa Walsh and Morgan Flanagan-Folcarelli.

Our thanks are also due to all those who participated in the two workshops held at SOAS and Brandeis in 2014. Thank you also to Tim Rivera, formerly of the British Council. Fareda would like to acknowledge the kindness and hospitality of the NYU Law School community during her sabbatical in the autumn (fall) of 2014. We have had the good fortune to work with an encouraging editorial team at Routledge: Annabelle Harris, Mark Sapwell and Olivia Manley. Thank you!

It goes without saying that without our contributors, this book would not have been possible. To all, our heartfelt gratitude for your time and contributions.

Introduction

Fareda Banda and Lisa Fishbayn Joffe

Religion and gender equality: defining the conflict

Required, rejected, regulated or relegated to the private sphere, religion is everywhere. Far from fading into insignificance following developments in scientific knowledge and the move towards an ill-defined "modernity", religions and religious discourses have taken even greater hold in all societies. It is telling that regardless of the framing of the state's relationship to religion, secular or devout, religion still manages to permeate public discourse and to regulate behaviour.

The struggle for gender equality is a key challenge in both domestic and international affairs. Every generation confronts the desires of members of various religious communities to follow their religious belief. Recent decades have seen the rise of human rights as the global normative framework seeking to direct relations amongst citizens and most importantly between citizens and governments. The intersections of gender, religion and human rights often give rise to competing claims that are difficult to reconcile in both domestic and international policy. Indeed, the global re-turn to religion(s) is also linked to dislocation and the heightened sense of physical and economic insecurity being experienced around the world. Human rights activists cannot afford to dismiss it as irrelevant, and to label religious adherents as irrational. Scope and space for meaningful conversations have to be found. Academics and policy makers have addressed these conflicts in the context of a range of issues including marriage and divorce, reproductive decision-making, violence against women and children and women's political participation.

This anthology also seeks to move beyond the focus of most lawyers and human rights scholars on comparative textual analyses and attempts to reconcile religion with human rights norms. It does some of that. However, the emphasis is on empirically grounded studies of religious law as it is being conceived, practised and interpreted in various communities, from the Hausa in Northern Nigeria to Muslim families in Montreal and Jewish communities in Beit Shemesh, Boston and Toronto. These snapshots of the lived realities of communities of faith provide important insights into the ways in which religious principles are being manipulated, co-opted, contested and reshaped to meet the evolving challenges that face the societies under review.

Gender, religion and equality are the fault lines of the twenty-first century. While both the right to profess and practise a religion and the right to live one's life free from discrimination, including on grounds of sex, are recognized in international and regional human rights, gender and its interpretation is more contested. While many choose to elide sex and gender using the two as synonyms, others interpret gender in more complex ways, including as encompassing plural sexual identities and other intersections.[1] The meaning of gender changes depending on who is using the term and in what context. For our purposes, we adopt the definition of gender within the international human rights framework:

> The term "sex" here refers to biological differences between men and women. The term "gender" refers to socially constructed identities, attributes and roles for women and men and society's social and cultural meaning for these biological differences resulting in hierarchical relationships between women and men and in the distribution of power and rights favouring men and disadvantaging women. This social positioning of women and men is affected by political, economic, cultural, social, religious, ideological and environmental factors and can be changed by culture, society and community.[2]

Of course, a view of gender that is rooted in a binary, male-female, sex model, misses a crucial element of gender that is its pluralism. Under secular law in some segments of the world, gender is arguably becoming less relevant. Widening recognition of a broad and fluid range of gender identities that are not correlated with sexual morphology (at birth, or at all) and advanced technologies that enable gender transition make invocations of gender more complex and challenging.[3] In previous centuries, secular law had to be concerned with the gender of its subjects because so many rights and privileges were gender differentiated. One could not establish rights to inheritance or family property, the capacity to perpetrate or be the victim of a sexual assault, or entitlements to vote and serve in public office, without knowing the gender of the claimant. In the twenty-first century, few of these gender differentiated legal categories remain intact. The recognition of gender equality in family law, criminal law, property law and citizenship render these issues moot. With the advent of same-sex civil marriage, perhaps the most significant context in which the law must concern itself with gender has fallen away. It is equally true to say that the growing recognition of same sex marriage has had a negative impact on gender relations in parts of the global South. Religion and culture have been invoked to denounce the developments in the North and as a justification for not extending rights to minorities.

Gender has not faded away in the context of religion to the same extent. Many of the rites and rituals associated with religious practice continue to be gender differentiated. These include rights to enter and exit marriage, rights and duties related to public religious worship and interpretation of sacred texts and obligations under codes of modesty and honour. Accordingly, areas of life that are regulated by religious norms continue to generate conflicts between gender equality and religious doctrine and to provide occasions for working out how changing notions of appropriate gender relations can be meshed with religious values.

States seeking to ensure that there is no normative dissonance between their international and regional commitments and arguably also religious ethos, do so by entering reservations to international human rights treaties. It is telling that the instrument most consistently reserved with reference to religion is the UN Convention on the Elimination of all Forms of Discrimination against Women, 1979 (CEDAW).[4] Concluding observations to CEDAW show that, in practice, there is little to distinguish between states with reservations and those without in their implementation of the Convention.[5] In part this may be explained by the elision of religion and culture identified by Raday.[6] While the formal legal position is that these reservations breach article 27 of the Vienna Convention on the Law of Treaties, which provides that national law must yield to international obligations, religious observers would note that "God is bigger than any state" so that one's obligation is to obey one's religion rather than either state or international law.[7] This in turn puts women of faith in an invidious position.

The meaning of gender as a concept thus lies at the fault line between orthodox strands of the three Abrahamic religions and nominally secular, but no less passionate, human rights advocates. Because gender reflects the ways in which all societies construct social norms, it is everywhere: in religious and secular spaces; in majoritarian faiths as well as ones practised by minorities; and of course in the ways in which people of no faith regulate their lives.

Many explorations of these conflicts have tended to focus disproportionately on Muslim women or women in Islam. They tend to dwell on two issues: dress (usually women and the veil) and women in the family.[8] It is true that many of these works offer important and challenging critiques of the increasingly narrow and male-centric interpretations of the religion.[9] Still, the impression created by the apparent deluge of literature, and case law, on "Muslim women" is of Islam as a uniquely oppressive religion, not least in Europe. Even books that seek to engage with the ways in which religion in general treats women, tend, in the end, to focus their attention on Islam. Examples of this trend are widely available. In the provocatively titled *Does God Hate Women?*, in a chapter which anticipates a charge of Islamophobia, the authors note: "It is not as though we've ignored the sins of other religions...but there's no denying that Islam is leading the pack in the misogyny stakes."[10]

Muslim feminist theorists have noted how the motif of a need to rise to the defence of the "imperilled Muslim woman" has been taken up by both western feminists and critics of Islam. Disappointment with the progress of domestic feminist projects led to a turn outward towards gender conflicts that could be characterized as "spectacularly oppressive and easy to organize around" in other cultures.[11] Forced veiling and murder or maiming motivated by concerns of honour are offered as the paradigm context of conflict between religion and human rights in liberal democracies.[12] But focus only on these extreme situations masks the more mundane and widespread role that traditional religions, including but not limited to Islam, play in perpetuating gender inequality. Moral panics about the impact of "creeping Shariah law" in the West have both exaggerated the role Islamic law adjudication plays and under-estimated the extent to which civil family law is enmeshed with a range of religious family law rules that also discriminate against women. This book, therefore, explores themes of gender, religion, equality and human rights under the law in Judaism, Islam, Catholicism, Scientology, Rastafarianism and indigenous belief systems.[13]

The expanding scope of this analysis is the focus of Part 1, *Gendered rites: gendered rights?* In the first chapter, *Culture, religion and women's international human rights*, Frances Raday provides a detailed historical account, describing the genesis of human rights protections for women and challenging the notion of a fundamental inconsistency between a commitment to gender equality and respect for religious faith. Raday's focus is on the three Abrahamic faiths. While the human rights regime is indeed "the child of secularism", it is based on a consensus affirmed by adherents to many different religious traditions. She traces the ways in which human rights norms have come into conflict with a range of religiously justified practices and describes twenty-first-century reactions against the success of these initiatives. She argues that the recurrence of these rearguard actions in the context of women's human rights work requires strict vigilance and caution lest the impulse to accommodate religious claims allows these gains to be lost.

Minority religions are often ignored or lack recognition and thus protection from religious discrimination for the adherents. Parties to marriages conducted under the auspices of these religions may therefore lack the benefits and protections of civil marriage. John Eekelaar's chapter, *Marriage, religion and gender equality*, uses discussion of English doctrine on the validity of marriage ceremonies to explore the role of the state in recognizing and validating religious marriage. While the recent decision of the United Kingdom Supreme Court in *Hodkin v. Registrar General*[14] recognized Scientology as a religion, allowing their churches to be registered for performing legally recognized marriages, Eekelaar points out that the system of requiring religious marriages to be performed in registered buildings in order to acquire state recognition creates anomalies and seems in practice to have restricted the recognition of marriages by many British Muslims. Women in these marriages may be subject only to Islamic legal norms and have no access to English courts.

Fareda Banda's chapter, *Gender, religion and human rights in Africa*, looks at feminist academic accounts of the shift in the understanding of gender from pre-colonial to colonial African States. She highlights how the imposition of colonialism and the religions that followed led to changes in gender relations. Banda's chapter also considers the decision of the regional human rights body, the African Commission, to recognize the rituals and practices, which included worshipping of their ancestors, of the Endorois indigenous group in Kenya as falling within the purview of "religion". In looking at national case law on the exclusion of Rastafari boys and men, Banda relies on the insights of masculinity studies, which have highlighted the disproportionate gendered impact of the stereotyping of men as breadwinners. Denying a man the right to work because he wears his hair in dreadlocks is, in effect, a form of emasculation. Men are the families' agents for securing livelihoods of the group at large. Additionally, requiring Rastafari to cut off their dreadlocks, which they sincerely believe to be a central tenet of their religion, not only negates their ability to practise and manifest their religion, but also leads to what Yoshino has termed enforced covering.[15]

The chapter by Mary Anne Case, *Implications of the Vatican commitment to complementarity for the equality of the sexes in public life*, traces the evolution of the use of complementarity by the Holy See in its gender discourse. This work helps to explain how the well-documented clashes over the meaning of gender that occurred between religious leaders led by the Holy See and more secular minded delegates at the fourth women's conference held in Beijing in 1995 and subsequent developments came to be. She traces a significant transformation in Catholic understandings of the nature of gender to a twentieth-century reaction against progressive claims from women's ordination, acceptance of contraception and toleration of homosexuality. She describes the impact these notions of gender have had on the Vatican's intervention in international law and domestic policy across Europe. She concludes that analysis of Pope Francis's attitude towards questions of gender does not suggest a change in the Church's approach to these issues or its role in international gender discourse.

The Holy See is not alone. It often acts in alliance with the Organisation of Islamic Cooperation (OIC), a group of 57 states straddling four continents.[16] Member states of the Organisation of Islamic Cooperation decided to incorporate a religious view of gender within a human rights framework, which took Sharia as its starting point.[17] This is exemplified by the Cairo Declaration on Rights in Islam, which makes religion the foundation and interpretive lens through which human rights are to be understood.[18] The situation is complicated by the fact that many OIC member States have also ratified international human rights instruments requiring equality between men and women, some with, and others without reservations, thus creating normative dissonance and uncertainty. This has negative consequences for women.

Part II, *Negotiating gender and religion in state law* presents case studies in Islam and Judaism that explore how a range of political and cultural factors shape the expression, understanding and resolution of disputes regarding women's rights and religious law. In *Between strict constructionist sharī'ah and protecting young girls in contemporary Northern Nigeria: the case of child marriage* (*ijbār*), Sarah Eltantawi presents the results of her field-work in Northern Nigeria investigating initiatives to outlaw child marriage. Nigeria, a Federal state, has a plural legal system. Eltantawi examines the reasons why some in the North are demanding that Sharia law should apply in both criminal and family law cases. Although not permitted by legislation protecting the rights of children, there is a high rate of (girl) child marriage which some justified by reference to the Sharia. Eltantawi's interviews showed that many people, including Islamic legal authorities, were appalled at the abuse of young girls. Her chapter traces the political tensions and legal interpretive strategies used to avoid the application of religious law in order to protect girls from early marriage and the health and emotional suffering it entails. Her analysis demonstrates how women's rights advocates invoking international human rights norms have sought to use the re-interpretation of Sharia as an occasion to encourage egalitarian change.

Celene Ibrahim also explores the resources Islamic legal authorities have at their disposal to resolve tensions between women's equality claims and Islamic laws regarding marriage and divorce. In *Family law reform, spousal relations, and the "intentions of Islamic law"*, Ibrahim describes how the strategy of identifying the potentially egalitarian "higher principles" which underpin discriminatory Islamic law norms has led to progressive family law reform, such as the expansion of opportunities to use premarital contracts to opt out of default marital conditions and the changing role of custom in the development of marriage norms. She suggests how such links can legitimate suspect feminist reforms, rendering them "halal" in the eyes of pious interlocutors.

In *The woes of WoW: the Women of the Wall as a religious social movement and as a metaphor*, Pnina Lahav explores a long-standing dispute in Israel over the right of women to pray as they wish at the Western Wall in Jerusalem. The wall is believed to be a remnant of the second Temple, destroyed by the Romans in 70 CE. Jewish worship is permitted at the site only in accordance with Orthodox practices. The area is split into a large section reserved for men and a smaller one for women. Women are forbidden to bring a Torah scroll on to the site or to read from it. Since the 1990s, women have lobbied and sued for the right to do so. Lahav describes the history of this legal conflict, which culminated in a 2012 court decision denying the rabbinate of the Western Wall in Jerusalem the right to exclude women who seek to read from the Torah and pray wearing tallit. She considers how this struggle reflects changes in women's advocacy for equality under Jewish law and changes in relations between the Jewish communities inside and outside Israel.

The final chapter in this section, by Sima Zalcberg Block, deals with another religion-based conflict over women's access to public space in modern Israel. *Religious coercion and violence against women: the case of Beit Shemesh* explains how a series of incidents ranging from vandalism and verbal abuse to more severe physical violence have been deployed to terrorize women and exclude them from the public sphere. These activities are perpetrated by local groups of radical Haredim (ultra-Orthodox), who see themselves as soldiers in the struggle for modesty, responsible for maintaining the purity of the community. Block links these developments to the rising demographic and political power of ultra-Orthodox Jews in Israel, analyzes the meanings behind these activities, identifies and characterizes the perpetrators, and describes how women's advocates are using the civil courts to push back against perpetrators and the timid, putatively secular, local governments which enable them.

Those seeking to re-interpret religious law and resist religiously based extremism are not necessarily secular people who reject the value of religion or the roles it assigns to women. Many theorists, activists and plaintiffs in legal cases are women who define themselves as traditionally religious but want to use progressive modes of interpretation and resources provided by the civil law to encourage adoption of more egalitarian conceptions of the tradition they cherish. From within religion come feminisms that demand respect for the inherent equality and dignity of women's roles as mothers, homemakers and caregivers. These voices echo the approach of difference feminists, also called cultural feminists with their insistence on different strengths and spheres of influence, grounded in mutual respect. A complex reading of the role of gender and religion in human rights struggles requires attentiveness to the ways in which religious women exercise agency in seeking remedies for inequality under religious norms, which allow them to remain connected to cherished religious communities and religiously mandated roles rather than to purport to offer only the possibility of exit from them. In Part III of this book, *Religious divorce in civil courts*, four authors explore the ways in which women seek to express themselves and manage the relationship between civil and religious law in the North America. They bring to these analyses very different expertise and perspectives.

Lisa Fishbayn Joffe begins the section, in Chapter 9, *The impact of "foreign law" bans on the struggle for women's equality under Jewish law in the United States of America* with an analysis of a troubling trend in legislatures across the US. A moral panic about the possibility of enforcement of inegalitarian Shariah laws has led many states to pass bans on the enforcement of foreign or religious law contracts in American courts. Joffe points out, however, that while there are some cases involving the enforcement of Islamic law contracts in the US, there is a much more substantial history of secular enforcement of contracts to accept rabbinical court arbitration. In particular, she notes the ways in which Jewish family law has become enmeshed with civil family law in order to provide protections to women denied a divorce or subjected to extortion in order to win their freedom from their Jewish marriage. Joffe cautions that the success of these laws that purport to have been passed in the name of vulnerable women may have the perverse effect of undermining the best protections they have.

A Jewish divorce can only be granted by a husband to a wife. A woman whose husband is unable or unwilling to grant her a divorce is an *agunah, (*a chained woman), chained to a marriage that is dead in all but name. Aryeh Klapper is an ordained Orthodox rabbi who sits as a judge on the Beit Din of Greater Boston, a rabbinical court serving the New England area. He is part of a panel of judges that hears approximately 40 divorce cases a year. In Chapter 10, *Systemic misunderstanding between rabbinical courts and civil courts: the perspective of an American rabbinical court judge*, he reflects on the challenges of navigating a path between commitment to the integrity of Jewish law and the Jewish legal process and a commitment to alleviating women's disadvantage under Jewish laws of divorce. Klapper argues that the modern agunah situation is best understood as resulting from the interaction between the Jewish and secular legal systems, rather than a function of flaws within the system of Jewish law itself. His chapter provides a unique insight into the doctrine and procedure of an American rabbinical court, analysis of common case types and recommendations for women, their lawyers and advocates seeking to manage the relationship between these two regimes.

In Chapter 11, *Socio-legal gendered remedies to* get *refusal: top down, bottom up*, sociologist Yael Machtinger reports on her research based on interviews with women who seek divorce before the Va'ad Harabbonim of Toronto, the Orthodox rabbinical court which deals with divorce proceedings. Her findings suggest that, while rabbinical courts have a range of remedies at their disposal, skepticism about the validity of women's claims and concerns about the effectiveness of their own authority make them reluctant to deploy these tools on behalf of women. Machtinger evaluates the civil legal remedies available to Canadian Jewish women and concludes by promoting the creation of opportunities for women to go around the rabbinical courts to find venues, including through sharing their narratives with her, to tell their stories of disadvantage to create pressure on the Jewish community and its legal authorities to respond to their needs.

In the final chapter, *Challenging stereotypes: gender-sensitive imams and the resolution of family disputes in Montreal*, legal anthropologist Anne Saris conducts a similar inquiry into the role played by imams in the resolution of family law disputes among Muslims in Montreal. She also identifies the ways in which women and religious authorities knit together aspects of civil and religious law in order to resolve their family law matters. Many Muslim couples seek out informal private dispute prevention and resolution processes, such as those conducted by religious authorities. Saris interviewed imams and the women who appear before them, finding that the desire to use faith-based mediation is rooted not only to religious conviction but also in practical concerns regarding costs, enforceability and efficacy of orders in the eyes of Muslim majority nations to which the women may be connected or wish to travel to. The imams act as counsellors and advisors, rather than adjudicators, and see it as their role to both educate and protect the parties who come before them. They refer parties to the civil court to process divorce petitions and testify as expert witnesses in order to aid interpretation of Islamic prenuptial and marriage contracts.

Religion is not the only source of gender inequality but is a persistent force in its perpetuation. Despite the ongoing challenges, it is important not to fall into the trap of taking a dichotomous approach that sets gender equality against monolithic "religions". A more nuanced approach is needed. While often involved in the perpetuation of gender hierarchies, religion can also be a source for powerful critiques of other factors that impoverish women's lives. We hope that this book contributes to understanding the complex ways in which religious law is enmeshed in cultural and secular legal norms and how feminist advocacy has opened up the possibility for reform in a range of traditions.

Notes

1 S. Baden and A.M. Goetz, "Who Needs Sex When You Can Have Gender? Conflicting Discourses on Gender in Beijing" in C. Jackson and R. Pearson (eds), *Feminist Visions of Development: Gender Analysis and Policy*, London, Routledge, 1998; S. Kuovo, "The United Nations and Gender Mainstreaming: Limits and Possiblities" in D. Buss and A. Manji (eds), *International Law: Modern Feminist Approaches*, Oxford, Hart, 2005, 673–682; *Report of the UN Special Rapporteur on the promotion and protection of human rights and fundamental freedoms while countering terrorism*, UN Doc. A/64/211, 3 August 2009, para. 20.

2 UN Committee on the Elimination of Discrimination Against Women (CEDAW), *General Recommendation No. 28 on the Core Obligations of States Parties under Article 2 of the Convention on the Elimination of All Forms of Discrimination against Women*, CEDAW/C/GC/28, 16 December 2010, available at: www.refworld.org/docid/4d467ea72.html [accessed 9 April 2015], para. 5.

3 For example, a student theatre group at all women Mount Holyoke College in the US discontinued the annual performance of the play, *Vagina Monologues*, put on to commemorate violence against women because they felt, in part, that the equation of the identity of "woman" with those who had vaginas offered too narrow a conception of female identity, Kaitlin Mulhere, "Inclusive Dialogues", *Inside Higher Education*, January 21, 2015. At the time of this book going to press, there has been saturation coverage (in the Western media) of the *Vanity Fair* magazine featuring Caitlyn Jenner, a former Olympic athlete, who transitioned from male to female, *Vanity Fair*, July 2015. Elinor Burkett's thoughtful comments on responses to Jenner's transition, expressing concern that breaking the link between embodied female experiences and the feminist movement, gave rise to a lively debate, "What Makes a Woman", *New York Times*, June 6, 2015.

4 Convention on the Elimination of All Forms of Discrimination against Women, 1249 UNTS 13.

5 Jane Connors, "Article 28: Reservations" in Marsha Freeman, Christine Chinkin and Beate Rudolph (eds), *CEDAW: A Commentary*, Oxford, Oxford University Press, 2012, 565–595.

6 Frances Raday, "Culture, Religion and Gender" 2003, 1 *International Journal of Constitutional Law* 663–715. Raday, "Culture, Religion and CEDAW's Article 5 (a)" in H.B. Schopp-Schilling and C. Flinterman (eds), *The Circle of Empowerment: Twenty Five Years of the UN Committee on the Elimination of Discrimination against Women*, Feminist Press, 2007, 68–85. See also Raday in this volume.

7 Vienna Convention on the Law of Treaties, 1155 UNTS 331.

8 Dominick McGoldrick, *Human Rights and Religion: The Islamic Headscarf Debate in Europe*, Oxford, Hart, 2006; Z. Mir-Hosseini (ed), *Gender and Equality in Muslim Family Law: Justice and Ethics in the Islamic Legal Tradition*, London, IB Tauris, 2013.

9 Ziba Mir-Hosseini, Mulki Al-Sharmani and Jana Rumminger (eds), *Men in Charge? Rethinking Authority in Muslim Legal Tradition*, London, One World Publishing, 2014. Cf. A. Hidayatullah, *Feminist Edges of the Qu'ran*, Oxford, Oxford University Press, 2014.

10 Ophelia Benson and Jeremy Stangroom, *Does God Hate Women?*, London, Continuum, 2009, 151.

11 Lila Abu-Lughod, *Do Muslim Women Need Saving?*, Cambridge, Harvard University Press, 2013, 7–8.

12 Sherene Razack, *Casting Out: The Eviction of Muslims from Western Law and Politics*, Toronto, University of Toronto Press, 2008.

13 The UN Human Rights Committee notes: "The terms "belief" and "religion" are to be broadly construed. … It is not limited in its application to traditional religions or to religions and beliefs with institutional characteristics or practices analogous to those of traditional religions." The Committee is also clear that the terms protect "theistic, non-theistic and atheistic beliefs, as well as the right not to profess any religion or belief." CCPR General Comment No. 22: *Article 18 (Freedom of Thought, Conscience or Religion)*, adopted at the Forty-eighth Session of the Human Rights Committee on 30 July 1993, CCPR/C/21/Rev.1/Add.4, General Comment No. 22. (General Comments), para. 2.

14 *R (on the application of Hodkin and another) (Appellants) v. Registrar General of Births, Deaths and Marriages (Respondent)* [2013] UKSC 77.

15 Kenji Yoshino, *Covering: The Hidden Assault on our Civil Rights*, New York, Random, 2006.

16 Organisation of Islamic Cooperation, "About OIC", at: www.oic-oci.org/oicv2/paget/?p_id=52&p_ref=26&lan=en [visited on 8 April 2015].

17 Banda discusses the impact of this on women in Sudan in her chapter in this volume.

18 Cairo Declaration on Human Rights in Islam, 1990 UN GAOR, World Conf. on Hum. Rts., 4th Sess., Agenda Item 5, UN Doc. A/CONF.157/PC/62/Add.18, 1993. See A. Mayer, *Islam, Tradition and Politics*, Colorado, Westview, 1999, 97–130. See also the Arab Charter on Human Rights, 2004, reprinted in 2005, 12 Int'l Hum. Rts. Rep. 893, preamble and arts. 3(3), 43.

Part I

Gendered rites

Gendered rights?

1 Culture, religion and women's international human rights

*Frances Raday**

Women's rights are human rights

The human rights regime mandates equality for women in all spheres of life. It recognizes the entitlement of women to equal personhood. Indeed, the UN Convention on the Elimination of all Forms of Discrimination against Women (CEDAW) has entrenched women's entitlement to equality in an international bill of women's human rights, requiring equality de jure and de facto. The primacy of women's right to equality under CEDAW flows, as noted in the preamble to the Convention, from "fundamental human rights and from the dignity and worth of the human person... among the human rights treaties, the Convention takes an important place in bringing the female half of humanity into the focus of human rights concerns".[1]

CEDAW introduced a concept of equality for women, which has remained radical even after 35 years, in part as a result of its own language; and, in part because of its interpretation by the CEDAW Committee and other human rights agencies and experts. Embracing all aspects of women's lives – political, public, and diplomatic; economic, employment, and rural; educational; health; marriage and family; and protection against violence, including domestic violence – CEDAW requires states to ensure both formal, substantive and transformative equality for women. It is notable that the Convention is openly committed to the goal of eliminating discrimination against women and does not assume a guise of gender neutrality. In its preamble, the Convention recognizes that "extensive discrimination against women continues to exist [and creates] an obstacle to the participation of women, on equal terms with men, in the political, social, economic and cultural life of their countries". CEDAW also expresses awareness of the need for a change in the traditional roles of men and women to achieve full equality between them.[2]

The modern human rights regime is based on a concept of human rights, which is the child of secularism. The significance of this nexus between human rights and secularism is on the plane of state constitutionalism. It is not the dictation of a secular agenda for individual belief systems but rather the setting of a neutral normative context for the thriving of pluralistic beliefs within a state. The secular character of the normative system embodied in human rights doctrine is essential to its comprehension. All its premises, values, concepts and purposes relate to the homocentric world and to ways of thought freed from transcendentalist premises and from the jurisdiction of religious authority. The concept of human rights which was central to the political philosophy of the Enlightenment made a radical departure from prior conceptualization of governmental morality, which was based on the community needs rather than individual freedoms and entailed individual obligations rather than rights.[3] This change of morality paradigm was a corollary to the technological, social and economic transformation of the industrial revolution. The factory employment of labour and the urbanization of families produced individualistic, pluralistic frameworks, which were regulated not by the hegemony of feudal status and religious dogma but by contract, at both the level of political philosophy and of individual occupation.

The shift to human rights was endorsed in the Universal Declaration of Human Rights in 1948, as an essential third pillar of the international community's two-pillar quest for peace and development, after the ravages of two world wars that had laid waste to human life and dignity on a massive scale. In the General Assembly the vote was 48 in favor, none against, and eight abstentions. Thus there was global consensus to endorse a normative international regime of human rights, giving universal expression to the rights to which all human beings are inherently entitled.[4] Subsequently, the UDHR has been gradually transformed from its declaratory status into a binding regime of international human rights law, by nine human rights treaties, with core treaties ratified by almost all states. As was noted by many states during the adoption of the Universal Declaration of Human Rights, the values underpinning the Declaration reflected diverse cultures and societies. For example, Ecuador stated that the "multiplicity of origin of human rights could be detected in reading the articles of the Declaration". China stressed that Chinese thought had influenced the evolution of ideas of the rights of man in the Western world. Brazil stated that "the Declaration did not reflect the particular point of view of any one people or of any one group of peoples. Neither was it the expression of any particular political doctrine or philosophical system. It was the result of the intellectual and moral cooperation of a large number of nations; that explained its values and interest and also conferred upon it great moral authority".[5] There is thus empirical support for the idea that human rights are indeed universal and indivisible, as predicated by the Vienna Conference on Human Rights in 1993. Thus, human rights have both moral universality, since human rights are held universally by all persons "simply because one is a human being", and international normative universality, meaning that human rights are universally accepted by governments through their commitments and obligations under international human rights law.[6]

The rights protected in the UDHR are based on the foundations of dignity, liberty, equality, and brotherhood, and on the non-distinction principle which prohibits discrimination on grounds of race, colour, sex, language, religion, political or other opinion, national or social origin, property, birth or other status. The protected rights include rights of the individual to life, the prohibition of slavery and torture, rights to fair trial, privacy, family, freedom of movement, a nationality, to own property, to freedom of association, thought, conscience, and religion, and to social, economic, and cultural rights, including the right to work with just and favourable conditions, an adequate standard of living, education, and health-care and to participate in cultural life. Culminating in a change of political paradigm, expressed in the norms of twentieth-century international and constitutional law, human rights have rightly been called the "single most magnetic political idea of the contemporary time".[7]

Religious patriarchy

Although patriarchy is strongly rooted in all traditionalist cultures, I focus here on religious patriarchy for two reasons. The first is that at the level of both international law and constitutional laws of many states, there is a high level of deference to religious norms or values which is not bestowed on cultural norms or values. The second is that religion is commonly recognized as an institutionalized belief system and as such it has a concentrated form of social or political power which in culture is diffused. Attempts to define religion categorically have failed because of the diversity between and within religions. However, I will not follow or add to these attempts, as the scope of my enquiry in this paper is limited to the impact of the three monotheisms, Judaism, Christianity and Islam, on the human rights agenda. These three religions are self-defined by their holy books, which lay down the source of their beliefs and the ground rules for regulation of their communities.[8] Religion was a major stepping-stone on the path to human rights. Religion developed the concept of men and women as being in the image of God, thus imbuing human beings with a common spiritual identity. But it stopped short of the human rights paradigm. While religion contributed to the pre-history of human rights by recognizing the common core of spiritual humanity in all human beings, it did not confer entitlement to equal treatment in religious or social institutions; and, at best, it regarded the Other with compassion or pity and predicated the good deed of charity.

The Abrahamic religions thus prescribed human dignity, compassion and community solidarity. They are however also deeply rooted in gender hierarchy, reserving public power to men and sacralizing the patriarchal family. The three monotheistic religions impose patriarchal regimes that disadvantage women in different ways, as variations on a theme. It has often been said that the religions all recognize the full humanity of woman. Woman was created in *imago dei (bezelem)*. Yet, notwithstanding acceptance of women's equal personhood as a spiritual matter, monotheistic religions have promulgated patriarchal gender relations.

Under the doctrine of all three monotheisms women have been excluded from public power and subjected to male domination within the family or in their sexual and reproductive lives.[9] The patriarchal domination of women is deeply rooted in the monotheistic conceptualization of womanhood. The Old Testament, the source book of the three monotheistic religions, forcefully frames gender as a patriarchal construct in the story of creation: "And Adam said: This is now bone of my bones and flesh of my flesh; she shall be called Woman because she was taken out of Man".[10] This story constitutes a paradigmatic expression of the "otherness" of woman,[11] as recounted by Simone de Beauvoir.[12] In the Old Testament, the punishment of womankind at the exile from the garden of Eden is quite explicitly patriarchal: "Unto the woman He said, I will greatly multiply thy sorrow and thy conception; in sorrow thou shalt bring forth children; and thy desire shall be to thy husband, *and he shall rule over thee*".[13] This patriarchal version of the story of creation and original sin was absorbed into Christianity in the guise of the original sin and, while not included in the Qur'an, was later included in Islamic tradition.[14] It will be said that there was an alternative version of creation in which "man and woman created He them". This version, however, does not correct the asymmetry as there is no equivalent matriarchal version to balance the story of Adam and Eve, no ongoing application of the egalitarian spirit and, indeed, the fate of the egalitarian version was to produce the she-witch Lillit and not an equal partnership between women and men. As commented by Elizabeth Cady Stanton in the time of the nineteenth-century Seneca Falls Convention, "To no form of religion is woman indebted for one impulse of freedom, as all alike have taught her inferiority and subjection".[15]

Women have been excluded from the hierarchies of canonical power and up until today, in almost all the branches of the three monotheistic religions, women are not eligible for positions of religious authority. The Special Rapporteur on freedom of religion has acknowledged: "It is a well-known fact that in many (not all) denominations, positions of religious authority, such as bishop, imam, preacher, priest, rabbi or reverend, remain reserved to males, a state of affairs that collides with the principle of equality between men and women as established in international human rights law".[16]

Under religious norms of all three monotheisms, women are not entitled to equality in family law and relations. In Judaism, the consequences of a spouse's refusal to agree to give a divorce are much more restrictive for a woman who wishes to establish a new family than for a man. In some branches of Christianity, a woman's right to reproductive choice is restricted by opposition to contraception and her right to life, health or choice is negated by strict prohibitions of abortion. Under Islam, women are not entitled to equal rights in marriage age, guardianship, custody of children, rights to remarry after divorce or widowhood or division of matrimonial property and in their freedom to participate, fully and autonomously, in public life, whether political, social, economic or cultural. Furthermore, much harsher penalties are imposed on women than on men for adultery, which is widely defined as any act of intercourse with a man who is not the woman's husband, and may thus include intercourse of an unmarried woman or an act of rape. Under the inheritance laws of all three monotheisms, men have a preferred status.[17]

Hermeneutic reform is possible and, in each of the three religions, there are dissenting voices that claim equal religious personhood for women. In both Christianity and Judaism, there were reform movements in Europe at the time of the Enlightenment, which tended to close the gap with human rights doctrine. There are also interpretations of Catholicism[18] and Islam,[19] issued by individual religious leaders, which are more consonant with a human rights approach. However, this hermeneutical endeavour is, in the best of cases, far from complete and it is demonstratively absent in those cases where the religious community is asserting a defence against human rights claims. Religious sects provide "a haven against social and cultural change, … defend the eroding authority of the family, sacralize ethnic loyalties, provide barriers against rationalized educational techniques and scientific explanations of nature".[20]

The traditionalist regimes of the orthodox religions pose an ideological and legal challenge to the human rights regime's clear mandate of equality for women. Traditionalist religious dogma designates women and men as "complements whose duties, though different, are socially comparable".[21] It propagates, at best, compassion to women but certainly not equal entitlement. This conceptualization of the role of women is in direct conflict with CEDAW's requirement of formal and substantive equality for women on the same terms as men and its call for transformative redistribution of resources and power between women and men. It is the religions themselves that have, in the human rights era, self-identified as the core of resistance to women's equality, as is clearly evidenced in states' reservations to CEDAW, which are almost exclusively addressed to the requirement of deference to religion.[22]

Currently, at both the international and at the state political level, institutionalized religious orthodoxy opposes women's modern right to equality and calls for the restoration of traditional values, forming a hard core of political resistance to equality for women. In states which allow the application of patriarchal religious law whether in hegemonic theocracies or in plural legal systems, women's right to equality is compromised, in both the private (family) and the public (political and economic) spheres of their lives.

Women's human rights to equality must prevail in the clash with religious patriarchy

The Vienna Declaration and Programme of Action in 1993, prioritized and guaranteed women's rights to equality in all contexts, including where discrimination derives from religion relying on Articles 5 and 18 of the Universal Declaration. Article 5 states that:

> All human rights are universal, indivisible and interrelated. The international community must treat human rights globally in a fair and equal manner, on the same footing, and with the same emphasis. While the significance of national and regional particularities and various historical, cultural and religious backgrounds must be borne in mind, it is the duty of States, regardless of their political, economic and cultural systems, to promote and protect all human rights and fundamental freedoms.

Article 18 also states the following:

> The human rights of women and the girl-child are an inalienable, integral and indivisible part of universal human rights. The full and equal participation of women in political, civil, economic, social and cultural life, at the national, regional and international levels, and the eradication of all forms of discrimination on grounds of sex are priority objectives of the international community.[23]

In 1980, CEDAW's Article 5 came into force, and expressly regulated the clash between culture and gender equality. Article 5 is regarded as cardinal to the normative regulation of the intersection of freedom of religion and women's human rights. The clash between cultural, customary and all other practices, including religious practices, on the one hand, and women's right to equality, on the other, is expressly regulated in Article 5(a) of CEDAW, which requires state parties to take all appropriate measures "to modify the social and cultural patterns of conduct of men and women, with a view to achieving the elimination of prejudices and customary and all other practices which are based on the idea of the inferiority or the superiority of either of the sexes or on stereotyped roles for men and women".

Furthermore, the interpretation of the ICCPR by the Human Rights Committee in General Comment 28 (para. 5) is clear in that where a clash occurs, for example, in Art. 27 ICCPR between the right of ethnic, religious or linguistic minorities to enjoy their own culture, to profess and practise their own religion, or to use their own language, with other human rights, as it does in the case of women's rights, it is the right to equality which prevails:

> Inequality in the enjoyment of rights by women throughout the world is deeply embedded in tradition, history and culture, including religious attitudes… States parties should ensure that traditional, historical, religious or cultural attitudes are not used to justify violations of women's right to equality before the law and to equal enjoyment of all Covenant rights … The rights which persons belonging to minorities enjoy under article 27 of the Covenant in respect of their language, culture and

> religion do not authorize any State, group or person to violate the right to equal enjoyment by women of any Covenant rights, including the right to equal protection of the law.[24]

The Human Rights Council's Special Rapporteur on freedom of religion and the Special Rapporteur in the field of cultural rights have repeatedly stated that freedom of religion cannot be relied on to justify discrimination against women. In 2005, Special Rapporteur on Religion Asma Jahangir identified the many ways in which religions rationalize and legitimize discrimination against women, remarking that "the longer we postpone tackling it the greater the risk of embedding gender inequalities in the field of human rights,"[25] and in 2009, Special Rapporteur on Religion Abdelfattah Amor emphasized that discrimination against women cannot be tolerated on the grounds of freedom of religion:

> Women's rights, even when involving cultural and religious aspects, form part of the fundamental rights of the individual.... universality arises out of a concept which is at the very root of human rights: the consubstantial and inherent dignity of the person.... When women's dignity is infringed, there is no place for sovereignty or for cultural or religious distinctions. This fundamental concept of dignity is the common denominator among all individuals, peoples, nations and States, irrespective of their cultural or religious differences or stage of development.[26]

Special Rapporteur on Freedom of Religion Heiner Bielefeldt highlights that gender-based discrimination has at least two distinct dimensions in the context of religion:

> On the one hand, women belonging to discriminated communities often suffer at the same time from gender-based discrimination, for example if a woman is discriminated against in the labour market because she has decided, from a religious conviction, to wear a religious symbol. On the other hand, religious traditions or interpretations of religious doctrine sometimes appear to justify, or even call for, discrimination against women. In this context, the Special Rapporteur would like to reiterate that it can no longer be taboo to demand that women's rights take priority over intolerant beliefs that are used to justify gender discrimination.[27]

The Special Rapporteur in the field of cultural rights includes religion within her analysis of cultural practices:

> Nevertheless, many practices and norms that discriminate against women are justified by reference to culture, religion and tradition, leading experts to conclude that "no social group has suffered greater violation of its human

> rights in the name of culture than women" and that it is "inconceivable" that a number of such practices "would be justified if they were predicated upon another protected classification such as race".[28]
>
> The justification for direct discrimination against women by reference to culture or religion – which, according to information provided to the Special Rapporteur, continues – should be eliminated.[29]

However, at the international level, an ideological challenge has been directed by strong religious lobbying against the universality of international human rights. In 2010, the member states of the HRC (Human Rights Council), voted by a majority to support a resolution proposed by Russia and the Organisation of Islamic Cooperation calling for reinterpretation of human rights in accordance with traditional values.[30] This resolution was strongly criticized as undermining women's hard won right to equality. Special procedures mandate-holders, treaty bodies and OHCHR have published many works that emphasize the importance of ensuring that "traditional values" are not elevated above universal human rights standards. They highlighted the use of such terms to justify the marginalization of minority groups and for maintaining gender-based inequalities, discrimination and violence, and the corresponding need to situate these terms within a human rights context.[31]

In 2012, the HRC Advisory Committee presented its preliminary study on promoting human rights and fundamental freedoms through a better understanding of traditional values of humankind. In a way which clearly pre-empted a retrogressive application of traditional values to the human rights regime, the Committee asserted the following:

> The international community has reached consensus that each and every person, regardless of that person's socio-economic, cultural and personal identity, belief, political views or physical location is entitled to all the rights and freedoms recognized in the Universal Declaration of Human Rights. Under international law, all States, regardless of their political, economic and cultural systems, have the responsibility to promote and protect all human rights and fundamental freedoms for all. Dignity is inherent to the human person, and is inextricably related to equality and non-discrimination. Freedom is the sphere of the individual's actions, beliefs and opinions, free from State interference…In order to build consensus and ensure that a better understanding and appreciation of such traditional values can contribute to the promotion and protection of human rights, the distinctive features of different cultures and religions should be accorded respect, so long as these are consistent with international human rights standards.[32]

Responding to the study, the International Commission of Jurists and International Service for Human Rights, non-governmental organizations in special consultative status, issued a joint written statement:

> While we believe that the revised report does an admirable job of responding to the mandate, we wish to reiterate our concern about Resolution 16/3. We believe that emphasising traditional values could lead to undermining the universality of human rights. International human rights law must take primacy over traditional values, and not the other way around. For these reasons, we believe that any future work on this issue should be recast as the implementation of human rights in diverse traditional and cultural contexts.[33]

In 2014, the Human Rights Council decided to convene a panel discussion on the protection of the family, "reaffirming that the family is the natural and fundamental group unit of society and is entitled to protection by society and the State [...]". The sponsors of the resolution expressed their cardinal motive as being the protection of the family so that it can fully assume its responsibilities within the community. The resolution[34] was passed by 26 votes to 14, with 6 abstentions. The concept note for the work of the panel emphasized the role that families play in development, expounding on the role of the family in "fostering social development, its strong force for social cohesion and integration, and...its primary responsibility for the nurturing, guidance, and protection of children". It envisages "designing, implementing and promoting family-friendly policies and services, such as...campaigns to sensitize public opinion on equal sharing of employment and family responsibilities between women and men... as well as developing the capacity to monitor the impact of social and economic decisions and actions on the well-being of families, on the status of women within families, and on the ability of families to meet the basic needs of their members".[35] It emphasised the structural problems of care responsibilities and the need not only to redistribute them between women and men, as required by CEDAW, but also between family and state, by provision of a protection floor for care services, which is a welcome departure and is in accordance with the recommendation of the Expert Group on DAW (Discrimination Against Women) to the Council on 16 June 2014. However, the resolution and the concept note raise grave concerns as they fail to reiterate women's right to equality in the family, referring rather to women's status within families.

The author of this article, as Chair-Rapporteur of the Expert Group on Discrimination against Women, sent a letter to the President of the Council requesting his intervention, pointing out that these documents produced a retrogression in women's human right to equality in the family, guaranteed under the 1948 UDHR, the 1966 ICCPR and the 1980 CEDAW Article 16:

> Silence in the Human Rights Council on the right of women to equality in the family is not innocuous. It is a denial of the crucial 20th century gain of women's right to equality within families, which had constituted a dramatic departure from the prior cultural and religious norm of the patriarchal family.

In the key messages from a Human Rights Council panel discussion on 15 September 2014, an important human rights move was made in acceptance that diversity of families should be respected and that violence within the family should be countered. However, the right of women to equality in the family was still not mentioned. In a statement made on 30 September 2014, the Special Procedures mandate holders took note of the developments in the Human Rights Council on the "protection of the family" and expressed concern regarding the fact that there had been no reference to women's and girls' right to equality within the family. The statement called on the Human Rights Council to ensure that in all future resolutions, concept notes and reports on the issue of the family, the right to equality between women and men, as well as between girls and boys, within the family must be explicitly included as a fundamental human right.[36]

Prohibition of cultural and religious practices that discriminate against women and girls

The experts of the Treaty Bodies, UN Women, the Expert Group on DAW of the Human Rights Council and hundreds of civil society organisations worldwide have called for the elimination of cultural practices which discriminate against women and girls, whether or not based on religious belief, and have asked governments to take measures to prevent such practices. These practices include child marriage; forced marriage; stoning, lashing or otherwise punishing for adultery; polygamy;[37] inequality in property rights during a marriage or after its dissolution; unequal rights of inheritance; prohibition of contraception; prohibition of abortion, at least in cases where the pregnancy threatens the woman's life or health, where the pregnancy is the result of rape or incest or where the fetus is not viable or suffers from a lethal defect; FGM; and restrictions on freedom of movement or freedom of occupation. Progress is being made steadily at the international level in recognizing the urgency of eliminating these practices.

The UN Resolution on Child, Early and Forced Marriage was adopted in 2013, a landmark resolution calling for a ban on child marriage.[38] This resolution marks a major breakthrough in the stop child marriage campaign, which a global partnership of over 400 civil society organizations has been leading. Every year, an estimated 15 million girls aged under 18 are married worldwide. In the developing world, one in nine girls is married before her 15th birthday and some child brides are as young as eight or nine. These girls are robbed of their childhood, deprived of their right to education, at great risk of domestic violence and marital rape, and also exposed to the problem of early pregnancy with its high level of threat to their health or life. Indeed, child marriage can often operate as a shield behind which slavery and slavery-like practices occur with apparent impunity.[39]

The HRC Expert Group on discrimination against women in law and practice issued a call to governments to repeal laws criminalizing adultery.

The Group notes that the enforcement of such laws leads to discrimination and violence against women in law and in practice.[40] The call by the Working Group is path-breaking. In many countries around the world, adultery continues to be a crime punishable by severe penalties, including fines, arbitrary detention, imprisonment, flogging and, in the most extreme instances, death sentences by stoning. Adultery laws have usually been drafted and almost always implemented in a manner prejudicial to women. Maintaining adultery as a criminal offence – even when, on the face of it, it applies to both women and men – means in practice that women will continue to face extreme vulnerabilities, and violation of their human rights to dignity, privacy and equality, given continuing discrimination and inequalities faced by women. The Group recognized that adultery may constitute a matrimonial offence bearing legal consequences in divorce cases, the custody of children or the denial of alimony amongst others. However, it should not be a criminal offence and must not be punishable by fine, imprisonment or death.[41]

The CEDAW Committee has long held that polygamous marriage contravenes a woman's right to equality with men and can have such serious emotional and financial consequences for her and her dependants that such marriages ought to be discouraged and prohibited.[42] In 2015, the Indian Supreme Court, reversing its earlier rulings, ruled that a Muslim's fundamental right to profess Islam did not include practising polygamy. What was protected under Article 25 (right to practise and propagate any religion) was the religious faith and not a practice which may run counter to public order, health or morality. Polygamy was not an integral part of religion and monogamy was a reform within the power of the state under Article 25, and the practice of polygamy did not acquire sanction of religion simply because it was permitted.[43]

Women's rights to equality in property, including matrimonial property, land rights and inheritance have been propounded in recent recommendations of UN expert bodies. UN Women in an extensive report in 2013 documented the way in which deprivation of the right to land ownership in some legal or customary systems has resulted in the denial of sustenance for women and their children and exposure to extreme poverty. The CEDAW Committee in GC (General Recommendation) 29 laid down the right of women to equality in property rights for the duration of marriage and after its dissolution and also, although CEDAW Article 16 did not expressly refer to inheritance rights, in intestate succession.[44] The GC adds that reservations to Article 16, whether lodged for national, traditional, religious or cultural reasons, are incompatible with the Convention and cannot justify violations of women's right to equality.[45]

There is growing pressure by international human rights experts to recognize that prohibition of contraception or abortion may amount to a violation of women's human rights. In some countries, access to abortion is absolutely prohibited, even where there is a threat to the life or health of the pregnant woman or girl or where the pregnancy resulted from rape or the fetus is not viable or has a lethal defect.

Although the human rights treaties incorporated women's right to health care without discrimination and to family planning, which clearly includes contraception, they do not explicitly refer to abortion. Article 12 of the International Covenant on Economic, Social and Cultural Rights obliges states parties to ensure that measures are taken to ensure that access to health services is available to everyone, especially the most vulnerable or marginalized sections of the population, without discrimination. Article 12 of CEDAW calls on states to ensure, on a basis of equality of men and women, access to health care services, including those related to family planning; and Article 16(1) of the Convention further holds that states should take all appropriate measures to ensure, on a basis of equality of men and women, the same rights to decide freely and responsibly on the number and spacing of their children and to have access to the information, education and means to enable them to exercise these rights. On this basis, statements made by ESCR and CEDAW Committees have, in the past, only indirectly asserted the "right to control one's health and body, including sexual and reproductive freedom", inferring the right at least to therapeutic abortions without naming abortion as such.[46] The Special Rapporteur on violence against women has emphasized that acts deliberately restraining women from using contraception or from having an abortion constitute violence against women by subjecting women to excessive pregnancies and childbearing against their will, resulting in increased and preventable risks of maternal mortality and morbidity.[47] Government failure to take positive measures to ensure access to appropriate health-care services that enable women to safely deliver their infants as well as to safely abort unwanted pregnancies may constitute a violation of a woman's right to life, in addition to the violation of her reproductive rights. Furthermore, government failure to provide conditions that enable women to control their fertility and childbearing, as well as to bring voluntary pregnancies to term, constitutes a violation of a woman's right to security of the person.[48] Additionally, the Special Rapporteur on the right of everyone to the enjoyment of the highest attainable standard of physical and mental health stated that the criminalization of sexual and reproductive health services for women generates and perpetuates stigma; restricts their ability to make full use of available sexual and reproductive health-care goods, services and information; denies their full participation in society; hinders their access to healthcare services; and disempowers women. Furthermore, criminalization of abortion results in negative physical and mental health outcomes for women and may increase the likelihood of women seeking clandestine abortions.[49] The need to allow rape survivors access to a safe abortion procedure has been recognized in situations of post-conflict by the Commission on the Status of Women[50] and as a general matter by the Special Rapporteur on torture and other cruel, inhuman or degrading treatment. The Special Rapporteur on Torture concluded that "international and regional human rights bodies have begun to recognize that abuse and mistreatment of women seeking reproductive health services can cause tremendous and lasting physical and emotional suffering, inflicted on the basis of gender".[51]

The growing urgency of ending practices which, although endorsed by traditionalist culture or religion, are harmful to women and girls was highlighted in 2014, when, for the first time, in Committees' Joint General Recommendation/General Comment,[52] two UN human rights expert committees joined forces to issue a comprehensive interpretation of the obligations of states to prevent and eliminate harmful practices inflicted on women and girls:

> Harmful practices are therefore grounded in discrimination based on sex, gender and age, among other things, and have often been justified by invoking sociocultural and religious customs and values, in addition to misconceptions relating to some disadvantaged groups of women and children. Overall, harmful practices are often associated with serious forms of violence or are themselves a form of violence against women and children. While the nature and prevalence of the practices vary by region and culture, the most prevalent and well documented are female genital mutilation, child and/or forced marriage, polygamy, crimes committed in the name of so-called honour and dowry-related violence.[53]

The GR/GC highlights other harmful practices such as virginity testing, stoning, widowhood practices, accusations of witchcraft, infanticide and incest. They also include body modifications that are performed for the purpose of beauty or marriageability of girls and women. The GR/GC regards these as "traditional, re-emerging or emerging practices" that are prescribed and/or kept in place by social norms that perpetuate male dominance and inequality of women and children, on the basis of sex, gender, age and other intersecting factors. It points out that they are imposed on women and children by family members, community members or society at large, regardless of whether the victim provides, or is able to provide, full, free and informed consent.

Concluding observation

The concept note of the conference in the context of which this paper was delivered called on us "to avoid a dichotomous approach that sets gender equality against monolithic "religions" and to recognize some very positive pro-women and pro-poor positions" in the religions. This call echoes the approach of the current Special Rapporteur on Freedom of Religion:

> Unfortunately, the impression that freedom of religion or belief and equality between men and women allegedly constitute two essentially

> contradictory human rights norms seems to be widely shared. This can cause serious protection gaps. For instance, efforts to explore and create synergies between freedom of religion or belief and gender equality are sometimes ignored or even openly discouraged. Moreover, the abstractly antagonistic misconstruction of the relationship between freedom of religion or belief and equality between men and women fails to do justice to the life situation of many millions of individuals whose specific needs, wishes, claims, experiences and vulnerabilities fall into the intersection of both human rights, a problem disproportionately affecting women from religious minorities.[54]

This conciliatory approach is not new nor is it confined to the feminist issue. This call echoes attacks on secular human rights as a "fighting creed" and for accommodation and support for religious values. However, there is no symmetry between religious values and liberal human rights values. While liberal values leave space for and even guarantee freedom of the religious individual and the religious community, to believe in and manifest their religion, religious values do not recognize the entitlement of the liberal individual to equality or freedom not countenanced by the religion. The claim for symmetry and for accommodation and support for religious values is, therefore, based on a demand for tolerance of inequality and lack of liberty for those deprived of a voice by, or within, the religious community.

In particular as regards women, the pervasive patriarchy in traditionalist cultures and religions regarding women's exclusion from power or even free access in the public space and subjection to male power in the family cannot provide individual women a choice between equality and inequality. In contrast, a human rights regime protects the right of a religious woman to choose to remain within the context of her religious beliefs and practices but carefully guards her right to claim equality either by right of exit or within the religion itself.

There is a growing body of feminist thought within religions, which demands redefinition, and reconstruction of religious hierarchies in order to secure equality for religious women within their religions. A woman's claim to equality within her religion may be through internal hermeneutics or it may be by constitutional claim against the state, in which the state may be asked to refrain from supporting, either directly or indirectly, the implementation of patriarchal edicts of a religion even against its own members.[55] While hermeneutic change is greatly desirable to bring about women's equality under religious precepts, it requires a transformative change in the dogma and the practices of each of the Abrahamic religions. In the interim until transformative change is achieved, states must provide access to justice for women who seek to enforce their right to equality, in all spheres of life, without the barriers created by religious patriarchy. Women's right to equal religious personhood in the leadership roles, functions and ritual of their religious communities should also be recognized by the state.

Secular human rights are not a fighting creed but rather a neutral facilitator of pluralistic life choices, which impose an obligation to recognize the equal entitlement for all members of society to fulfill their potential without barriers based on their identity, including race or sex. This is a regime of universal normative empathy, beyond that required by any one religion. Women are at the hub both of the transformative concept of the human rights regime and of the ideological backlash emanating from cultural or religious traditionalism. The recognition of women's right to equality under the human rights regime represents a shift of perception. Its transformation into the ruling paradigm can be achieved only through the sustained thriving of secular human rights.

Notes

* With warm appreciation to Professor Fareda Banda, who invited me to participate and present my work on culture, religion and women's international human rights at the SOAS-Brandeis workshop on Gender, Religion and Equality in Public Life: sponsored by the British Council, held at SOAS, 19 May 2014.

1 Frances Raday, 'Gender and Democratic Citizenship: the Impact of CEDAW' 10 *International Journal of Constitutional Law* 512–15 (2012) I.

2 Convention on the Elimination of all Forms of Discrimination Against Women, 1979, 1249 UNTS 13.

3 Frances Raday, 'Culture, Religion, and Gender' 1 *International Journal of Constitutional Law* 663 (2003); Yehoshua Arieli, 'The Theory of Human Rights, its Origin and its Impact on Modern Society' in Daniel Gutwein and Menachem Mautner (eds.), *Mishpat ve-Hisroryah [Law and History]*, (Jersusalem, Merkaz Zalman Shazar le-Toldot Yisra'el, 1999), p. 25 (in Hebrew).

4 Johannes Morsink, *The Universal Declaration of Human Rights: Origins, Drafting, and Intent* (Philadelphia, University of Pennsylvania Press, 1999). See especially Renee Cassin at p. 33.

5 Human Rights Council Advisory Committee, *Preliminary study on promoting human rights and fundamental freedoms through a better understanding of traditional values of humankind*, UN Doc. A/HRC/AC/9/2, 6–10 August 2012, para. 33.

6 Jack Donnelly, *Universal Human Rights in Theory and Practice*, 2nd ed. (Ithaca and London, Cornell University Press, 2003), p. 1.

7 Zbigniew Brzezinski, *The Grand Failure: the Birth and Death of Communism in the Twentieth Century* (New York, Macmillan Publishers, 1989), p. 256.

8 The three religions are linked conceptually, historically and geographically. God is the One God. The Bible is a sacred book for Judaism and Christianity and a book of inspiration for Islam. Abraham is the historical Father for the three religions and he came from Ur Kasdim in Mesapotamia. Moses came from Egypt across the Sinai desert to the borders of Canaan and the Jewish people founded their settlement there in Jerusalem and the Galilee. Jesus Christ was born in Bethlehem, preached in the Galilee and was crucified and resurrected in Jerusalem. Mohamed was born in Mecca, ruled from Medina and mythically rose to the Heavens on a white horse from Jerusalem. In the late Roman Empire, which extended over Europe and Mesopotamia, Christianity was embraced by the Emperor of Constantinople, Christianity and Judaism became the only religions to be permitted by the Emperor Theodosian, and Christianity became the dominant religion of the European Empire and a powerful presence amongst the Copts of the Eastern Empire. It was against

this backdrop that Mohammed was born in the Arabian Peninsula in the sixth century. Mohammed imposed Islam on the population of Mecca, and by Dimmi agreements followed by military conquests, overpowered the previous multiplicity of religious and pagan communities in the region. The struggle between Christianity and Islam continued in the Middle Ages with failed attempts to encroach on each other's territory. In the eighth century Muslim forces conquered and occupied the Iberian peninsula, governing the Christian and Jewish communities with considerable tolerance in what is known as Cordoba's Golden Age of Islam and Judaism until the eleventh century. However, freedom of religion was not equality of religion, and Islam was the governing religion. It was not until the fifteenth century that Islam was ousted from Europe, when Granada fell to the Catholic monarchs Ferdinand and Isabella. The Christian Crusades in the eleventh to thirteenth centuries attempted to restore the dominance of Christianity in Jerusalem and the Holy Land.

9 Much has been written in defence of the humanism of the Bible's treatment of women in the context of biblical times. See Michael S. Berg and Deborah E. Lipstadt, 'Women in Judaism from the Perspective of Human Rights,' in John Witte and Johan D. van der Vyver (eds.), *Religious Human Rights in Global Perspective: Religious Perspectives* (The Hague, Martinus Nijhoff Publishers, 1996), pp. 304, 310. Indeed, women were in some respects protected by Biblical law against abuse. However, protections for women were paternalistic, given to them as unequals like those given to slaves or children; thus, for instance, women were given protection against excesses of physical violence by their husbands when exercising the right of chastisement. Such protections enhanced the prospects of health and survival of women, but they did not bestow autonomy or power. The basis remained unchanged: an image of women marked by inferiority and as being of instrumental worth to men rather than having their own intrinsic worth.

10 Genesis 2:23.

11 There have been subsequent interpretations that express the view that the story is not one of domination and inequality. Rabbi Meir Zlotowitz (ed.), *Ibn Janach, Bereishis/Genesis – A New Translation with Commentary Anthologised from Talmudic, Midrashic and Rabbinic Sources*, 1 Artscroll Tanach Series 104 (Mesorah Publications, 1977). There is also an alternative version of the creation of men and women in an earlier chapter of Genesis. According to that version, "So God created man in his own image, in the image of He created He him; male and female created He them", Genesis 1:27; V 1–2. This paragraph has been interpreted as allowing the fundamental equality of men and women in the Jewish tradition. However, the relationship of this version of the Creation to the story of Adam and Eve is a subject of much controversy. See W. Gunther Plaut, *The Torah: A Modern Commentary* (Union of American Hebrew Congregations, 1981), p. 32. In any case, it is incontrovertible that there are only two versions, one androcentric and one neutral, while there is no female-centred alternative version and so the patriarchal theme remains clear.

12 Simone de Beauvoir, *The Second Sex*, H.M. Parshley trans. and ed., (Knopf, 1989) (1952), p. 718.

13 Genesis 3:16; italics added by the author.

14 The story of Eve's role in the fall from the Garden of Eden was not reproduced in the Qur'an, and Riffat Hassan has, on this basis, persuasively argued that there is no justification at source for attributing Eve's guilt to women in Islam. Nevertheless, Hassan concludes: "Underlying the rejection in Muslim societies of the idea of man-woman equality are the three deeply rooted beliefs ... namely, that women are inferior to men in creation (having been created from a crooked rib), and in righteousness (having helped Ash-Shaitan in defeating God's plan

for Adam), and in having been created mainly to be of use to men who are superior to them", John Witte and Johan van de Vyer, *Religious Human Rights in Global Perspective: Religious Perspectives* (The Hague, Martinus Nijhoff, 1996), p. 385.

15 Elizabeth Cady Stanton, *Eighty Years and More: Reminiscences 1815–1897* (1898), Project Gutenberg, April 2004, www.gutenberg.org/files/11982/11982-h/11982-h.htm (accessed June 2015).

16 Heiner Bielefeldt, *Interim report of the Special Rapporteur on freedom of religion or belief*, UN Doc. A/68/290, 7 August 2013, para. 58, www.ohchr.org/Documents/Issues/Religion/A.68.290.pdf.

17 See full discussion in Raday, 'Culture, Religon, and Gender' (2003).

18 Pope John Paul II, 'Letter to Women', *Libreria Editrice Vaticana* (29 June, 1995), at: http://w2.vatican.va/content/john-paul-ii/en/letters/1995/documents/hf_jp-ii_let_29061995_women.html (accessed 12 June 2015).

19 Martha Nussbaum, *Sex and Social Justice* (Oxford, Oxford University Press, 1999), p. 86.

20 Richard Fenn, *Toward a Theory of Secularization* (Storrs, Conn., Society for the Scientific Study of Religion, 1978), p. 36.

21 Nkiru Nzegwu, 'Gender Equality in Dual-Sex System: The Case of Onitsha', 1(1) *JENdA: A Journal of Culture and African Women Studies* (2001), ISSN: 1530–5686 (online).

22 Raday, 'Gender and Democratic Citizenship', pp. 512, 515–517 (2012).

23 UN World Conference on Human Rights. Vienna Declaration and Programme of Action reproduced in (1993) 33 *International Legal Materials* 1661. The UN reference is UN Doc. A/CONF. 157/23 (1993).

24 Human Rights Committee, General Comment 28, *Equality of rights between man and women* (Article 3), UN Doc. CCPR/C/21/ Rev 1/Add.10, 2000, paras. 5, 32.

25 Asma Jahangir, United Nations Special Rapporteur on Freedom of Religion or Belief, speech given at The Parliamentary Assembly of the Council of Europe, available at http://assembly.coe.int/Main.asp?link=/Documents/Records/2005/E/0510041000E.htm#5t.

26 Abdelfattah Amor, 'Civil and Political Rights, Including the Question of Religious Intolerance' (E/CN.4/2002/73/Add.2), Fifty-eighth Session, 24 April 2009, para. 29.

27 Heiner Bielefeldt, *Freedom of Religion or Belief: Thematic Reports of the UN Special Rapporteur 2010–2013*, Religious Freedom Series (IIRF) vol. 3 (Germany, Culture and Science Publications, 2014), para 16, at www.bucer.org/uploads/tx_org/Heiner_Bielefeldt_-_Freedom_of_Religion_or_Belief.pdf.

28 Farida Shaheed, *Report of the Special Rapporteur in the field of cultural rights*, UN Doc. A/67/287, 10 August 2012, para. 3.

29 Ibid., para. 62.

30 Human Rights Council, Resolution 16/3 'Promoting human rights and fundamental freedoms through a better understanding of traditional values of humankind', UN Doc. A/HRC/RES/16/3, 8 April 2011, available at http://daccess-ods.un.org/TMP/2258836.92502975.html.

31 HRC Advisory Committee, UN Doc. A/HRC/AC/9/2, para. 39.

32 Ibid., paras. 76, 80.

33 Human Rights Council Advisory Committee, UN Doc. A/HRC/AC/9/NGO/4, 6–10 August 2012, available at www.ohchr.org/Documents/HRBodies/HRCouncil/AdvisoryCom/Session9/A-HRC-AC-9-NGO-4_en.pdf.

34 Human Rights Council, Resolution 26/11 Protection of the family, UN Doc. A/HRC/26/L.20/Rev.1, 25 June 2014, available online at www.family2014.org/HRC25062014EN.pdf.

35 HRC, panel discussion at its 27th session on Protection of the Family, 15 September 2014.

36 Frances Raday, 'The Family Agenda: Promoting Traditional Values in the Human Rights Council', *Oxford Human Rights Hub*, 8 January 2015, available online at http://ohrh.law.ox.ac.uk/the-family-agenda-promoting-traditional-values-in-the-human-rights-council/.

37 CEDAW, General recommendation on Article 16 of the Convention on the Elimination of All Forms of Discrimination against Women, UN Doc. CEDAW/C/GC/29, 26 February 2013, para. 27. See also CEDAW General Recommendation No. 21, para. 14.

38 General Assembly Resolution 68/148 'Child, early and forced marriage' UN Doc. A/RES/168/148 18 December 2013.

39 Catherine Turner, 'Out of the Shadows: Child Marriage and Slavery', *Anti-Slavery International*, April 2013, available online at www.antislavery.org/includes/documents/cm_docs/2013/c/child_marriage_final.pdf.

40 Statement by the United Nations Working Group on discrimination against women in law and practice, 18 October 2012, available online at www.ohchr.org/EN/NewsEvents/Pages/DisplayNews.aspx?NewsID=12672&LangID=E.See also Frances Raday, 'Decriminalizing Adultery: Eliminating Discrimination and Violence against Women', *Oxford Human Rights Hub*, 2 November 2012, available online at http://ohrh.law.ox.ac.uk/decriminalizing-adultery-eliminating-discrimination-and-violence-against-women.

41 Ibid. There have been some constitutional court decisions which struck down the penal code's punishment of marital infidelity or adultery on the basis both of the constitution's equality guarantees and human rights treaties, including the Convention on the Elimination of All Forms of Discrimination against Women (CEDAW): 1996, the Guatemalan Constitutional Court; 2007, the Ugandan Constitutional Court; 2015, the South Korea Supreme Court (reversing its previous rulings). It should be added that European countries have all decriminalized adultery.

42 CEDAW, UN Doc. CEDAW/C/GC/29, para. 27, and CEDAW General Recommendation 21, para. 14.

43 Amit Choudhary, 'Polygamy not integral part of Islam: SC', *The Times of India*, 10 February 2015, available online at http://timesofindia.indiatimes.com/india/Polygamy-not-integral-part-of-Islam-SC/articleshow/46180105.cms.

44 CEDAW, UN Doc. CEDAW/C/GC/29, paras. 38, 47, 53.

45 Ibid., para. 54.

46 Committee on Economic, Social and Cultural Rights in its General Comment No. 14 on the highest attainable standard of health, CESCR, article 12 of the CESCR, E/C.12/2000/4, 1 August 2000 made clear that the right to health contains both freedoms and entitlements and holds that "the freedoms include the right to control one's health and body, including sexual and reproductive freedom, and the right to be free from interference, such as the right to be free from torture, non-consensual medical treatment and experimentation", para. 8.

47 Radhika Coomaraswamy, *Report of the Special Rapporteur on violence against women, its causes and consequences*, UN Doc. E/CN.4/1999/68/Add.4, 21 January 1999, para. 57.

48 Ibid., para. 66.

49 Letter to the High Commissioner for Human Rights, UN Doc. AL Health (2002–7) G/So 214 (89–15) IRL 1/2013, 8 February 2013. See also Anand Grover, *Interim report of the Special Rapporteur on the right of everyone to the highest attainable standard of physical and mental health*, UN Doc. A/66/254, 3 August 2011, para. 17.

50 Commission on the Status of Women, Elimination and Prevention of all Forms of Violence against Women and Girls: Agreed Conclusions, 57th session, March 2013.
51 Juan E. Méndez, *Report of the Special Rapporteur on torture and other cruel, inhuman or degrading treatment or punishment*, UN Doc. A/HRC/22/53, 1 February 2013, para. 46.
52 'Joint General Recommendation No. 31 of the Committee on the Elimination of Discrimination against Women/General Comment No. 18 of the Committee on the Rights of the Child on harmful practices', UN Doc. CEDAW/C/GC/31-CRC/C/GC/18, 14 November 2014.
53 Ibid., para. 7.
54 Bielefeldt, UN Doc. A/68/290, Summary.
55 Frances Raday, 'Claiming Equal Religious Personhood: Women of the Wall's Constitutional Saga', in *Religion in the Public Sphere, A Comparative Analysis of German, Israeli, American and International Law*, in Winfried Brugger & Michael Karayanni (eds.), (Max Planck Institute, Heidelberg, 2007), p. 255.

2 Marriage, religion and gender equality

John Eekelaar

The recognition of marriage and gender equality

Marriage has long been viewed as a prime location of gender inequality, and for good reason. I am not going to question that at all; nor, that it is still a common site where gender inequalities persist. However, the assumption of this contribution is that, in many jurisdictions, gender equality is more likely to be promoted if unions which the parties and their communities see as marriages are also accepted as marriages by the civil law than if they are not. In that way, the norms of the civil law relating to marriage become available to the parties, should either wish (and be able) to access them.

This is not an argument that being married is 'good' for people, in the sense of improving health or relationships. I think such arguments are largely spurious because of the difficulty of separating the benefits flowing from the underlying relationship from the status of marriage.[1] Similarly, while evidence supports claims that parties who marry show more commitment to one another than those who live together without marrying, the comparison is of little value because of the extremely diverse circumstances in which people cohabit without marrying. What this paper does maintain, though, is that if people *do* marry, it is better for gender equality if they do so under the jurisdiction of the civil law than if they do not. The reason is that the civil law is on the whole more committed to gender equality, although it may not always achieve this, than the norms of many religious or other forms of community groups.

A radical view argues that equality can be achieved only by removing marriage from the public sphere and replacing the legal aspects by contracts between the parties.[2] An opposite view, but reaching the same conclusion, argues that, in the US, at any rate, the public institution of marriage has become so liberal and individualised, especially after the recognition by some courts of gay marriage, that it should be removed from state jurisdiction and 'returned to the churches'.[3] I think both positions undervalue the public importance of marriage. While it is well known that the rate of marriage has declined in many 'westernised' societies (across the EU, for example, the crude marriage rate (per 1,000 population) declined from 5.9 to 4.4 between

1991 and 2011[4]) marriage is still important for many people, though the reasons for this, and the place of marriage in a relationship, vary greatly. A study based on a sample of 39 people, born between the late 1960s and late 1970s, revealed that of the 32 who had been (or were still) married, 18 had done so primarily for what were classed as 'conventional' reasons: that is, in order to conform with religious or cultural reasons or parental expectations.[5] Others saw it as expressing their own wish to 'confirm' their relationship to the outside world, or as a framework within which their relationship could grow. In all these cases, the approval of family and the wider community was an important feature. Even those who saw marriage as primarily an event that 'transformed' or added an extra dimension to their relationship, often combined this with 'conventional' reasons.[6]

So, one of the key roles of marriage is to demonstrate the acceptance and approval of the couple's relationship by their community and peers. The significance of social acceptance lies behind the public ceremonials and the conferment of gifts present in almost all weddings. It explains why the right to marry appears in many international instruments,[7] and why removal of legal bars to marriage, whether based on status (for example, slavery), religion, race or gender (as in the case of same-sex couples), has such significance. This acceptance is reinforced if the state gives legal recognition to the religious or cultural act that is seen by the parties and their community as bringing the marriage into being. If the state recognises the legality of a marriage contracted according to the practices of the couple's community, it not only demonstrates its acceptance of the special nature of the couple's relationship but also of the couple's group as an integral part of the pluralistic nature of civil society.

Since such recognition allows either of the couple, should they wish, to access the civil law relating to marriage, gender equality is promoted the more widely such marriages are recognised. But the state has to tread carefully. It cannot risk importing gender inequality into its law. So it is important that fundamental principles regarding the conditions for recognising marriage (primarily age, consent, degrees of relationship and monogamy) and its legal consequences are maintained. This paper considers how far this strategy is followed in the law of England and Wales. It does this by explaining the current provisions governing the formation of marriage, focusing on the circumstances in which they allow for the legal recognition of marriages performed by religious groups, and then considering their weaknesses and how they may be improved.

The religious/secular divide in English marriage law

The English law on formation of marriage operates under an historical shadow projected from the period when the Clandestine Marriages Act 1753 (Lord Hardwicke's Act) gave the Church of England a 'virtual monopoly'[8] over the procedures for the solemnisation and recording of marriages. While it became possible to marry according to entirely secular procedures in 1836, this civil system operates alongside a religious system, an inheritance of that history. On the religious side of the divide are: (1) marriages according to the rites of the Church of England which are sufficient in themselves to formalise a marriage; (2) Jewish and Quaker marriages, which are likewise sufficient; and, (3) marriages in other religions that can be contracted in a registered building which is a 'place of meeting for religious worship'.[9] The third group must be attended either by two witnesses, and a registrar or an 'authorised person', usually a cleric in the relevant religion. Certain words must be used at some point, the marriage registered and information about the registration supplied to the superintendent registrar, and civil preliminaries must have been fulfilled.[10]

On the secular side of the divide, the marriage can take place in a register office or, after 1994, on premises approved by a local authority. In either case, the ceremony must be entirely secular.[11] A prescribed form of words must be used and a superintendent registrar, registrar and two witnesses must be present. The premises (which must be a fixed structure; a marquee would not do[12]) must 'have no recent or continuing connection with any religion, religious practice or religious persuasion'.[13] At least one local authority has interpreted this as extending to the presence of furniture and furnishings with such connection, and it certainly applies to any 'reading, music, words or performance which forms part of a ceremony, including material used by way of introduction to, in any interval between parts of, or by way of conclusion to the ceremony'.[14] These are usually referred to as 'civil' marriages. In both civil and religious cases (except for marriages according to the rites of the Church of England, in which case it is optional), the parties must have satisfied certain 'civil' preliminaries, fulfilled by giving notice of the intended marriage at a marriage register office.[15]

This dual system posed serious problems for the proposal to introduce gay marriage. Various religious leaders were concerned that the legislation would compel them to perform gay marriages, but if such marriages were confined to the civil sector, same-sex couples would not be able to introduce a religious element into the ceremony. The government's solution was to allow 'religious' gay marriage only in the event that the proper authorities of the religion expressly 'opted-in' to this power. However, the Church of England (but not the Church in Wales) was not given this power, since this would imply that Parliament had purported to amend the canons of that Church.[16]

The result is that a gay marriage can be performed by a religious ceremony in a registered building if the appropriate authorities have applied for registration for this purpose.[17] However, the use of many places of worship is shared between different religious authorities, some on a formal and others on an informal basis. Section 44A(6), inserted into the Marriage Act 1949 by Schedule 1 of the Marriage (Same Sex Couples) Act 2013, requires the consent of each of the authorities formally sharing the place to such an application. A government response to a consultation regarding shared buildings[18] proposed that the same provisions should apply to 'informally' shared buildings as well as to formally shared ones, except that, if the building was 'informally' shared, the provisions would apply only to a religious body that used the building for 'public religious worship' on two or more occasions in each calendar month.[19] The purpose is, of course, to prevent a religious group that uses the building less than that having a veto over an application by the group using it more often, should that group wish to make one.

These regulations could require some difficult, even bizarre, types of decisions, which the UK Supreme Court has confirmed,[20] would need to be made by the Registrar-General. Apart from the question of deciding what constitutes a 'building' (e.g. is it a whole complex or just part of it), the Registrar-General might have to decide such issues as whether preceding a cake sale by saying prayers would or would not amount to use for 'public religious worship', and whether a wedding or a funeral is an occasion for 'public religious worship'. It was with such large questions that the Supreme Court was faced in the *Scientology* case.

The Scientology case: what is a religion?

In *R (on the application of Hodkin and another) (Appellants) v Registrar General of Births, Deaths and Marriages (Respondent)*,[21] the UK Supreme Court heard an appeal from the decision of Ouseley J who considered himself bound by the Court of Appeal decision in *R v Registrar-General, ex parte Segerdal*[22] to hold that a chapel of the Church of Scientology was not a 'building' which was a 'place for religious worship'[23] and therefore could not be used to celebrate a marriage.

In the Supreme Court, Lord Toulson (with whom Lord Neuberger, Lord Clarke and Lord Reed agreed) considered that it was first necessary to consider whether Scientology was a 'religion', and that had to be decided according to contemporary understandings, and not those of the original legislators. Having considered judicial and academic discussion, he gave the following 'description' of his understanding of religion for the purposes of the relevant legislation:

> I would describe religion in summary as a spiritual or non-secular belief system, held by a group of adherents, which claims to explain mankind's place in the universe and relationship with the infinite, and to teach its adherents how they are to live their lives in conformity with the spiritual understanding associated with the belief system. By spiritual or non-secular I mean a belief system that goes beyond that which can be perceived by the senses or ascertained by the application of science. I prefer not to use the word 'supernatural' to express this element, because it is a loaded word that can carry a variety of connotations. Such a belief system may or may not involve belief in a supreme being, but it does involve a belief that there is more to be understood about mankind's

> nature and relationship to the universe than can be gained from the senses or from science. I emphasise that this is intended to be a description and not a definitive formula.[24]

The key to Lord Toulson's description is the statement, derived from the judgments of Wilson and Deane JJ in the High Court of Australia in *Church of the New Faith v Commissioners of Pay-Roll Tax*:[25] 'By spiritual or non-secular I mean a belief system which goes beyond that which can be perceived by the senses or ascertained by the application of science'. This appears to be consistent with Ronald Dworkin's view[26] that 'religion' can comprise acceptance of certain moral and aesthetic values as an objective ('ungrounded') reality that exists apart from empirical facts or sensory perception, and is not dependent on theism. Not everyone will be persuaded that such values (if they are a 'reality') will be perceived or interpreted in a uniform way, so they could encompass a wide range of behaviour. It also seems to make speculation central. Could it imply that the further the conclusions are removed from sensual perception and science the stronger is their claim to be a religion? That could be a dangerous invitation. It would also seem strange to *privilege* such beliefs over those that are based on sensory perception and the application of science.

Conversely, there are those who argue that their religious beliefs are in fact supported by empirical evidence and sensory perception. Proponents of 'intelligent design' claim this has a scientific basis. Although the US courts eventually rejected the claim,[27] it can be argued, as Thomas Nagel does,[28] that the argument for 'intelligent design' can be regarded as an engagement in 'science'. Yet it is seen as supporting belief in a supreme being. It seems that if they wished to have their world view accepted as a religion according to Lord Toulson's description of religion, they would need to argue for it on grounds that contradicted their beliefs.

One might use a different approach and try to determine the matter on grounds similar to those supporting religious freedom. The difficulty is that these grounds seem also inevitably to support freedom of conscience on a broader base, as the framing of Article 9 of the European Convention on Human Rights demonstrates.[29] Two commentators on the protection of religious freedom in the United States characterise that protection as one that gives equal liberty to religious and non-religious beliefs: 'groups and individuals are entitled to be free from discrimination on the basis of the spiritual foundations of their deep commitments and important projects.'[30] They argue that it breaches the equality principle to give protection to such commitments and projects only if they have a religious basis. Webber has criticised this position, saying that such freedom can only be justified on the understanding that there is something especially valuable about religious belief.[31] However, he conceded that 'the very idea of religious freedom presupposes a willingness to recognise commitments that operate in a comparable way whether or not they conform to a preconceived idea of religion'.[32]

Dworkin has argued similarly that protection of religious freedom should be seen as merely an aspect of a general right to 'ethical independence'.[33]

Perhaps a more promising approach is one that sees religion as a practice, part of social and cultural norms of a community and communities. For example, the sociologist Emile Durkheim described religion as:

> A unified system of beliefs and practices relative to sacred things, that is to say things set apart and surrounded by prohibitions – beliefs and practices that unite its adherents in a single moral community called a church.[34]

A 'cultural' definition does not need to go as far as specifying the usage of the word 'church' or its equivalent, or to expect uniformity or even the open display of what is believed. An important element of Australian Aboriginal culture appears to be confining knowledge of appropriate rituals and sacred places to small groups of people, and restricting communication of certain matters to one or the other gender. This has caused difficulties in dealing with government authorities, for in seeking protection (for example, of sacred sites) they need to disclose what is to be protected, thereby breaking their own religious precepts.[35] While religious practices of that kind are perhaps unlikely to be found in the United Kingdom, the examples show that religion for these purposes may be better understood in terms of social practice rather than the nature of the beliefs, which may not even be known. But that immediately raises the challenge: which social practices are religious, and which are not? Durkheim's reference to 'sacred' things and 'moral community' are helpful, but perhaps it should be accepted that there could be no clear dividing line between the religious and secular. That would not matter, and perhaps should not matter, unless the law makes it matter by specifying that certain consequences are contingent on making the distinction, as does the law of marriage.

However that problem is resolved, a second problem needed resolution in the *Scientology* case: once Scientology had been held to be a religion, it became necessary to decide whether that church's premises were a 'place for religious worship'. Lord Toulson gave this a wide interpretation, holding the expression to be 'wide enough to include religious services'.[36] But what counts as a 'service' could also be a matter for debate.

Overcoming the division

So perhaps it is time to review our marriage law. The decline in marriage could not, of course, be attributed to defects in the laws regarding formation of marriage. However, it would be regrettable if those laws were an obstacle to the legal recognition of marriage. For example, if a Muslim marriage is to be recognised, it must take place in a registered building (just as the Scientologists' marriages now can be) and be notified as required. However, it seems that Muslims are reluctant to seek registration of their premises. For example, in 2010, there were 899 Certified Muslim Places of Worship, but only 198 registered for marriage.[37] Although the process of registration is relatively straightforward (signatories of 20 local householders must be acquired), it is possible that it is seen as intrusive in some communities. The result is that English matrimonial law will not be available to many married Muslims. There may be other people who, for various reasons, may be marrying 'outside' the law because they want to marry in ways that do not comply with the complexities of the law.

The 'continental' solution

In 1973 a Working Party of the Law Commission considered that the law fell 'woefully short … particularly perhaps as regards simplicity and intelligibility' of the conditions necessary for a good marriage law,[38] and this was before the further complications introduced by the Marriage Act 1994 and the Marriage (Same Sex Couples) Act 2013! The Commission thought that the 'simplest and most effective' solution would be to enact that only civil marriages would be legally recognised, 'on the Continental model', but felt this would be generally unpopular, especially with the churches.

Legally recognising only civil marriage could be a clear and simple solution. There would be no state 'intrusion' into designating in which buildings the religious marriages must take place in order for it to be recognised, or which officials from community groups are authorised to perform them. The state would be concerned only with the civil marriage, which would be held in a public building (as in the French and German model), or effected by a public official. It is possible that some couples would not regard the civil marriage as a marriage at all,[39] but they would remain free to hold a subsequent religious ceremony, which would be an entirely private matter.

Comparisons with other jurisdictions are difficult because of the impact of different cultural traditions. Some might argue that such a model promotes cultural assimilation, and that that is a desirable policy goal. These are large issues, and this paper does not take a concluded position on them. However, the case will be made for an alternative approach, which has distinct merits of its own.

An alternative approach

The alternative approach to the 'continental' solution modifies and expands the present English system. This rests on an appreciation of the role of marriage in demonstrating approval and acceptance of relationships and of local communities within the wider community represented by the state. The present English system partially achieves this to the extent that the state recognises religious marriages, but does so in a clumsy way, and is vulnerable to the uncertainties discussed above over the understanding of religion. There are a variety of ways in which it might be adjusted or developed.

One way is to abandon the provisions concerning religious buildings, and replace them with a measure requiring non-civil marriages to be carried out before authorised representatives of a religion. This is the solution adopted in the Marriage (Scotland) Act 1977. Under that Act, apart from civil marriages, marriages can be solemnised by 'a minister, clergyman, pastor, or priest of a religious body prescribed by regulations' which may 'nominate to the Registrar General any of its members who it desires should be registered under this section as empowered to solemnise marriages'.[40] It does not matter where this solemnisation happens. Civil preliminaries (such as notice) must be complied with.[41]

Nevertheless, this retains the difficulty of defining what qualifies as a 'religious' body. The issue was partially circumvented by the use of section 12 of the 1977 Act, which allows the Registrar General 'to grant to any person a temporary written authorisation to solemnise (a) a marriage or marriages specified in the authorisation; or (b) marriages during such period as shall be specified in the authorisation'. This was used to permit the Humanist Society in Scotland to solemnise legal marriage. The Society explains: 'In January 2001, the Society lodged a petition with the Scottish Parliament calling for the Marriage (Scotland) Act 1977 to be amended to allow legal humanist wedding ceremonies, alongside religious and civil ones'. Although the Act was not amended, section 12 of the Act allows the Registrar General for Scotland to authorise temporary additional celebrants. In 2005, the Registrar agreed to authorise 12 celebrants from the Humanist Society, in part because of a concern that allowing legal religious weddings but not legal humanist ones might not be consistent with the right to 'freedom of thought, conscience and religion', which includes non-religious belief, in Article 9 of the European Convention on Human Rights. The first legal humanist wedding took place at Edinburgh Zoo on 18 June 2005 between Karen Watts (from Ireland) and Martin Reijns (from the Netherlands). Humanist weddings have since becoming increasingly popular and, in 2010, with over 70 celebrants authorised to conduct them, 2,092 legal humanist weddings took place in Scotland, becoming the third most popular form of wedding in Scotland after Registrars and the Church of Scotland.[42]

In response to this development, the Marriage and Civil Partnership (Scotland) Act 2014 will, when brought into effect, amend the 1977 Act by substituting the expression 'religious body' with 'religious or belief body', the latter being defined as an 'organised group of people the principal object of which is to uphold or promote philosophical beliefs and which meets regularly for that purpose'.[43]

In June 2014 the UK government initiated a consultation as to whether, and if so, how, marriages conducted in England and Wales in accordance with the usages of 'non-religious belief organisations' should be legally recognised.[44] The Consultation Document put forward three suggestions. One was to 'permit non-religious belief organisations to solemnize marriages within their own buildings or buildings where the organisation meets to manifest its beliefs and that are certified for this purpose'; another was to 'permit non-religious belief organisations to solemnize marriages anywhere (other than religious premises) meaningful to the couple, including outdoors'; the third was to permit non-religious belief organisations to solemnize marriages at 'approved premises' (other than religious premises), such as a stately home or hotel. A 'belief organisation' was defined as being an organisation 'whose principal or sole purpose is the advancement of a system of non-religious beliefs which relate to morality or ethics'.

These proposals maintained the distinction between 'religious' and 'non-religious' beliefs or systems, and the first and third retained the need to solemnise the marriage within buildings. The first followed the model used for buildings registered for religious weddings, while the third followed the system for approving premises for civil weddings. In the event, the government deferred making any decision on the matter by referring it to the Law Commission, saying any resolution demanded review and potential reform of the 'legal and technical requirements of marriage ceremonies and registration in England and Wales'.[45]

Discussion

Gender equality is promoted by the civil law extending its reach to cover as many unions in which the parties consider themselves 'married' as possible. It is arguable that current English law falls short in this regard. While it is important for the state to provide some sort of screening process as to who enters marriage, this could be performed at the preliminary stage. The remaining question is whether there is reason for the state to seek to control how and where marriage is formalised. Should people be permitted the widest scope for choosing their own forms, subject only to the requirement of providing a proper record of its completion?

There is a strong case that the presence of some authorised person, regarded as legitimate within the community of the couple, should be required when a 'non-civil' marriage is formalised. Four reasons may be suggested for this. One is to provide added security to that provided by the civil preliminaries regarding the contracting of the marriage, the age and status of the parties and presence of consent. Another is to provide a certain degree of control over the nature and place of the event. A third is that the authorised person acts as a representative of the couple's community, and therefore is a manifestation of the community's acceptance of the union. A fourth is that using a person authorised by the state enhances the interlocking of approval of the union by both the couple's immediate community and the wider community.

The options put forward in the government consultation were much more restricted. The first and third options retained the strategy (which is not followed in Scotland) of seeking to control the place where the marriage is celebrated. The second abandoned that (apart from excluding the use of 'religious' premises), limiting its control (apart from through preliminary formalities) to approval of the celebrant. The government was concerned that this second option could be criticised as giving belief organisations greater freedom than religious bodies. This prompts the observation that the strategy of controlling the place of celebration of religious marriages is misplaced. It does not in any case apply to Quakers and Jews. Provided preliminary formalities have been followed, an authorised celebrant is present and proper records are kept, why should the place of celebration be subject to legal control? The administration and costs involved in satisfying these requirements are unnecessary and could be a deterrent to compliance by some religious communities.

Retaining the religious/secular divide further compromised the government's proposals. Hence, even under the second option, where the marriage need not take place in authorised premises, it was specified that 'religious' premises should not be used. That would of course require definition, with the pitfalls that involves. The division was carried into the definition of a 'belief' organisation. The Consultation Paper, drawing on section 14 of the Marriage (Same Sex Couples) Act defined a belief organisation as one 'whose principal or sole purpose is the advancement of a system of *non-religious* beliefs which relate to morality or ethics'. That seems to have been drafted with the Humanist Society in mind. However, the requirement that the beliefs be 'non-religious' opens the way for essentially irresolvable debate as to what is a 'religious' and a 'non-religious' belief. There may be concern that failure to maintain this distinction could lead to 'religious' organisations avoiding the registration requirements for religious weddings. But why should this matter? If the second option were available to organisations 'whose principal or sole purpose is the advancement of a system of *religious or philosophical* beliefs which relate to morality or ethics', organisations of either kind could use its more liberal framework. The new Scottish legislation changes the definition of persons who may solemnise marriage from 'a minister, clergyman, pastor, or priest of a religious body' to 'a priest or other celebrant of a religious or belief body'.[46] Hence, as nothing will turn on whether the authorised person is from a religious or a 'belief' body, the significance of the distinction falls away.

The remaining question is how widely the authority to solemnise marriages should be conferred on communities. If the argument made above that when the state recognises a marriage, it not only shows its approval of the couple's relationship but also of the community solemnising the marriage, is accepted, then the state has some interest in the nature of that community. While the requirement that it should have a principal or sole purpose to advance philosophical beliefs relating to morality or ethics might exclude, say, a football supporters' club, difficult decisions may still need to be taken. What about political movements, or even political parties? Since the Registrar-General may presently need to decide what a religion is, it may not be unreasonable to allow this official the discretion to decide whether an organisation falls within the stated definitions. This could be assisted by regulations and guidelines. For example, it would seem appropriate to exclude political movements and commercial enterprises since marriage can be seen as expressing identification between the couple and a community in a deeper, more permanent, sense than provided by such organisations. It could be stated that the community must be of significant size, and that it provides guidance or reflection on a worldview and norms of behaviour. It is also important to ensure that approval is not given to anti-social groups. A further requirement, for example that it provides a public benefit (a concept taken from charity law), would be necessary.

Conclusion

For many people, entering marriage has a wider dimension than the solely personal. It is the outward sign of a personal relationship that is, or seeks to be, in accord with the expectations of the wider community. While it is possible that people can solicit and obtain this approval in ways other than by marriage, marriage remains an important means of achieving this. By legally recognising a marriage that is solemnised following the processes accepted by a group simultaneously with the group, the state indicates its acceptance of the group as an integral part of a diverse society. At the same time it is plausible to suggest that recognising marriages solemnised in accordance with community customs will be a more effective way of enhancing the reach of civil marriage law among the population, and therefore enhance gender equality while at the same time respecting diversity. By making this contingent on preliminary notification it seeks to ensure conformity to certain fundamental conditions it deems necessary for the well-being of both parties.

I have argued that this may be best done by authorising celebrants put forward by communities assessed to possess certain characteristics, though an alternative that requires only that a solemnisation of any kind is witnessed could also be considered. The need to obtain official approval of the celebrant in the former approach may provide some additional protection to potentially vulnerable parties, although the two approaches might also be combined in some way.

Notes

1 See John Eekelaar, 'Evaluating Legal Regulation of Family Behaviour,' *International Journal of Jurisprudence of the Family* 1 (2011): 17–34, http://heinonline.org/HOL/Page?handle=hein.journals/ijjfl&id=1&collection=journals

2 See for example Martha Albertson Fineman, 'The Meaning of Marriage,' in *Marriage Proposals: Questioning a Legal Status*, ed. Anita Bernstein (New York and London: New York University Press, 2006); Cass R. Sunstein and Richard H. Thaler, 'Privatizing Marriage,' *The Monist* 91 (2008): 377–87.

3 Stephen B. Presser, 'Marriage and the Law: Time for a Divorce?' in *Marriage and Divorce in a Multicultural Context: Multi-Tiered Marriage and the Boundaries of Civil Law and Religion*, ed. Joel A. Nichols (Cambridge: Cambridge University Press, 2013).

4 Eurostat, *European Social Statistics 2013 edition*, p. 35.

5 John Eekelaar and Mavis Maclean, 'Marriage and the Moral Basis of Personal Relationships,' *Journal of Law and Society* 31 (2004): 510–38. This was particularly strong in the case of members of ethnic minorities: Mavis Maclean and John Eekelaar, 'The Significance of Marriage: Contrasts between White British and Ethnic Minority Groups in England,' *Law & Policy* 27 (2005): 379–98.
6 People who choose not to marry may be developing alternative ways of receiving peer and community approval, such as where people who have been living together have an 'engagement' party, or in announcements about 'status' in the social media.
7 Universal Declaration of Human Rights (1948), Article 16; European Convention on Human Rights and Fundamental Freedoms (1950), Article 12; International Covenant on Civil and Political Rights (1966), Article 23.
8 *R (on the application of Hodkin and another) (Appellants) v Registrar General of Births, Deaths and Marriages (Respondent)*, [2013] UKSC 77, para. 6.
9 Places of Worship Registration Act 1855, s 2.
10 Marriage Act 1949, ss 44, 53–57.
11 Marriage Act 1994, introducing ss 46A and 46B into the Marriage Act 1949.
12 The Marriages (Approved Premises) Regulations 1995, s 2, defines 'premises' as 'a permanently immovable structure comprising at least a room, or any boat or other vessel which is permanently moored'.
13 Ibid., schedule 1, para 4.
14 Ibid., schedule 2, para 11.
15 Marriage Act 1949, ss 5 and 27.
16 Marriage (Same Sex Couples) Act 2013, ss 2–5.
17 See Marriage Act 1949, s 43A, inserted by Marriage (Same Sex Couples) Act 2013, Schedule 1. Some religious denominations have done this, see: www.theguardian.com/society/2014/apr/14/first-church-wedding-gay-couple-uk
18 Marriage (Same Sex Couples) Act 2013 Shared Buildings Regulations Consultation Paper (23 January 2014).
19 Ibid., 14.
20 See especially the judgment of Lord Wilson.
21 [2013] UKSC 77.
22 [1970] 2 QB 697.
23 Marriage Act 1949, s 41 (1).
24 [2013] UKSC 77, para 57.
25 (1983) 154 CLR, 156, 174.
26 Ronald Dworkin, *Religion Without God* (Cambridge MA: Harvard University Press, 2013).
27 See Peter Radan, 'From Dayton to Dover: the Legacy of the *Scopes Trial*,' in *Law and Religion in Theoretical and Historical Context*, ed. Peter Cane *et al.* (Cambridge: Cambridge University Press, 2008), Chapter 7.
28 See Thomas Nagel, 'Public Education and Intelligent Design,' *Philosophy and Public Affairs* 36 (2008): 187–205.
29 'Everyone has the right to freedom of thought, conscience and religion.' This was however restrictively interpreted in *Pretty v UK*, 2346/02, but without much analysis.
30 Christopher Eisgruber and Lawrence Sager, *Religious Freedom and the Constitution* (Cambridge MA: Harvard University Press, 2010), 95.
31 Jeremy Webber, 'Understanding the Religion in Freedom of Religion,' in *Law and Religion*, Chapter 3.
32 Ibid., 43.
33 Dworkin, note 26 above, 128–137.
34 Carol Costman, trans. *The Elementary Forms of Religious Life* (New York: Oxford University Press, 2001), 46.

35 See E. Willheim, 'Australian Legal Procedures and the Protection of Sacred Aboriginal Spiritual Beliefs: a Fundamental Conflict,' in *Law and Religion*, Chapter 10.
36 [2013] UKSC 77, para 62.
37 Office for National Statistics, Marriages in England and Wales 2010, Area of Occurrence, Type of Ceremony and Denomination, Tables 6 and 7: for other denominations the discrepancy is much smaller.
38 See the discussion in Stephen Cretney, *Family Law in the Twentieth Century: A History* (New York: Oxford University Press, 2003), 24–28.
39 See the discussion by Jane Mair, 'Belief in Marriage' in *International Journal of the Jurisprudence of the Family* 5 (2014): 63–88.
40 Marriage (Scotland) Act 1977, ss 8(1)(ii) and 9 (1)(b).
41 Marriage (Scotland) Act 1977, s 4.
42 "Humanist Society Scotland," Wikipedia, accessed 17 April 2014, http://en.wikipedia.org/wiki/Humanist_Society_Scotland
43 Marriage and Civil Partnership (Scotland) Act 2014, s 12(4).
44 As required by the Marriage (Same Sex Couples) Act 2013, s 14. See *Marriages by non-religious belief organisations* (Ministry of Justice, 26 June 2014).
45 House of Commons: Written Statement (HCWS152), Ministry of Justice, Written Statement made by: The Minister of State for Justice and Civil Liberties (Simon Hughes) on 18 December 2014.
46 Marriage and Civil Partnership (Scotland) Act 2014, s 12(2)(a)(ii).

3 Gender, religion and human rights in Africa

Fareda Banda

In 1989 I was awarded a scholarship to study in England. Two days before my departure, my grandmother and aunt came to my parents' home in Harare to bid me farewell. On the eve of my departure, my grandmother asked me to get a clean, empty jam jar from the kitchen and accompany her to the garden. In the garden, she gathered some soil which she put in the jar. When she had half-filled it, my grandmother handed the jar to me and asked me to take it to England with me. On arrival at my new home, I was to take soil from that garden, and fill the jam jar to the top. In this way she told me, I would not be homesick. My spirit would be settled and would not wander in search of home. The blending of the soil of my home of origin and that of my new adopted home would ensure emotional and spiritual harmony.

That evening, my aunt also called me and holding a brand new razorblade asked me to sit at her feet while she carved a small cross in the hollow of my neck just above the meeting of my clavicle. This is known in Shona as *kutema nyora*. She rubbed some powder on this. This was to ward off malign spirits. I have to confess to submitting under protest. While feeling under a cultural obligation to respect my elders, I did so with the internal eye rolling of a 22-year-old sophisticate who considered herself to be "above" these strange ways. If I am honest, I found it all a bit embarrassing and "passé".

Finally, on my last day, my grandmother called the whole family together. We knelt on the carpeted floor of my bedroom and she prayed as only a Methodist lay preacher used to having a captive congregation can pray: with passion, at length and speaking in such a way that left one without any doubts that she must have a direct connection to God, who must exist. I remember feeling both loved and protected. I was ready for my onward journey.

In my grandmother's life and work, I see all the complexities of gender and religion on the continent. Her story reminds me that, just as she did, people can hold more than one set of religious beliefs simultaneously. Yes, my grandmother was a fervent convert to the Christian faith. She also brewed beer to commune with the ancestors as a cultural duty and to ensure the safe passage of her mother's spirit to the other side after her death. When visiting us in town, she did not scoff when my mother's friend told her about her infertility which she was getting treated by using a combination of Western medicine and the divination efforts of several traditional healers. Even when she did not subscribe to certain beliefs, for example in negative ascriptions of witchcraft, my grandmother understood that someone might genuinely hold the view that a negative turn of events in their lives could be explained in this way. Where some might see disciplinary dissonance, she saw logic. One sought help and solace where help was available. My grandmother's ability, or more accurately need, to negotiate plural legal orders: colonial law, ecclesiastical teachings and customary normative frameworks tell me that she was an early proponent of that which Sousa Santos was to later term inter-legality where:

> [D]ifferent legal spaces superimposed, interpenetrated, and mixed in our minds as much as in our actions, in occasions of qualitative leaps or sweeping crises in our life trajectories as well as in the dull routine of eventless everyday life. We live in a time of porous legality or legal porosity, of multiple networks or legal orders forcing us to constant transitions and trespassing. Our legal life is constituted by an intersection of different legal orders, that is, by inter legality.[1]

On gender within the African context

To start, a disclaimer: part of the role of this chapter is to examine the place of gender and religion on the African continent and how they interact with the law. Clearly one cannot hope to do justice to a continent of 54 states with plural legal systems, multi-ethnic and multi-religious communities, all with shifting and contested ideas about gender, and, indeed, about religions and their multiple interpretations.[2]

Oyewumi has warned against mapping Western[3] gender theory onto African societies. Focusing on the Yoruba in Nigeria she sets out to challenge five commonly held assumptions grounded in what she argues is Western epistemological hegemony:

1. Gender categories are universal and timeless and have been present in every society at all times. This idea is often expressed in a biblical tone, as if to suggest that 'in the beginning there was gender.'
2. Gender is a fundamental organizing principle in all societies and it is therefore always salient. In any given society, gender is everywhere.
3. There is an essential, universal category 'woman' that is characterized by the social uniformity of its members.
4. The subordination of women is a universal.
5. The category 'woman' is pre-cultural, fixed in historical time and space in cultural space in antithesis to another fixed category 'man'.[4]

For Oyewumi, the concept of "gender" as currently used, did not exist in pre-colonial Yoruba societies. Status and influence was grounded, in part, on seniority. The hierarchies of status of roles which have produced Western gender categories did not exist.

A number of other works have chartered societal organisation of sex roles on the African continent.[5] The classic is Ifi Amadiume's ground-breaking studies of Igbo societies. She noted that roles were not always fixed: women's status, influence and positions within a family were dependent, in part, on whether they were direct descendants or incomers by marriage.[6] Discussing practices such as woman to woman marriages in *Male Daughters and Female Husbands*, she argued for a concept of 'gender flexibility'.[7]

Other studies have relied on archival and ethnographic work to challenge the assumption of African women's universal and perpetual oppression by patriarchal fathers and husbands. Gaidzanwa and Nzegwu prefer what they see as a non-hierarchical dual sex model of analysis, giving agency and equal weighting to the different roles played by men and women in society. For Gaidzanwa, gender roles are neither static nor fixed for either sex.[8]

Building on Gaidzanwa, Schmidt's study of Shona women in Zimbabwe showed that in the period preceding colonialism, women were autonomous and sometimes held positions of power and influence, including as spirit mediums.[9] Indeed a female spirit medium known as Mbuya Nehanda, is credited with having waged the first *Chimurenga*, or war of resistance against British occupation. El Feki's recent, much lauded study of sexuality in North Africa, highlights how societies can move from openness to plural sexualities and identities, to repression. Religion and its politicization is at the centre of this regression.[10]

Mama shows that the ongoing negative constructions of the powerlessness of African women are a direct result of the transposition of both colonial and gender hierarchies that saw whiteness as normative and "entitled" and blackness and femaleness as inferior.[11] Chanock has argued that the sexism suffered by African women post-colonialism is traceable, in part, to the low status accorded to white women at the time of colonisation.[12] Roman law-derived constructions of men, fathers or husbands, as *pater familias*, or heads of the family, resulted in women as daughters, sisters and wives being regarded as always in need of guardianship. They could not be trusted with full legal capacity because they did not have the intellectual or other faculties to exercise this capacity responsibly. This limited view of *all* women's competence was influential in the colonisers' situation of African women as neither white, nor entitled to the limited privileges of maleness awarded to African men.[13] Ogundipe-Leslie's work shows how African women activists have fought to challenge these western gendered ascriptions.[14] To this category, I would join Kolawole in acknowledging the role African writers of fiction including Adichie, Ba, Mukasonga and Ndebele have played in presenting a complex view of women of the continent and the different strategies they employ for discussing gender.[15] Also growing in influence has been the emerging literature on masculinity.[16]

While acknowledging the dangers of inappropriate or indeed poor translation or application of Western gender theory in different contexts, Tamale argues that it still makes: "a lot of sense in using existing theoretical bases as a starting point and then correcting/revising them in light of the contextual evidence collected in current studies."[17] Tamale's pragmatism is grounded in an acknowledgement of the changes wrought by colonialism and capitalism to those societies. To this I would add religion, specifically the imposition of Christianity and Islam through slavery and colonialism.[18] Oyewumi also acknowledges that there have been enormous changes wrought by both colonialism, and preceding it, the Atlantic slave trade. Referencing Foucault's history of sexuality, Oyewumi starts by highlighting the importance of excavating the "history of gender – that is, the history of what functions in academic discourse as a specific field of truth – must first be written from the viewpoint of a history of discourses."[19] She also identifies the hegemony of western education and training on African intellectuals as in part responsible for an uncritical absorption and acceptance of western perspectives and scholarship as creating *the* leading or dominant discourse in any field.[20]

It is true that issues of cultural hegemony and dominance of voice in the academy and elsewhere remain.[21] However, it may be an over-simplification of any "Western" theory to say that claims of universality are made, or indeed assumed to apply everywhere. If anything, the comparisons drawn between the "enlightened" West and the more gender-oppressive "Other" have been challenged and pluralism accepted, at least rhetorically, in this ill-defined "Western" gender discourse. It remains important to mark the ways in which African scholarship has conceptualized gender and the ways in which distinctions have been drawn with dominant "Western" theories. The situation has been changing as can be seen by the work of Arnfred and others on the Rethinking African Sexualities project.[22] Oinas and Arnfred note that investigating African society:

> Can enhance theoretical thinking in the North by providing connections and contrasts that reveal our local blind spots. Studies of sexuality and politics in Africa can alert us to issues of sex and politics being interconnected in ways we might not otherwise have noticed and which, in turn, can enhance our understanding of the political in sexualities, also in the North.[23]

Understanding religion in Africa

A proper understanding of religion in Africa would require an historical survey starting with pre-colonial polities before moving on to consider the impact of trade, slavery, colonialism and their associated imports: religions.[24] Judaism in Ethiopia is said to be more than 15 centuries old,[25] certainly pre-dating Arab and European colonialism with their dissemination, some might argue imposition, of Islam and Christianity respectively. Indigenous religious beliefs had always existed, and have continued despite vigorous attempts to challenge and undermine them.[26] This chapter cannot hope to do justice to the vast literature on the history of religions on the continent and so will content itself on concentrating on contemporary developments focusing on gender and law.[27]

Religion, and specifically the spread of Christianity (initially Church of England Anglicanism and Roman Catholicism) and Islam have also had a major impact on the position of women within African societies. Writing about how colonial laws made their way to Africa, many of my colleagues describe it as "the reception theory of law." Having been at the receiving end, most Africans I know, prefer to call it the imposition theory of law. In many ways the spread of the Abrahamic religions to Africa can be classified as initially an imposition. However, it is equally true to say that in modern times, they have been, and continue to be, enthusiastically received. The passion of the converts for the conversion has outstripped the source. The reason for the resurgence of religion in Africa, as compared to its diminishment in Europe, is that it offers hope to people. This should be seen in the light of failed states and the inability or unwillingness of many governments to provide education, jobs and decent livelihoods.

Growing in power and influence have been the Pentecostal churches. These new versions are charismatic, literalist and suggest that the congregant has greater agency to change their lives than might actually be the case.[28] Moreover, they are able to accommodate a pluralist understanding of the spiritual world. Explaining the popularity of the Zionist Christian Church in the Northern Province in South Africa, Oomen notes: "This church has shot to popularity because of its ability to combine classic 'Christian' and 'Africanist' discourses, and to include in its theology and practice ancestors, traditional healers, witchcraft beliefs and traditional leaders."[29]

Gender and religion

Again, as with contestations over the role of women within African societies pre- and post-colonialism, so too there is a huge literature on the impact of religion in the (re)construction of relations between men and women within African societies. Did religious adherence help or hinder women's self-actualization? Were religious frameworks liberatory or oppressive? Were religions a seamless continuation of the colonial project of domination or did religion offer an alternative discourse that both challenged and changed both local cultures and practices and the colonial project itself? Does the answer depend on who was interpreting the religion? How did it translate into local conditions? Was there a successful transplantation from the place of origin, to the new sites of practice?[30] How is success to be measured, by the number of adherents, changed social behaviours or a more humane colonial policy? Are any phenomena ever that clear cut?

In terms of gender and religion, it seems true to say that religious leaders (Christian and Muslim), have continued to encourage conservative, heteronormative relations. The privileging of male authority and decision making is still revered, as is the submission of women.[31] While men are asked not to be abusive in the exercise of their power, in many instances, this injunction is not enforced or prioritised. If anything, the changed post-colonial cultural landscape dovetails neatly with the masculinised religious frameworks in the construction of gender relations. The two, religion and culture, act as mutually reinforcing forces providing justification and legitimacy for the maintenance of unequal gender relations. Continuity of masculine dominance is guaranteed by the exclusion of women from leadership in religious, cultural and indeed public institutions. Writing on the right to conscience, Dickens perceptively argues:

> Religious institutions and hierarchies that, for instance, do not include women, and that expressly exclude women from positions of doctrinal authority, may be considered conscientiously flawed, and to lack relevance in their pronouncements, particularly on a matter such as abortion, in which women's health and interests are centrally involved.[32]

If one does not have a voice in the determination of policies that affect one, then one cannot easily influence those policies. It offends against dignity and equality and reinforces stereotypes of women as incapable of leadership.[33] Some faiths seem to demand disproportionately high personal sacrifice from women, when compared to men. The use of familial imagery, "the Christian family" and the idea of the common good which should override personal "selfishness" is deployed effectively to silence women who feel duty bound to conform to the gender stereotype of women as caring, outward looking and willing to privilege others over self.

A countervailing voice is Van Klinken, whose empirical research on the sermons of a Zambian male pastor in the Pentecostal church showed a more nuanced version of gender being propagated. Specifically, in a series of lectures on male headship, Pastor Banda (no relation) enjoined his flock to reject an oppressive model of male headship, not least because it showed an abdication of leadership. In its stead, he promoted a 'constructive exercise of power' which he framed as grounded in Christ's example of 'servant leadership'.[34]

Is Pastor Banda's approach, in asking for benign exercise of male headship, failing to dislodge the presumption of male supremacy over women? As Van Klinken notes, African feminist theologians and scholars have joined their northern sisters in pointing out that far from challenging gender ascriptions, continuing to insist on male headship merely reinforces the misuse of patriarchal power, leading to husbands seeking to rationalize violence against wives. They further argue that the HIV crisis can be explained, in part, by the continued religious insistence on demands made on women to "submit themselves", literally, to their diseased husbands.[35] These discussions are not new, or unique to Protestantism, for as Doris Lessing observes in her memoir/travelogue of Zimbabwe, of the Roman Catholic nuns that she meets on her journey: "They are feminists, critical of male authority of the Church and the Pope." They remind her of the nuns who ran the Convent school that she had attended in the 1920s, in then capital Salisbury: "I wonder what Mother Patrick would make of them? Kindred spirits, I think."[36]

Squaring the circle: gender equality, religion and human rights

The methodology for the re-constructionist project varies depending on its authorship. Some favour an approach that privileges human rights as the means to achieve gender equality, while others see it as important to work from within the religion.[37] Those in the latter category demand an historical contextualization of texts noting that one cannot ignore the period in which religious texts were written. They further argue that often those charged with recording the words of key figures in the religion and with interpreting the texts have put narrow constructions on the words. The effect disfavours women because it confers the privilege of leadership in family, religion and public life exclusively on men. Groups like Musawah, point to empirical research as debunking the myth of men meeting all the responsibilities associated with male guardianship. The lived realities of women show that often they contribute financially to the family, and in some instances are solely responsible for maintenance. The invocation of rights of male authority without the concomitant responsibilities itself points to the grafting onto religion of patriarchal cultural frames of reference, and is not a religious injunction as some claim.[38]

Change is of course under way, but it is often slow and patchy and sometimes subject to violent resistance.[39] Those women who do seek to challenge the exclusivity of power and the mis-interpretation of religious and other texts, are labelled 'outlaws' and subjected to public shaming which itself acts as a deterrent to other women who may aspire to greater gender equality and rights of access and participation in all spheres, including that of work. Examples of these phenomena can be found in discussions during legal reform. In 1996 the Namibian Parliament passed the Married Person's Equality Act. The purpose of the law was to remove the legally enshrined discrimination against married women. Prior to the passage of the law, women marrying under the Roman-Dutch law came under the guardianship of their husbands. They lacked legal capacity and could not own property in their own right or indeed enter into contracts. They were, like their children, minors. Unlike their sons, whose minority ended at 21, their minority was perpetual. The post-independence Constitution which had been drafted after Namibia had attained freedom from its mandated status from a racist South African state, provided for equality for all before the law. Surprising then was the response of some male parliamentarians to the Equality Bill's proposal to equalize status between husband and wife with one saying: "Even in a game of cards, the King counts more than the

Queen" and another "A hen cannot become a cock and it remains so." Finally, a personal favourite: "Man is the image of god and we pray Our Father in Heaven but not our mother in heaven. That means that man is more powerful than women."[40] Becker notes that the public opposition to the Bill was led exclusively by men who argued that both tradition and religion were against equality between the sexes.[41]

Writing about the passage of the Domestic Violence Act in Zimbabwe, Christiansen identifies the same tensions. Using the Hansard (parliamentary) record and media reports, she paints a picture of the deployment of religion and culture as swords to defeat claims for equality and the enactment of the law. The counter-narrative, provided by women's rights advocates, also employed religion as a shield to argue that violence was a breach of Christian principles. One Member of Parliament said: "I stand here representing God Almighty. Women are not equal to men." To this, the Zimbabwean Lawyers for Human Rights responded in a letter: "The Domestic Violence Bill advocates for mutual respect in families, a principle that runs through the Bible and Zimbabwean Culture. 1 Corinthians 7 vs. 3."[42]

Sexual minorities are often classed as religious and cultural "deviants" and thus not entitled to either consultation or consideration. The labelling of gay men as "women" suggests that they have forfeited their male privilege and must thus content themselves with the inferior female role. The de-classification of gay men is a manifest example of oppressive gender stereotypes which also embed the idea of woman as a second-class citizen.[43] Again one sees the deployment of both religion and culture in legal reform that seeks to criminalize homosexuality.

A great deal has been written about violations of LGBTI rights on the African continent.[44] At heart it is a debate premised on sexuality and its uses: for pleasure certainly but, more central, is the belief that sexuality should serve procreation which can only take place within a heterosexual, preferably marital, relationship.[45] There is little point therefore in recognizing the rights of same sex people. Religion, often intermingled with nationalist politics, has been central to the framing of the debate.[46] For political groups such as the Muslim Brotherhood, "dissident sexualities" threaten masculinist gender frameworks which privilege male control of women. Recognition of sexual diversity runs the risk of creating dissident gender categories and rebellious women, all of which pose a threat to the heterosexual family.[47]

Also important has been the elision of religious norms and "nature." Natural law cannot support "unnatural" behaviour. The conundrum as Lemaitre notes, is between competing visions of the moral order:

> The most important exponents of Catholic legal thought, and the church itself, claim that human rights are nothing more than natural law recognized and reproduced in legal documents. This claim is not easily rejected because human rights activists themselves make similar appeals to an objective moral order – the human rights order.[48]

While there has been discussion about the legacy of British colonial laws on homosexuality in post-colonial African states, it is religious pressure and rationalizations that have kept them in place. The irony of the politicians' anti-imperialism call to resist Western pressure to repeal laws of Western origin, is coupled with the invocation of Christian and Islamic norms, equally alien to Africa, to justify the maintenance of laws banning homosexuality.[49] Lost are discussions about autonomy, social justice, compassion and memory.[50] Given the importance of religion in both political and private life, an insistence on the decoupling of religion and rights, an insular secularity, may prove counter-productive. More persuasive may be a framing of the issues within religious ethics of compassion and kindness for all humanity which is the position adopted by Archbishop Desmond Tutu, thus putting paid to the idea of a unitary religious view.[51] Asked about a "gay lobby" within the Vatican, the Pope is reported to have said:

> There's a lot of talk about the gay lobby, but I've never seen it on the Vatican ID card...When I meet a gay person, I have to distinguish between their being gay and being part of a lobby. If they accept the Lord and have goodwill, who am I to judge them? They shouldn't be marginalized. The tendency [to homosexuality] is not the problem ... they're our brothers.[52]

Human rights and religion in Africa

I now move on to consider the human rights norms that govern religion on the Continent.[53] The African Charter on Human and Peoples' Rights, 1981[54] frames article 8, the right to religion in this way:

> Freedom of conscience, the profession and free practice of religion shall be guaranteed. No one may, subject to law and order, be submitted to measures restricting the exercise of these freedoms.

There are *no* reservations to this provision. The African Commission which oversees the Charter has considered this provision in respect of challenges to state denial of the religious rights of various groups and found violations in each case. The first concerned people belonging to the Jehovah's Witness group in Zaire. They were subjected to arbitrary arrests, appropriation of church property, and exclusion from access to education. The Commission ruled that state action could not be justified by reference to public order as it was excessive and inordinate.[55] Another case concerned Christians in Sudan (pre-partition). The authors complained about the "oppression of Sudanese Christians and religious leaders, expulsion of all missionaries from Juba, arbitrary arrests and detention of priests, the closure and destruction of Church buildings, the constant harassment of religious figures, and prevention of non-Muslims from receiving aid." They further noted that there were forcible attempts to convert Christians and that Christian prisoners were denied food in an attempt to blackmail them.[56] The Commission identified a breach of both article 8 and article 2 on discrimination noting that respecting the Muslim religious rights, "should not be done in such a way as to cause discrimination and distress to others."[57]

The final case involved the Endorois indigenous group in Kenya who were arbitrarily evicted from their land, making it impossible for them to perform traditional rites at Lake Borgoria.[58] Access to the Lake and surrounding forests was central to the community. The ancestral burial grounds needed tending. Moreover, in addition to marriages, initiation and circumcisions, there was an annual seasonal ritual around the Lake to mark the survival of the Endorois from an earlier catastrophic event. All these comprised religion under international law.[59] The government failed to put in place access to the Lake or indeed to consult or compensate them.

The Endorois case is significant because it is the first time that the African Commission considered indigenous religious beliefs. Recalling Raday's contention that there is often an overlap between religion and culture, the Endorois also brought a claim under article 17 of the Charter for a breach of their cultural rights. By turning their home into a game reserve the government had denied them their right to practise their culture. They noted that unlike article 8, this provision was not hedged by the subject to law and order clause.[60] Finding for the Endorois, the African Commission noted: "This Commission is aware that religion is often linked to land, cultural beliefs and practices, and that freedom to worship and engage in such ceremonial acts is at the centre of the freedom of religion."[61] It noted that the denial of access to the Lake and the surrounding forest meant that they could not perform the ceremonial rituals which were central to their spiritual framework. This constituted a breach of article 8 of the Charter.[62]

In both the Endorois and Sudanese case, the Commission was clear that the actions taken by the state were neither reasonable nor proportionate and could not be interpreted in any other way than as direct violations of the authors' article 8 rights.

African states are also party to a number of UN Conventions including the Convention on the Elimination of All Forms of Discrimination against Women (CEDAW).[63] The African states seeking to limit their obligations under CEDAW on grounds of religion all cite the Sharia.[64] While it may well be that these states are at least honest in their acknowledgement of state deference to religion, it has the unfortunate effect of reinforcing a common stereotype of "Islamic law as a form of legitimized oppression of women." It goes without saying that this view is partial and biased: gender discrimination is not unique or confined to one religion or culture.

The "African CEDAW" is the African Protocol on Women's Rights. Although it does not address religion directly, it has made some concessions to religion, not least in permitting polygyny. The Protocol tries to bridge religious and cultural male claimed entitlements to polygyny, by noting that while monogamy is the preferred model of family, polygyny will be acknowledged.[65] Moreover, it acknowledges, and, arguably reinforces, religious discrimination against women in the inheritance of property and on the dissolution of marriage, by providing that property should be shared equitably.[66] The equity here is closely allied to complementarity anticipated by religious frameworks, not least the Sharia and customary laws. While successful legal challenges have been mounted on differential property entitlements justified by reference to custom or culture, dislodging or renegotiating religious precepts seems much harder.

Controversial has been the inclusion in the Protocol of article 14(2)(c) which permits abortion in defined circumstances: "sexual assault, rape, incest, and where the continued pregnancy endangers the mental and physical health of the mother or the life of the mother or the foetus." This provision has been objected to by states such as Rwanda, which is predominantly Catholic, Senegal, Sudan, and more recently Uganda. While the African Protocol is the first international human rights instrument to recognize the right to abortion, the reality is that there is little provision.[67] Case law from South Africa shows that when faced with a challenge brought by a Christian organization to the right to terminate pregnancy on grounds of a right to life, the Constitutional Court upheld the abortion law noting that independent life rights did not begin until after birth.[68]

Ten African states are members of the Arab League which has a separate human rights treaty, the Arab Charter, 2004.[69] They all also belong to the Organisation of Islamic Cooperation (OIC) which was responsible for the Cairo Declaration on Human Rights in Islam. Both documents take, to different degrees, Islamic Sharia as their guide on issues of equality or equity between the sexes.[71] The impact of what Cismas calls "religionalism" can be seen in the discussions over gender and sexuality.[70] At the regional level, co-existence, of international, regional and "religional" frameworks, creates challenges of normative dissonance when different standards apply to the same issue depending on which human rights instrument is invoked.

It is noteworthy that Sudan is one of the few African states not to have ratified CEDAW or the African Protocol on Women's Rights. It is a member of the Arab League, the OIC and the African Union and is also the site of much of the litigation on public order "morality crimes" in regional human rights law. Much has been written about how the responsibility for maintaining "honour" in this context is placed on women who are seen as the repositories of culture, modesty and morality. Male relatives are forced into a supervisory role.[72] The policing of this "honour", in Sudan at least, seems to be almost exclusively in the hands of men, whether religious leaders, moral police or anyone else who chooses to take offence.

Doebbler v. Sudan was about the arrest of eight female university students for immoral behaviour under article 152 of the Criminal Law 1991. They had applied for permission to hold a picnic in a local park but were arrested for "kissing, wearing trousers, dancing with men, crossing legs with men, sitting with boys and sitting and talking with boys."[73] The young women were convicted of public order violations and sentenced to between 25–40 lashes and ordered to pay fines. The lashes, on bare skin, were administered in public. There was no medical supervision. The complaint to the African Commission cited a violation of article 5 of the African Charter which protects the dignity of the person and outlaws degrading, inhuman treatment and torture. The students claimed that their punishment had been disproportionate, and also, that the punishment had exceeded the prescribed Sharia penalties for minor crimes.[74]

The Commission found for the complainants. In so doing, the Commission was at pains to note that it was not passing judgment on the Sharia but on the Criminal Law which founded the action. This seems disingenuous, not least because the 1991 statute which falls within the Public Order framework, is subtitled "Offences of Honour, Reputation and Public Morality."[75] In a Memorandum to the Bill, the government noted:

> Thus the first thing that the Revolution for National Salvation has paid attention to…was asserting the country's identity and the promulgation of the original Sudanese Laws derived from Islamic Law in response to the Sudanese people's aspiration and in fulfilment of the promise made by the revolution.[76]

Sezgin advances the view that once religious law is incorporated into state law, it loses (or should be seen to lose) its character as religious law, for it becomes an instrument of the state.[77] Equally disappointing was the Commission's silence with respect to the targeting of the women, but not the men.[78] Of course the punishment was wholly unnecessary. Lubna Hussein, the UN journalist prosecuted under article 152 for wearing trousers has said:

> Islam does not say whether a woman can wear trousers or not. The clothes I was wearing when the police caught me – I pray in them. I pray to my God in them. And neither does Islam flog women because of what they wear. If any Muslim in the world says Islamic law or sharia law flogs women for their clothes, let them show me what the Qur'an or Prophet Muhammad said on that issue. There is nothing. It is not about religion, it is about men treating women badly.[79]

In 2014 another case was filed against Sudan at the African Commission on behalf of a Christian woman charged with apostasy and adultery.[80] Born to a Christian mother and Muslim father and a Christian by choice, the complainant married a Christian man born in Sudan, but now a United States resident and citizen. She was sentenced to death for apostasy and ordered to be lashed 100 times for adultery. Pregnant, she was imprisoned with her toddler son. While awaiting her appeal to be heard, she gave birth, while shackled, to a daughter in prison. An application for provisional measures (interim stop on the execution of the punishments) was sent to the African Commission on her behalf. Ultimately the case was resolved by diplomatic and media pressure. She was released and flew out to the United States with her husband and children, meeting the Pope at the Vatican en route. The gender discrimination against Meriam was two-fold; her case highlighted the distinction between men and women, mothers and fathers with respect to the transmission of religion. Her mother's Christianity did not count when put against her father's faith. Moreover, while Muslim men can marry non-Muslim women, women are denied the right to marry outside of the faith, even if it is an imposed rather than chosen faith. The charge of adultery brought against her was in itself a moral claim of religious "ownership" over her body, mind and decision-making. In the case of *Amnesty International v. Sudan* discussed earlier, the African Commission noted:

> Another matter is the application of Shari'a law. There is no controversy as to Shari'a being based upon the interpretation of the Muslim religion. When Sudanese tribunals apply Shari'a, they must do so in accordance with the other obligations undertaken by the State of Sudan. Trials must always accord with international fair-trial standards. Also, it is fundamentally unjust that religious laws should be applied against non-adherents of the religion. Tribunals that apply only Shari'a are thus not competent to judge non-Muslims, and everyone should have the right to be tried by a secular court if they wish.[81]

Most religious discrimination cases are argued in national courts. The next section considers the issue of dress and presentation.

Religious rights for Rastafari

While in Europe the focus is on the wearing of religious dress, in other regions, the issue of appearance is not just one that only affects Muslim women.[82] Kenji Yoshino has explored the demands made of religious minorities to obscure or "cover" their religious identity in order to fit in with majoritarian demands. He notes that there are similarities with the demands made of gay people in the workplace to mute their gay selves with demands made of people of religious faith not to wear outward symbols of their faith, or to openly discuss that faith within the work environment. The rendering invisible of the religious self is the price to be paid for entry to some public spaces.[83]

In Southern and Central Africa, men and boys professing the Rastafari faith have been denied rights to participate in education and employment, in part because they refused to cut off their dreadlocks to conform with the rules and regulations of schools and employment practices.[84] They have even been asked to justify that Rastafarianism is indeed a religion. The adherents cite the Bible, which they say is the source of the religion and claim that it enjoins them not to cut their hair.[85] The case law on Rastafari traverses a lot of ground: colonialism, race and the framing of religious authority; could a black man (the Ethiopian Emperor Haille Selassie) really have founded a legitimate religion, what are the key elements for a set of beliefs to be classified as a religion, by whose definition and through which aesthetic lens can the wearing of dreadlocks be seen as untidy or unacceptable in the public sphere?

National courts have in all cases recognized Rastafarianism as a religion, some because they focus on the sincerity of belief of the adherents[86] and others because they have ascertained that the practice sought to be protected is a central tenet of the belief system. However, they have also noted that smoking marijuana (another practice said to be central to religious observance) cannot be condoned because it breaches criminal law.[87]

Although not explicitly explored, there is also a gender dimension. The case law focuses exclusively on men. The demands made of men to conform to an aesthetic ethic in the workplace is not expected of African women who wear dreadlocks.[88] The demand that men cut their hair under pain of losing their jobs, or forfeiting their education, was a breach of their economic, social and cultural rights and impacted on their ability to earn a living. Furthermore, gender stereotypes of men as breadwinners extended the resultant disadvantage beyond the individual man and also impacted on the wider family and dependents. Even if a Rastafari did want to "cover" or "mute his religious affiliation", the challenge is that dreadlocks cannot be disguised, or cut for public engagement during the day, and then re-grown by night for private religious observance. Compared to other groups, Rastafari are disproportionately impacted by the assimilationist demands made of them.[89]

Perhaps one of the more challenging questions in post-colonial African states has been the seeming inability of both state law and religion to control some practices. The final section examines some of the issues.

Indigenous or cultural-religious practices: the limits of religious authority and secular law

There are practices such as Female Genital Mutilation (FGM), slavery and witchcraft which appear to be beyond the control of both state and religious leaders, although both entities seek to influence them. FGM is the issue that has received the most attention from lawyers, policy makers and even religious leaders. The African Protocol on Women's Rights is the first international treaty explicitly outlawing FGM and calling on states parties to prevent the practice from occurring, and when it has happened, to provide counselling and rehabilitative services to survivors.[90] At a conference on FGM held in Cairo in 2003 both the Sheik of Alzhar (the pre-eminent Islamic authority) and the Patriarch of the Coptic Church in Egypt noted that neither Islam nor Christianity required girls or women to be cut.[91]

Despite the legal, NGO and religious consensus on the issue, FGM remains prevalent.[92] The reasons for the continuation of the practice are manifold: key is the desire to control young girls and to ensure that their sexuality is harnessed to marriage and to fulfilling gender stereotyped roles. The issue of control is central for, as the CEDAW/CRC general recommendation notes, even when people move to new communities, the practice persists: "in particular in destination countries where gender roles provide women and girls with greater personal freedom."[93]

The solution, transformative equality, requires attitudinal change in all sectors of society. However, as long as gender-based discrimination persists, laws remain unenforced, police and judges remain unwilling to take seriously these violations as constituting breaches of human rights, community and religious leaders continue to assert, albeit incorrectly that the practice is required by the religion or custom and women remain dependent on marriage for survival, then the practice will continue.

The case of *Hadjiatou Mani v. Niger*[94] illustrates what happens when the above conditions are not met. Hadjiatou and her parents lived in Niger which had, until it was outlawed in 2003, a caste-based system of slavery. At age 12 she was handed over to her parent's master who raped her at 13. He already had four wives. She was not formally married. She went on to bear him three children before he issued her with a certificate of liberation. When she tried to marry another man by choice, her former master reported her for bigamy. Although successful in the first court, Hadjiatou lost the case on appeal and was sentenced to imprisonment. It was only when a human rights NGO heard of her case and became involved that she was freed. Her case was brought before the West African regional tribunal, ECOWAS, which ruled that slavery was a breach of human rights. They ordered Niger to pay her compensation which the state did with impressive rapidity.

Helen Duffy, one of the lawyers involved in the case, has bemoaned the ECOWAS tribunal's silence on the gendered discrimination that made the slavery of the young woman particularly heinous.[95] Commenting on the case, Duodo highlights the challenges facing an enslaved woman seeking to free herself:

> Yet unless a woman has access to an influential person, especially one who holds a judicial office, she cannot make him realise that the man who worships in the same mosque as himself has a way of life that does not accord totally with the tenets of universal justice, as preached by their common religion.[96]

As with FGM, so too with slavery. State law may ban it (or indeed deny its very existence), while state practice continues, by its inaction, to condone it. Religious leaders may condemn it as not being of the religion, while doing nothing to castigate or cast out those within their flocks whom they know to be enslaving other human beings.[97] The intersection of gender and race-based discrimination reinforced by the system of slavery means that black women are disproportionately impacted. As the Mani case showed, for a young girl, slavery was not only about labouring without pay in the fields and home, but also coerced sex which led to three pregnancies.[98]

The final example concerns witchcraft and specifically accusations of witchcraft. The anecdotal evidence seems to point to two groups as particularly vulnerable: children, often accused of being possessed by demons by renegade Pentecostal priests, and older women, often widowed, who are accused of ill-intent whenever something goes wrong, or indeed someone wants to move a widow off her deceased husband's land or to win an inheritance dispute.[99] The cost to both is high: painful exorcisms and ostracism from the community. While law and human rights protect both, it is clear that often this protection is meaningless, for without access to resources (legal, emotional and financial) both are vulnerable to abuse.[100] A life-cycle analysis shows that just as widows are women without male protection from a husband, so too often the children accused are homeless street children, or orphans or living with relatives. It goes without saying that accusations made in the name of religion (imposed or indigenous) are almost impossible to challenge.

Conclusion

I started this chapter by telling you about my grandmother. I wanted to finish it by telling you about the birth of my first daughter in London in October 2007. My mother came from Zimbabwe to help with the new baby. On her return, I gave her my daughter's umbilical cord in a little matchbox. I asked her to take it back with her and to bury it in my grandmother's grave in the village where I grew up. It was in remembrance of the many happy years that I had spent with my granny. I was comforted by the thought that my grandmother would watch over my daughter, and later, her sister as she had done my brother, cousin and me. The 22-year-old sophisticate who rolled her eyes at these strange ways, is no more. In her place is a middle-aged woman who likes to believe that justice is both a legal and supernatural concept.

This chapter has considered the meaning of gender from an African feminist perspective. It concluded that the impact of colonialism and the spread of foreign religions had all played an important part in forcing an evolution in gender relations. This chapter has also considered how human rights bodies and courts on the continent have both defined religion and its impact on a range of areas of life. While both law and religion are growing in importance in African societies, the continuation of practices such as FGM, slavery and witchcraft accusations remind us of Allott's limits of law, religious and secular.[101] Conversely, the tangible changes wrought within African societies by both human rights and religion tell us that the possibilities of positive transformative change exist.

Notes

1 B. Sousa Santos, "Law: A Map of Misreading. Towards a Postmodern Conception of Law" *Journal of Law and Society* 14, 1987, 279–302, 289.

2 M. Kolawole, "Re-Conceptualizing African Gender Theory: Feminism, Womanism and the *Arere* Metaphor" in S. Arnfred, *Re-thinking Sexualities in Africa*, Uppsala, Nordic Africa Institute, 2004, 251–266. She adds to the category of nationality, other considerations that need to be taken into account including: "class, culture, ethnicity religion and politics and the attendant result that African women's progressive gender consciousness differs from one African society to another." p. 253.

3 I have kept "Western" as a term to mirror the terminology used by many of the authors considered in this piece. It is of course true that terms such as global south and north, third world, developing and developed, industrial and industrialising, are also used in other contexts. See for example R. Rao, *Third World Protest: Between Home and the World*, Oxford, Oxford University Press, 2010, 24–30.

4 O. Oyewumi, *The Invention of Women*, Minneapolis, University of Minnesota, 1997, xi–xii. See also S. Arnfred, "Introduction" in S. Arnfred (ed), *Re-thinking Sexualities in Africa*, Uppsala, Nordic Africa Institute, 2004, 7–29.

5 See generally A. Cornwall (ed), *Readings in Gender in Africa*, Oxford, James Currey, 2005.

6 For the impact of patriliny or matriliny descent systems on gender role construction and also receptivity to the Christian missionization, see J. Davison, *Gender, Lineage and Ethnicity in Southern Africa*, Colorado, Westview, 1997, 100–103.

7 I. Amadiume, *Male Daughters, Female Husbands*, London, ZED, 1987. Cf. O. Oyewumi (1997) 185 n 4. See also I. Amadiume, *African Matriarchal Foundations: The Case of Igbo Societies*, London, Martins, 1987.

8 R. Gaidzanwa, "Bourgeois Theories of Gender and Feminism and their Shortcomings with Reference to Southern African Countries" in R. Meena (ed), *Gender in Southern Africa: Conceptual and Theoretical Issues*, Harare, SAPES, 1982, 92. See also C. Obbo, *African Women: Their Struggle for Economic Independence*, London, ZED, 1981.

9 E. Schmidt, *Peasants, Traders and Wives: Shona Women in the History of Zimbabwe 1870–1939*, Oxford, James Currey, 1992.

10 S. El Feki, *Sex and the Citadel: Intimate Life in a Changing Arab World*, London, Vintage, 2014.

11 A. Mama, "Gender Studies for Africa's Transformation" in T. Mkandawira, *African Intellectuals: Rethinking Politics, Language, Gender and Development*, London, ZED, 2005, 94, 104–5.

12 M. Chanock, "Neither Customary, Nor Legal: African Customary Law in an Era of Family law Reform" *International Journal of Law, Family and Policy* 3, 1989, 72.

13 See also R. Grosfoguel, L. Oso and A. Christou, "Racism, Intersectionality and Migration Studies: Framing Some Theoretical Reflections" *Identities: Global Studies in Culture and Power*, 2014, 1–18, 9–10, 14–15.

14 M. Ogundipe-Leslie, *Recreating Ourselves-African Women and Critical Transformation*, Trenton, Africa World Press, 1994.

15 M. Kolawole (2004) 254 n 2. C. Adichie, *Purple Hibiscus*, New York, Fourth Estate, 2003. M. Ba, *So Long a Letter*, London, Heinemann, 2008. N. Ndebele, *The Cry of Winnie Mandela: A Novel*, Oxford, Ayebia-Clarke, 2004. S. Mukasonga (English translation by M. Mauthner), *Our Lady of the Nile*, Brooklyn, Archipelago Books, 2014. For non-fiction, see also, C. Adichie, *We Should all be feminists*, London, Harper Collins, 2014.

16 L. Ouzgane and R. Morrell (eds), *African Masculinities: Men in Africa from the Late Nineteenth Century to the Present*, Basingstoke, Palgrave MacMillan, 2005. M. Epprecht, *Hungochani: The History of a Dissident Sexuality in Southern Africa*, Montreal, Mc Gill-Queen's University Press, 2004. See also the Special Issue on "Masculinities in Southern Africa" *Journal of Southern African Studies*, 24 (3), 1998.

17 S. Tamale, "Researching and Theorizing Sexualities in Africa" in S. Tamale (ed), *African Sexualities*, Oxford, Pambazuka Press, 2011, 11–37.

18 Epprecht argues that Christianity was introduced to the African continent by Mark, one of the disciples of Jesus, and not by Europeans as often claimed. He later asserts that the Portuguese were the first Europeans to take Catholicism South of the Sahara "in the fifteenth to seventeenth centuries". M. Epprecht, *Sexuality and Social Justice in Africa: Rethinking Homophobia and Forging Resistance*, London, ZED, 2013, 82, 84.

19 O. Oyewumi, *The Invention of Women: Making an African Sense of Western Gender Discourse*, Minneapolis, University of Minnesota, 1997, xi.

20 Ibid. 22–27.

21 R. Connell, "Rethinking Gender from the South" *Feminist Studies*, 40, 3, 2014, 518–539. Hawthorne and van Klinken note that even postcolonial studies are not immune from this Western dominance. S. Melville Hawthorne and A. van Klinken, "Catachresis: Religion, Gender and Postcoloniality" *Religion and Gender*, 3, 2, 2013, 159–161, 163–167.

22 See generally the papers in S. Arnfred (ed), *Re-thinking Sexualities in Africa*, Uppsala, Nordic Africa Institute, 2004.

23 E. Oinas and S. Arnfred, "Introduction: Sex & Politics-Case Africa" *Nordic Journal of Feminist and Gender Research* 17, 3, 2009, 149–157, 149.

24 See for example J. Davison, *Gender, Lineage, and Ethnicity in Southern Africa*, Colorado, Westview Press, 1997, 65–94.

25 S. Weil, "The Ethiopian Jews: Background" Jewish Women's Archive, at: http://jwa.org/encyclopedia/article/ethiopian-jewish-women. My thanks to Lisa Fishbayn-Joffe for this reference.

26 See for example the discussions over colonial attempts to criminalize the belief in witchcraft and the conflation of traditional beliefs in healing via an intercession of a traditional healer and ancestor connection with "backwardness". M. Bourdillon, *Where are the Ancestors? Changing Culture in Zimbabwe*, Harare, University of Zimbabwe, 1993, 71–126. T. Petrus, "Defining Witchcraft related Crime in the Eastern Cape Province of South Africa" *International Journal of Sociology and Anthropology*, 3(1), 2011, 1–8.

27 D. Maxwell, "Writing the History of African Christianity: Reflections of an Editor" *Journal of Religion in Africa*, 36, 2006, 379–399.

28 A. Mbe, "New Pentecostalism in the Wake of the Economic Crisis in Cameroon" *Nordic Journal of African Studies*, 11, 3, 2002, 359–376; D. Parsitau and P. Mwaura, "God in the City: Pentecostalism as an Urban Phenomenon in Kenya" *Studia Historiae*, 36, 2, 2010, 95–112.

29 B. Oomen, *Chiefs in South Africa: Law, Power & Culture in the Post-Apartheid Era*, Oxford, James Currey, 2005, 153.

30 See also Chanock on the face-off between colonial courts, missionaries and African men and women on the issue of marriage, and, specifically polygyny. M. Chanock, *Law, Custom and Social Order: The Colonial Experience in Malawi and Zambia*, Portsmouth, Heinemann, 1998, 150–159. See also J. Amoah and T. Bennett, "The Freedoms of Religion and Culture under the South African Constitution" *African Human Rights Law Journal*, 8, 2, 2008, 357–375, 359–367.

31 J. Lemaitre, "Catholic Constitutionalism on Sex, Women and the Beginning of Life" in R. Cook, J. Erdman and B. Dickens, *Abortion Law in Transnational*

Perspective, Pennsylvania, Penn Press, 2014, 239–257, 242. See also S. Razavi and A. Jenichen (eds), "The Unhappy Marriage of Religion and Politics – Problems and Pitfalls for Gender Equality" in a Special Issue of *Third World Quarterly*, 31, 6, 2010.

32 B. Dickens, "The Right to Conscience" in R. Cook, J. Erdman and B. Dickens *Abortion Law in Transnational Perspective*, Pennsylvania, Penn Press, 2014, 210–238, 211, 220–221.

33 R. Cook and S. Cusack, *Gender Stereotyping*, Philadelphia, University of Pennsylvania Press, 2010, 17, 86, 92, 101.

34 A. van Klinken, "Male Headship as Male Agency: An Alternative Understanding of a 'Patriarchal' African Pentecostal Discourse on Masculinity" *Religion and Gender*, 1, 1, 2011, 104–124.

35 Ibid. 107-112. See also A. van Klinken, "God's World is not an Animal Farm. Or it it? The Catachrestic Translation of Gender Equality in African Pentecostalism" *Religion and Gender*, 3, 2, 2013, 240–258.

36 D. Lessing, *African Laughter: Four Visits to Zimbabwe*, Harper Collins, London, 1993, 163. Although an atheist, she writes about her boarding school years at the Dominican Convent and being a homesick child who had climbed onto the lap of a nun: "and wept in arms that turned out, after a first stiffness of surprise, to be kind, warm, close, hospitable." p. 164.

37 UNRISD, "Religion, Politics and Gender Equality" *Research and Policy Brief* 11, 2011, 4. See also Raday in Chapter 1 in this volume.

38 See generally Musawah, *Men in Charge? Rethinking Authority in Muslim Legal Tradition*, London, Oneworld, 2014.

39 See generally F. Raday, "Culture, Religion and CEDAW's Article 5(a)" in H-B. Schopp-Schilling and C. Flinterman (eds), *The Circle of Empowerment: Twenty Five Years of the UN Committee on the Elimination of all Forms of Discrimination against Women*, New York, Feminist Press, 2007, 68–85.

40 Legal Assistance Centre (LAC), *Guide to the Married Person's Equality Act*, Windhoek, LAC, 2009, 22, 23.

41 H. Becker, "A Concise History of Gender, 'Tradition' and the State in Namibia" in Konrad Adenaur Foundation, *State, Society and Democracy*, 171–200. Available at: www.kas.de/upload/auslandshomepages/namibia/State_Society_Democracy/chapter6.pdf.

42 L. Bull Christiansen, "'In our Culture' – How Debates about Zimbabwe's Domestic Violence Law became a 'Culture Struggle'" *Nordic Journal of Feminist and Gender Research*, 17, 2, 2009, 175–191, 179, 183.

43 Question Time following Statement by Special Rapporteur on Promotion and Protection of Human Rights and Fundamental Freedoms while Countering Terror, 64th General Assembly, Third Committee, DPI, GA/SHC/3959 (26 October 2009), para 16, available at: www.un.org/News/Press/docs/2009/gashc3959.doc.htm. Report of the Special Rapporteur on the Promotion and Protection of Human Rights and Fundamental Freedoms while Countering Terrorism, Part III, *A gender perspective on countering terrorism*, UN Doc. A/64/211, para 18–53 (3 August 2009).

44 S. Tamale (ed), *African Sexualities*, Oxford, Pambazuka, 2011; M. Epprecht, *Hungochani: The History of a Dissident Sexuality in Southern Africa*, Montreal, McGill-Queen's University Press, 2004.

45 Epprecht's study on the "heterosexualisation" of African societies provides an important counter-narrative. M. Epprecht, *Heterosexual Africa? The History of an Idea from the Age of Exploration to the Age of AIDS*, Ohio, Ohio University Press, 2008. S. Murray and W. Roscoe, *Boy-Wives and Female Husbands: Studies in African Homosexualities*, New York, St. Martin's Press, 1998.

46 A. van Klinken, "Homosexuality, Politics and Pentecostal Nationalism in Zambia" *Studies in World Christianity*, 20, 3, 2014, 259–281.
47 Muslim Brotherhood, "Muslim Brotherhood Statement Denouncing UN Women Declaration for Violating Sharia Principles", Cairo, 13 March 2013, www.ikhwanweb.com/article.php?id=30731 (last accessed 7 April 2015).
48 J. Lemaitre, "Catholic Constitutionalism on Sex, Women and the Beginning of Life" in R. Cook, J. Erdman and B. Dickens, *Abortion Law in Transnational Perspective*, Pennsylvania, Penn Press, 2014, 239–257, 252. See also N. Scott, "The Clash of Unprovable Universalisms: International Human Rights and Islamic Law" *Oxford Journal of Law and Religion*, 2, 2, 2013, 307–329.
49 T. Adams, "Binyavanga Wainaina interview: coming out in Kenya" *The Observer*, London, 16 February 2014. It has been noted that much of the anti-homosexuality talk that is underway is itself an import of Christian fundamentalist ideology from the United States. The export of hate has resulted in a legal action brought by US-based Centre for Constitutional in the United States and the group Sexual Minorities Uganda (using the Alien Tort Statute) against Scott Lively, one of the US preachers associated with public comments against homosexuality in Uganda. A. Warner for the Centre for Constitutional Rights, "The Case against Scott Lively-Illustrated" reprinted in *Huffington Post*, 2 May 2014. Available at: www.huffingtonpost.com/the-center-for-constitutional-rights/the-case-against-scott-li_b_4732099.html. I am grateful to Scott Skinner-Thompson, one of the attorneys involved in filing suit, for bringing this case and cartoon to my attention.
50 R. Rao, "Re-membering Mwanga: Same-sex Intimacy, Memory and Belonging in Postcolonial Uganda" *Journal of Eastern African Studies*, 9:1, 2015, 1–19.
51 D. Tutu and J. Allen (ed), *God is not a Christian and Other Provocations*, London, Harper Collins, 2011, 53–58. Chapter 6 is titled: "All are God's children: On including Gays and Lesbians in the Church and Society".
52 J. Allen, "Pope on Homosexuals: Who am I to Judge?" *National Catholic Reporter*, 29 July 2013. This statement has been multiply analysed and not all are agreed that the Pope was indeed affirming support for the human rights of gay people.
53 See generally J. Van der Vyver and M. Christian Green, "Law, Religion and Human Rights in Africa: Introduction" *African Human Rights Journal*, 8, 2, 2008, 337–356. This is a part special edition volume of the journal focusing on religion in select Sub Saharan African states. See also N. Sultany, "Religion and Constitutionalism: Lessons from American and Islamic Constitutionalism" *Emory International Law Review* 28, 2014, 345–424. The paper considers the different approach to religion and its place within national constitutions taken by two North African states, Egypt and Tunisia.
54 African Charter on Human and Peoples' Rights, 1981 *International Legal Materials* (1982) 59.
55 Communications 25/89, 47/90, 56/91, 100/93 *Free Legal Assistance Group and Others v. Zaire*, African Commission on Human and People's Rights, (1995), para 3. Finding at para 45.
56 Communications 48/90, 50/91, 52/91, 89/93 *Amnesty International and Others v. Sudan*, (1999) *African Commission on Human and People's Rights*, paras 74 and 76.
57 Ibid. para 72.
58 Communication 276/03 *Centre for Minority Rights Development (Kenya) and Minority Rights Group (on behalf of Endorois Welfare Council)*, paras 77–85, 163–164.
59 Ibid. para 164.
60 Ibid. paras 78, 114–117. See also para 156; F. Raday, "Culture, Religion, and CEDAW's Article 5 (a)" in H-B. Schopp-Schilling and C. Flinterman (eds), *The Circle of Empowerment*, New York, Feminist Press, 2007, 68–85, 71.

61 Ibid. para 166.
62 Ibid. paras 167–78. The Commission also cited at para. 164, the Human Rights Committee, General Comment 22, Article 18 (Forty-eighth session, 1993), "Compilation of General Comments and General Recommendations Adopted by Human Rights Treaty Bodies", UN Doc. HRI\GEN\1\Rev.1 (1994), 35. It notes that religion is not limited "8 is not limited in its application to traditional religions or to religions and beliefs with institutional characteristics or practices analogous to those of traditional religions". The Commission also cited, "Declaration on the Elimination of All Forms of Intolerance and of Discrimination Based on Religion or Belief" (Thirty-sixth session, 1981), UN GA Res. 36/55, African Commission, para 165.
63 Convention on the Elimination of All Forms of Discrimination against Women, 1979, 1249 UNTS 13.
64 J. Bond, "CEDAW in Sub-Saharan Africa: Lessons on Implementation" *Michigan State Law Review* 2014, 241–263.
65 Protocol to the African Charter on Human and Peoples' Rights on the Rights of African Women, 2003, OAU AHG/Res.240, art. 6 ©.
66 Ibid. arts. 7(d) and 21.
67 C. Ngwenya, "Reforming African Abortion Laws and Practice: The Place of Transparency" in R. Cook, J. Erdman and B. Dickens, *Abortion Law in Transnational Perspective*, Pennsylvania, Penn Press, 2014, 166–186.
68 *Christian Lawyers Association v. Minister of Health* 1998 (4) SA 1113. The statute under review was the Choice on Termination of Pregnancy Act 92 of 1996.
69 League of Arab States, Arab Charter on Human Rights, May 22, 2004, reprinted in 12 *Int'l Hum. Rts. Rep.* 893 (2005).
70 I. Cismas, *Religious Actors and International Law*, Oxford, Oxford University Press, 2014, 253.
71 Arab Charter, 2004. Arts 3(1) and 11 provide for equality while art 3(3) provides positive discrimination for women as provided in the Sharia. There is confusion about whether this gives women more, the same as, or less than men. Interpretation of the Charter is made subject to a mixture of international and domestic law thus reinforcing the confusion (art 43). Organization of the Islamic Conference (OIC), *Cairo Declaration on Human Rights in Islam*, 5 August 1990, available at: Preamble, arts 6, 20 and 21.
72 A. Appiah, *The Honour Code*, New York, Norton, 2011, 137–172; L. Welchman and S. Hossain, *Honour: Crimes, Paradigms, and Violence against Women*, London, ZED, 2005.
73 Communication 236/2000 *Doebbler v. Sudan*, para 3.
74 Ibid. para 40.
75 Amnesty International Sudan: *Abolish the Flogging of Women* (2010) AFR 54/005/2010. The cases brought under the statute include the arrest of Lubna Hussein, a female UN official for wearing trousers while out at a restaurant (she was with 12 other women, 10 of whom admitted guilt and were lashed) and the arrest of a 16-year-old girl for wearing a skirt and many others.
76 In The Name of God The Compassionate the Merciful Memorandum to the Penal Code 1991 available at: www.ecoi.net/file_upload/1329_1202725629_sb106-sud-criminalact1991.pdf.
77 Y. Sezgin, *Human Rights under State Enforced Religious Family Laws in Israel, Egypt and India*, Cambridge, Cambridge University Press, 2013. I am grateful to John Eekelaar for introducing me to this book.
78 Report of the Special Rapporteur on Freedom of Religion or Belief, Heiner Bielefeldt, on violence committed in the name of religion, A/HRC/28/66, 29 December 2014, paras 12, 21.

79 J. Copnall, "I'm not afraid of being flogged. It doesn't hurt. But it is insulting." *The Observer*, London, 2 August 2009.

80 Redress, Letter to Commissioner Maiga, Urgent Appeal in respect of Ms. Meriam Yahiya Ibrahim, London, 10 June 2014.

81 Communication 89/93 *Amnesty International v. Sudan*, para 73.

82 C. Elkay am-Levy, "Women's Rights and Religion: The Missing Element in the Jurisprudence of the European Court of Human Rights" *University of Pennsylvania Journal of International Law*, 35(4), 2014, 1175–1222. In South Africa, religious discrimination has been found to have occurred with respect to school uniform. See *Pillay v. MEC for Education, Kwa-Zulu Natal and Others* 2006 10 BCLR 1237. This was a case involving a female Hindu student who was denied the right to wear a nose ring because it was not part of the uniform. Unfair discrimination was found to have occurred.

83 K. Yoshino, *Covering: The Hidden Assault on our Civil Rights*, New York, Random House, 2006, 168–170.

84 *Farai Dzova v. Minister of Education, Sports and Culture and Others* (2007) ZNSC 26 (7-year-old schoolboy sent home); *Prince v. President, Cape Law Society and Others* (2002) 2 SA 794 (CC) (lawyer denied the right to practise law); *In Re Chikweche* 1995 4 BCLR 533 (ZSC) (denied registration as a lawyer because unkempt and not a fit and proper person to be a lawyer). M. Mhango, "The Constitutional Protection of Minority Religious Rights in Malawi: The Case of Rastafari Students" *Journal of African Law*, 52, 2, 2008, 218–244, (hereafter Mhango 2008a); M. Mhango, "Upholding the Rastafari Religion in Zimbabwe: *Farai Dzvova v. Minister of Education, Sports and Culture and Others*" *African Human Rights Law Journal*, 8, 2, 2008, 221–238 (hereafter Mhango 2008b).

85 King James Bible, the book of Numbers Chapter 6, verses 1–6. Cited in M. Mhango (2008b) 223.

86 Mhango (2008b) 227, and Mhango (2008a) 224.

87 See also A. Renteln, *The Cultural Defense*, Oxford, Oxford University Press, 2004, 82–84.

88 For a consideration of the pressure on placed on minority black women in some workplaces to wear their hair in certain 'acceptable styles' (i.e. not cornrowed or braided) see Caldwell's discussion of the US case of *Rogers v. American Airlines* 527 F. Supp. 229 (S.D.N.Y 1981), P. Caldwell, "A Hair-Piece: Perspectives on the Intersection of Race and Gender" *Duke Law Journal*, 2, 1991, 365–396. See also K. Yoshino, *Covering*, New York, New Haven, 2006, 130–136.

89 K. Yoshino, *Covering*, New York, New Haven, 2006, 168–182, 180.

90 African Protocol on Women's Rights, 2003, art. 5. See also African Charter on the Rights and Welfare of the Child, 1990 OAU Doc. CAB/LEG/TSG/Rev.1 art 21; Joint general recommendation No. 31 of the Committee on the Elimination of Discrimination against Women/general comment No. 18 of the Committee on the Rights of the Child on Harmful Practices, CEDAW/C/GC/31/CRC/C/GC/18, (14 November 2014) para 19.

91 See the Cairo Declaration on the Elimination of FGM, 2003, preamble at: Afro-Arab Expert Consultation on Legal Tools for the Prevention of Female Genital Mutilation, Cairo, June 2003, 21–23. Available at: http://www.npwj.org/FGM/Afro-Arab-Expert-Consultation-Legal-Tools-PREVENTION-FEMALE-GENITAL-MUTILATION.html, Accessed 1 May 2015.

92 The joint CEDAW/CRC general recommendation/ general comment 31/18 cites figures of 100 to 140 million girls cut, para 19.

93 Ibid. paras 17 and 18.

94 *Hadjiatou Mani v. Niger* ECOWAS Court. H. Duffy, "*Hadijatou Mani Koroua v Niger:* Slavery Unveiled by the ECOWAS Court" *Human Rights Law Review*, 9, 1, 2009, 151.

95 Ibid.
96 C. Duodu, "One in the Eye for West African Slaves" *New African*, 23 November 2008 available at: http://newafricanmagazine.com/one-in-the-eye-for-west-african-slavers/ (site last visited 11 May 2015).
97 This best describes the situation pertaining in Mauritania. See Special Rapporteur on Contemporary Forms of Slavery, Including its Causes and Consequences, on her Mission to Mauritania, UN Doc. A/HRC/15/20/Add 2, (15 August 2010) para 34.
98 On the gendered dimensions of slavery see Special Rapporteur, ibid. para 38.
99 World Health Organization, *World Report on Violence and Health*, Geneva, World Health Organization, 2002, 128; A. Cimpric for UNICEF, *Children Accused of Witchcraft: An Anthropological Study of Contemporary Practices in Africa*, Dakar, UNICEF, WCARO, 2010. I am grateful to Nonny Onyekweli for this reference.
100 The African Protocol on Women's Rights, 2003 art 22 provides special protection for elderly (sic) women as does CEDAW General Recommendation No. 27 on older women and protection of their human rights, 16 December 2010, CEDAW/C/GC/27; African Charter on the Rights and Welfare of the Child, 1990, art. 16 (child abuse and torture) and art 21 (harmful practices); CRC General Comment No. 13, the right of the child to freedom from all forms of violence, 18 April 2011, CRC/C/GC/13.
101 A. Allott, *The Limits of Law*, London, Butterworth, 1980.

4 Implications of the Vatican commitment to complementarity for the equality of the sexes in public life

Mary Anne Case

In November 2014, just a month after concluding a much more widely publicized and liberally inclined Extraordinary Synod on the Family, Pope Francis personally welcomed an international who's who of self-described proponents of traditional marriage and opponents of same-sex marriage from diverse faith traditions and continents to the Vatican for an International Colloquium on the Complementarity between Man and Women ("Humanum Conference")[1] sponsored by the Vatican's Congregation for the Doctrine of the Faith ("CDF"), at which they could all strategize and watch a new series of films "On the Meaning of Marriage" across cultures.

For the Vatican, complementarity entails that "man and woman" have "equal dignity as persons" but that this equal dignity is premised on and manifest in essential and complementary differences, "physical, psychological and ontological."[2] The differences the Vatican has in mind as essential include most of what American constitutional law since the mid-1970s would characterize as sex stereotypes,[3] a term many activist proponents of complementarity embrace rather than repudiate.[4]

In this chapter,[5] I will trace developments over the course of the last half century that first brought the Vatican to embrace complementarity as the foundation of its theological anthropology and then to mobilize that anthropology in an attempt to influence secular law in settings as diverse as the United Nations and the French Manif Pour Tous, the protest movement that first brought hundreds of thousands of French citizens onto the streets of Paris to demonstrate against the inclusion of same-sex couples in a law extending "Marriage Pour Tous" (Marriage for Everyone) in the spring of 2013.

Over the course of the same half century, the Vatican and those operating under its influence around the world came to view the English word "gender" as anathema and to associate it with what it terms an "ideology" or "theory of gender" it sees as linking feminism and gay rights in a worldwide effort to redefine, not only secular laws governing the sexes, sexuality, reproduction, and the family, but human nature itself. As a result, the Vatican, in venues ranging from the United Nations to legislative bodies and protest movements in every part of the world, has opposed not only these changes in secular law and the NGOs and activists it sees as conspiring to bring them about, but the very use of the word "gender" itself, whether in scholarly work or in legal documents.

My chapter will argue that, far from being longstanding Catholic orthodoxy, complementarity is a mid-twentieth century innovation imported into Catholicism at a theoretical level through the work of converts such as the married Protestant Dietrich von Hildebrand and at a more pastoral and political level by members of the Catholic hierarchy trying to reconcile commitments to separate spheres and the equality of the sexes. The move from the invention of complementarity to the anathematization of gender is largely a tale of three popes: Paul VI, who, in response to what he saw as dangerous trends of the times, promulgated documents newly entrenching Catholic opposition to women's ordination (Inter Insigniores), to contraception (Humanae Vitae) and to homosexuality (Persona Humana); John Paul II, who brought the philosophical work he had done as Carol Wojtyla to a Theology of the Body;[6] and Benedict XVI, who combined concerns about feminism, the new reproductive technologies and LGBT rights he had voiced as a connected whole as early as his 1984 Ratzinger Report[7] into his notion of a human ecology at risk of destruction by all he saw as encompassed by the term gender.

In addition to the invention of complementarity, a second crucial component to the intellectual history on which this chapter rests is the parallel development of two different meanings for the term "gender" among the sort of feminist intellectuals and activists Ratzinger, the future Pope Benedict XVI, set his face against. Also in the mid-twentieth century, English-speaking scholars of women's studies and scientific researchers into sex differences used "gender" to distinguish cultural or attitudinal characteristics associated with the sexes from biological characteristics (i.e. to distinguish masculine and feminine from male and female). Simultaneously, Ruth Bader Ginsburg, in the 1970s the leading US litigator for constitutional sex equality and now a Justice of the US Supreme Court, used the term "gender" interchangeably with "sex" in legal documents, to ward off from the minds of judges what she feared might be distracting associations with what happens in porn theaters.[8] These two uses of the term may seem antithetical, with the first stressing the distinction between sex and gender, the second using the terms interchangeably and synonymously. But from the Vatican's perspective, there was the same reason to be concerned about both usages: each is associated with what Ratzinger condemned as "the obscuring of the difference or duality of the sexes" in the Letter to the Bishops of the Catholic Church on the Collaboration of M[a]n and Wom[a]n in the Church and in the World (2004 Letter)[9] he wrote in his capacity as head of the CDF.

A third component of the history is how, in reaction, the Vatican anathematization of gender spread through the world, beginning with preliminary concerns of Catholic activists at the United Nations Rio, Cairo, and Beijing conferences in the first half of the 1990s; and continuing through the proclamations of Harvard Law professor and Vatican ambassador to the 1995 Beijing conference, Mary Ann Glendon, subsequent polemics of figures like the French Lacanian psychoanalyst priest, Tony Anatrella, and documents such as the Pontifical Council on the Family's massive Lexicon of Ambiguous and Debatable Terms Regarding Family Life and Ethical Questions; to influence debates about secular law reform in venues such as the UN, the EU, and the French National Assembly, including debates about specific law reforms such as recognition of same-sex marriage and broader approaches to sex equality in law and policy such as what came to be known as gender mainstreaming.[10] The Vatican's campaign has even made new work for lexicographers, with the English word "gender" declared 2013's word of the year in Poland[11] while German-speaking Catholic activists now warn of "Genderismus" and "Genderwahn" (gender craziness).

The chapter will conclude with an analysis of the effect of Pope Francis's own ideology on the Vatican's opposition to what it calls the ideology of gender, detailing evidence that leads to pessimistic conclusions about the likelihood of the new Pope committing his Church to a new vision of freedom or equality when it comes to gendered rights or gendered rites.

The invention of complementarity

In his book *The Invention of Sodomy in Christian Theology*, Catholic theologian Mark D. Jordan claims to be able to find "no trace of the term before the eleventh century" when it was "invented by medieval theologians."[12] Similarly, neither I nor the staunchest Catholic supporters of an ideology of complementarity, despite their heroic efforts to seek its roots in prior centuries, have found any trace of the term "complementarity" before the twentieth century. Consider for example, the work of Sister Prudence Allen, recently named by Pope Francis to the overwhelmingly male International Theological Commission, which advises the CDF. Sr Allen was one of the principal speakers at the Humanum Conference. Although she has published nearly twelve hundred pages in two volumes of a history of *The Concept of Woman* from 750 B.C. to A.D. 1500, the word "complementarity" appears in none of the cited sources. As she herself documents, in prior centuries, those who stressed the equality of the sexes also stressed their essential sameness, while those who focused on essential differences between the sexes also asserted the superiority of men, whether it be the Pythagoreans who associated male with goodness and light, female with badness and darkness; Aristotle, who thought of women as misbegotten males; or Thomas Aquinas, who followed Aristotle in this and who gave as his principal reason why a woman could not become a priest that, because "it is not possible in the female sex to signify eminence of degree, for a woman is in the state of subjection, it follows that she cannot receive the sacrament of" ordination. (*Summa Theologica*, Q 39 A 1 Body).

The closest Sr Allen comes to early traces of what later became complementarity is in the work of the twelfth-century abbess, mystic and composer Hildegard von Bingen, who, according to Sr Allen, "developed a theoretical framework within which sex complementarity could be articulated as a philosophy of sex identity."[13] It is therefore no accident that one of Pope Benedict XVI's last major acts, in October of 2012, before announcing his resignation in February 2013, was to declare Hildegard to be, like Thomas Aquinas, a Doctor of the Church, that is to say one of now 4 women and 32 men whose writings are to be seen as authoritative and influential, albeit not infallible.[14]

I can find no trace of sexual complementarity in the Gospels. Even the Virgin Mary, the model of "the woman" for complementarians like John Paul II, displays few stereotypically feminine traits and a fair degree of feistiness.[15] Not only do the apostles display few identifiably masculine traits, both Jesus's treatment of women and the behavior attributed to women in the Gospels is remarkably free of gender stereotypes. As for sex role differentiation, far from endorsing it, Jesus explicitly repudiates it, sending women out to preach, and rebuking Martha for demanding that her sister Mary be forced to join her in household tasks. Mary, who has taken on what in ultra-Orthodox Judaism is still today a role confined to males, sitting at the feet of a great teacher, has, according to Jesus, "chosen the best part, which shall not be taken away from her."[16]

In the Epistles there is more fodder for complementarians, particularly in the discussion of marital roles and in the analogy, crucial for the theological anthropology of complementarity, between husband and wife on the one hand, and Christ and the Church on the other. But, true to form, when Paul speaks of difference between the sexes, he also speaks of subordination ("Wives, be subject to your husbands, as it behoveth in the Lord. Husbands, love your wives, and be not bitter towards them." Colossians 3:18, 19). When he speaks of equality, it is equality in sameness or non-differentiation ("There is neither Jew nor Greek: there is neither bond nor free: there is neither male nor female. For you are all one in Christ Jesus." Galatians 3:28). Importantly, the language of Colossians leads many Protestant denominations and their theologians, including, for example, the Southern Baptists and the President of their Ethics and Religious Liberty Commission, Russell D. Moore, who was a principal speaker at the Humanum Conference, explicitly to reject egalitarian marriage in favor of "patriarchy" and the doctrine of "male headship and wifely submission."[17] As will be discussed further below, prioritizing that aspect of its theological anthropology of complementarity that stresses essential differences between the sexes over the part that also stresses the essential equality of the sexes leads the Vatican to strange bedfellows[18] and contradictions.

With respect to the Scriptures, the Vatican is in the difficult position of having simultaneously to argue that texts that imply subordination are really egalitarian – that Colossians can be read to support what the Southern Baptist Russell dismisses, i.e. "'mutual submission' within an equal marital partnership"[19] – and that texts like Galatians 3:28 also mean the opposite of what they seem to say. Thus, in his 2004 Letter, Ratzinger, immediately after quoting Galatians 3:28, goes on to insist:

> The Apostle Paul does not say that the distinction between man and woman, which in other places is referred to as the plan of God, has been erased. He means rather that in Christ the rivalry, enmity and violence which disfigured the relationship between men and women can be overcome and have been overcome. In this sense, the distinction between man and woman is reaffirmed more than ever.[20]

I am a lawyer experienced in litigation, which means that I am well trained in how to make words do whatever my client needs them to do, but even I cannot extract a "reaffirm[ation]" of "distinction" from a text asserting that there "is no" differential categorization, rather "all are one." Making Ratzinger's point is especially difficult considering that the three sets of categories are all what lawyers would call *in pari materia* with one another. A single sentence links three pairs of categories denying their continued existence with parallel use of the word "neither" and ending by saying "all are one." Each pair consists of what would have been viewed by the writer and his audience as a hierarchy composed of a superior and a subordinate. Whatever happens textually to one in this series happens to all. Would Ratzinger ever suggest that Galatians merely puts an end to "the rivalry, enmity, and violence which disfigured the relationship between [master and slave]" while "the distinction between [master and slave] is reaffirmed more than ever?" I doubt it.

In addition to its tortured textual interpretation, what is remarkable about Ratzinger's argument in the 2004 letter is the extent of its reliance on "sola scriptura," a quintessentially Protestant form of argumentation rarely found in authoritative Catholic texts, which typically supplement or even replace citation to scripture with citation to Church teaching from the Fathers, the Doctors of the Church, the prior Popes or other magisterial sources. The text of the 2004 Letter cites only once a work by a Church father.[21] It cites the work of only one Pope, the then reigning John Paul II, but cites him repeatedly, in the overwhelming majority of the footnotes. In addition, all citations to curial authorities are to work produced during the papacy of John Paul II, i.e. extremely recently.[22] This is strong evidence for the fact that "complementarity" is a very recent doctrinal innovation, and also support for the proposition frequently advanced that the theological anthropology of complementarity is largely the work product of John Paul II, building on his philosophical and theological influences, such as the theory of personalism and the work of Dietrich von Hildebrand and Edith Stein.

I do not deny the importance of John Paul II and his sources from the first half of the twentieth century. But it is important, in my view, to consider the crucial role other modern popes have played, including both his predecessors Pius XII, John XXIII and Paul VI, and, most importantly, his successor Benedict XVI, in his work as Pope, but also in his earlier work as the theologian Joseph Ratzinger and as the head, during John Paul II's papacy, of the CDF. Before going on to consider the influence of these other popes in shaping the doctrine of complementarity, let me say a few words about the relevant philosophical influences on John Paul II.

Again, the first central point to observe is how recent John Paul II's sources are. It is only, perhaps, in the modern era, when for the first time, according to Thomas Laqueur, "reproductive organs went from being paradigmatic sites for displaying hierarchy ... to being the foundation of incommensurable difference"[23] that equality in difference can be asserted, in particular equality in difference that goes all the way down. For the pre-modern church it would have been heresy to suggest that souls have a sex or that sex is essence not accident, but that seems just what complementarity, with its stress on ontological, psychological, and spiritual sex differences, does seem to assert. And, although the nineteenth century did hold out to feminists outside the Church some notion of the possibility of equality in separate spheres, the early modern period saw a step backwards from the essentially egalitarian Catholic medieval canon law of marriage to an emphasis on the "subjection of wife to husband" which persisted as late as Pope Pius XI's 1930 Encyclical On Christian Marriage, Casti Connubii.[24]

A second central point is that even in the twentieth century, where Sr Allen's yet to be published third volume on the Concept of Woman situates the word "complementarity" in the work of Dietrich von Hildebrand and Edith Stein,[25] it is noteworthy how late the term emerges as a term of art. Several things are significant about Hildebrand and Stein's writings in this regard. First, neither actually uses what has now become the standard German word "Komplementaritaet", instead, they each speak of "Ergaenzung"[26] (completion) which is not quite the same thing. So how and when did the term of art become "complementarity"?[27] Second, significantly, Hildebrand is a married convert from Protestantism and Stein a convert from orthodox Judaism. Complementarity sits much better with each of those faith traditions than with the Catholicism of a celibate male priestly hierarchy, the glorification of virginity, and sex-segregated monasticism (the era of the double monasteries having ended in the middle ages). In Protestantism, everybody should be married; in orthodox Judaism, role differentiation goes all the way down. Just as for Jews one is born rather than becoming a woman,[28] one is born rather than becoming a priest; it is not a vocation but an inheritance, genetically determined. More importantly, however well complementarity may work for married life, the ideal for all Jews and all Protestants, it is a poor fit with the current structure of the Catholic Church, run by a celibate male hierarchy from which women are excluded and served by those consecrated to celibate life in single-sex religious communities. This raises a number of questions, such as why parity in the magisterium (even if not in the ministerial priesthood) isn't logically entailed by complementarity, and how to reconcile John Paul II's assertion that the complementarity of the sexes models the trinity with his Church's proclamation that the godhead must always be translated by masculine pronouns regardless of the genders of the scriptural Greek or Hebrew words (*Sacrosanctum Concilium*, art 36).

One way of turning complementarity to feminist purposes would be to accept, at least *arguendo*, its premises and some of the conclusions the Vatican has recently declared follow well-nigh infallibly from them, such as the exclusion of women from the ministerial priesthood, and to work on seeing what can fruitfully be accomplished with or in spite of them. One could thus argue, following William of Ockham, that women should not be excluded from a general council, especially in matters of faith which concern all.[29] One could argue, as Catholic feminist theologian Elisabeth Schuessler Fiorenza once did, that, even if women cannot be ordained, they can be appointed as cardinals,[30] a position not requiring ordination, and that in the interests of parity only women should henceforth be appointed to the College of Cardinals. One could argue, as even members of the current Church hierarchy have done, that the voices of women are required to develop a more adequate theology of "the woman."

The more different women and men essentially are, the more humanity is only a complete whole when the two of them are collaborating equally using their complementary attributes, and thus the more essential it becomes to include women in decision-making and teaching authority. This is an argument the Vatican has, since the second half of the twentieth century, pressed strongly with respect to the collaboration of men and women in the world, but it has not applied that argument to their collaboration in the Church. It is the sort of argument used to good advantage by feminists in the nineteenth-century zenith of separate spheres ideology, such as those suffragettes who, whether genuinely or strategically, claimed that precisely to the extent women had special gifts, the polity stood in great need of those gifts in public life and hence women should be able to vote and encouraged to assume public office.[31] Although making such arguments is the sort of work I have been trained to do as a lawyer, I will note that they have thus far been of relatively little interest to practicing Catholics or Catholic theologians. Even Schuessler Fiorenza has more recently substituted for her earlier calls for women's ordination and appointment to the Church hierarchy a categorical rejection of all hierarchy to replace what she condemns as a kyriarchal church.[32]

Let me now return to the precise term "complementarity" which is clearly a Latinate word which migrates from either French or Italian into, e.g. English and German. In the first half of the twentieth century Catholic-influenced Vichy French activists spoke of the "complementary roles of men and women"[33] in terms quite consistent with later Vatican pronouncements.

The same sort of language occurs in a series of speeches to women's organizations made by mid-century Popes from Pius XII to Paul VI. These speeches all have a somewhat similar and by now familiar character – they acknowledge that woman's roles are expanding, as is the recognition of her equality with men; they do not condemn (indeed often encourage or at worst recognize as inevitable) her greater participation in public life, but stress nevertheless her special responsibilities for the family and urge that in working out her new role her complementary particularities be fully taken into account.

I will quote extensively from one of these speeches, which not only pre-dates any pronouncements by Carol Wojtyla/John Paul II on the subject, but sets forth far more clearly than his Theology of the Body the practical implications of complementarity for secular law and life, of the sort John Paul II first began pronouncing on at any length in his 1988 Mulieris Dignitatem (Dignity of Woman) and then in documents he prepared in direct anticipation of the 1995 UN Beijing Conference on Women.[34] On October 21, 1945, Pope Pius XII gave an Address To Members of Various Catholic Women's Associations on Women's Duties in Social and Political Life[35] which included the following section:

Distinctive and complementary qualities of the sexes

> What, then, is this God-given dignity of woman? The answer lies in human nature as God has fashioned it.... As children of God, man and woman have a dignity in which they are absolutely equal.... To have vindicated and proclaimed this truth, and to have delivered woman from a slavery as degrading as it was contrary to nature, is one of the imperishable glories of the Church. But man and woman cannot maintain or perfect this equal dignity of theirs unless they respect and make use of the distinctive qualities which nature has bestowed on each sex: physical and spiritual qualities which are indestructible, and so co-ordinated that their mutual relation cannot be upset without nature itself intervening to re-establish it. These peculiar characteristics which distinguish the sexes are so obvious to everybody that nothing short of willful blindness, or a doctrinaire attitude as disastrous as it is utopian, can ignore or fail to see their importance in the structure of society.
>
> Indeed, this co-ordination of the sexes through the characteristics peculiar to each is such as to extend its influence to every single manifestation of the social life of man. Two of these, and only two, We mention here because of their special importance: marriage, and voluntary celibacy .... The benefits of true wedded life do not consist only in ...offspring ... nor only in the material and spiritual blessings which family life confers upon humanity. The whole of civilization in all its ramifications–nations, the community of nations, the Church herself–in a word, all human values feel the good effects of married life when it is in a flourishing and orderly condition...

> Where, on the contrary, the sexes disregard the intimate and harmonious relations which God has established and willed to subsist between them, and indulge instead in a perverse individualism;... where they do not co-operate in mutual harmony to serve humanity according to the designs of God and nature; where youth... renders itself morally and physically unfit for the holy life of matrimony–here the common welfare of human society, spiritual and temporal alike, is seriously compromised, and even the very Church of God trembles–not for her own existence, since she has the Divine promises–but for the greater success of her mission among men.
>
> Motherhood is woman's natural function. Be she married or single, woman's function is seen clearly defined in the lineaments of her sex, in its propensities and special powers. She works side by side with man, but she works in her own way and according to her natural bent. Now a woman's function, a woman's way, a woman's natural bent, is motherhood. Every woman is called to be a mother, mother in the physical sense, or mother in a sense more spiritual and more exalted, yet real none the less. To this end the Creator has fashioned the whole of woman's nature: not only her organism, but also and still more her spirit, and most of all her exquisite sensibility. This is why it is only from the standpoint of the family that the woman, if she is a true woman, can see and fully understand every problem of human life. And this is why her delicate sense of her own dignity causes her a thrill of apprehension whenever the social or political order threatens danger to her vocation as a mother, or to the welfare of the family.

Conditions unfavorable to the family and the dignity of woman:

> And in fact social and political conditions today are, unfortunately, fraught with this danger. Indeed, the sanctity of the home and therefore the dignity of woman threatens to become more and more precarious. This is your hour, Catholic women and Catholic girls. Public life needs you ... It is for her to work with man for the welfare of the civitas in which she enjoys a dignity equal with his, and here each sex has its part to play according to its nature, its distinctive qualities, its physical, intellectual, and moral capabilities. Both sexes have the right and the duty to work together for the good of society... But it is clear that while man is by temperament more suited to deal with external affairs and public business, generally speaking the woman has a deeper insight for understanding the delicate problems of domestic and family life, and a surer touch in solving them–which, of course, is not to deny that some women can show great ability in every sphere of public life.
>
> It is not so much that each sex is called to a different task; the difference is rather in their manner of judging and arriving at concrete and practical applications. Take the case of civil rights, for example; at the present time

> they are equal for both sexes. But just think how much more intelligently and effectively these rights will be used if men and women pool their resources in using them. The sensibility and delicacy which are characteristic of the woman may perhaps bias her judgment in the direction of her impressions, and so tend to the prejudice of wide and clear vision, cool decision, or far-sighted prudence; but on the other hand they are most valuable aids in discerning the needs, aspirations, and dangers proper to the sphere of domestic life, public assistance, and religion.

Why do I quote so extensively from this obscure document? One reason is to advance the possibility that to look to theologians for the origins of the theological anthropology of complementarity might be to look in the wrong place. Complementarity may have started out, not just ended up, in a sphere closer to the political than the noumenological. Another is to suggest how early in the post-World War II period the concept develops, simultaneously with the incorporation of dignity – which for Catholics remains a status-based dignity – as a central feature of the development of an international human rights regime in which the equality of the sexes was included.

I could have cited similar quotations from John XXIII[36] and Paul VI,[37] as counterevidence to another hypothesis I have entertained in trying to come to terms with the development of the Vatican's simultaneous rejection of what it groups under "gender" and embrace of what it calls complementarity. The hypothesis was that there was a moment in the immediate aftermath of Vatican II when it might have all turned out differently – when, having already embraced the equality of the sexes, in, for example, the documents of Vatican II, the Church could have avoided turning to complementarity and accepted that much of what it came to demonize as the "gender agenda" was in fact perfectly consistent with and indeed prefigured by Christian teaching on the sexes from the Gospels on down. Its view of what sex equality entailed, in the world and in the Church, thus could and should have been not unlike that of Ruth Bader Ginsburg (whose view of gender underlay, for example, the 1995 Beijing Declaration which so upset the Vatican), allowing Catholic and liberal feminists to continue in common cause.

The moment I'm thinking of is before Paul VI's proclamation of Humanae Vitae, Inter Insigniores and Persona Humana, when an overwhelming majority of the Pontifical Commission on Birth Control saw no conflict between use of birth control and Catholic teaching, when a majority of the Pontifical Biblical Commission saw no scriptural obstacle to the ordination of women, and when Paul VI accepted a women's equality symbol from the hands of Betty Friedan.[38] One sign of both the possibility and its failure is the way the debate between complementarist theologians, like Ignaz de la Potterie on the one hand and a group of female dissenters and Karl Rahner on the other, played itself out in the meetings of the ill-fated Pontifical Commission On Women in Society and in the Church in the mid-1970s.[39] (Significantly, this is exactly the time that Ruth Bader Ginsburg's use of the term "gender" and the rejection of sex stereotypes which underlay it, was becoming constitutional orthodoxy in the United States on its way to international export.)

I also cite such early papal language as counterevidence to the proposition that it is John Paul II alone, with his Theology of the Body, to whom we owe complementarity as the new Catholic orthodoxy. One should not underestimate Ratzinger's contribution: a) to the way in which the theological anthropology of the sexes has become what Carol Gilligan in another context called "math problems with humans,"[40] b) to the assembling of the component parts of what becomes for the Vatican the "gender agenda" and c) to the shifting of emphasis away from influencing the behavior of the faithful and onto an insistence on shaping secular law. Let me now to turn to Benedict XVI before concluding with Francis.

The contribution of Benedict XVI/Joseph Ratzinger to the invention of complementarity and the anathamatization of gender

It seems to have only been a decade after the 1984 Ratzinger Report, when he was personally presented post-Beijing by the American activist and later blogger Dale O'Leary with her position paper "Gender: The Deconstruction of Women, Analysis of the Gender Perspective in Preparation for the Fourth World Conference on Women" Beijing, China, September 1995 (later revised and published as *The Gender Agenda*) that Ratzinger cathected onto the word "gender" and sent it out into the polemic-generating machinery of the Vatican. But he had already at the time of the interviews that became the Ratzinger Report put all the pieces together – radical feminism, gay rights, abortion, reproductive rights, new family forms, even transsexuality – without yet having the word "gender" to attach them to.

Already in 1984, Ratzinger had thought it:

> necessary to get to the bottom of the demand that radical feminism draws from the widespread modern culture, namely the "trivialization" of sexual specificity that makes every role interchangeable between man and woman… Detached from the bond with fecundity, sex no longer appears to be a determined characteristic, as a radical and pristine orientation of the person. Male? Female? They are questions that for some are now viewed as obsolete, senseless, if not racist. The answer of current conformism is foreseeable: "whether one is male or female has little interest for us, we are all simply humans." This in reality has grave consequences even if at first appears very beautiful and generous.[41]

By the time of his 2004 Letter, he had the word gender to attach to and blame for these grave consequences, which he saw as proceeding in the first instance from feminism:

> Recent years have seen new approaches to women's issues. A first tendency is to emphasize strongly conditions of subordination … A second tendency emerges in the wake of the first. In order to avoid the domination of one sex or the other, their differences tend to be denied, viewed as mere effects of historical and cultural conditioning. In this perspective, physical difference, termed sex, is minimized, while the purely cultural element, termed gender, is emphasized to the maximum and held to be primary. The obscuring of the difference or duality of the sexes has enormous consequences on a variety of levels. This theory of the human person, intended to promote prospects for equality of women through liberation from biological determinism, has in reality inspired ideologies which, for example, call into question the family, in its natural two-parent structure of mother and father, and make homosexuality and heterosexuality virtually equivalent, in a new model of polymorphous sexuality.
>
> While the immediate roots of this second tendency are found in the context of reflection on women's roles, its deeper motivation must be sought in the human attempt to be freed from one's biological conditioning. According to this perspective, human nature in itself does not possess characteristics in an absolute manner: all persons can and ought to constitute themselves as they like, since they are free from every predetermination linked to their essential constitution.[42]

Several things are of note in Ratzinger's mobilization of the Vatican against what it terms "the gender agenda." First, very few interventions against "gender" are undertaken by the Catholic Church as a religious body attempting to influence the hearts and minds of believers. Rather, even when the addressees of warnings against "gender" are, for example, Catholic clergy, as in Ratzinger's 2004 Letter, the emphasis is on the imperative to influence secular law and policy in line with the Vatican vision. In international and multinational settings, the Vatican acts first and foremost as a state actor, the Holy See; as such it can make common cause with other state actors, notably members of the Organization of the Islamic Conference (known today as the Organization of Islamic Cooperation) who share some of the concerns it situates in relation to the term "gender."[43] Within Europe, by contrast, the Vatican can act as an insider, stressing the importance of its Christian contribution to European heritage and values. More broadly, acting both in its own name and through a multitude of individual and organizational actors, the Vatican can effectively position itself vis-à-vis the women and the nations of the Third World as one who understands and supports them by contrast with those feminists and sexual rights advocates it paints as focused on issues of interest only to a small minority and far removed from the real, material needs and the preferences of most poor women. Thus, for example, in presenting the "Holy See's Final Statement" at the 1995 Women's Conference in Beijing, Harvard Law Professor Mary Ann Glendon, head of the Vatican delegation, expressed regret at an "exaggerated individualism" and "the colonization of the broad and rich discourse of universal rights by an impoverished, libertarian rights dialect," saying, "Surely this international gathering could have done more for women and girls than to leave them alone with their rights!"[44] Perhaps the most interesting of all the Vatican's modalities of opposition to the "gender agenda" are its attempts to speak as what Ratzinger, in his 2004 letter, called "an expert in humanity [with] a perennial interest in whatever concerns men and women."[45]

When the Vatican does speak for a faith community in promoting complementarity and opposing the gender agenda, as at the Humanum Conference, it does so together with members of other faith communities many of which are much less committed than it is to egalitarianism between the sexes. Just as its alliance with the Organization of the Islamic Conference at the UN beginning in the 1990s is particularly disturbing, given many of the organization's member states' views and laws on women, so it is particularly disturbing that the Humanum Conference was sponsored by the CDF, the Catholic Church's guarantor of doctrinal orthodoxy (previously known as the Inquisition) and that at the time of the Colloquium the CDF, infamously, was investigating the United States Leadership Conference of Women Religious (LCWR) for alleged heresies including "radical feminism" and "tak[ing] a position not in agreement with the Church's teaching on human sexuality."[46] As between the positions attributed to the LCWR and those openly espoused by, for example, the Mormon Church, the Southern Baptists, Islam, and Orthodox Judaism, all of whom had representatives invited to speak at the Humanum Conference, those attributed to the LCWR are more easily reconciled with Catholic orthodoxy.

The Vatican sees, and assumes its opponents also see, a tight connection between and among all the components it incorporates under the "gender agenda," such as the dismantling of sex roles, the acceptance of homosexuality, the recognition of a diversity of family forms and of sexual and gender expression, and access to the new reproductive technologies, condoms, other contraceptives, and abortion – in short, most of what goes under such diverse headings as women's sexual and reproductive rights, SOGI (sexual orientation and gender identity), family law reform, and the elimination of sex stereotyping. Unfortunately, however, the feminist and sexual rights advocates on the other side of the "gender agenda" from the Vatican too rarely make common cause or even seem to see the connections between the issues to which they are committed, instead engaging in silo-ing. Whether these metaphorical silos are seen as hoarding grain in the form of funding or protecting missiles to be lobbed against the opposition, their downsides are that each silo (the SOGI silo, the reproductive rights silo, etc.) tightly encloses a set of issues and constituencies far from fruitful interaction with others and some constituencies are left without a well-filled and fortified silo of their own.

Not only do many advocates for components of the "gender agenda" tend to draw too few of the connections the Vatican does between and among their causes, they also tend to misinterpret the Vatican itself as being almost exclusively obsessed with homosexuality and transsexuality (i.e. with the standard components of the SOGI silo) even when a careful reading of the Vatican's pronouncements makes clear much broader concerns about sex and gender are often at issue. Consider one dramatic example. When interested observers reported on the 2008 Christmas speech Pope Benedict XVI made to the members of the Roman Curia, the headlines tended to read along the lines of "Pope says saving heterosexuality like saving the rainforest."[47] What he actually said was far more sweeping and more interesting.[48] According to Benedict XVI, the Church:

> Has a responsibility towards creation, and must also publicly assert this responsibility. In so doing, she must not only defend earth, water and air as gifts of creation belonging to all. She must also protect man from self-destruction. What is needed is something like a human ecology, correctly understood.
>
> If the Church speaks of the nature of the human being as man and woman, and demands that this order of creation be respected, this is not some antiquated metaphysics. What is involved here is faith in the Creator and a readiness to listen to the "language" of creation. To disregard this would be the self-destruction of man himself, and hence the destruction of God's own work.
>
> What is often expressed and understood by the term "gender" ultimately ends up being man's attempt at self-emancipation from creation and the Creator. Man wants to be his own master, and alone – always and exclusively – to determine everything that concerns him. Yet in this way he lives in opposition to the truth, in opposition to the Creator Spirit.
>
> Rain forests deserve indeed to be protected, but no less so does man, as a creature having an innate "message" which does not contradict our freedom, but is instead its very premise.[49]

Taking seriously the notion of a "human ecology" put at risk by the "gender agenda" has a number of fascinating implications. First, it indicates that Benedict XVI thinks of people like me – feminists and advocates for sexual rights – in much the same way as environmentalists think of logging companies: we are on the verge, if we are not stopped, of clear-cutting human nature the way loggers are the rainforest. This imagines a level of power and influence, not only on law but on lived human experience, that even the most hopeful supporters and severest critics of what Janet Halley calls "governance feminism"[50] have not hitherto ascribed to feminists or to SOGI activists. It also helps make sense of the Vatican's emphasis on shaping secular law: the Vatican is seeking the equivalent of an endangered species act for the traditional family.

Even more intriguing, it suggests that, in Benedict XVI's view, just as it would be possible to destroy the rainforest, it would also be possible, though similarly inadvisable and contrary to the will of the Creator, for human beings to effect the "self-destruction of man himself" by destroying what the Vatican sees as "the nature of the human being as man and woman." His argument here echoes similar arguments made, for example, in twentieth-century French family law reform debates by public intellectuals with Catholic connections, including Vaticanists like Tony Anatrella, but also a host of other politicians and scholars who invoked, inter alia, Lacanian psychoanalytic theories and philosophical anthropology to argue that any move to eliminate traditional sex distinctions in French family law (for example, through recognition of same-sex couples, new reproductive technologies, gay and single parent adoptions) could, by disrupting the symbolic order, "bring about a generalized state of social chaos and psychic distress,"[51] in a worst case scenario turning society and all within it psychotic.

How much, if any, of this apocalyptic vision does Pope Francis share with his predecessor? How committed is he to promoting a vision of complementarity and opposing the vision his predecessor associated with gender in the Church and in the world? As I shall conclude, his pronouncements to date, when read together, seem to indicate that Francis, while not nearly as obsessed with affirming the essential complementarity of the sexes as was John Paul II, or with opposing gender as Benedict XVI, shares his predecessors' views and objectives when it comes to gendered rights and gendered rites.

Pope Francis between choice and echo on complementarity

From the moment of his election to the papacy in 2013, Vatican watchers of all backgrounds and ideological stripes have been fiercely debating and frantically watching to see to what extent Pope Francis shares his predecessors' conservative views on many matters, but particularly on those related to gender and sexuality. By now there seems little doubt that the emphasis during Francis's papacy will be elsewhere than on opposing the gender agenda, and that, when he does turn to gender, it will by and large be in a kindler, gentler manner than that of his predecessors. Advocates for the LGBT community, for example, have taken heart from his private meetings with a Spanish transman and from his oft-quoted question, "If someone is gay and he searches for the Lord and has good will, who am I to judge?"[52] But, as with his approach to the divorced and remarried and to women who have had abortions, it is important to note that Francis's approach is less of acceptance, it is rather that of "accompany[iment] with mercy."[53] As Francis himself is the first to tell us, this signals no change in fundamental doctrine, only in pastoral approach.

Similarly, advocates of what the Vatican thinks of as the gender agenda might initially take heart to hear Francis observe early on, "We cannot insist only on issues related to abortion, gay marriage and the use of contraceptive methods," even more so when he described these issues, not, as his predecessor did, as part of a coherent whole ideology, but rather as a "disjointed multitude of doctrines [not] to be imposed insistently." Yet in the very same sentence in which he urged that "it is not necessary to talk about these issues all the time," Francis acknowledged that "the teaching of the church, for that matter, is clear and I am a son of the church."[54] In context, what Francis again appears to be urging is a change in emphasis, not in position, and again, in the interests of what a cynic might call better salesmanship for the Church.

Pope Francis's opening remarks to the Humanum Conference might again awaken hope for change, since he took as his model for complementarity the non-sex specific notion in 1 Cor. 12 that "the Spirit has endowed each of us with different gifts" and went on to stress:

> When we speak of complementarity between man and woman in this context, let us not confuse that term with the simplistic idea that all the roles and relations of the two sexes are fixed in a single, static pattern. Complementarity will take many forms as each man and woman brings his or her distinctive contributions to their marriage and to the formation of their children–his or her personal richness, personal charisma.[55]

But he went on to speak, like his predecessor Benedict XVI, of "the crisis in the family ha[ving] produced a crisis of human ecology, for social environments, like natural environments, need protection."[56] Like Benedict XVI, Francis sees the threat posed by what both call "gender theory" in apocalyptic terms, comparing it to nuclear war, Nazism and one of the "Herods that destroy, that plot designs of death, that disfigure the face of man and woman, destroying creation."[57] But his view of the threat is less abstract than his predecessor's: Francis draws on concrete experience with what he calls "ideological colonization" by, for example, those who tie grants for the education of the poor to the condition that "gender theory [be] taught."[58]

Like John Paul II with his Theology of the Body, but again characteristically in a more down-to-earth way, Francis has devoted a series of weekly audiences to a catechesis on the family. In them, as well, grounds for hope of change seem to be extended, only to be qualified or withdrawn. For example, Francis insisted in a general audience that "it is necessary that woman not only be listened to more, but that her voice carry real weight, a recognized authority in society and in the Church."[59] But when asked by journalists in interviews about concrete ways of giving women such recognized authority, Francis described the idea of women cardinals as a bad joke[60] and suggested he saw no need to appoint women to head Vatican departments because "priests often end up under the sway of their housekeepers."[61] His more serious responses to questions of female authority are no more comforting to those, like me, who see complementarity as an unnecessary limit on the equality of the sexes in public life. "Women in the Church must be valued not "clericalised,"[62] he said in response to the bad joke about women cardinals. But he proposes to value them largely in the abstract and largely insofar as they are different from men, saying, on the one hand:

> I ask myself, if the so-called gender theory is not, at the same time, an expression of frustration and resignation, which seeks to cancel out sexual difference because it no longer knows how to confront it. Yes, we

> risk taking a step backwards. The removal of difference in fact creates a problem, not a solution.[63]

And on the other:

> We have not yet understood in depth what the feminine genius can give us, what woman can give to society and also to us. Maybe women see things in a way that complements the thoughts of men. It is a path to follow with greater creativity and courage.[64]

Perhaps, however, the true risk of a step backwards lies not in being open to the removal of difference, but rather in resolutely insisting that there is such a thing as "the feminine genius." If there is indeed a path to follow through complementarity to the equality of the sexes in public life, Pope Francis has yet to show us what it might be, let alone to lead the way along such a path.

Notes

1 Links to the films and speeches at the Colloquium, together with further information about the so-called Humanum project of which the Colloquium forms a part can be found at http://humanum.it/.

2 Letter from Joseph Cardinal Ratzinger, Prefect, Congregation for the Doctrine of the Faith, to the Bishops of the Catholic Church on the Collaboration of Men and Women in the Church and in the World (May 31, 2004), available at www.vatican.va/roman_curia/congregations/cfaith/documents/rc_con_cfaith_doc_20040731_collaboration_en.html.

3 A stereotype in this context amounts to an imperfect proxy: it is something normatively or descriptively associated with one sex or the other, but is not categorically true of all members of that sex and/or not categorically false with respect to all members of the other sex. Stereotypes, or "fixed notions concerning the roles and abilities of males and females" should not, in the view of the Supreme Court and of feminists, be used to limit the opportunities of individuals of any sex. For further discussion see Mary Anne Case, " 'The Very Stereotype the Law Condemns': Constitutional Sex Discrimination Law as a Quest for Perfect Proxies," *Cornell Law Review* 85 (2000) 1447, 1473.

4 For example, German activist Gabriele Kuby warned in a Vatican publication that a resolution by the EU Parliament "to promote equality between women and men" by encouraging the elimination of "sexual stereotyped images" from advertising and the media threatened "to break the innermost core of the culture, namely the different identities of men and women." Kuby asked, "Why do women not see that their freedom to be wives and mothers is about to be mercilessly strangled? Why do men not understand that the raging battle of the sexes is seeking to take away their male power and identity?" Gabriele Kuby, "Gender Mainstreaming – The Secret Revolution," *Vatican Magazine* (November 6, 2008).

5 This chapter is part of a much larger project on the Vatican and gender, which includes, inter alia, my prior publications "After Gender The Destruction of Man? The Vatican's Nightmare Vision of the Gender Agenda for Law", *Pace Law Review* 31 (2012) 802 and "The Role of the Popes in the Invention of Sexual Complementarity and the Anathematization of Gender", in *Religion & Gender, Habemus Gender* special issue (2015).

6 Catechesis on the Theology of the Body available at www.totus2us.com/vocation/jpii-catechesis-on-theology-of-the-body/.
7 For the English edition, see Joseph Cardinal Ratzinger and Vittorio Messori, "The Ratzinger report: an exclusive interview on the state of the Church" (1985) 95.
8 Ruth Bader Ginsburg, *Gender in the Supreme Court: The 1973 and 1974 Terms*, 1975 SUP. CT. REV. 1, 1 n 1.
9 2004 Letter, supra n 2. I have made the alteration in the title of this document because, although the official English translation speaks of the "Collaboration of Men and Women," the Italian and every other official language I can read speaks of the sexes in the singular – as "Uomo e … Donna' as "Mann und Frau," i.e. as "Man and Woman." The use in particular of "woman" in the singular, as an essential or ideal type, is one of the most problematic aspects of the theological anthropology of complementarity.
10 Gender mainstreaming became a term of art for the UN and many of its member states following the 1995 Beijing Final Report and Platform for Action's repeated recommendations that "[g]overnments and other actors should promote an active and visible policy of mainstreaming a gender perspective in all policies and programmes," See e.g. Beijing Declaration and Platform for Action, Fourth World Conference on Women, September 15, 1995, A/CONF.177/20 (1995).
11 See e.g. Slawomir Sierakowski, "The Polish Church's Gender Problem, " *New York Times* January 26, 2014, available at www.nytimes.com/2014/01/27/opinion/sierakowski-the-polish-churchs-gender-problem.html.
12 Mark D. Jordan, *The Invention of Sodomy in Christian Theology*, University of Chicago Press: 1997, 2.
13 Sr Prudence Allen, *The Concept of Woman, Vol. I: the Aristotelian Revolution, 750 B.C. to A.D. 1250*, p. 253. But note, that Hildegard wrote that "Woman is weak and looks up to man to provide for her, just as the moon receives its strength from the sun. For this reason she is subject to man and should always be prepared to serve him." (De Operatione Dei, I. 4, 65). See Barbara Newman, *Sister of Wisdom, St. Hildegard's Theology of the Feminine*, Berkeley, University of California Press: 1987, 95.
14 It is noteworthy that among Benedict XVI's classmates when, as Joseph Ratzinger, he studied theology at the University of Munich, was Elisabeth Goessman, who, as a professor specialized in Hildegard von Bingen and in the long history of arguments for the equality of the sexes. Goessman reports that the consistent reaction of her fellow students was that Hildegard "appears to have been not merely (!) a mystic, but a mature theologian," but that nevertheless Hildegard's works were then studied as literature, not theology. See Rebecca L.R. Garner, Elisabeth Goessman (1928–), "Overcoming Obstacles" in *Women Medievalists and the Academy*, Jane Chance ed., University of Wisconsin Press: 2005, 857–872 at 863.
15 See e.g. her cross-examination of the angel of the Annunciation, Luke 1:34, and her refusal to take her son's "no" for an answer at the wedding feast in Cana. Note also that at the Annunciation, she speaks of not having known a man rather than of a man not having known her, thus taking on for herself the active description of the sex act as knowledge usually ascribed to males.
16 Luke 10:40–42, Douay-Rheims trans. (as are all other English quotations from the Bible in this chapter).
17 Russell D. Moore, "After Patriarchy, What? Why Egalitarians Are Winning The Gender Debate," Jets 49/3 (September 2006) 569–76 at 570.
18 See discussion infra.
19 Russell D. Moore, supra n 17.

20 2004 Letter, supra n 2 at II.12.
21 See 2004 Letter, supra n 2 (citing Iraneus's *Adversus haereses*, for the relatively uncontroversial point that the New Testament goes beyond the Old because "with Jesus Christ 'all newness' appears").
22 See e.g. 2004 Letter at note 2 ("On the complex question of gender, see also The Pontifical Council for the Family, Family, Marriage and 'De facto unions'" (July 26, 2000)).
23 Thomas Laqueur, *Making Sex: Body and Gender from the Greeks to Freud*, Harvard University Press: 1992, 149.
24 Pius XI did acknowledge that "the degree and manner [of this subjection] may vary according to the different conditions of persons, place and time. In fact, if the husband neglect his duty, it falls to the wife to take his place in directing the family."
25 See e.g., Prudence Allen, "Man-Woman Complementarity: The Catholic Inspiration," 9.3 Logos (2006), 87, 92. I am grateful to Sr Allen for sharing her unpublished drafts with me.
26 See e.g. Dietrich von Hildebrand, *Die Ehe*, Müller: 1929.
27 See infra for some suggestions. Even if only the word and not the concept were new, this, by Ratzinger's own account, would be a strong reason not to rely on it. In the Ratzinger Report, supra note 7 at 78, he asserts, "It's always very dangerous to change religious language. Continuity here is of great importance."
28 Cf. Simone de Beauvoir's "One is not born but rather becomes a woman," seen by Vatican opponents of gender as a sort of reverse proof text: "one is not born, but rather becomes, a woman." Simone de Beauvoir, *The Second Sex*, New York: Vintage Books: 1973, 301.
29 William of Ockham. Dialogus, Book 6, Chapter LXXXV in *Auctores Britannici Medii Aevi*, John Kilcullen et al., eds., available at www.britac.ac.uk/pubs/dialogus/ockdial.html. Ockham's Magister repeatedly suggests women are part of *omnes* for purposes of the maxim of canon and later of secular law "quod omnes tangit" ("what touches all must be debated and decided by all"). For further discussion of the uses of the maxim in making feminist arguments from the middle ages to the present, see Mary Anne Case, "The Ladies? Forget About Them. A Feminist Perspective on the Limits of Originalism", *Const. Comment* 29 (2014) 431.
30 For a discussion of the evolution of her thought on this issue, see generally, Elisabeth Schuessler Fiorenza, "We are Church – A Kingdom of Priests," Keynote Address for Women's Ordination Worldwide (WOW) Second International Conference Breaking Silence, Breaking Bread: Christ Calls Women to Lead, Ottawa, Canada, July 22–24, 2005, available at http://womensordinationworldwide.org/ottawa-2005/2014/2/2/elizabeth-schussler-fiorenza-we-are-a-church-a-kingdom-of-priests.
31 See Mary Anne Case, "The Ladies? Forget About Them. A Feminist Perspective on the Limits of Originalism", *Const. Comment* 29 (2014) 431.
32 See supra n 30.
33 Quoted in Francine Muel-Dreyfus, *Vichy and the Eternal Feminine: A Contribution to a Political Sociology of Gender*, Duke University Press: 2001.
34 See e.g. Pope John Paul II, Mulieris Dignitatem [Apostolic Letter on the Dignity and Vocation of Women] (1988) available at www.vatican.va/.../apost_letters/documents/hf_jp-ii_apl_15081988_mulieris-dignitatem_en.html - 156k - 1988-08-15 and Pope John Paul II, Letter to Women, 1995 available at www.vatican.va/holy_father/john_paul_ii/letters/documents/hf_jp-ii_let_29061995_women_en.html - 31k - 1995-06-29.

35 "Questa Grande Vostra Adunata", Address of His Holiness Pope Pius XII To Members of Various Catholic Women's Associations, October 21, 1945, available at http://catholictradition.org/Encyclicals/questa1.htm.
36 "Discorso Del Santo Padre Giovanni XXIII Ai Partecipanti Al Corso Di Studio La Donna E La Professione Promosso Dall'universit Cattolica Del Sacro Cuore" 6 settembre 1961 http://w2.vatican.va/content/john-xxiii/it/speeches/1961/documents/hf_j-xxiii_spe_19610906_donna-professione.html.
37 "Discorso Del Santo Padre Paolo Vi Alle Partecipanti Al Congresso Nazionale Del Centro Italiano Femminile (Cif)," Lunedì, 6 dicembre 1976.
38 See Betty Friedan, *It Changed My Life: Writings on the Women's Movement*, Harvard University Press: 1998, 77–78.
39 For a detailed discussion of this debate, see Dirkje Donders,"The Tenacious Voice of Women." *Rie Vendrik and the Pontifical Commission On Women in Society and in the Church*, Utrecht: 2002.
40 Carol Gilligan, *In a Different Voice*, Harvard University Press: 1982, 26.
41 Joseph C. Ratziner and Vittorio Messori, supra n 7.
42 Ratzinger, 2004 Letter, supra n 2.
43 See e.g. Doris E. Buss, "Robes, Relics and Rights: the Vatican and the Beijing Conference On Women", *Social and Legal Studies* 7 (1998) 339, 343, 347 (describing cooperation between the Vatican and Islamic states at the Cairo and Beijing conferences).
44 *Statement of the Holy See in Explanation of Position on the Agreed Conclusions*, The Permanent Observer Mission Of The Holy See To The United Nations, available at: http://www.holyseemission.org/statements/statement.aspx?id=73.
45 Ratzinger, 2004 Letter, supra n 2.
46 Congregation for the Doctrine of the Faith, Doctrinal Assessment of the Leadership Conference of Women Religious, available at http://www.usccb.org/upload/Doctrinal_Assessment_Leadership_Conference_Women_Religious.pdf.
47 See e.g. *Pope says saving heterosexuality like saving the rainforest*, Reuters (Dec. 22, 2008, 1:18 IST), http://blogs.reuters.com/faithworld/2008/12/22/pope-says-saving-heterosexuality-like-saving-the-rainforest/; Foreign staff, "Pope: Saving world from homosexuality like saving rainforests, " *Daily Telegraph* (December 22, 2008, 6:33 PM), http://www.telegraph.co.uk/news/worldnews/europe/italy/3902931/Pope-Saving-world-from-homosexuality-like-saving-rainforests.html.
48 Confirming this broader interpretation, "[a] Vatican spokesman said that the pope did not want to attack homosexuality or transsexualism per se, but 'was speaking more generally about gender theories.'" Jason Farrago, "Pope: Save Rainforest and Heterosexuality, Too: Benedict's Christmas Message Decries Erosion of 'Traditional' Gender Roles," *Newser* (Dec. 23, 2008, 8:08 AM), www.newser.com/story/46091/pope-save-rainforest-and-heterosexuality-too.html ("Benedict's speech focused on the blurring of gender roles, which he said could lead to the 'self-destruction' of the human race.").
49 Pope Benedict XVI, Address of His Holiness Benedict XVI to the Members of the Roman Curia for the Traditional Exchange of Christmas Greetings (Dec. 22, 2008), available at www.vatican.va/holy_father/benedict_xvi/speeches/2008/december/documents/hf_ben-xvi_spe_20081222_curia-romana_en.html.
50 See Janet Halley, Prabha Kotiswaran, Hila Shamir and Chantal Thomas, "From the International to the Local in Feminist Legal Responses to Rape, Prostitution/Sex Work and Sex Trafficking: Four Studies in Contemporary Governance Feminism", *Harvard Journal of Law and Gender* 29 (2006) 335, 340 (defining governance feminism as "the incremental but by now quite noticeable installation of feminists and feminist ideas in actual legal-institutional power").

51 See Camille Robcis, "French Sexual Politics from Human Rights to the Anthropological Function of the Law" *French Historical Studies* (2010) 129, 132.
52 Apostolic journey to Rio de Janeiro on the occasion of the XXVIII World Youth Day press conference of Pope Francis during the return flight *Papal Flight* Sunday July 28, 2013 available at http://w2.vatican.va/content/francesco/en/speeches/2013/july/documents/papa-francesco_20130728_gmg-conferenza-stampa.html.
53 See e.g. Synod14, "Relatio Synodi" of the III Extraordinary General Assembly of the Synod of Bishops: "Pastoral Challenges to the Family in the Context of Evangelization" (October 5–19 2014), 18.10.2014, 24.
54 Antonio Spadaro, S.J., "A Big Heart Open to God: The exclusive interview with Pope Francis" *America Magazine*, September 30, 2013 available at http://americamagazine.org/pope-interview.
55 Pope Francis, "Not Just Good, but Beautiful," Opening Address Humanum Conference, available at http://humanum.it/talks/pope-francis-opening-address-humanum-conference/.
56 Ibid.
57 Lisa Fullam, "'Gender Theory,' Nuclear War, and the Nazis", *Commonweal*, February 23, 2015 available at www.commonwealmagazine.org/blog/gender-theory-nuclear-war-and-nazis-0.
58 "Apostolic Journey Of His Holiness Pope Francis To Sri Lanka And The Philippines (January 12–19, 2015) In-Flight Press Conference Of His Holiness Pope Francis From The Philippines To Rome Papal Flight," accessed on Monday January 19, 2015, available at http://w2.vatican.va/content/francesco/en/speeches/2015/january/documents/papa-francesco_20150119_srilanka-filippine-conferenza-stampa.html. (Citing the funding conditions placed on a woman of his acquaintance in 1995 and the more recent complaints of the African bishops at the 2014 Synod).
59 Pope Francis, "The Family – 10. Male And Female (I)," General Audience, Wednesday April 15, 2015.
60 See e.g. John L. Allen Jr., "Francis shoots down women cardinals," *NCR Today* Dec. 15, 2013, available at http://ncronline.org/blogs/ncr-today/francis-shoots-down-women-cardinals.
61 John Hooper, Pope Francis jokes 'woman was from a rib' as he avoids vow to reform church, *The Guardian*, June 29, 2014 available at www.theguardian.com/world/2014/jun/03/pope-tells-couples-have-children-not-pets (detailing Pope's remarks in interview with Il Messaggero's Franca Giansoldati).
62 Andrea Tornielli, "Never be afraid of tenderness". In this exclusive interview, Pope Francis speaks about Christmas, hunger in the world, the suffering of children, the reform of the Roman Curia, women cardinals, the Institute for the Works of Religion (IOR), and the upcoming visit to the Holy Land, *La Stampa Vatican Insider*, available at www.lastampa.it/2013/12/14/esteri/vatican-insider/en/never-be-afraid-of-tenderness-5BqUfVs9r7W1CJIMuHqNeI/pagina.html.
63 Pope Francis, "The Family – 10. Male And Female (I)," General Audience, Wednesday April 15, 2015.
64 Ibid.

Part II

Negotiating gender and religion in state law

5 Between strict constructionist sharī'ah and protecting young girls in contemporary Northern Nigeria

The case of child marriage (ijbār)

Sarah Eltantawi

Introduction

Starting in November 1999, Northern Nigerians took to the streets to demand that full Islamic penal law be (re)introduced in their societies. They believed that this Islamic penal code would re-enliven the ḥudūd, or punishments that derive from the Qur'an, which would at last alleviate the poverty and corruption that had reached desperate levels. Hundreds of thousands of people filed out onto the street assuming that nothing less than the unyielding laws of God stood a chance of bringing justice and order to a Nigerian society whose laws of man had failed. Sharī'ah penal codes were reintroduced in twelve Northern Nigeria states starting in 1999.

This essay analyzes a fault line within this perception of widespread support for the strictest iteration of Islamic penal law. I contend here that while Northern Nigeria witnessed widespread support for "idealized" sharī'ah, once this idealization expressed itself through the existing governmental system – a process I call "political sharī'ah" – this support became far less monolithic and more fractured. To illustrate this fissure, I concentrate on the example of ijbār, or child marriage, often of children as young as eight or nine years. I show in this essay that even within a context of a society like Northern Nigeria, that witnessed a grassroots revolution demanding the implementation of the strictest iteration of Islamic penal law, that law can be sidelined when society agrees that the law presents an ethical conflict. That this is true in the case of ijbār, which I will show here, foregrounds the larger philosophical and theological issue of how orthodoxy is constructed. This essay lends credence to the idea that the notion of "orthodoxy", often presented as timeless, cannot be understood outside human, historical processes.

In 2010, I conducted fieldwork across Northern Nigeria, concentrating on the states of Kaduna, Zaria, Sokoto, and Kano. My aim was to interview the lawyers and judges involved in the infamous case of Amina Lawal, a peasant woman from Katsina state, who in 2002 was sentenced to death by stoning for committing the crime of adultery (zinā), and who was later acquitted in an Islamic court. I interviewed these actors and many more people, including academics, journalists, NGO workers, Islamic scholars of all persuasions, including various forms of Islamist and adherents to traditional sūfī orders, and Christian leaders in the North. This paper is based on this fieldwork in addition to archival research.

Unlikely opponents

In today's Northern Nigeria, there is a well-documented societal drive to outlaw ijbār. We observe in this drive both a desire to reinstate a strict constructionist understanding of Mālikī law (the school of Islamic law practised in Northern Nigeria) and a desire to outlaw ijbār – which is prescribed by Mālikī law. I investigate in this essay how these instincts can co-exist in a society thought to be strictly "religious", and in the context of twelve northern Nigerian states that oppose the UN Convention on the Rights of the Child.

Contemporary Nigeria's opponents of ijbār are surprisingly ideologically diverse. They even include some Islamists who participated in writing Northern Nigeria's first penal code after the grassroots revolution demanding the implementation of full Islamic sharī'ah from 1999. Ijbār, however, is sanctioned in Mālikī fiqh, which dominates Northern Nigeria, and its practice has been justified on that basis (in part) for generations in Hausaland. Ijbār is widespread among poorer, rural families, whose economic hardship necessitates the early marriage of daughters.[1]

To explain this incongruence, I look at the driving forces behind both sharī'ah reimplementation and the desire to outlaw ijbār. The first, the drive to reintroduce sharī'ah at this moment in Northern Nigeria, rests at a more abstract, rhetorical level and depends on a notion of sharī'ah as both locally and globally "legitimate." The second, on the question of ijbār, depends on localized micropolitics to drive the activism to oulaw it. Put another way: while a return to sharī'ah invigorates Northern Nigerians at the abstract and ethical level, and while the drive for sharī'ah enjoyed wide cultural appeal, the issue of child marriage reveals different sets of ethical and social priorities. These ethical priorities are not best realized through strict constructionist Islamic law.

The sharī'ah revolution in contemporary Northern Nigeria

In November 1999, tens of thousands of Nigerians crowded into *tashar motaci* (transport stations) across Northern Nigeria to make their way mostly westward to Zamfara state to witness its Governor, Ahmed Sani Yerima, launch sharī'ah – the reintroduction of full Islamic penal law in twelve northern states. Some sold their belongings to afford the journey, and in a widely remarked upon development, taxi drivers reduced their fares in celebration. Governor Yerima – known for his sharp political instincts, if not for his special Islamic piety – had struck a geyser of popular support in his announcement that Zamfara state was to restore full sharī'ah penal law for the first time since the British High Commissioner for the Protectorate of Northern Protectorate of Northern Nigeria, Lord Frederick Lugard, issued a native courts ordinance in 1900 declaring some aspects of Islamic penal law – including stoning and hand amputations – "antithetical to natural justice."[2]

While conducting ethnographic research in Northern Nigeria in 2010 I found that the return to sharī'ah in 1999 was an effort first and foremost to assert Northern Nigerian independence from the federal state structure, whose corruption had by that point condemned many ordinary Nigerians to a life of intolerable poverty and injustice. Nigeria's political hegemony had moved southward since Olusegun Obasanjo was elected in 1999, the first time a Christian had held the office. The contrast between the extremely lavish lifestyle of governors (who regularly grab the nation's commercial and petrol earnings) and regular people were readily observable by the Nigerians who took to the streets to demand sharī'ah as they were to anyone else. Governors often have second, third, or forth homes on unpaved streets behind fortress-like gates, where the maid's quarters alone are of a splendor these ordinary Nigerians could only dream of.

History

To return to sharī'ah is to return to a past that is understood to enact an alternative system of morality and justice that enjoys wide legitimacy in Northern Nigeria – namely the local and global history of "Islam." On the global level, Nigerians observe the splendor of mosques, charitable organizations and schools funded by wealthy Gulf states and associate these material riches with austere Islam. Intellectually and morally, Islamic traditions enjoy a transcendent position as universal truth, an epistemological state that has been deeply rooted at least since the Sokoto Caliphate took root in 1809. Many Northern Nigerians (who before the colonial period were referred to as the Hausa, and their region, Hausaland, though the actual ethnicities and languages spoken in Northern Nigeria are multiple) look back with awe and fondness at the legacy of the nineteenth-century Sokoto Caliphate, known locally as "the jihad." The Sokoto Caliphate is a proud instance of rule by "native sons" – for Africans, by Africans.

The jihad and its leader, Uthman Dan Fodio (d. 1817), are often thought of as attentive to justice and social prosperity and focused on bringing Hausaland in line with surrounding literate Islamic cultures. I formed this impression of how the jihad is remembered both through a study of modern historiography of the jihad period and through a study of the polemical and theological works produced in Arabic by the jihad leaders of that era. These histories reflect less the complexities of the jihad era – which include a rich history of resistance to the caliphate alongside welcoming the caliphate (a dramatic case in point is the Kano civil war of 1893–1894 CE) – but rather an idealized image of the caliphate in circulation today in Northern Nigeria.

The Sokoto Caliphate was defeated in 1903 by the British colonial army, a legacy that today many Nigerians blame for their contemporary governmental and economic problems, though I think that blame has been intensified in the present as conditions worsen and a search for historical antecedents for this state of affairs also intensifies. This simplification of 19th century jihad history coupled with lingering resentment over British colonialism were deployed from 1999 to justify a contemporary return to sharī'ah.

"Thirteen useless drunkards came along and took away our law": contemporary reception of British colonialism

While 1900 signaled the death-knell of the Sokoto Caliphate, 1959, a year before independence, ended Islamic penal law as Hausaland had known it for generations. In that year, a new Penal Code came into effect that effectively ended the use of Islamic penal law. It was based on the Indian (1860) and Sudanese (1899) Penal Codes, but was essentially an English code. The decision to adopt this code was made on the basis of a 1958 conference held in Nigeria seeking to preserve Islamic law in the north while comporting with the "general pattern of legal jurisprudence" at that time. This meant that Islamic law would be effectively limited to civil law, though the Sudanese and Indian laws incorporated some sharī'ah offences while simultaneously subjecting them to ordinary common law procedures.[3] The conference argued that this should be acceptable, as it was working for "millions of Malays, Sudanese, and Indians."

The above history marks the ascension of "imposed" law by the federal government. Northern Nigerian legal scholars supportive of sharī'ah remarked to me that in a truly Federal system, regions would be able to follow their own laws; and the Nigerian constitution does indeed hold that states are responsible for the maintenance of criminal law, not the federal government. The so-called Native Courts Proclamation of 1900, for example, offers a stark illustration of the roots of this distrust. The proclamation, issued by British High Commissioner Lord Frederick Lugard, outlawed the stoning punishment using arguments in support of "natural justice."[4] Note, however, that Joseph Schacht, a leading western scholar of Islamic law, in a mission to Northern Nigeria for the British crown, reports that the Caliphate never carried out the stoning punishment.[5] The result of outlawing stoning, therefore, was to create defensiveness and fear among the native populace about the disruption of their Islamic societal order, which was thought to have been legitimately established through trade with Africans (especially trade from the Maghreb in North Africa down to Kano and other commercial centers in today's Northern Nigeria). Because the British colonial authorities insisted on control over capital punishment (in addition to taxation and land rights), reclaiming this lost legacy of Islamic penal law was seen as a reclamation of sovereignty. I contend that this instinct toward self-determination underpinned support for the stoning punishment much more than a desire to see the punishment carried out in reality.[6]

A professor I interviewed in Zaria summarized this history thus: "Thirteen useless drunkards came along and took away our law."[7] As if to conceptually leap over the ensuing history of Nigerian independence, the political dominance of Muslims in the country since independence, and the fact that the north enjoys southern oil wealth, the professor then cited a quote from *Surat al-Ahzab* in the Qur'an by way of settling the issue once and for all: "No believing men and women have any choice in a matter after God and his Apostle have decided it. Whoever disobeys God and his apostle has clearly lost the way and gone astray."[8]

This lack of respect for the Nigerian constitution is repeatedly discussed alongside justifications for a return to sharī'ah in Northern Nigeria, but often quick to follow were denunciations of the poverty and corruption plaguing Nigerian political culture. The frequency of this juxtaposition has led me to form a theory outlining the divergence between "idealized sharī'ah" and "political sharī'ah"; "idealized sharī'ah" seems to directly result from and reflect the desperation Northern Nigerians feel in the face of massive government corruption, deepening poverty, and social ills such as increased prostitution and instant divorce. The federal system – which is seen as representing contemporary Nigerian political culture as a whole – is blamed for these problems. This system is described, as we saw above, as essentially colonial in its genesis and structure, and bound to a western worldview and geopolitical relationships seen by northerners as a major cause of their problems. The "silver bullet" version of sharī'ah, therefore, in which God's law will usher in sweeping and swift change, signals a level of desperation that made it clear that the time for recourse to holy miracles had arrived.

The eminent Nigerian historian of the Sokoto Caliphate, Ibrahim Suleiman – insisted that the terminology should be changed from "reintroducing" sharī'ah to "reenlivening" sharī'ah – for sharī'ah had existed since the jihad in some form, albeit in part interrupted by colonialism, and always in the deepest yearnings of Muslims. "Every society is responsible for itself", he told me. "Sharī'ah in the north is merely an expansion of an existing system." In Suleiman's view, independence from the British came at a very difficult price – the suspension of ḥudūd (Islamic penal laws). "When the ḥudūd was weakened", he added, "crime rates increased." Their hope was always for ḥudūd to return.

Islamic law and ijbār

Now that we have an understanding of the instincts that fuelled a return to sharī'ah, let us look at the question of child marriage (ijbār) whose problematic aspects disrupt the easy certainty of this choice. A question at the heart of this inquiry is: what prompts or causes ijbār? Is ijbār best explained by particular circumstances such as poverty, or is ijbār better understood as conditioned behaviour that finds its origin in primary text sources such as the Qur'an and ḥadīth? This question takes on an epistemological aspect when the classical intellectual history of the legal formation of ijbār is examined as well. The discussion of ijbār in classical Islamic legal texts itself shows it to have both sociological elements (known in Islamic legal discourse as '*urf*, or custom) and theological thinking.

The fact that the practice of ijbār is contested by a surprisingly wide swath of Nigerian society suggests that the call for sharī'ah is more a framework, a symbol, and a message of a desire above all to apply Islamic family law in all respects without regard to local custom. Like many issues involving gender norms, the question of ijbār pierces through the constructed fiction of an idealized, perfect Islamic tradition by bringing us back to present reality with its problems and injustices. Women in Nigeria are at the front of this process of piercing idealized sharī'ah and insisting on looking at the practical consequences of politicized sharī'ah – the version that actual people negotiate and live.[9]

"Ijbār" is the coercive authority given to fathers in Mālikī Islamic law to marry off their young offspring.[10] The term derives from two phrases in the legal literature: *al-wilāyat al-ijbāriyyah* (compulsory guardianship) and *al-walī al-Mujbir* (compulsary guardian). The root W-L-Y (forming wilāyat) in Arabic denotes a helper, caretaker, or protector, while the root J-B-R (forming *mujbar*) denotes forcing or compelling (someone to do something). The underlying logic of the concept of the wilāyat is the notion that the ward is a person of restricted capacity. With the etymologies of these two words in mind, *al-walīyah al-ijbāriyya* thus conveys the sense of a duty on guardians imposed by law. While a father has the power of ijbār to marry off both young girls and boys, this power ends when the children fulfill the conditions of "emancipation" (*rushd*); a standard that is different for boys and girls. According to Mālikī jurist al-Dardīr[11] (d. 1201CE) in his *Sharh al-Kabīr*, (a commentary of the fourteenth century *Mukhtasar* of Sīdī Khalīl, which is very important in Northern Nigeria)[12], a male child is automatically emancipated upon reaching social and biological maturity, which is generally interpreted as having reached the age of puberty. A male adult is considered to automatically possess the required capacity.

A female, on the other hand, is not considered emancipated without a judicial decision that she is rashīda, or emancipated – the default assumption being that she is not a rashīda, and thus her father can compel her to marry. Failing this judicial decree, a girl can be emancipated upon satisfying the following two conditions: she must enter a marital home (i.e., marry), and become the subject of two reliable witnesses testifying to her ability to manage her property.[13] A ward, as just mentioned, could apply to a court of law for intervention, but I would assert that this is all but unthinkable in reality in contemporary Nigeria for both social and logistical reasons.

Contemporary practice of ijbār

It is difficult to pinpoint with certainty how long the ijbār has been practised in Northern Nigeria. When I was in Nigeria in 2010, ijbār was often cited as a major cause for concern not only among women's rights advocates but among Northerners more generally. Even Islamist activists, who generally react defensively to attempts to reform sexual practices, often concede that in the end, ijbār is a result of poverty, ignorance, and an incorrect understanding of Islam.

The sources of ijbār are both textual and social, owing to factors such as poverty and patriarchal family structures. To my knowledge, Masud[14] was the last to undertake a systematic study of the sources of ijbār that gathers empirical data from Islamic societies where the practice is known to occur. Masud sets out to explain why the practice is declining in some societies while remaining in others. The fact that this disparity in practice exists is explained, for Masud, as a triumph of "informal sources" (e.g. social and local factors) over formal sources (e.g. Qur'an and ḥadīth)[15] as the cause of fluctuation in the practice.[16] Many of his examples are Nigerian.

That contemporary Northern Nigerians should mobilize to combat ijbār at this particular moment in their history is noteworthy in itself. The sharī'ah revolution in Nigeria aimed to interpolate an unruly society – into a narrative of an always already perfect Islamic one. This was manifested through incantations of an ahistorical conception of sharī'ah that is simultaneously narrowly constructed as the only solution to Nigerian problems. In this structure, it is essential that conceptions of "Islam", "sacred texts", "religion" and "sharī'ah" remain stable – indeed, that is entirely the point. "Islam" as a symbolic category is the most powerful legitimizer in Northern Nigerian society for both political change and moral discipline, conformity, and spiritual reflection. In a time of great uncertainty, sharī'ah – even if invoked in name only – is the ultimate "silver bullet" solution. Despite all of this, objections to the practice and consequences of child marriage have not stopped Nigerians from fighting back against the practice. Objections to child marriage emerge from a different ethical place, one strong enough to engage a surprisingly diverse swath of political actors in Northern Nigeria.

Forces that fight child marriage

Women's rights advocates such as WRAPA (Women's Rights Advancement and Protection Alternative), have taken up the cause against ijbār as part of an overall women's empowerment agenda.[17] WRAPA, along with the British Council and the DFID (Department for International Development (UK)) sponsored a report called, "Promoting Women's Rights Through Sharī'ah in

Northern Nigeria. Centre for Islamic Legal Studies, Ahmadu Bello University, Zaria." It begins by saying, "With the widespread conviction of many states in Northern Nigeria to reform society based on Sharī'ah, an opportunity had presented itself to improve the position of women, and to improve their means to face the challenges confronting them in this global age and ever-changing Muslim society."[18] What is noteworthy about the sponsoring organizations is that, while they are composed of Nigerian feminists and western NGO's, the report was written and promoted by a leading and well-respected Islamic jurist in Nigeria, Ibrahim Naiya Sada, who was one of the chief authors of the Zamfara legal code in post-1999 Northern Nigeria.[19]

VVF (Vesicovaginal Fistula) is one of the main problems that concern girls' and women's advocates in Northern Nigeria and one of the main issues addressed in the report. VVF is an abnormal fistulous tract that is found between the vagina and bladder that causes involuntary discharge of urine into the vaginal vault. The problem can be caused in childbirth or as a result of hysterectomies and other cancer treatments, but in Nigeria the problem has been identified as resulting most often from sexual activity, often forceful, with girls whose vulvas and reproductive systems are not yet fully formed. The VVF condition can cause leakage of fecal matter into the vaginal area, which is then often used by husbands as a ground for divorce.

Because of ijbār's identification with VVF (in addition to other reasons), its designation as a problem to be targeted by non-governmental organizations in Northern Nigeria has attracted negative reactions from Islamist forces there, who are not only concerned that traditional forms of marriage remain in place, but cite considerable distrust of non-profit organizations – particularly with "Islam" in the title – that involve themselves in these issues. These NGO's[20] are seen as a form of western soft-power whose implications for the disruption of traditional forms of social order is all the more exaggerated by the disproportionate amount of money that can be placed into those efforts. For Ibrahim Aliyu, Professor of Islamic Law at Ahmadu Bello University, Zaria, for example, VVF is western propaganda: "Girls can get pregnant by age 12 in Europe", he told me in Zaria. But having said that, he then interestingly pivoted to an analysis of the "problem", locating its genesis in poverty and a failure of education: "the under 18 marriage situation is purely due to poverty. Schools are not working – this is also a measure of poverty."[21]

Journalist and prominent Kano activist Balqisu Yusuf, on the other hand, who is a founding member of the Federation of Muslim Women's association and has as of 2010 been its national president, begs to differ. Yusuf considers VVF among her chief concerns, and rejects the notion that her acceptance of money from NGOs compromises her causes. She would welcome the transparent funding of issues dear to her like maternity rights and VVF. I described to Yusuf some of my conversations with Islamist activists who attacked her efforts largely because of her acceptance of NGO money. Her reply: "These guys don't like that I take NGO money? Bring King Fahd's money![22] I have child mortality to deal with! I can't wait until money comes from the Federal government!"[23] The implication here is that these same

Islamist critics regularly accept money from King Fahd of Saudi Arabia. If they have a source of funding, she needs one as well.

Indeed, they organize intrepidly. Nigerian NGOs such as the Federation of Muslim Women's Associations in Nigeria (FOMWAN), whose mission is, "to propagate Islam, educate Muslim women and ensure that they live according to the tenants of Islam and make positive impact on national matters, both religious and secular," takes up reproductive rights as one of its chief platform issues. The Adamawa state chapter, for example, organized a two-day workshop on sex education and parental relationships which was held in the city of Yola. Writing about such a conference in Bauchi state, the report reads: "Quite a number of VVF patients benefited from successful VVF repairs under the sponsorship of FOMWAN Bauchi State CHSP (Community Health Services Program) through provision of community Health Services to two communities in Zaki LGA and Itas LGAs of Bauchi State. These are interspersed with da'wah (proselytization) services and Islamic schools."

FOMWAN's funding appears to include foreign funding,[24] which makes their efforts for girls' and women's health and education instantly rife for suspicion by Islamist conservatives despite the fact that they, as Yusuf pointed out above, have their own sources of foreign funding. The reason the Islamist critique might "stick" more on a cultural level is that in contemporary Northern Nigeria, all activist activities must be framed within the language of "Islam" to have any chance of gaining wide acceptance. Reference to "Islam" as a proper noun, a cultural heritage, and a moral system is simply the only workable currency for social change on the rhetorical level. However, what I am attempting to show here is how this system ("Islam") can also be manipulated to advance goals that are outside strict constructionist Islamic law. In the case of ijbār, it was.

In support of efforts to outlaw ijbār was the Chairman of the north's largest state's sharī'ah commission (Zamfara) and the Chief Judge of Kaduna State, among many other prominent figures of the Nigerian Islamic legal scene, were also signatories.[25]

Arguing against the practice of ijbār, the authors write:

> Parents who do this (ijbār) rely on the jurisprudential ruling of Imam Malik to the effect that a father may compel his previously unmarried daughter to marry a man he chooses for her. All the Jurists agree though that it is recommended and always necessary to seek to consent of the girl before she is given in marriage. Nowhere does the Qur'an or the Prophet (SAW) speak with approval of coercive authority. There are authentic reports in the traditions of the Prophet (SAW) where some parents gave their daughters in marriage without the daughter's consent, but when the women concerned objected to them before the Prophet (SAW), the daughters were given the option to revoke the marriage.[26]

This reasoning relies on an analysis of matn (substantive meaning) of the ḥadīth (sayings and practices of the Prophet Muhammad). The report goes on to cite several aḥadīth portraying girls who were forced to marry, only to have those marriages annulled after complaining to the Prophet.[27] One such ḥadīth is the following: "Ibn Abbas reported that the Prophet (SAW) said: 'A matron (i.e. a woman previously married) has more right regarding herself than her guardian, and a virgin's consent should be sought and her silence is her consent.'" This ḥadīth, however, sidesteps the question of ijbār, for, as mentioned earlier, the practice is only valid for pre-emancipated women, and this ḥadīth clearly states that a "woman previously married" is the one subject to "more right regarding herself than her guardian." As for the virgin, "her silence is her consent", and the sources are clear that she has no means of disputing her father's wishes outside an onerous legal process that I would argue is essentially unthinkable in practical terms in contemporary Northern Nigeria – that is, if regular Nigerians are aware of this option at all, which I very much doubt. More to the point, this report clearly sidesteps fiqh to achieve its aims of arguing for an ethics-based approach to marriage based on the comparatively more gracious spirit of the ḥadīth in this case. A different WRAPA report[28] is more explicit in its rejection of jurisprudence: "Ijbār is a product of Islamic jurisprudential thought. It has no basis either in the Holy Qur'an or Sunnah of the Holy Prophet (PBUH)". The report continues: "Ijbār is in the main practised by the Malikis", and "other schools of Fiqh do not apply it as the Malikis do." By pointing out that ijbār is prescribed as it is in just one school of law among many, the authors and signatories of this report send a clear message that the rationale behind the punishment is contingent, man-made and thus disputable.

The stoning punishment: a similar rationale

Another of FOMWAN's publications addresses the stoning punishment in particular. The language is winding, as if hesitating to take a clear position, but the reader does emerge with one fact that is repeatedly emphasized: the stoning punishment is not found in the Qur'an. The article[29] begins simply by quoting verses 17:33 and 24: 1–11 from the Qur'an, which address adultery.[30] These Qur'an verses are conflated in the subsequent discussion with the "the sharī'ah": "The injunction: 'Do not go near adultery' is clearly a comprehensive and effective commandment according to the sharī'aht,[31] where the concept of "sharī'ah" traditionally encompasses fiqh in addition to Qur'ānic revelation." The article goes on to interpret the Qur'anic text. It is only near its end that it mentions in passive construction: "As regards stoning for adultery, according to the Merciful, Almighty Allah, (sic) in the Holy Quran 24:3, it is flogging for adultery culprits."[32] This subsequent sentence does not make sense:

> The conviction that is actually imposed on adultery must be according to the established Islamic law, sharī'ah. That is with the prescribed evidence of the combined four eyewitnesses who were physically present at the

> same time, and testified to the engagement in actual adultery. All these must first and foremost be verified before sentence."[33]

The brochure goes on to make itself more clear:

> On the other hand, Allah further said among others in the Holy Qur'an 4:26 that, in the case of married ones who are found guilty of lewdness, half of the due punishment is prescribed. Such a culprit is also forbidden to the believers in marriage but eligible only to the adulteress or idolatress or vice versa. The divine orders are a clear indication that apart from flogging, stoning to death was never contemplated in the Holy Qur'an as penalty for adultery.

Let us, therefore, take note that a victim stoned to death cannot according to the Holy Qur'an 4:16,17 and 24:4 be confined, repent, amend or married to anybody, after his or her death or adultery:

> May the Merciful Allah, continue to guide us in the straight path of those on whom you, Allah, has bestowed your favours, Ameen. (Culled from the *Guardian*, Friday March 15, 2002)[34] (Nigerian newspaper).

In this example of stoning, the authors employ the same logic we just saw employed with regard to child marriage; foreground the Qur'an and render the legal tradition anthropomorphic, thus displacing its authoritative aspect and creating room for different interpretation. What is really happening is that Islamic law is rendered here practically irrelevant without explicitly stating this position.

Post-modern Islamic law, activism and primary sources

Clearly, then, from the examples of child marriage and the stoning punishment, when expedient, the jurisprudential tradition, and specifically the Mālikī school, are argued by interested Nigerian actors as human constructions that do not carry the same authoritative weight as the Qur'an and Sunnah. 'Urf, or custom, is also described as illegitimate: "The practice of ijbār is traceable to the 'urf wal adat (sic) of the people of Medina as exemplified by the practice of some Sahabas namely: Qasim Ibn Mulid, and Salim Ibn Adullahi." Finally, with respect to Prophetic tradition, the report says, "all of the Imams of Mudhahibs (sic) are by consensus agreed that any of their Fatwas that is contrary to any Prophetic Tradition or the Holy Qur'an should be disregarded."[35]

This sidestepping of fiqh is interesting for at least two reasons: one, as mentioned earlier, sidestepping Islamic law in this context is promoted by leading thinkers of the post-1999 reintroduction of sharī'ah (Islamic legal) penal codes in Northern Nigeria. Secondly, this move seems to break from the time-honoured tradition in Northern Nigeria of identification with the Mālikī school.

This flexibility has a nineteenth-century antecedent that is worth mentioning. Abdullahi Ibn Fūdī, son of the fabled jihad leader of the Sokoto Caliphate Uthman Dan Fodio, made explicit his desire to align Hausaland with the Mālikī to intellectually solidify the newly-emerging caliphate against the predilections of his father, who wrote in his late eighteenth-century *Iqāmat al Sunnah wa-Izālat al Bid'ah* that he was partial to a robust policy of *istishān*, or juridical preference. Ibn Fūdī, considered the most fiqh-inclined of the early jihad leaders, prevailed. This Sokoto tradition was widely invoked in the post-1999 sharī'ah debate – but as with many other traditions that were rhetorically resurrected, including, I would argue, Islamic law itself – the evidence suggests these were reduced to symbolic categories whereby their very invocation is hoped to accelerate divine intervention. This is another instance in which the Islamic tradition can be seen to function more at the symbolic than the practical level.

Conclusion: an alternative ethical system in an age of strict constructionist Islamic law

What I have shown so far are segments of a culture that wants to end the practice of child marriage, and the best of the jurists on the ground cannot find a way to do so with finality within the jurisprudential tradition. And so they dropped it – in writing and in public. I would argue, significantly, that this is a culture that is among one of the least likely to have done so. Therefore, we must contend with the question of multiple planes of morality in a society that has not only very recently reintroduced Islamic penal codes via a massive grassroots demand – indicating broad support for "Islamic law", and one with a tradition of juridical "strict constructionism" that can be traced back to the eighteenth century.

My thoughts on this problematic stuation are the following: sympathy for young girls in precarious situations and the attendant instinct to combat ijbār is sincere across the ideological spectrum in Northern Nigeria, despite some arguments, made mostly by Islamists, that the (relatively) massive western funding for this cause precedes the "concern". At the same time, there is no question that the Islamists are right in their critique that the material means sought for this activism in the form of western NGO funding quite simply introduces a form of western soft power into the equation in a society that is extremely averse to the merest sign of "intervention."

The inability to resolve the ijbār problem with finality and legitimacy using jurisprudential means creates a lacunae that is easily filled with western forms of soft power, including not only funding, but all of the bureaucratic strings that are attached: compulsory reports indicating "progress", adoption of "NGO language" including "stakeholders" and "change agents", the continuing diminution of traditional forms of learning and rhetoric, and, finally, the abandonment of jurisprudence itself where necessary.

Hence, we must account for that plane of experience – which we can perhaps call "collective emotion" – that would motivate a culture that has given every indication of maximal fidelity to the Islamic legal tradition to nonetheless work to overcome a clear legal ruling in the interests of accommodating immediate, pressing concerns. One might well ask why a maslaha (public good) legal argument was not proffered in this cause, despite the qualifications and power on the part of many participants in this report to do so. While it is undeniably simply easier to label the jurisprudential tradition as "man made" and emphasize the Qur'ān and ḥadīth, my guess is that the strategy of foregrounding ḥadīth, which in this case (but of course, not all cases) softens the legal ruling, was deemed to be a quicker and more effective strategy to convince the Nigerian public. What is noteworthy here is that the dozens of judges that adopted this method to address ijbār placed a strategy of maximal public persuasiveness over remaining within a legal framework. Scholarship of the modern period has yet to account for a such a privileging of public concern – especially at the hands of jurists who themselves wrote, advocated for, and reintroduced sharī'ah penal codes – when that concern clearly challenges a plain legal ruling.

There is another potential explanation for the decision not to critically engage the jurisprudential tradition – fear. As Dean of the Law Faculty at the University of Jos, Jamila Nasr told me, "Justice does not exist outside the Qur'an. Muslims are afraid of their reasoning." Attorney Ahmed Garba of Jos said to me simply, "If you ask questions the teacher is not comfortable with, you get beaten." I recorded the following conversation I had with a lead attorney in Abuja on the topic of stoning:

> Aliyu Yauri's demeanor was strange. I told him some of the Islamic arguments against stoning, because he had mentioned, a bit nervously: "some say it's not in the holy Qur'an." I said, yes, this is the case. Then he said, "but it is all over the ḥadīth of the Prophet, and in Sahih al-Bukhari." The he added, tentatively, "do you think some of these are forged?" I said, "yes, some are weak, but the point is, the early fuqaha' (jurists) used takhsīs (specification) to resolve this contradiction." He then said, "I am very proud of Islam and I am willing to ignore all of this. It is just academic."

Saudatu Mahdi, Secretary General of WRAPA, helped me interpret the above conversation. She said of Yauri: "He's using the legal system to do what he can, but a lot of people are afraid of scholarship and reluctant to challenge the laws themselves. One focuses on interpretation and education because the actual text is a 'no go' area and absolutely off the table."[36]

In sum, one can argue that the jurisprudential tradition in Northern Nigeria has become ossified as a result of intimidation. Ironically, this climate of intimidation operates in the service of preserving a notion of a stable and unchanging Islamic law to offset the climate of chaos and insecurity present in modern Northern Nigeria. Under such circumstances, one would expect the very Nigerians who clamoured for the reintroduction of sharī'ah penal codes – to say nothing of the judges who wrote and promoted those codes – to fall into line with the strong local tradition of strict-constructionist jurisprudence. Instead, ethical concerns about ijbār were considered so pressing that jurisprudence was cast aside, creating an ethical lacunae that one could argue the western tradition of human rights was invited to fill. While the rhetorical gesture for sharī'ah can be very strong on the symbolic and even material level through the establishment of courts, as the sharī'ah experiment in Northern Nigeria continues to unfold and weave its way through the inevitably more complex ethical terrain of Northern Nigerian society, especially with respect to concerns over rights for women and girls, scholars should continue to monitor whether jurisprudence can keep up with the times.

Notes

1 Chimaroaoke O. Izugbara and Alex C. Ezeh, "Women and High Fertility in Islamic Northern Nigeria" *Studies in Family Planning*, vol. 41, no. 3. (September 2010), 193–204.
2 For a comprehensive study of the constitutional challenges involved in unilaterally declaring Islamic penal law northern states within a larger federal structure, see: Andrew Ubaka Iwobi, "Tiptoeing through a Constitutional Minefield: the Great Sharia Controversy in Nigeria" *Journal of African Law*, 48 (2004), 111–164.
3 A.G. Karibi-Whyte, *History and Sources of Nigerian Criminal Law* (Ibadan: Spectrum, 1993), 190. Cited by: Sam Amadi, "Religion and Secular Constitution: Human Rights and the Challenge of Sharī'ah" (paper written for the Carr Center for Human Rights Policy, Harvard University, 2003).
4 "Native Courts Proclamation" administered by Lord Frederick Lugard, British High Commissioner for the Protectorate of Northern Nigeria, 1900 (Kaduna National Archives).
5 Joseph Schacht, "Islam in Northern Nigeria" *Studia Islamica*, no. 8 (1957), 123–146.
6 Sarah Eltantawi, "Stoning in the Islamic Tradition: The Case of Northern Nigeria" (Dissertation, Harvard University, 2012).
7 Aliyu Ibrahim, interview with professor, April 2010, Zaria, Nigeria.
8 Qur'an 33:36, (Translated by Ahmed Ali, Princeton: Princeton University Press, 1993).
9 For a deeper discussion on the question of Islamic feminism, see: Valentine M. Moghadam, "Islamic Feminism and its Discontents: Toward a Resolution of the Debate" *Signs: Journal of Women in Culture and Society* vol. 27, no. 4 (2002). A more detailed study of gender and religion in Kaduna, Northern Nigeria is provided by: Colette Harris, "Masculinities and Religion in Kaduna, Nigeria: A Struggle for Continuity at a Time of Change" *Religion and Gender*, vol. 2, no. 2 (2012), 207–230.
10 Ijbār is present in all four schools of sunni Islamic law. The debate over the intellectual historical origins of the practice continues to be an open one that implicates a larger debate concerning the origins of Islamic law. M.K. Masud (1985) advances the argument that the practices' historical background can be traced to

"tribal norms" of the early period of Roman Law: "The source of the power of the guardian in these systems was the power (potestas) of the head of the family or tribe (paterfamilia) which was absolute and compulsive."

11 Al-Sharh al-Kabīr by Ibn Dardır al-'Adawi (d.1201) which is in itself a Mukhtasar commentary on the Mukhtasar al-Khalīl and it is a very relied upon book; published with the Hāshiyyah of al-Dasūqī (d.1230).

12 Dardīr's commentary on Khalīl is particularly instructive to consult, as Sīdī Khalīl's Mukhtasar (thirteenth century CE) plays a important historical, theological and, most importantly for our purposes, legal role in contemporary Northern Nigeria. The Zamfara penal code, the first post-1999 Sharī'ah penal code applied in the northern state of Zamfara, was a reduction of Khalīl's bāb al-hudūd. Historically the Mukhtasar has been the most important legal compendium in Hausaland Maliki history.

13 See: Mohammad Fadel, "Reinterpreting the Guardian's Role in the Islamic Contract of Marriage: The Case of the Maliki School" *The Journal of Islamic Law*, vol. 3, no. 1 (Spring/Summer 1998). See footnote 20: "Al-Dardīr 382–83 ("wa al-sabī maḥjūr 'alayhi.li-bulūghihi rashīdan wa zīda…fī al-unthā dukhūl zawj bihā. wa shahādat al-ʿudūl bi-ḥifẓihā mālahā.) A minor male is legally incapacitated until he attains puberty, in a sound state of mind…It is also required in the case of a woman that she enter her marital home…and the testimony of upright witnesses that she can manage her property." [Note, this condition is for female children that have not been deemed rashīda by a judge.]

14 M. K. Masud, "The Sources of the Maliki Doctrine of Ijbar" *Islamic Studies*, vol. 24, no. 2 (Summer 1985), 215–253.

15 For the sake of reference, I include here the "formal sources" i.e. Our'apic verses and abadith referenced by jurists. I Qur'an: 1. "Marry those among you who are single and who are pious among your slaves and maids." (XXIV: 32) 2. "Do not marry unbelieving women till they believe…Nor marry the unbelieving men till they believe." (II: 221) 3. "Oh believers, when believing women come to you having migrated from their homes, examine them…when you are sure they are believing women do not return them to believers. These women are not lawful to the unbelievers nor are they lawful of these women. Pay them what they have spent on these women. It is no sin for you to marry these women when you have paid them their dues." (IX: 10). 4 "And whoso is not able to afford to marry free, believing women, let him marry from the believing maids whom your right hand possesses…. Marry them with the permission of their folk." (IV: 25) 5. "If you divorce them, before you have touched them, and you had fixed for them a portion (dower), then pay half of what was fixed unless they agree to forego it or he in whose hands is the marriage tie agrees to forego." (II, 237) 6. "And when you have divorced women and they reach their term, do not prevent them from marrying their husbands, if it is agreed between them in kindness." (For more discussion on the uses of these verses by various jurists in different schools, see Masud.) II. HadithL 1. Any woman who is married (or marries herself) without the permission of her guardian, her marriage is void, void, void. If the marriage is consummated, the woman is entitled to dower because the man took her as lawful wife. If they are in dispute, the ruler is guardian for those who have no guardian. (Reported by A'ishah) [Tirmidhi, I, 141; Abu Da'ud, I, 284, Al-Mustadrak, II 168 vide Zayla'I, Nasb al-Ra'yah, p. 182.] (Masud supra note 14 pg. 248) 2. No marriage without a guardian. (Reported by Ibn 'Abbas) Ibn Majah, 136, vide Zayla'a op. cit, p. 188, Zurqani, pg. 6. 3. A single (al-ayyim) who had been previously married is entitled regarding herself more than her guardian. The virgin's consent regarding herself must be sought, her silence is her consent. (Reported by Ibn

'Abbas) Muslim, I. 455, Tirmidhi, I 143, Abu Da'ud I, 286, Al-Nas'I, II 77, Al-Muwatta'. 189, Zayla'I, op. cit., 182.

16 Masud, 216.

17 WRAPA is a non-profit organization set up by the former first lady of Nigeria, who was described to me as, "the wife of Abdulsalam Abubakr." This designation is not just significant because of the identification of the woman with her husband, but because it highlights the organization's ties to Nigerian state power. WRAPA held a conference on 5–7 August of 2009 in Dutse, Jigawa State, called, Islamic family law (IFL) and practices in Northwestern Nigeria: Documentation and Intervention Strategies.

18 *Promoting women's rights through Sharī'ah in Northern Nigeria*, Centre for Islamic Legal Studies, Ahmadu Bello University, Zaria (Zaria: Ahmadu Bello University, Centre for Islamic Legal Studies, (1990) 1).

19 Ibid. (see title page).

20 For more on the politics of NGO's and Human Rights Discourse, see: Makau W. Munta, "Savages, Victims, and Saviors: The Metaphor of Human Rights" *Harvard International Law Journal*, vol. 42, no. 1 (2001), 201–245.

21 Zaria Aliyu Ibrahim, interview March 2010, Nigeria.

22 The King of Saudi Arabia. Saudi Arabia has been known to fund Islamist causes in Northern Nigeria.

23 Balkisu Yusuf, interview April 2010, Kano, Nigeria.

24 The following is the information FOMWAN makes public regarding their funding sources: "Hithero FOMWAN has been funding its activites from membership dues, sales of publications, donations, Zakat and grants from donor agencies. FOMWAN is the 34 States of the Federation keep accounts with various banks while the Headquarters has Habib bank as her bankers in Abuja, Kaduna and Lagos. All states give account of their activities during the quarterly National Executive Council Meeting. FOMWAN accounts are regularly audited. The organization has fixed assets and is currently not indebted to any individual or organizaton." FOMWAN Brochure, "20 Years of Service to Islam" 20th Anniversary edition (1985–2005). Acquired in Kano, Nigeria.

25 Motion for the adoption of the communiqué was moved by Professor Sani Zaharadden and seconded by Qadi Shehu Ibrahim Ahmed, Nurudeen A. Mashi, and Fatihu Yassar. Signed: Professor Sani Zahradden, Chairman, Sharī'ah Commission Kano State; Hon. Justice Saddik A. Mahuta, Chief Judge, Katsina State; Hon. Justice Tijjani Abubakr, Chief Judge, Jigawa State; Hon. Justice Shehu Ibrahim Ahmad Qadi, Sharī'ah Court of Appeal, Kaduna; Barrister Rufa'i Aminu, Ministry of Justice, Birnin Kebbi; Dr. Abubakar Nababa Umar, Permanent Secretary, Ministry for Religious Affairs, Sokoto State; Alhaji Sani M. Maradun, Permanent Secretary, Ministry for Religious Affairs, Zamfara State; and Dr. Nasiru Musa Yauri, Secretary, Communique Committee. (Copy of communiqué obtained during fieldwork research.)

26 FOMWAN Report, 3.

27 The report says, for example: "Hassana bint Khaddan was married by her father against her wish. She complained to the Prophet, who repudiated the marriage."

28 A one-page newsletter I picked up in Abuja, Nigeria in February of 2010 while meeting with WRAPA's president Saudatu Mehdi.

29 "Is Stoning to Death Penalty for Adultery?" from, *The Muslim Woman: Magazine of the Federation of Muslim Women's Association of Nigeria*, Issue 6 (2006), 25.

30 As quoted in the magazine: Verse 17:33: "And go not near unto adultery, surely, it is a manifest indecency and an evil way," and verse 24: 1–11, "The adulteress and the adulterer flog each of them twain with a hundred stripes, and let not pity for them the twain. Both of them detain you not from obedience to Allah in

execution Sharī'aht the judgement, if you believe in Allah and the Last Day and let a party of the believers witness their chastisement." "The adulterer cannot have marital relationship with any, but an adulteress or an idolatress; and the adulteress, none can have intercourse relations with her but an adulterer or any idolater; and it is forbidden to the believers." "And those who accuse free women and bring not four witnesses, flog them with eighty stripes and never accept their evidence ever after, and, therese are the transgressors. Except those who afterwards repent and act aright, surely, Allah is Most Forgiving, Merciful. As for those who accuse their weives of adultery and have no witness except themselves, let one of them testify four times solemnly affirming and bearing Allah to witness, that he is of those who speak the truth. And at the fifth time that the curse of Allah be on him if he is of those who lie." "And it shall avert the chastisement from her, if she testifies four times, bearing Allah to witness, that he is of those who speak not the truth. And at the fifth time, that the wrath of Allah be upon her if he has spoken the truth." "And were it not for Allah's grace upon you and His mercy and that Allah is compassionate oft-returning to mercy, Wise, otherwise you would have come to grief" (24: 1–11).

31 English transliterations of "Sharī'ah" in Northern Nigerian publications are often transliterated "Sharī'aht", with the additional "t" reflecting the Northern Nigerian practice of pronouncing Arabic grammatical 'arāb in spoken Arabic. This practice is commonly found in the pronunciation of proper names.

32 Ibid.

33 Ibid.

34 Ibid.

35 *Promoting women's rights through Sharī'ah in Northern Nigeria*, Centre for Islamic Legal Studies, Ahmadu Bello University, Zaria (Zaria: Ahmadu Bello University, Centre for Islamic Legal Studies, 1990, www.ungei.org/resources/files/dfid_promoting_womens_rights.pdf).

36 Saudatu Mahdi, interview February 2010, Abuja, Nigeria.

6 Family law reform, spousal relations, and the "intentions of Islamic law"

Celene Ibrahim

Introduction

Islamic scholars have transformed classical religious rules in areas of finance, while still remaining conscientious of and loyal to core religious principles such as the aversion to usury.[1] A similar enterprise, with equally global ramifications, is now underway with regard to conception of sex and gender within Muslim history, formative texts, and contemporary communities. In the same way that transformations in technology and global financial markets present new horizons and challenges for religious laws and ethics, family and gender equity is also presenting new challenges as societies evolve and as Muslims settle into new geographic and cultural vistas. On the ground, the interplay between religion, gender, and law is exceedingly complex. I focus here on marital relations due to the central role of marriage in defining and structuring the parameters of family life. Drawing upon women-affirming scholarship on Islamic family law by reform-minded Muslim intellectuals, as well as others who have challenged the normative frameworks for marital relations within religious law, I describe how a renewed emphasis on classical frameworks of religious law, rather than an abandonment or disparagement of them, may prove effective in catalyzing family law reforms.

Sociopolitical location informs scholarship agendas, and hence, I will offer a few remarks on my own context and motivations: I came of age in a world in which women – including in the wealthiest nations – are still lacking representation in the upper echelons of science, government, and business and where the odds remain weighted that my male colleagues will be offered substantially more in salary and be offered tenure more readily. I came of age in an era where hard-won gains for women's legal rights remain in jeopardy; an era when stronger legal rights for women are advocated against by women themselves, and an era in which women's bodies and sexualities continue to be the symbolic battleground for postcolonial and nationalist power struggles. My scholarship is situated in the context of a globalized feminist struggle for legal and economic justice, yet at the same time, as a practicing Muslim, I draw inspiration from the texts and traditions of the Islamic heritage in ways that aim to nuance and enrich feminist understandings of sex, gender, sexuality, religious law and ritual, piety, political activism, suffering and healing. The aim is to contribute to ongoing efforts to reappraise foundational sources and assumptions in Islamic family law, to eschew misogynist rhetoric, and to forward paradigms that are not only religiously legitimate but that are also culturally responsive to a plurality of institutional frameworks, family structures and individual situations. This is a tall order, but it is not impossible; the risk of complacency with the status quo of gender-based oppression is much greater than the risks involved in trying to devise new, workable models and more equitable, alternative systems.

Rationales for religious family law reform

Feminist movements have mobilized for decades around the idea that gender, like other markers of identity, is constructed along axes of privilege. Global women's movements have labored to debunk faulty perceptions about biological sex and gender in favor of recognizing the social and cultural constructions of identities and the power dynamics at play. Religious debates on sex and gender are an important, yet often underappreciated, part of these feminist discussions. Given the fluidity between cultural norms and religious norms, attention to the role of religion in achieving larger societal shifts toward gender equity is essential; this is especially true in regions where postcolonial dynamics have generated deep ideological divisions regarding the role of religion in public life.

Muslim feminist perspectives that address disparities in capital distribution and intellectual production have been gaining traction in the academy since the early 1980s,[2] and the discourse has developed to a very sophisticated level.[3] Still, a considerable share – perhaps the most vociferous – of Muslim legal opinions involving gender relations still rely on hackneyed and sometimes bigoted formulae.[4] Painting at the outset with such broad strokes minimizes important counter-examples, but nonetheless, belittling notions of womanhood are manifest in a range of institutions and within cultural perspectives on family affairs. For instance, in religious and civil courts of law, rulings may be arbitrated on a case-by-case basis to the benefit of wives and mothers, but default rulings regularly privilege males over females, such as child custody and divorce,[5] inheritance,[6] familial authority and sexual gratification,[7] and personal liberties.[8] Muslim gender-reformers often describe the body of Islamic family law discussions – consisting of the works of medieval legal authorities, as augmented their premodern successors, and as stridently defended by contemporary, overwhelmingly male-dominated Muslim religious institutions – as overwhelmingly chauvinistic and blatantly oriented toward maintenance of a patriarchal social order.[9] For instance, reformers point to the presumption that men are *de facto* heads of households and to exclusively male rights to religiously sanctioned polyandry within and beyond the framework of marriage, to just name a few contested issues.[10]

Do Islamic rulings for spousal relations inherently disadvantage the female partner in the marriage? When probed by anti-Muslim antagonists, a common counter argument is that the Prophet Muhammad was a reformer and sought to institute gradual reforms to improve the status of women and other disenfranchised persons.[11] Debate has also coalesced around the extent to which later generations of Muslims upheld, advanced, or corrupted reforms that were initiated by the Prophet Mohammed. The Qur'an and Prophetic Sunnah in some instances explicitly treat males and females, men and women, wives and husbands in the same way, and at other times different measures are prescribed for different sexes.[12] Thus, it is not possible to make overarching statements about gender equality writ large from these primary sources, and debates rage over interpretations of particular Qur'anic verses (such as Q. 2:228, 4:1, and 4:34).[13] Some interpreters argue that gender differences prescribed by the Qur'an are partially a response to the social atmosphere and cultural norms at the time that the Qur'an was revealed.[14] A related line of reasoning holds that the "higher principles" *(maqāṣid al-sharīʿa)* may be inferred from Qur'anic statements; the specific letter of the text should be considered holistically for guiding principles, but the letter of the law may require modification for contemporary contexts. Hence, some rulings that were appropriate to the initial Qur'anic generation may not be appropriate for contemporary contexts.[15] These ideas about the letter and spirit of the law are not, in fact, novel to the modern period. Context and circumstance, have consistently been important in understanding the Qur'anic and Prophetic mandates, according to the earliest methodologies for deriving Islamic law as fleshed out by the earliest generations of legal scholars.[16]

Muslim scholars invested in progressive gender reform are reinforcing and reiterating such principles in their efforts to deduce value-driven, context-based ruling grounded in Islamic text and traditions. At the same time, they are pushing for rulings that are conducive to bringing about gender justice within legal systems and society more broadly.[17] A widespread push on the part of reformers is to consider the sociological context much more robustly, taking into full consideration both the milieu of the original revelation as well as the particular circumstances in which a given rule is to be applied at present. For instance, in approaches that rely on identifying the "higher principles of the law," a productive balance is needed between the textual evidence from Qur'an and ḥadīth and consideration for the common good.

Challenges to this methodology lie in the overarching complexity of extending religious laws to apply to new circumstances as well as entrenched attitudes about what is "normal" or "natural" with regard to gender. The dominant, mainstream paradigm for gender relations posits "complementary" gender roles, i.e. gender-based divisions of spousal rights and responsibilities where men have "a degree over" women, a principle which can also be described as unwelcome paternalism, or what some social psychologists have called "benevolent sexism".[18] Political and social pressures to conform to precedent, as well as salient and well-meaning fears of potentially straying from the Qur'anic and Prophetic guidance, produce a reticence on the part of many scholars of religious law to tinker with any of the medieval principles, particularly in the areas of gender and family law where the principle of male supremacy in familial affairs is seen as part of the natural order and are therefore, by definition, just.[19]

Even if many core aspects of the marital rulings – particularly those that involve sex and marital finances – differentiate between female and male roles in normative jurisprudence, the early generations of Muslim legal scholars, to their credit, recognized a number of injunctions that they identified as being incumbent on both spouses, such as kind and compassionate conduct.[20] Guiding principles for Islamic marriage, and familial ethics broadly speaking, are vested in the promotion of families as cohesive social units that beget progeny successfully. The prospects for wives within the religious imaginary are not entirely bleak. For instance, wives entering into Islamic marriages retain independent finances and were never thought of as the legal property of husbands as they had been in some contemporaneous societies; a husband owes a wife a mutually agreed upon monetary or symbolic marital gift (*mahr*) to enhance the wife's material and marital security; wives have a stipulated inheritance; these are set alongside other such measures intended to enhance women's social capital. Women's rights in the context of marriage also went beyond purely socioeconomic considerations; according to dominant schools of legal thought, wives generally also possess legal rights to sexual and emotional satisfaction.[21] In a practical sense, court records even provide anecdotal evidence that, in certain societies and epochs, family law did serve to safeguard the economic interests and integrity of wives.[22] Courts that apply Islamic law in different regions have long recognized a variety of circumstances for wife-initiated judicial divorce, some of which bear resemblance to contemporary "no fault" paradigms based on the irrevocable breakdown of the marriage.[23] At the very least, wives have had some recourse to divorce in cases of a husband's protracted absence, or in the regrettable cases where a husband caused marked harm to her person. While advances are still needed, there are many principles within family law that do have the wellbeing of the wife as the underlying concern, and the "system" should not be vilified, but engaged in constructive ways. In short, classical epistemologies need not be seen as utterly inimical to the interests of women, even when some areas warrant redress.[24]

Indeed, according to many reform-minded Muslim activists, classical Islamic family laws have inherent flexibility and need not be utterly eschewed.[25] Continuing to take marriage as an example, it is a contract where both parties have the opportunity to stipulate their own legally binding expectations and conditions for the marriage. These conditions, if violated, can nullify the marriage or be grounds for separation. Hence, even in societies where homage is paid to a range of classically formulated rulings and customary practices, adding conditions and expectations to the contract provides some means to quash more ingrained practices that are not conducive with the Prophetic example, for instance.[26] Yet, simply adding conditions or provisions to marital contracts is not a panacea. On a practical level, women are frequently discouraged from enforcing – or are simply unaware of – their legal rights. Furthermore, the long-term benefits of adding pro-women conditions, such as a husband stipulating his wife's right to unilateral divorce, might not be a practicable option given the enduring patriarchal nature of many societies. A further limitation is that conditions cannot be added which are deemed to be in opposition to the fundamental purpose or structure of the Islamic marriage contract, as defined by classical Muslim family law. Hence, even with the potential of adding various stipulations to eschew male-biases, there is still an overarching need for recalibrating the classical normative paradigm.[27]

If the parameters of the marital contract are one potential area of focus for purposive reform, the second area of focus is the role of custom (*ʿurf*) in the development and perpetuation of classically devolved marriage-related rulings.[28] For example, some "customary" marriages are conducted without a written contract or witnesses, a phenomenon that can severely disadvantage females, not only in cases where paternity is not clearly established, but also in cases where divorce has occurred but the correct monetary compensation from the former husband to the former wife has not properly transpired.[29] Another legal conundrum that can arise due to the religious recognition of unregistered, orally contracted marriages and divorces is how to handle cases where a husband divorces a wife without witnesses, later denies that he divorced her, and then sexually overpowers his former wife in an act that amounts to penetration outside marriage by force or by threat of force or coercion (fornication or rape). Here, she has been divorced, but she has limited means to secure a ruling against her former husband as her divorce was unilateral, oral, and without witnesses. Other aspects of marital legal rulings that have incorporated custom to a large extent include the concepts of guardianship (*wilāya*), maintenance (*nafaqa*) and the marital gift (*mahr*), which were fleshed out based on religious texts and the prevailing local customs of late antiquity and the medieval period. These customary formulae and legal approaches are often problematic for gender equity when they are transposed onto contemporary legal systems. However, with constructive consideration of context and higher purposes, it is possible to find workable solutions.[30]

At the same time, the legal consideration for custom is not entirely dissolute; it has, for one, allowed for malleability within and across jurisdictions and attests to the potential of Islamic law to be responsive to localized, exigent needs.[31] However, more holistic, inductive, and outcome-driven frameworks are in order to discern which customs engender marital and familial harmony, and which do not. Promising work is already being done in this regard using maqāṣid *al-sharīʿa* frameworks as one tool in the discernment and recalibration process to reform socio-religious attitudes and legal rulings related to sexual and fiscal relations between spouses.[32]

Potential application for women's fiscal empowerment

Within and beyond Muslim societies, women are often seen as the default primary caregivers, a role that, while potentially emotionally, psychologically, and spiritually rewarding, is also labor intensive and can encumber women's advancement in other spheres, such as fiscal and professional advancement. In Islamic family law, there is no general religious command for women to be the primary or exclusive caregivers; both the husband and the wife are jointly responsible for childcare within dominant understandings of the law. In Islamic law, there are no general prohibitions on women's compensated work, so long as it meets basic conditions for safety, and does not interfere with other religious obligations. The Qur'an can be read as valuing women's compensated labor.[33] Despite these religious views, women are often fiscally disadvantaged by a cultural over-emphasis on female domesticity.[34] On account of these socio-religious dynamics, wives, and women in general, can be discouraged from pursuing compensated labor, or can be outright forbidden from doing so by their husbands or male guardians. This ostensibly deprives women and girls of opportunities to self-actualize, hold offices of civic or public import, or procure meaningful and dignified labor.[35] These phenomena are again by no means unique to Muslim societies, but they can serve to reify husbands' socio-economic dominance at wives' expense.[36] Concern for women's protection and honor is generally commendable, and children have the right to attentive caregivers, but these priorities need to be weighed alongside a wife's potential for fiscal self-actualization.

The very legitimate and worthwhile goals of caring for children and protecting women from harm could be better balanced with the goals of fostering spaces for women's effort, intellect, and creativity in and beyond the familial sphere.[37] In the classical model for familial finances the husband is responsible for procuring the financial means to support the spouse and children of the marriage. Yet, in many contemporary contexts more than one breadwinner is needed to support a family, and socio-religious stigmas on husbands who cannot provide singlehandedly for their families can be demeaning to the husbands and produce detrimental tension within the marriage.[38] If the higher intentions of the law are to seek out marital harmony on a microcosmic level, and social welfare on a macrocosmic level, then a more nuanced, holistic approach to spousal relations is needed in place of totalizing, normative paradigms. This is simply one of many contexts where *maqāṣid*-based approaches to gender reform have potential to assess a variety of socio-religious priorities in order to emphasize spousal cooperation.[39] Rather than relying on generic ideas of gender complementarity,[40] a purposive model for deriving law asks: What rules and guidelines for spousal relations contribute to stability and lead to marital satisfaction? How do different social and societal factors affect the structure and function of marriage on local, national, or regional levels? Such practical questions do not *replace* the revealed texts or wholly throw out juridical precedents; the idea is to fully integrate the spheres of revelation and reason.[41]

Maqāṣid al-sharīʿa approaches in postcolonial contexts

To a profound extent, colonizing processes disrupted institutional life in many Muslim majority societies. Colonizing processes not only weakened the educational systems that produced learned scholars and jurists, but colonial systems supplanted many of the institutions of law and social order within which traditionally trained religious jurist consultants could conduct legal and bureaucratic affairs. While such colonizing processes differed in character and extreme from one majority-Muslim society to the next, this colonizing process and its aftermath has been a defining force in shaping the position and manifestation of Islamic law in the contemporary world.[42] Meanwhile, misinformed, xenophobic feminism has, to no small extent, turned attention away from causes of immediate, practical relevance to actual women who most need resources. For example, resources and attention given to saving Muslim women from the clutches of Muslim men has caused a fiery reaction from sectors of indigenous actors, who, in turn, overemphasize the need to preserve "traditional" gender roles in the face of a real, or perceived, western cultural invasion.[43] This postcolonial power struggle diverts attention away from addressing the experiences, interests, and concerns of the wider section of the Muslim populace. The production of knowledge in the academy is part and parcel of this struggle, and scholars, at times, debate the roles and rights of women in Islam while blatantly overlooking the long-lasting effects of colonizing experiences in Muslim societies. It is also common for such academic discourses on Islam and gender to draw on centuries-old polemics, couched in a civilizing mission, to buttress a neo-conservative, hegemonic, or neo-imperialist agenda.[44] It is not my aim to replicate or reinforce such trends here. Rather, my aim is to suggest how *maqāṣid al-sharīʿa* principles have promise in constructively rethinking gendered constructs within normative religious law, as well as in informing civil law reform in places where the two are intertwined.

Pro-women reforms that are grounded in secular frameworks may be perceived as western impositions that have little to do with religious values.[45] Here *maqāṣid al-sharīʿa* principles can help ground reforms in Islamic texts and traditions in order to win more public and indigenous backing.[46] Due to the political currency of Islamist ideas in many parts of the world, policy specialists transnationally are becoming increasingly attuned to the ways in which a wide variety of development based interventions must in fact take grassroots Muslim views on gender relations into consideration in order to be effective in designing and implementing interventions on the ground.[47] If "halal" solutions for gender-reform are indeed the way that international development practitioners and trends are moving, which preliminary observations suggest they are, intelligible *Maqāṣid al-sharīʿa* arguments can help to forward reforms that serve the welfare of women on any number of social issues by providing palatable, Islamically grounded reform frameworks. While it has drawbacks, the *maqāṣid al-sharīʿa* guided approach to reform enables a great degree of sensitivity for the intentions and integrity of classical epistemology, while still leaving room to tune conceptions of spousal relations to be temporally, culturally, and situationally appropriate.

Cautionary notes on gender and family law reforms

Supporting and encouraging the framing of gender issues according to *maqāṣid al-sharīʿa* methodology could prove to be a pragmatic and effective approach for transnational feminist activists. Namely, *maqāṣid al-sharīʿa* discourses could foster a culturally relevant reform framework that is palatable to a larger cross-section of Muslims than purely secular reforms. The methodologies could also be appealing to the sensibilities of the non-religious, as *maqāṣid al-sharīʿa* frameworks stress goal-driven outcomes and with overt attention to the role of reason and context in deriving law. Also due to this stress on the role of empirical knowledge, there is room at the table for Muslim women from a wide array of professional backgrounds to have more influence in debating Islamic law and ethics than they have hitherto had in shaping the foundations of Islamic jurisprudence. Finally, transreligious and transcultural conversations could more readily ensue regarding commonalities in "higher principles" and regarding the role of empirical knowledge in shaping law. Stressing common aims allows for greater integration between disparate legal systems.

Women have a long history of near-complete exclusion from the ranks of influential jurist consultants and have not been afforded equitable input in the direction of Islamic family law. If women are excluded from the conversations regarding *maqāṣid al-sharīʿa*, women's interests will likely remain marginalized in the ongoing formulation and exercise of the law. Quite plainly stated, more men need to recognize that it is not their exclusive right to legislate on behalf of half the human population, and individuals with political and religious influence must make a point of elevating women's expertize and contributions within existing forums, even if it means sharing the authority and the limelight.[48] Until women religious scholars and professionals are fully integrated in meaningful ways – and in truly representative numbers – on high-level religious and political forums, it will be necessary to support and enhance the visibility of women-dominated forums of scholarly exchange.[49] At the same time, as much as feminism and the women's movement have done to raise discourse on women and gender, blind imitation or hegemonic enforcement of western cultural norms and values will not assist in creating substantive women-friendly reforms. This is true particularly when discourses around gender reform focus on abstract notions of gender equality that have little bearing on the lived realities of most women. Moreover, western, secular-liberal and feminist paradigms are not without their own limitations: western, liberalized societies have their own pressing gender-related issues that are in need of attention.[50] It is beneficial for feminists more broadly to consider if and when there is value in differentiating roles and privileges of spouses. It may be that *difference* in and of itself does not inexorably lead to bias.[51]

Along similar lines, a potential pitfall of some *maqāṣid al-sharīʿa* debates is the propensity to overlook ways in which sexuality and gender are socially constructed and embedded in localized webs of meaning. For instance, it is a biologically observable fact that in the sphere of human reproduction men and women are complementary. Yet, if or how woman is the complementary opposite of man in respects *other* than biological reproduction is open to debate. Here, various cultural and stereotyped gender roles need diligent, critical examination, as sex-stereotyping is a major problem that could easily affect even well intentioned *maqāṣid al-sharīʿa* paradigms. As I have argued above, there is a pervasive need to value the inherent personhood of a woman that includes, but ultimately transcends, her role as wife or caretaker within a familial structure.[52] Lest it need reiteration, women are, in fact, much more than domesticated beings whose ambitions are exclusively directed at correct performance of ritual, unquestioning service of husband, production and rearing of children, and good-tempered support of charitable causes.[53]

Some proponents of *maqāṣid* frameworks restrict the application only to instances in which there is no explicit precedent in *fiqh*, or they see *maqāṣid al-sharīʿa* as an entirely separate domain of legal thought. Others see the *maqāṣid al-sharīʿa* as ultimately integrated within (*uṣūl al-fiqh*), where texts, for instance, provide indications to the higher objectives of the law. Particularly in the realm of gender-based rulings, it is the latter outlook that is more promising.[54] Applying *maqāṣid al-sharīʿa* frameworks only in the absence of prior precedent could simply serve to reinforce tendencies toward ossification rather than engender the productive dynamism that is necessary to bring about substantive and lasting reform in gender-based religious rulings.

The balance between how to weigh individual interests against the collective benefit is challenging.[55] Much of the theoretical discourse is mired in technical minutiae, such as discussions of how many levels of *maqasid* should be recognized. Such discussions, in my view, will only engender more elite academic exchanges and will not bring about the practical results that they were intended to provoke. Sophisticated theoretical discussions are valuable, but these discussions cannot stand in the way of devoting intellectual and fiscal resources toward deriving practical, workable models. For example, the extent to which human beings can use reason, innate moral knowledge, and experience to discern the higher purposes of the law is one question that continually surfaces in theoretical *maqāṣid al-sharīʿa* works, from the formative period to the present.[56] The question is tautological but for the purposes of practical reform efforts legal scholars should presume that humans are able to infer and deduce higher purposes to a sufficient degree. If there is a metaphorical leap of faith involved in advocating for reform based on *Maqāṣid al-sharīʿa*, it is a faith that collective reason, innate human nature, and experience can in fact discern justice from injustice. This is conceivably the leap of faith implicated in any legal system, and it is not unique to Islamic law.

While considerable anti-women biases exist in many classical formulations of family law, with attention to context and circumstance, laws could be more responsive to a broader range of circumstances. Non-cisgender sexuality and gender identity is an avenue for further inquiry.

Family and gender involve complex socio-political phenomenon, and there are not simple cookie-cutter formulae for securing social and economic justice. Yet, it is a priority to work towards constructive and systematic paradigms within which to pursue thoughtful, substantive, enduring reform. *Maqāṣid al-sharīʿa* should not be conceived of as a universal remedy for gender injustice, but rather as a conceptual framework to allow competing ideological, doctrinal, cultural, and religious conceptions to be vetted and debated with reference to guiding texts, values, and goals.

Notes

1 For a discussion of how legal scholars address contemporary needs, see Craig Nethercott and David Eisenberg, eds., *Islamic Finance: Law and Practice* (Oxford: Oxford University Press, 2012).

2 For a concise overview of the field see Celene Ayat Lizzio, "Continuing Momentum in Muslim Critical Gender Scholarship," *Journal of Muslim World Affairs* 1, no. 1 (Sept. 3, 2013), available online: www.muslimworldaffairs.com/2013/09/continuing-momentum-in-muslim-critical.html.

3 For the most recent developments see Ziba Mir-Hosseini, Mulki Al-Sharmani, and Jana Rumminger, eds., *Men in Charge? Rethinking Authority in Muslim Legal Tradition* (London: Oneworld, 2015).

4 For an example of such normative religious opinion, geared for an American public, see Ali Gomma, "Gender Equality in Islam," *The Washington Post*, July 21, 2007.

5 See Susan A. Spectorsky, *Women in Classical Islamic Law: A Survey of the Sources* (Leiden; Boston: Brill, 2010), and Jamal J. Nasir, *The Status of Women Under Islamic Law and Modern Islamic Legislation,* 3rd ed. (Leiden; Boston: Brill, 2009).

6 For an extended analysis of this issue, including Qur'anic verses 4: 11–12 and 4:176, see Ahmed Souaiaia, *Contesting Justice: Women, Islam, Law, and Society* (Albany: State University of New York Press, 2008), 59–86.

7 See Kecia Ali, "Obedience and Disobedience in Islamic Discourses," *Encyclopedia of Women in Islamic Cultures*, ed. Suad Joseph (Leiden; Boston: Brill, 2007), 309–313.

8 See Ann Elizabeth Mayer, *Islam and Human Rights: Tradition and Politics*, 5th ed. (Boulder, Colorado: Westview Press, 2013), 85–97 and 99–129.

9 For one critique and constructive argument for gender reform see Sa'diyya Shaikh, "In Search of al-Insān: Sufism, Islamic Law, and Gender," *Journal of the American Academy of Religion* 77, no. 4 (Dec. 2009), 781–822; see especially 787 for a persuasive call for systematic reform.

10 For analysis of the classical formulation of marriage rulings, see Kecia Ali, *Marriage and Slavery in Early Islam* (Cambridge: Harvard University Press, 2010). For extensive analysis of polygamy, see Ahmed E. Souaiaia, *Contesting*

Justice: Women, Islam, Law, and Society (Albany: State University of New York Press, 2008), 48–57.

11 A lengthy and polemical debate abounds on the veracity of this claim. For instance, see the arguments of Tariq Ramadan to this effect in *Radical Reform: Islamic Ethics and Liberation* (New York: Oxford University Press, 2009), 210–211.

12 See Karen Bauer, "The Male is Not Like the Female (Q 3:36): The Question of Gender Egalitarianism in the Qur'an," *Religion Compass* 3, no. 4 (2009), 637–654.

13 For full details see Aysha A Hidayatullah, *Feminist Edges of the Qur'an* (Oxford: Oxford University Press, 2014).

14 See for instance, Mohammad Fadel, "Two Women, One Man: Knowledge, Power and Gender in Medieval Sunni Legal Thought," *International Journal of Middle East Studies* 29 (1997), 185–204; see also discussion of other thinkers who take this approach in Jasser Auda, *Maqasid al-Sharia as Philosophy of Islamic Law: A Systems Approach* (London; Washington: International Institute of Islamic Thought, 2008), 184–188.

15 For full details of this method see Gamal Eldin Attia, *Towards Realisation of the Higher Intents of Islamic Law, Maqasid Al Shari'ah: A Functional Approach (Naḥwa taf'īl maqāṣid al-sharī'a)*, trans. Nancy Roberts (London; Washington: International Institute of Islamic Thought, 2008); see also Jasser Auda, *Maqāṣid al-sharī'ah as Philosophy of Islamic Law: A Systems Approach* (London; Washington: International Institute of Islamic Thought, 2008).

16 See Bernard G. Weiss, *The Spirit of Islamic Law* (University of Georgia Press, 2006). See also Wael B. Hallaq, *A History of Islamic Legal Theories: An Introduction to Sunni Usul al-Fiqh* (Cambridge: Cambridge University Press, 1997).

17 See for instance Adis Dujerija, "A Case Study of Patriarchy and Slavery: The Hermeneutical Importance of Qurānic Assumptions in the Development of a Values-Based and Purposive Oriented Qurān-sunna Hermeneutic," *HAWWA Journal of Women in the Middle East and the Muslim World* 11, no. 1 (2013), 58–87.

18 I adopt the term "benevolent sexism" from Peter Glick and Susan T. Fiske, "The Ambivalent Sexism Inventory: Differentiating Hostile and Benevolent Sexism," *Journal of Personality and Social Psychology* 70, no. 3 (1996), 491–512.

19 For a discussion of the classical scholars and their attitudes toward women, see Ramadan, *Radical Reform*, 211–212.

20 For discussion of the Qur'an's verses on marital harmony, including Qur'an 2:187 and 30:2, see Azizah al-Hibiri, "An Islamic Perspective on Domestic Violence," *Fordham International Law Journal* 27, no. 1 (2003), 195–224. See also Kecia Ali, "'A Beautiful Example': The Prophet Muḥammad as a Model for Muslim Husbands," *Islamic Studies* 43, no. 2 (2004), 273–291. There are even some provisions in classical law that could give contemporary women inspiration; for example, a wife of a Muslim husband is not *a priori* religiously bound to perform domestic labor, and under certain circumstances, it is legally possible that the husband can be compelled to compensate her monetarily for her voluntary household labor.

21 For a full discussion of the rights of wives and husbands in marriage according to dominant schools of thought, as well as some minority positions, see Kecia Ali, *Sexual Ethics in Islam: Feminist Reflections on Qur'an, Hadīth and Jurisprudence* (Oxford: Oneworld, 2006), see Chapter 1, "Marriage, Money, and Sex," 1–21.

22 For one anecdote see Judith E. Tucker, "'And God Knows Best': The Fatwa as a Source for the History of Gender in the Arab World," in *Beyond the Exotic: Women's Histories in Islamic Societies*, ed. Amira El Azhary Sonbol (Syracuse, NY: Syracuse University Press, 2005), 168–179. For further historical analysis, see also Wael B. Hallaq, *Sharī'a: Theory, Practice, Transformations* (Cambridge, Cambridge University Press, 2009), 184–196, and Amira El Azhary Sonbol ed., *Women, the*

Family, and Divorce Law in Islamic History (Syracuse, NY: Syracuse University Press, 1996).

23 See Kathleen Portuan Miller, "Who Says Muslim Women Can't Divorce? A Comparison of Divorce under Islamic and Anglo-American Law," *New York International Law Review* 22, no. 1 (2009), 201–248.

24 For a survey of Muslim feminist positions on both sides of the debate over whether or not Islamic law is fundamentally inimical to the interests of women, see Mounira Charrad, "Gender in the Middle East: Islam, State, Agency," *Annual Review of Sociology* 37 (2011), 427–28.

25 For a discussion of immutable versus the changing facets of Islamic law, see Tariq Ramadan, *Radical Reform: Islam Ethics and Liberation* (New York: Oxford University Press, USA, 2009), 17–22.

26 For a theoretical discussion of how to regard the cultural, geographical, and historical context of the prophet revelation in determining rulings, see Jasser Auda *Maqasid al-Sharia as Philosophy of Islamic Law: A Systems Approach* (London; Washington: International Institute of Islamic Thought, 2008), 186–88.

27 For an example of such a reform-minded position based on *maqāṣid* principles see Sayed Sikandar Haneef, "Treatment of Recalcitrant Wife in Islamic Law: The Need for a Purposive Juridical Construct," *Global Jurist* 12, no. 2 (2012). For a discussion of the potential roles of *maqāṣid* in familial contexts, see Ramadan, *Radical Reform*, 224–29.

28 For a persuasive account of the relationship between the higher intentions of the law and custom see Auda, *Philosophy of Islamic Law*, 196 and 202–4. For a thorough discussion of the role of custom in Islamic legal frameworks, see Ayman Shabana, *Custom in Islamic Law and Legal Theory: The Development of the Concepts of `Urf and `Adah in the Islamic Legal Tradition* (Palgrave Series in Islamic Theology, Law, and History, New York: Palgrave Macmillan, 2010).

29 For comprehensive analysis of divorce laws see Judith E. Tucker, *Women, Family, and Gender in Islamic Law* (Cambridge, UK; New York: Cambridge University Press, 2008), 38–83.

30 For promising scholarship on how to integrate *mahr* into contemporary legal frameworks, by taking into account lived realities and higher principles, see Lene Løvdal, "*Mahr* and Gender Equality in Private International Law: The Adjudication of *Mahr* in England, France, Norway and Sweden," in *Embedding Mahr (Islamic Dower) in the European Legal System*, ed. Rubya Mehdi and Jørgen S. Nielsen (Copenhagen: Djoef Publishing, 2011) 77–112.

31 For a helpful review of country-specific sources on contemporary family law, see Charrad, "Gender in the Middle East: Islam, State, Agency," 420–421.

32 For instance, in his discussion of the role of *maqāṣid al-sharīʿa* in reforming Islamic legal thought regarding women, Traiq Ramadan argues that the "higher goals" for gender reform include: dignity, integrity, autonomy, development, education, intelligence, welfare, health, and inner balance; see *Radical Reform* (2009) 212–214. For ruminations specifically on the American context, see Zainab Alwani, *Al-Usra fī maqāṣid al-sharīʿa: qirāʾa fī qaḍāiyā wa-l-ṭalāq fī amrīkā* (Herndon, VA: The International Institute of Islamic Thought, 2012).

33 For example, Qur'an 4:32 and 3:195 can be read pertaining not only to the rewards that one earns for righteousness, but to actual fiscal earnings. See also the discussion in Alwani, ibid., 56–57.

34 For an example of such rhetoric, see the views of the late Egyptian political activist Zaynab al-Ghazali (1917–2005), who had a central role in the Muslim Brotherhood. For al-Ghazali, women's primary social responsibility and function is to "build" the "kind of men" that are wanted to "fill the ranks of the Islamic call," p. 236, in Valerie Hoffman, "An Islamic Activist: Zaynab Al-Ghazali," in

Women and the Family in the Middle East, ed. Elizabeth Fernea (Austin: University of Texas Press, 1985), 233–254.

35 There are, of course, many structural problems related to women's employment and civic participation that need to be addressed on a global scale, including sexual exploitation, sexual discrimination, and gender disparities in wages empowerment, not to mention the dismal state of worker rights in many industries. Nonetheless, the solution is arguably to address these problems in the workplace, not to curtail the self-actualization of women and girls.

36 This is a long-standing critique made by feminist thinkers. See for instance Simone de Beauvoir, *The Second Sex, (Le Deuxième Sexe)*, trans. and ed. by H. M. Parshley (New York: Vintage Books, 1974, 1st ed. 1949).

37 The "higher goals" of Islamic law that Ramadan cites with relevance to gender reform include: dignity, integrity, autonomy, development, education, intelligence, welfare, health, and inner balance. *Radical Reform* (2009), 212–214. See also the observations of Mahnaz Afkhami, "Rights of Passage: Women Shaping the Twenty-First Century," *The Future of Women's Rights: Global Visions and Strategies*, ed. Joanna Kerr *et al.* (London: Zed Books, 2004), 56–68, especially 66–68.

38 For instance, in a recent work on civil and religious conceptions of marriage among European Muslims, Zainab Alwani and I argued that in times of increasing global financial insecurity and widespread unemployment, particularly among young adult and migrant populations, the unilateral model for family finances is no longer practicable and sustainable. We suggested that in light of current economic and social realities and exigent needs, flexible, responsive paradigms and language for conceiving of spousal responsibilities are needed to help create a bridge between the tradition of family law and social realities. We also argued that European Muslims should abide by European civil laws regulating marriage. In making these arguments we made regular appeals to the higher intentions of the law. See "Religion, Gender, and Family Law: Critical Perspectives on Integration for European Muslims," with Zainab Alwani, in *Applying Sharia in the West: Facts, Fears and the Future of Islamic Rules on Family Relations in the West*, ed. Maurits S. Berger (Leiden; Boston: Brill, 2013), 227–240.

39 Ramadan writes particularly eloquently on the value of partnership and mutual fulfillment, see *Radical Reform* (2009), 226–227.

40 Along these lines, Alwani argues that "instead of relying on technical and material dictations," what should be stressed is ethics, virtues, and values (*qiyām*), alongside proper behavior (*maʿrūf*); see "The Qur'ānic Model on Social Change: Family Structure as a Method of Social Reform," *Islam and Civilisational Renewal* 3, no. 1 (2011), 55.

41 As Tariq Ramadan explains, the "revealed book" (scriptural sources) and the "book of the universe" (historical-social-scientific knowledge as derived from experience) must be considered in tandem in order to develop the higher principles of the law. In turn, religious scholars use the higher principles of the law, taking into consideration text and context, to elaborate applied Islamic ethics. Ramadan, *Radical Reform* (2009), 126–133.

42 For a detailed account of the onset of colonial modernity in Muslim societies and the affect on law, see Hallaq, *Sharīʿa* (Cambridge: Cambridge University Press, 2009), 357–499. For a survey of scholarship on gender and the legacies of colonialism, see Charrad, "Gender in the Middle East," 419–420. For a discussion of negative Western stereotypes of Muslim women, see Nikki R. Keddie, *Women in the Middle East: Past and Present* (Princeton: Princeton University Press, 2007), 57–59.

43 On this power dynamic with regard to family law in North Africa, for instance, see Yakaré Oulé-Jansen, "Muslim Brides and the Ghost of *Shari'a*: Have the Recent Law Reforms in Egypt, Tunisia, and Morocco Improved Women's

Position in Marriage and Divorce and Can Religious Moderates Bring Reform and Make it Stick?" *Northwestern Journal of International Human Rights* 5, no. 2 (2007), 181–212.

44 See for example, Jasmine Zine, "Between Orientalism and Fundamentalism: The Politics of Muslim Women's Feminist Engagement," *Muslim World Journal of Human Rights* 3, no. 1 (2006), 1–24. See also Christina Scharff, "Disarticulating Feminism: Individualization, Neoliberalism and the Othering of "Muslim Women," *European Journal of Women's Studies* 18, no. 2 (2011), 119–134.

45 For a reflection on this dynamic see Ramadan, *Radical Reform* (2009), 152.

46 For examples of such practical applications see essays by Zinah Anwar, Marwa Sharafeldin, and others in Mir-Hosseini *et al.* eds., *Gender and Equality in Muslim Family Law* (New York: I.B. Tauris, 2013), 37–126. Additionally, see Mohammad Hashim Kamali, "Islamic Family Law Reform: Problems and Prospects", *Islam and Civilisational Renewal* 3, no. 1 (2011), 37–52, and Jana Rumminger *et al.*, *Cedaw and Muslim Family Laws: In Search of Common Ground* (Selangor, Malaysia: Musawah, 2011).

47 For an explanation of this phenomenon see Ziba Mir-Hosseini, "Justice, Equality, and Muslim Family Laws: New Ideas, New Prospects," (esp. 24–25), in Mir-Hosseini *et al.* eds., *Gender and Equality in Muslim Family Law* (New York: I.B. Tauris, 2013) Chapter 1, 7–34.

48 As Tariq Ramadan notes: "it is women who must, from within, refuse to accept that religious discourse about them should be merely legal and, in effect, curtailed, since it deals with interpersonal relations without elaborating anything about *womanhood*," *Radical Reform* (2009), 217, emphasis original. Ramadan mentions the necessity of including women in "constructive critical work" regarding "the text reading process" and the "study of the social contexts in which they live," 215. Later he speaks of the necessity for more women on religious councils, "both as text scholars and as experts specializing in social dynamics and daily realities," 232.

49 Muslim women scholars are making some progress in etching out forums for female-stream and reformist scholarship; see for example the anthology of Elif Mendeni, Ednan Aslan, and Marcia Hermansen, eds., *Muslima Theology: The Voices of Muslim Women Theologians* (Frankfurt am Main: Peter Land Verlag, 2013).

50 These include domestic violence, economic disparity, sexual harassment, racial discrimination, deficient political representation, and so on. See Anissa Hélie, "Risky Rights? Gender Equality and Sexual Diversity in Muslim Contexts," in Anissa Hélie and Homa Hoodfar, eds., *Sexuality in Muslim Contexts* (London: Zed Books, 2012), 302. See also Ramadan, *Radical Reform* (2009), 220.

51 For an engagement with this issue and a historical overview of Muslim considerations of gender equality vs. difference, see Anver M. Emon, "The Paradox of Equality and the Politics of Difference," in Mir-Hosseini, *et al.* eds., *Gender and Equality in Muslim Family Law* (New York: I.B. Tauris, 2013), 237–58. See also Ahmed E. Souaiaia, *Contesting Justice: Women, Islam, Law, and Society* (Albany: State University of New York Press, 2008), 121–122.

52 For more on the influence of sex stereotyping see Ann Elizabeth Mayer, *Islam and Human Rights*, 5th ed. (Boulder, CO: Westview Press, 2013), 128–30. See also Ramadan, *Radical Reform* (2009), 211.

53 Likewise, there is also a need to acknowledge the non-binary nature of sex and gender identities, a point that classical jurists were possibly more attuned to than some of their modern and contemporary counterparts.

54 See Attia, *Towards Realization*, 241–244. Attia writes: "As for the view held by Ibn Ashur in favor of establishing an independent science of *maqāṣid al-sharīʿah* while leaving the science of *uṣūl al-fiqh* as it is, my own view is that this would be

harmful to both sciences, since it would, in effect, freeze *uṣūl al-fiqh* in its present state and deprive it of the spirit of *maqāṣid;* in addition, it would exclude *maqāṣid* from the practical role which they perform at present, a role which we must do our utmost to support, sustain and develop," 244.

55 This concept of a hierarchy of aims has been key to religious formulations of *maqaasid* since the formative stages; although, individual scholars differ with respect to how aims are prioritized. For a detailed discussion of current debates, see Gamal Eldin Attia, *Towards Realization of the Higher Intents of Islamic Law* (London; Washington: International Institute of Islamic Thought, 2008), 77–149.

56 On different juristic opinions on the human ability to use reason and experience to understand the higher objectives of the law, see Gamal Eldin Attia, *Towards Realization of the Higher Intents of Islamic Law*, 1–16. The ability to discern higher objectives of the law is also predicated on the notion of *fiṭra*, the primordial human inborn disposition that allows humans to also discern correct belief and morality.

7 The woes of WoW*

The Women of the Wall as a religious social movement and as a metaphor

Pnina Lahav†

Introduction

The Women of the Wall (hereafter WoW) and their struggle for space at the Western Wall in Jerusalem offer a metaphor for Israel's evolving national identity as well as for the place of women in both Judaism and progressive society. This chapter elaborates on the substance of this metaphor.

WoW has recently risen to national and international headlines. In the past they were considered an esoteric group but of late major media began to pay attention to them. People are beginning to comprehend the general as well as the particular meaning of their cause.

WoW is a group of women, Israeli as well as citizens of the Jewish Disapora (American, Canadian, Australian, French, Brazilian and more), who wish to hold communal prayers in the women's section of the holiest of Jewish sites, the Western Wall in Jerusalem. Because some of them are orthodox, they all adhere to the orthodox custom of gender segregation during prayer. They wrap themselves in a tallit, the traditional prayer shawl, and read from the Torah, chanting and singing, in keeping with the traditional service of worship.

Their claim, that women's communal prayer is not prohibited by Halacha (Jewish Law, hereafter Halacha) is no longer novel. Many rabbis have validated this claim and the practice of women's prayer groups has been accepted in many orthodox synagogues around the world. But the orthodox in Jerusalem, who are in charge of the Wall, view this practice as heresy and use any means at their disposal to stop it.

The struggle of WoW has triggered litigation, deliberations by commissions, parliamentary debates and legislative bills, cabinet crises and arrests of women as they pray. More recently, the various Jewish religious movements in the United States came to be actively involved in the struggle. Also recently, a solution has been found, which involves exiling the WoW from the women's section into an adjacent space, known as the Robinson Arch. Whether this solution will indeed materialize and how it will affect the WoW remains to be seen.

Why do the orthodox in Jerusalem consider the practice of WoW a heresy? Because the traditional Jewish service requires a minyan, a group of ten individuals. Traditionally and historically, in keeping with patriarchal values, the requirement of ten was translated into a requirement of ten men. Women were excluded, except perhaps on very special occasions.[1] Some rabbis in Jerusalem do not deny that Halacha indeed does not ban the practice, but they profess loyalty to custom. Custom in Jewish communities taught that only men will serve in a minyan, therefore, they argue, women are welcome to pray as individuals but are banned from praying as a group.

For a long time this confrontation, between WoW and the leaders of the orthodox community in Jerusalem, simmered on a very low burner and attracted little attention. Why has it come to international public scrutiny? Why has it become an urgent issue demanding a resolution? The answer lies in the evolving understanding of the status of women in Israeli society as well as in the closer attention paid to the matter by Diaspora Jews.

Makom: the Western Wall and WoW as a metaphor

WoW is not only a social movement and an important contributor to religious life. It is also a metaphor. Let me start with the concept of Makom.

The Hebrew word Makom has multiple meanings. In liturgy it stands for God. Jewish tradition holds that the ancient location of the Jewish Temple is where God's spirit resides.[2] In modern Hebrew, Makom means space, a place. Zionist ideology holds that the right place for Jews is the State of Israel. This is the justification that Zionists give for the stubborn insistence on the right of the Jewish people to inhabit the land, claimed too by the Palestinian people.

Makom as a place is an important analytic tool in feminist theory. The traditional division of labor between the sexes was based on the expectation that women had a place, a particular place, and that place was the home, the private not the public realm. When Israeli Rabbis embarked on their project of gender segregation (e.g., in buses, on sidewalks, in cemeteries) they were trying to re-enforce the ideology that there is a special place – "makom" – for women. The back of the bus has been one such place.

In rejecting WoW's request for a place at the women's section of the Wall, the State of Israel agreed that the Wall was not "their place." If a woman wants equality of worship, she has to go elsewhere. The act of exiling the women to the Robinson Arch, taken after considerable agony and controversy, therefore captures the tragedy of Zionism and of the State of Israel itself. Israel cannot grant space – "makom" – for its women.[3] They must go elsewhere, to a "makom acher". The contradiction is glaring. On the one hand, as a Zionist state, Israel insists that the only right place for Jews is Israel itself, on the other hand it wants its women to go to "another place." Inevitably, the message is that women are worth less. WoW is driven to the margins, to an alien place (the Robinson Arch) where they may be comfortably ignored. Thereby, the core of Zionist ideology is compromised.

Original Zionist ideology professed allegiance not only to the principle of gender equality but also to the principle of the separation of Church and State. Current Israeli Law states that Israel is a Jewish and Democratic State. WoW exposes a dangerous compromise of principles. When the notion of "Jewish" in the "Jewish State" is limited to a reified world view of orthodoxy, Israel as a State distances itself from the great progressive principles that fueled its existence. WoW is a metaphor for the clash between the Israel built on utopian ideals and a gender-based orthodoxy bent on protecting patriarchy.

WoW is a metaphor because it stands for a concept of Jewishness that fits well with Zionist ideals, with the democratic component of the State of Israel, and with a forward-looking and inclusive Judaism, that stands for pluralism, for accommodation, for inclusion, and for dignity. WoW also stands for the Jewish pluralism practiced by the majority of Jews around the world. Furthermore it also stands for the morality of the rule of law – both the secular and the religious – a notion of law that is based on dignity and a profound sense of morality.

The wave of gender-based segregation so evident in Israel today, for which the segregation in buses is only one example, should be understood and explained through the lens of WoW. The rejection of tolerance, pluralism and gender equality began with them. It is therefore particularly important to understand their story.

Twenty-first century developments concerning the status of women in Israel

Either as a result of growing religious fundamentalism around the world, or because of increasing confidence in their ability to run communal life as they desire, or perhaps out of fear that secular forces are taking over and unduly changing their culture, rabbis in religiously inhabited areas in Israel began to develop an agenda of gender segregation. They wanted segregation in streets (one pavement for men, another for women), in classrooms, in military service, in supermarkets, in medical facilities and most notably in public buses.[4] In buses, they insisted that women take the back seat, which they perceived was the appropriate women's place.[5] A woman, they reasoned, was inherently seductive and in order to protect both herself and men in her environment, she should be clad with modesty in person as well as spatially.

The practice that particularly vexed the secular public was bus segregation. A counter movement developed to challenge the practice, which secular Israelis see as damaging women's rights and women's dignity. The legendary American hero of the civil rights movement, Rosa Parks, who refused to go to the back of the bus, served as inspiration. IRAC, an Israeli organization committed to religious pluralism, launched a campaign of "freedom riders" who would go on bus lines and make sure that the secular law prohibiting segregation is observed. As this chapter is being written, the secular and the orthodox camp are still sparring over these issues. At stake is the question whether Israel is a Jewish-orthodox state where Rabbis make important decisions regarding everyday life or whether it is a secular, liberal democratic state, where law is made by the people's representatives and interpreted by judges committed to the rule of law.

The outrage at the movement to segregate women in the public sphere and the international attention it has received brought WoW to the attention of the public. People did not fail to see the similarity between their claim, to be accepted as equal citizens in Jewish religious worship, and the need to guarantee gender equality on Israeli soil.[6] Men and women from Israel proper and from the Diaspora came to Jerusalem, to participate in both the freedom riders' campaign and in the practice of communal prayer by women at the Wall. This most recent development, one taking place in the second decade of the twenty-first century, brought the issue of the Women of the Wall to world public attention.

For two decades, the WoW were involved in court litigation, trying to persuade Israel's High Court of Justice to recognize their wish to worship at the Wall. The Court had some sympathy for their claim, but ultimately withheld its support. But the WoW kept coming, practicing civil disobedience and insisting on their rights. Frustrated, the rabbis sought police assistance. The police, either receiving orders from above (say, from religious ministers or from officers schooled in tradition, who could not comprehend the WoW message of gender equality) complied. When the police at the Wall Plaza identified a woman wearing the traditional praying shawl or planning to begin a communal service, they would arrest her and bring her to the police station. There she would be jailed with other criminal suspects overnight, perhaps in an effort to "teach her a lesson" and deter such activity in future.

In May 2013, five women were arrested at the Wall Plaza. As discussed below, the District Court held that the women should be set free and that they have a right to pray "in accordance with their custom" at the Wall.

Context mattered. The public outrage at segregation, Israeli law as interpreted by the judiciary in the bus segregation case (and other cases) and an increasingly astonished international public opinion unable to digest the Israeli practice of segregation probably prompted Israel's government to respect the District Court's order, or at least to understand that the time has come to address the claims of WoW.

WoW: a collective biography

In 1988 an international conference dedicated to women's issues was held in the City of Jerusalem.[7] The conference attracted women from many corners of the Jewish World. Rivka Haut, an orthodox woman from New York, had an idea: the participants should borrow a Torah scroll from one of Jerusalem's progressive synagogues and make a pilgrimage to the Western Wall, there to conduct a communal prayer service. Haut, mother of two daughters, was passionate about Jewish life. Her study of Halacha raised her awareness of its complexity and ambiguity: it was not at all clear that Halacha prohibited women's communal prayer. Rather, the rabbis, as creatures of a patriarchal world view interpreted the law as patriarchal.

With her husband, a rabbi and a man comfortable with gender equality, she developed an alternative reading of the rabbinic sources, one that legitimated the communal prayer.[8] She mastered the art of leading the religious service as well as the art of chanting from the Torah scroll. Throughout the 1980s, in New York, she actively spread the idea of the legitimacy and desirability of the women's prayer groups.[9] Haut was a pioneer in the orthodox world, and her prayer groups are now practiced in many modern orthodox communities, including in Israel.[10] But in 1988 her project was novel, attractive to few and startling to many.

Haut persuaded conference participants, women and men, to join her in making a pilgrimage to the site of the Wall in Jerusalem, and there hold the very first women's only prayer service at the Wall's women's section. The space of the Wall, the most sacred in Judaism, is presently operated as a traditional orthodox synagogue. In keeping with tradition, the plaza adjoining the Wall is divided into a large section for men, and a rather narrow section for women. A fence separates the two sections.[11] When Haut's group unfurled the Torah scroll and began the communal service, the worshippers present at the site were at first flabbergasted. What they witnessed was so alien to their world view as to defy comprehension. But soon enough they concluded that they were witnessing the essence of heresy. Perceiving themselves as "guardians of the faith," they took the law into their own hands, determined to nip the practice in the bud. There and then WoW was born.

The participants at the 1988 conference came mostly from abroad, primarily from the United States. Not all of them were religious, and their religiosity itself was diverse. They reflected the pluralistic and tolerant nature of American Jewry.[12] Some were modern orthodox like Rivka Haut, some conservative, a few were reform, while others were interested in Israel but were solidly secular. However, they did have something in common: all were committed to gender equality. As Americans, the members of the original group had already been sensitized to feminism, to women's struggle to partake in all spheres of life, including religious life, and to the activism that life in civic society entails (that's why they traveled to Jerusalem). As Americans, too, they were accustomed to a constitutional order. The ethos of American constitutionalism is that the constitution enshrines certain universal principles that cannot be violated. Among them is the free exercise of religion (the First Amendment), and the equal protection of the law (the Fourteenth

Amendment).[13] The American ethos also holds that in a case of violation one may petition the courts, and that if the petition is valid a court of law will declare the practice unconstitutional. Once the Court delivers its verdict, Americans expect the executive branch to back the Court and implement the Court's decree.[14] Thus, for the American women in the group the problem was rather simple: the fundamental law of the land was violated and litigation was likely to bring relief.

But that was true in the United States. Was Israeli fundamental law violated as well, and would an Israeli court declare the practice invalid? Did their analysis apply to Israel as well? The American members had some reason to believe that this was so.[15]

Indeed, Israel is one of the few democracies in the world which does not have a formal constitution, but both the principles of free exercise of religion and of equality, particularly of gender equality, have been recognized as being part of the Israeli constitutional system.[16] Furthermore, just as the WoW were beginning to articulate their cause, Israel's High Court of Justice was gaining a reputation as a court that actively defends political and civil liberties. I shall not elaborate on this development, but only note in passing that it was a part of a larger transformation of Israeli society into a more civic and rights oriented polity.[17] Two examples, directly relevant to our subject matter, are presented here.[18] In 1987, a modern orthodox woman, Leah Shakdiel, challenged the refusal of the Minister of the Interior to consider her application to serve on a religious council. The minister had statutory authority to convene such local councils and appoint its members.[19] Never before had a woman been included in such a local body. The issue was extremely controversial, but the Court held that women were perfectly eligible to serve and ordered the minister to consider Shakdiel's application on the merits.[20] That same year the city of Tel Aviv was preparing to elect its chief rabbi. The orthodox parties opposed the idea that women council-members would vote in the election of a rabbi. The women petitioned the Court and won: the Court held that women were entitled to participate in the election of a rabbi, who was a government employee and subject to the laws of the state.[21] These recent (in 1988) gains in gender equality could persuade the skeptics – both Americans and Israelis – that the ground was ripe for another round of litigation which would vindicate WoW's right to pray at the Wall.[22] After all, what did they want? Merely to pray in accordance with orthodox principles, confined to the women's section and behind the mehtiza.

In the United States, the American group formed ICWoW (International Committee for the Women of the Wall). In this group were experienced veterans of the civil rights movement and the feminist movement, who knew well how to organize a social movement and to galvanize public opinion in support of their cause. Prominent in the group was Phyllis Chesler, a well-known author, psychologist, feminist, activist, and theoretician of women's issues.[23] Chesler was a formidable force in establishing and nurturing the ICWoW, and in forming the policy it would pursue in its campaign to get access to the Wall. But at the moment that the ICWoW began to contemplate what steps to take, the nascent social movement confronted the constraints of being not only women, not only Jewesses, but members of the larger community of American Jews. The loaded question of the relationship between the Diaspora and Israel was placed on the table.

The ICWoW were ardent supporters of the State of Israel, and looked upon Israel as a progressive polity which shared American values and sensibilities.[24] They were not sufficiently aware of the complex reality of Israel, where constitutionalism was only beginning to assert itself, and where orthodoxy was reified, fundamentalist, patriarchal and in possession of increasing political power. Their challenge to this form of powerful orthodoxy brought them into conflict not only with the orthodox, who expected women to be deferential in matters of religious rites, but also with Israel's foreign affairs.

How did the matter of prayer at the Wall relate to foreign affairs? As soon as ICWoW embarked on their campaign, a potential conflict with the leadership of the American Jewish community emerged. This leadership is largely devoted to defending the State of Israel in the context of the Arab-Israeli conflict. It is therefore quite sensitive to any issue that may cast a negative light upon Israel, thereby swaying American public opinion against it. Furthermore, when defending Israeli interests, the US Jewish community strives to present a united front. The issue of WoW was divisive. Reform, conservative, and modern orthodox found themselves on one side of the divide, with the fundamentalist orthodox on the other side. ICWoW was urged to display awareness of this sensitivity. Like any minority group, Jews have historically avoided issues which might cast a negative light on the community (known as "hanging dirty laundry in public"). Airing the conflict between traditional orthodox and progressive Jewry in the matter of gender, and providing details of the callous treatment WoW was getting at the Wall, could "cast a bad light" on Jews. A vocal movement calling attention to the fact that in Jerusalem, Israel's capital and the holiest Jewish space, Jewish women were denied freedom of religious worship, flew in the face of the claim that Israel alone could be trusted with maintaining equal access to the holy sites. ICWoW's and WoW's very existence, let alone vocal protest, were perceived as disloyal to the larger agenda of supporting the State of Israel on the political front.[25] It is quite likely that ICWoW was urged to "be discreet" and to avoid the general media so as to refrain from giving ammunition to those critical of Israel.[26]

Thus, as a social movement, the members of ICWoW placed themselves at a disadvantage. They did not, perhaps could not, use the tools and skills that they possessed in order to alert American and world public opinion to the strange phenomenon: freedom of Jewish worship, the freedom of women to pray in accordance with their legitimate (if controversial) beliefs, is denied by the State of Israel – the same state that claims it is the better guardian of religious worship in the old City of Jerusalem and that, at least formally, is proud of its long standing commitment to gender equality. But in the process of subordinating their rights to what they perceived as the "Jewish interest", they tragically walked in the footsteps of their mothers and grandmothers: women's rights were again sacrificed to a perceived greater good, defined largely by men.[27]

The Israeli women who were among the original group had much in common with their international sisters, but they were also markedly different. Their concern was for their civil rights in their own country of residence. Citizenship does make a difference, and the difference is no less meaningful when religious experience is concerned. The Israelis felt about the communal prayer at the Wall in exactly the same way Chesler and her sisters felt about any issue of gender equality in the United States. Their Israeli citizenship immunized them to the subtle pressures experienced by their sisters abroad, who were fully integrated in the civil society of their respective countries, but were also painfully vulnerable when they engaged in criticizing the State of Israel.[28] For them, the politics of the American-Jewish community and its worries about American public opinion in matters of American foreign affairs were less relevant.[29] Furthermore, they were accustomed to challenging Israeli policy in the arena of public opinion for purposes of advancing their collective interests. They also had other differences with the American group of WoW founders.

First, religious pluralism, while taken for granted in the United States, has been (and to a large degree still is) a marginal phenomenon in Israel. Israeli "Jewish identity" and American "Jewish identity" are not the same. Most of the founders of Zionist ideology, from Benjamin Z. Herzl to David Ben-Gurion and Zeev Zabotinsky, sought to develop an alternative to the religious lifestyle. So too did Zionism's founding mothers, from Henrietta Szold to Rachel Kagan and Golda Meir distance themselves from religion. Religion was a relic of the past. National revival was taking its place. Therefore, the emerging Israeli society was encouraged to embrace a secular lifestyle and distance itself from "the dark clerical past" of rabbinic rule. A small space was carved out for the orthodox minority, and it is not an exaggeration to say that a metaphorical wall has been separating the two Jewish communities. Secular Israeli Jews transformed Jewish religion into a civic religion but rejected Halachic meaning of rites and rituals. The conservative and reform movements, which outside of Israel served as a bridge between a religious lifestyle and modernity and represented the Jewish majority, failed to take root in Israel, and were rejected by the State.[30] Conservative and reform religious lifestyles were practiced in tiny local communities, mostly by immigrants who came from English-speaking countries and were not supported by the state apparatus. Tension existed between traditional orthodoxy and modern orthodoxy, but by and large it did not concern the secular public which turned a blind eye to the differences between the two. The religious part of the Israeli public, including those who call themselves "traditional" (masorti – selectively observing the principal tenets of the religious way of life), has been predominantly orthodox, especially when it came to the status of women. Most secular Israelis, encouraged by state ideology, view Zionist ideology as the legitimate modern heir of Judaism.[31]

Second, and not less important, theories of feminism and gender equality have been slow to penetrate the Israeli consciousness. By 1988, the Israeli public was still indifferent to or uncomfortable with feminism and most well-accomplished women felt an inner desire to keep their distance from it. Thus, most of the Israeli women, conscious activists, who attended the 1988 conference were more interested in the agenda of promoting gender equality in the secular Israeli world, and less aware of the significance of women's communal prayer. To make a commitment to the cause of WoW, Israeli feminists had to embrace the concept of Jewish religious pluralism, which at that time had a weak hold on their consciousness. Many Israeli feminists viewed the controversy as an internal religious affair – a controversy about the meaning of Jewish law and modern orthodoxy in which they were not interested. The agenda of feminist reform was ferociously crowded and its priority list quite long. The issue of WoW was quite low on the Israeli agenda.

The reluctance of the Israeli feminist camp to rally around WoW could have deeper causes. Israeli feminists have lamented the control exercised by the rabbinical establishment in the most profound aspect of their being – in matters of marriage and divorce. Many have been angry and frustrated by this state of affairs.[32] The practice of communal prayer, in the women's section, appeared alien and esoteric, even blind, to the suffering of the individual Israeli woman in need of divorce or other family matters. WoW were both a reminder of their own helplessness in fighting the rabbinical establishment and a dangerous return to religious practice (prayer), when the goal should be to break religion's hold on a woman's freedom and dignity (getting a divorce or an adequate financial settlement upon divorce). Indeed, the Israeli members of WoW did not see it this way. They sought Halachic change and reform across the board, and believed that just as they could show that communal prayer was permissible, so they could show that Halachic reform was necessary to make divorce more harmonious with women's dignity and rights.[33] The Israeli feminist agenda was itself a major woe of WoW as they sought support for their cause among feminists.

It is important to re-emphasize that WoW itself is diverse and complex. At a minimum, it is divided into two groups, the Israeli chapter, and the international chapter. The fence separating them is low and somewhat invisible. Members move from one group to the other as they change their place of residence or their interpretation of current or past events. But they do have their differences, and the milieu within which they operate (Israel for WoW, and mainly the US for ICWoW) affects them in different ways. As shall be discussed shortly, the opposition among WoW to the "egalitarian plaza" as presently (2013) conceived by the Israeli government is led mostly by ICWoW. These constraints add to the woes of WoW, referred to in the title.

The woman endowed with natural leadership gifts, and who eventually became the Israeli leader of WoW, Anat Hoffman, represented WoW's agenda.[34] A member of Meretz (the Civil Rights Party, advocating a rigorous separation of church and state similar to the American model), she gradually adopted the reform movement of progressive Judaism and developed a passion for restoring a place for Jewish religious life in Israeli identity. With the help of the reform movement in the United States she established IRAC and developed a plan to transform the Israeli cultural landscape into one more accepting of Jewish religious practices which are inclusive and progressive. These have been presented as solid and attractive alternatives to the Orthodox way of life.

In doing so she has been fighting an uphill battle with the hostile orthodox camp, with the indifferent secular public, and with the State which eventually came to side with the orthodox. At the same time she had to negotiate with her partners in the United States (the ICWoW). All of the above illustrate the woes of WoW. The maze in which they have been forced to navigate is formidable indeed.

WoW was forced simultaneously to confront two legal systems, each with its own dynamics and limitations: the Israeli legal system and Halacha as understood by the orthodox camp. The woes of WoW have not only been sociological and geographical. They were also distinctly and significantly legal.

The road to litigation

Situated within a Western-style democratic state, Israeli constitutional law generally claims loyalty to the principle of the separation of church and state as well as the principle of the free exercise of religious worship.[35] Haut's concept of women's prayer groups has never been prohibited in Israel. Women could always congregate in a private space of their choice, or indeed establish their own synagogue and fulfill their yearning for the experience of communal prayer.[36] The controversy erupted because WoW has been insisting on holding their communal prayers at the site of the Wall – the most public sacred space in Israel, indeed in the Jewish world. WoW wanted access to the public space in order to assert their equal citizenship in religion, to make the point that their "place" was not only in the private home or private synagogue, but in the public realm as well.[37]

For centuries Jews were discouraged from coming to the Wall for prayer. In the early twentieth century, when Britain came to occupy Palestine, access was partially permitted (this article does not address that history, which also involved considerable violence). Photographs from that period reveal that men and women mixed at the site of the Wall, i.e., the separation of men and women was not a part of the custom at the Wall. In 1948 the kingdom of Jordan took control of the Wall, and banned Jewish presence there. The 1967 War united the city and brought the Wall under Israeli control. Within days a vast plaza was created. After fierce deliberations, the government placed the administration of the Wall under the jurisdiction of the Ministry of Religions and the Ministry established a mehitza to separate men from women in keeping with orthodox practice.[38] The lion's share of the space was allocated to men. Less than one-third was allocated to women. The men's section was well-stocked with Torah scrolls and folding tables appropriate for conducting the Jewish religious rituals. The women's section was allocated a small room stocked with regular prayer books (siddurim). No Torah scrolls or tables were furnished as women were expected to pray only as individuals, not as a group. This was the situation that Haut's group encountered when it first arrived at the Wall to conduct a communal prayer.[39]

Since 1967, Israel's government has emphasized the significance of the Wall in Jewish heritage and history, and encouraged tourists to make a pilgrimage to the Wall. Therefore it is small wonder that Haut felt the Wall would be the most appropriate place to hold the group prayer. An ordinary synagogue would not open the deep wells of yearning and inclusion as the Wall could. Nor could it send the message that women have arrived, that they are equal citizens of the Jewish people, and that they are accorded the equal protection of Israeli laws. The connection between women's rights, the State of Israel, and Jewish heritage could best be communicated through the communal prayer at the women's section at the Wall.

At this junction, it is important to consider the concept of "orthodoxy." Jewish orthodoxy is a continuum. One extreme is ultra-orthodox, a fundamentalist movement denying the legitimacy of the State of Israel. The other extreme is modern orthodoxy attempting to reconcile the Jewish lifestyle and modern society.[40] Haut was a radical within the modern orthodox camp, a pioneer of women's prayer groups, a concept that in the 1980s was still meeting resistance in the orthodox world. The Wall-synagogue was administered and controlled by men who were closer to ultra-orthodoxy on the continuum of orthodoxy, and who therefore could not empathize with Haut's demands.[41]

A large measure of naïvete lay at the core of Haut's high expectations. Haut and her friends underestimated the fierce opposition the orthodox generally hold against anything new or untraditional. Nor did they understand the political dynamics of the relations between church and state in Israel, or the impact of this dynamic on Israeli law.

When the worshippers at the site of the Wall unleashed their rage at the conference participants, Haut and her fellow worshippers expected police protection as well as sympathy. After all, they were modernizing Jewish religion and bringing it to exist more in tune with its glorious heritage of equality and justice. Thereby, they were more in tune with the best hopes of Zionism itself. At the scene of the Wall, startling verbal abuse and invective soon culminated in physical assault. Men hurled metal chairs at the WoW (from the men's section), threw them to the ground in anger and even discharged tear gas grenades (originally meant to disperse Arab-Palestinian demonstrations).[42] The police, always present at the site of the Wall, chose the role of passive observers. They allowed the rage to sizzle for a while, and finally moved to arrest a few of the women participants, on the ground that it was they who had broken the law (breach of the peace) by offending the feelings of the worshippers.[43]

Thereafter, the Rabbi of the Wall, using his statutory authority, issued a regulation prohibiting any prayer on the premises of the Wall which contravened "custom" (literal translation, "the custom of the place", or in Hebrew "minhag hamakom").[44]

For American women in particular, heirs of the civil rights movement and accustomed to judicial protection of First Amendment rights under the US Constitution, these events were quite upsetting. The State's complicity, putting secular law at the service of the orthodox, opened their eyes to the vast gap between themselves and the "others" and ignited a determination to fight and eradicate one more vestige of patriarchy and sex discrimination.

Back in the United States, ICWoW made plans to sue, and it persuaded its Israeli sisters to join in.[45] Thus far, they were dealing with the executive branch of the government. Now they petitioned the Judiciary. The international flavor of WoW again became apparent. Much of the financing of this protracted litigation arrived from sources outside of Israel. ICWoW intimately identified with the struggle, which concerned their identity as Jewish women. Furthermore, support for WoW was yet another aspect of the general US effort to cultivate a civic society in Israel, thereby deepening its democratic culture and perhaps making it more similar to the United States. Thus began a protracted litigation before Israel's High Court of Justice.

The legal battle

What was the legal framework of the controversy? The Rabbi of the Wall was serving two masters. On the one hand, he was a government employee (of the ministry of religious affairs), and therefore required to abide by secular Israeli law. On the other hand, he was a distinguished rabbi, well respected in orthodox circles, and committed to live within the four corners of Halacha.

The Rabbi's refusal to allow WoW freedom of religious worship at the women's section placed Halacha in direct conflict with Israel's secular law. WoW and ICWoW petitioned Israel's High Court of Justice to enforce the following well-accepted principles of Israeli constitutional law: all government employees must abide by the law of the State; State law includes the principles of separation of church and state, of free exercise of religion and of gender equality.[46] Therefore, the Rabbi of the Wall must honor these rights and facilitate the presence of the Women's Prayer Group in the women's section.

However, these principles, so easily accessible to the modern citizen of a secular state, at least on the abstract level, are not as accessible to someone wholly immersed in the religious social worldview. The orthodox tolerate a duality of legal systems only if there is no perceived conflict between the two.[47]

The government (and its justice department) faced a hard choice: uphold the well-articulated principles of the rule of law (equality, free exercise of religion) and respect WoW's rights, or side with the orthodox and reject WoW's petition. Of course, representatives of the secular government of Israel would not go as far as to state that they are bound by Halacha and therefore feel compelled to violate cherished constitutional principles, but they could and did resort to the justification that the WoW practice "offended the feelings of the worshippers at the Wall" and therefore may be prohibited. This argument continues to be voiced by the opponents of WoW in the current confrontation.

Many of the cabinet ministers at the time were agnostic about the issue of women's prayer groups; still, they sided with the orthodox camp. The need for the political support of the orthodox, combined with the failure to understand notions of gender equality and puzzlement at WoW's request tilted the balance against WoW. It was easy to ignore the feelings of the women while empathizing with the feelings of the patriarchy. If a secular male politician, does not value his own right to pray, why should he value the right of a woman to the same practice?

But things were even more complicated. The conflict opened a controversy between rabbis and scholars of Halacha. Some held that Halacha categorically limited communal prayer to men, whereas others insisted, with equally learned scholarship, that in fact Halacha is either supportive of the notion or at least is ambiguous about it.[48]

In between these interpretations of Halacha, should the secular Court take a stand? The conflict furthermore triggered disagreement about secular Israeli law. Should the Court view this issue as a case of first impression and analyze it with analytical tools from feminist legal theory and civil rights theory? Or should the Court defer to the concept of the "status quo", whereby the orthodox sector of Israel has been recognized as the guardian of the religious lifestyle and therefore its feelings are entitled to particular deference?[49]

Moreover, the hard question of territorial identity was raising a stubborn head. If Israel was the homeland of all Jews, then certainly members of ICWoW had a right to petition the Court for redress of grievances. But if Israel was a state "like all states", with a distinct "Israeli" culture and citizenry, then members of ICWoW were foreigners trying to intervene in domestic affairs.[50] Their Israeli sisters were likewise "otherized", because many of them had ties to the United States and they were adopting a practice born in the United States and not yet familiar in Israel. The rumor spread that WoW is a group of American women who want to bring their reform customs to the site of the Wall.

One should not be surprised to hear that at the sacred space of the Wall, operating as an Orthodox synagogue, the Jewish pluralism from which WoW sprang, appeared as a direct assault on Halacha, a radical departure from the natural order of things.[51] Well aware of the enormous resistance, WoW asked for permission to pray only once a month, on Rosh Hodesh, at 7:30 in the morning. Rosh Hodesh, the beginning of the lunar month, is halachically observed as a day entirely dedicated to the welfare of women, hence the expectation that respecting the rights to pray as a group on that day would get especial lenience, even in orthodox circles. WoW also expected that this extremely modest request would make it easy for the Court to accept their petition. After all, they were asking for only a very tiny bite of the pie.[52] Still, the rabbis resisted. Several, not merely two, worlds collided and challenged the Justices in acute ways.

The first three rounds of the legal battle lasted from 1989 to 2003, and ended in a compromise. In the end of this cycle, WoW was asked to leave the women's section and move to an adjacent space. After protracted controversy and endless negotiations, the government agreed to prepare an alternative site, at an archeological park known as the Robinson Arch. The Robinson Arch, formally a part of the ancient Wall of the Jewish Temple, has not been perceived to be as sacred as the Wall area, and it is located at a distance from the Wall itself. It is also a space difficult to renovate, because it contains precious archeological treasures and is subjected to strict Israeli laws governing archeological sites.[53] The Robinson Arch was mildly renovated to allow access for the women (including the disabled). Members of the reform and conservative denominations, where mixed-gender prayers are the norm, were invited to pray at the Robinson Arch (as a mixed gendered group they are banned from the Wall itself, which strictly segregates men and women).[54] But no one denies that at present the site looks like a makeshift location, lacks the dignity of a place of worship and does not invoke the deep spiritual feelings associated with the Wall.

Back to the trajectory of the legal battle. Like in any other democracy, law enforcement is a matter for the executive branch, and there is no doubt that the government agonized about the matter. It is not clear precisely what went into the deliberations, but two factors must have weighed heavily in favor of the status quo and against the WoW. First, the orthodox camp in Israel is more than a sizable religious group. Several political parties represent orthodox interests, and they hold significant leverage in the Knesset (Parliament), and often in the cabinet.[55] An important example of leverage is the peace process. It is doubtful that a peace process involving the end of occupation can move forward without the support of at least some of these parties. Any change in the status quo at the Wall may well result in withdrawal of political support on the diplomatic front. The second factor is Israeli secular consciousness. Until very recently, Israelis felt comfortable with the grand compromise of Zionism: the orthodox would define religious practice, while the majority of Israelis would be secular. This may have been changing of late but during the 1990s, Israel's secular majority could not appreciate the WoW's arguments or evaluate their significance for Israeli and Jewish life. One may even go as far as to say that until the beginning of the twenty-first century the majority would have wanted these women to disappear and remove the annoying issue from the crowded agenda. These factors fed the government's decision to side with the religious camp rather than with WoW.

ICWoW took the lead in launching the legal battle. They hired a very prominent male attorney and planned to petition the High Court of Justice for an injunction. The Israeli WoW did not happily comply; they wanted to have their say. They were hoping for a woman attorney to represent them. Again, this episode, which deserves further documentation, illustrates the internal woes of WoW. A movement wishes to form a united front but one should never underestimate disagreement, even discord, underneath. Ultimately, a very fine woman attorney, Hebrew University Law Professor Frances Raday, agreed to represent WoW.[56]

As Raday was fighting on behalf of WoW, she was conducting an array of other legal battles before the Court. WoW's battle must be evaluated in the context of the larger struggle of Israeli women for equality. In the late 1980s and early 1990s, gender-based discrimination was rampant. Women's income was significantly lower than men's; very few women (the formidable career of Golda Meir honoring the breach of the norm of sex equality) rose to positions of power; age discrimination in the workplace compelled women to retire before men; leadership positions in the military, the apple of Israel's eye, were closed to women; and sexual harassment was perceived as the material entitlement of men. WoW was competing in a very crowded space; given the secular context of the Israeli women's movement, it could be expected that their struggle would get a low place on the priority list.[57] No one should be surprised to learn that the High Court did not display too much enthusiasm to spend its capital on supporting WoW's petition.

The litigation yielded three opinions by the High Court of Justice. One in 1994, the second in 2000 and the third in 2003. The third opinion was delivered by a sharply divided Court, five justices in the majority and four in the dissent.

The First Round: Israel's Court typically sits in panels of three justices. Three male justices were appointed (at that time there were two women justices in the Court), to review the petition: Chief Justice Meir Shamgar and Justice Shlomo Levin, both secular men, and Deputy Chief Justice Menahem Elon, an international authority on Halacha and a modern orthodox man.

The petition was submitted in 1989, and the decision was delivered in 1994. The Court, as was increasingly its policy in political controversies, decided to postpone the legal resolution of the case.[58] Chief Justice Shamgar held that indeed, WoW's claim had merit, but because of the sensitivity of the issue, he recommended that the government establish a commission, which would develop an appropriate solution. Justice Shlomo Levin joined him, but his rhetoric displayed a more resolute commitment to the free exercise of religion. Justice Menachem Elon delivered a lengthy, opinion, analyzing in great detail the women's claim that Halacha did not ban women's communal prayers and concluding that indeed they were right.[59] But then Elon made a surprising U-turn. Custom, he opined, expected only men to conduct a communal prayer. The site of the Wall required unity of worship thereby requiring deference to custom, and WoW should sacrifice its valid claim so as to perpetuate that precious unity. By a 2:1 margin, the High Court sent the ball to the government's court. The executive branch was told to develop an appropriate solution to WoW's petition.

Time passed. Prime Minister Yitzhak Rabin was assassinated (by a young man determined to derail the peace process which he understood to violate Halacha), and in the ensuing 1996 elections the orthodox gained more power. Commissions were appointed, dragged their feet, and could not reach conclusions. The issue was both low on the priority list, and too explosive to address. A petition to expedite review was denied. The Court preferred to wait for the commissions to articulate a solution, but the commissions stalled because of lack of consensus. In 1999, almost ten years after the initial event of communal prayer at the Wall, the Court agreed to re-hear WoW's petition.[60]

The Second Round: As the twenty-first century dawned, the Court issued a unanimous opinion in favor of WoW. Three justices, one man – Justice Eliyahu Matza, who wrote the opinion for the Court – and two women (Justice Tova Strassberg Cohen and Justice Dorit Beinish, later appointed as Chief Justice, now retired), authored a well-reasoned, superbly crafted, opinion explaining that, under Israeli constitutional law, it is the duty of the government to protect the women as they exercise their right to freedom of worship. However, mindful of the explosive ramifications, the Court refrained from providing the customary remedy of ordering the government to let the WoW pray at the Wall. Rather, it postponed the final order, calling upon the government to make appropriate arrangements within six months.[61]

In June 2000, the Attorney General requested the Court to grant the State a "further hearing", a chance to challenge the opinion and the Court acquiesced. The Attorney General's request could only be explained in the context of the volatility of the conflict and its high profile.

By the year 2000 the High Court of Justice was no longer in the position of an invincible, revered institution. A backlash was taking place, targeted among other things at the Court's liberal position in matters of the separation of church and state or of freedom of worship.[62] One may imagine (although this author has no proof) that the then Attorney General, Eliakim Rubinstein, an orthodox man, must have experienced external as well as internal pressure to derail the Court's opinion. The Court itself must have understood the volatility of the situation when it granted the Attorney General's request for a further hearing.[63]

One may pause to indulge in counterfactual scenarios. What would happen if the government, led by a Prime Minister committed to the right to freedom of worship, decided to go forth and implement the second Court decision? After all, WoW was aware of the sensitivity of its claim, and therefore made a very modest request, to pray at the Wall in the early morning hours, once a month, excluding the period of heavy traffic during the high holidays. If WoW's request were implemented by the government, the burden on the orthodox worshippers would have been miniscule indeed. One may imagine, counterfactually, a prime minister using leadership skills, explaining to the orthodox camp, the Israeli public, world public opinion, that Israel must be true to its commitment to democratic values, indeed, Zionist values, and therefore it was honor bound to uphold the right of the tiny minority in its midst. One can also imagine, counterfactually that, had the police been instructed to protect the women steadfastly, the orthodox camp would have acquiesced after a few arrests for breach of the peace. Such a scenario is not altogether fantastical.[64] But context matters. In Israel in the first decade of the twenty-first century, the orthodox camp enjoyed considerable power, especially when it came to defining what is Jewish. Protracted violence and a political crisis were also possible.

The Third Round: Nine Justices sat on the panel that reviewed the unanimous opinion. Among them were the then Chief Justice, Aharon Barak, and Justice Mishael Cheshin, both secular men, known for their brilliant legal skills as well as for their commitment to the separation of religion and state. Again, the Court took its time, and there were rumors that behind-the-scenes intense negotiations were taking place to find a compromise. In 2003, the Court issued its opinion: a sharply divided Court recognized WoW's right to freedom of worship, but sided with the government's argument that the Wall should be kept under the patriarchal umbrella. The majority did not explicitly hold that WoW does not have a right to group prayer at the women's section of the Wall, but opined that under the circumstances they should go someplace else. The Court did, however, warn the government that if it failed to provide an adequate alternative the Court may intervene and issue an injunction on behalf of the women[65]

WoW and the concept of the rule of law

The case of WoW deserves a dissertation (not to be offered here) at least about the trials and tribulations of the rule of law. In every stage of the struggle, the matter of principle (equality, freedom of worship), well entrenched in Israel's legal system, has been compromised because of fierce pressure by orthodox circles, prevailing upon the Israeli government to take their side. Even the High Court of Justice was dragged into the practice of ignoring the straightforward meaning of these principles as well as a unanimous opinion delivered by three of its own justices, in order to avoid a gathering storm.

When the orthodox first heard of WoW's claim, they retorted that Jewish law – Halacha – prohibits it. When they were challenged and shown that in fact Halacha is not against the practice, they elevated custom into an entrenched and sacred principle that could not be compromised.

After the Israel's High Court gave its blessing to the Robinson Arch as an alternative venue, the orthodox adopted another argument. If until then they argued that between Israeli rights law and Halacha denying rights the latter prevails, they now piously wrapped themselves in the tallit of secular law. The Court, they reminded everyone, sent the women to Robinson's Arch, and its verdict must be obeyed.

Judge Sobel's opinion, holding that WoW does have a right to pray at the women's section of the Wall (infra, p. 142), upset the cozy relationship between secular and religious law. Now the orthodox were again in square one, facing a secular judicial opinion that negated their claim to monopoly at the Wall. The orthodox therefore abandoned the haughty argument that the law of the land must be obeyed and again insisted that only Halacha as interpreted by their rabbis is the supreme law of the land.

One wonders if this is another metaphor for the troubles affecting the State of Israel. From the beginning WoW offered a version of Halacha that was in harmony with the secular law. This version recognized women's equality and dignity (women, too, were created in the image of God). If adopted by the rabbis, the entire conflict could have been avoided. But the orthodox rabbis in Jerusalem could not accept that even Halacha requires change, and thereby brought about a conflict between the two legal systems, tilting of the balance against equality and in favor of patriarchal values.

2013: an unending saga

By 2004 WoW seemed to be losing in Court and in the legislative arena generally. And yet, this group of determined women proved to be remarkably resilient. An argument has been raging in the legal academy as to whether the quest for controversial rights (race equality, the right to abortion) is better off being fought in Court or whether social mobilization is essential for a successful outcome. It appears that WoW's leadership was mindful of this argument. Once they understood the limits of litigation, and became aware of negative attitudes in the Knesset and the Court, WoW turned to social action.

They have harnessed technology to their cause. WoW has a website and an electronic newsletter, they are on Facebook, they tweet, they try to mobilize support through various projects, such as selling hand-made tallitot (prayer shawls) with the names of the four Jewish matriarchs embroidered in the four corners, encouraging tourists to hold bat mitzvas and other celebrations with them. They spread the message of gender equality and rally support against segregation. Two film documentaries track the struggle, and are available to the general public.[66]

For a while, WoW attempted discreetly to hold their ritual at the site of the Wall. For a while, the police turned a blind eye, and on occasion even chilled the enthusiasm of the worshippers who wanted to sabotage the ritual (was this another indication of the ambivalence of the executive branch?). WoW pointed out that the government was lax in its renovation of the Robinson Arch and that therefore the Robinson Arch was not a viable alternative to the Wall. They kept invoking the image of Rosa Parks, who refused to defer to segregation. Also, they were the beneficiaries of numerous rabbinical scholars, men and women, who expanded the study of this subject matter and offered more learned reasons to support their claim. This scholarship strengthened WoW's argument that they were within the four corners of the law, and that they were the victims of grave injustice.[67]

But the opposition to their appearance on Rosh Hodesh did not abate. This opposition must be understood in the context of the campaign, expanding at the end of the first decade of the twenty-first century, to broaden gender segregation and limit women's presence in the public square.

The more WoW was rebuffed, the more it became the harbinger of the general theme of gender equality in Jewish religious life in general and in Israel in particular. For its part, the opposition also rallied its troops and its influence. I shall address the opposition first and then move to discuss two important events occurring in 2013.

At first, the opposition to WoW was made of men only. Women were confined to the role of "informers", alerting the men from behind the mehitza that the WoW has arrived. But while the opposition is wedded to patriarchal custom, they do not lack modern sophistication and probably enjoy the help of savvy PR professionals. Orthodox women were soon recruited to voice vocal disapproval of WoW. Already during the litigation before the High Court of Justice orthodox women filed a brief to voice disagreement with WoW. An organization called Women for the Wall (as distinct from Women of the Wall) waxes eloquent about the need for unity and for deference to rabbinic authority required by that concept of unity.[68] In a way reminiscent of the suffragists' struggle at the end of the nineteen century and the beginning of the twentieth century, groups of women are pitted against each other, one carrying the torch of inclusion, progress and change, the other insisting on the supreme value of tradition and the status quo.

It stands to reason that at a certain point during the second decade of the twenty-first century, someone instructed the police to change course and begin to enforce a ban on women's prayer groups. As discussed above, members of WoW who tried to hold their service at the women's section were arrested by the police and brought to jail.[69] They would be forced to spend a night incarcerated, along with other criminal suspects (such as prostitutes) presumably in the hope that the experience and the humiliation would chill further activity. Jail was the place – "makom" – these women deserved if they did not adhere to the ban. The women would then be brought before a Justice of the Peace on charges of breach of the peace and a restraining order would issue, to refrain from attending the Wall for a period of time. Instead of being deterred, WoW widely spread pictures of their sisters being dragged by the police, wrapped in a tallit and holding a Torah scroll. These were not pretty pictures and they alarmed progressives in Israel and elsewhere. More visitors started attending the Rosh Hodesh events to support WoW. It appears that in the course of these developments, at least some secular Israeli women were transformed too, spiritually discovering the beauty and meaning of the Jewish service and of the power of praying together.[70]

In April 2013 five women who participated in the Rosh Hodesh prayer were detained by the police. They were brought before Judge Sharon Larry-Bavli (a woman) of the Jerusalem Court of the peace, who reviewed the evidence (video) presented by the police and determined that none of the detainees engaged in violence or in breach of the peace. The judge therefore dismissed the government's request for a restraining order. In other words, the claim that the mere appearance of WoW at the women's section, without more, amounts to a legal provocation to violence was rejected. The government appealed. The State of Israel thus positioned itself formally against WoW, in the case known as State of Israel v. Rus.[71]

The appeal came before Judge Moshe Sobel of the Jerusalem District Court.[72] On April 24, 2013 he delivered an opinion that served as a lightning rod across the Jerusalem sky, shaking and reordering the previous balance of power. Judge Sobel held that Israeli law requires proof of actual provocation before the offense of breach of the peace may be applied. In this case, no such evidence existed. This holding strengthened the findings made by the Justice of the Peace. Furthermore, he held that the High Court opinions in the matter of the Women of the Wall did not explicitly prohibit women's prayer groups at the Wall. He pointed out that a majority of the Justices did recognize WoW's right to worship at the Wall. The fact that they also urged all parties to opt for an alternative has not cast doubts upon the right itself. Therefore WoW were not violating any law when they were practicing group prayer at the Wall. It was a formidable opinion, superbly crafted and well written. In my view, the fact that it was legalistic and devoid of rhetoric only added to its power.[73]

Israel is a country quite respectful of the rule of law, and once Sobel's opinion was announced the government ordered the police to protect the women. In addition, and quite likely against this background, Israel's attorney general also issued a set of recommendations to combat gender segregation in the public sphere, including a recommendation to criminalize such segregation.[74]

The orthodox felt they were losing ground, at the site of the Wall as well as elsewhere. Their response was an unprecedented counteroffensive against WoW. Rabbis summoned young seminary girls to take a day off of school and fill the women's section of the Wall, thereby leaving no room for WoW's members to practice their prayer.[75] They did not hide their determination to derail WoW by all available means. It is too early to tell whether this move is successful or whether it is bound to backfire. These orthodox seminary girls, less complacent than they used to be, may well be radicalized by the experience, and draw the conclusion that they have collective power (or at least a potential) to prevail upon the rabbis in important matters such as family planning, education and even religious ritual.[76]

At the same time, the government did understand that the public outrage, especially outside of Israel, hurts Israel's reputation as a democracy as well as a Jewish state, committed to all Jews rather than to the particularly narrow sector of orthodoxy. If until the events of 2013 the cabinet was in no hurry to find a solution, it now felt the heat. Together with Nathan Scharansky, head of the Jewish Agency, the option of the Robinson Arch was again placed on the table.

A plan was submitted to the Prime Minister, to expand the Wall Plaza. The Wall itself would remain in orthodox hands, but an equally large plaza will be constructed, called "Ezrat Yisrael", where members of WoW, the reform and the conservative movements could hold prayers in accordance with their own customs.

WoW was not happy about this solution, because it required their consent to discontinue worship at the women's section at the Wall. In particular, WoW's orthodox members objected that the new plaza will have no mehitza or women's section, a situation unacceptable to them from their modern orthodox Halachic perspective (recall that group prayers meet Halachic requirements, but still requires a mehitza). Behind the scenes, it appears that pressure was put on leaders of the reform and conservative movements in the United States to prevail upon WoW to accept a compromise and move to the Robinson Arch under the new plan.

WoW did not have enough time to relish the victory of Sobel's opinion or the increasing support it got from the domestic and international public. In deliberating the offer to move to a renovated Robinson Arch, a rift became visible within WoW's membership. The orthodox members of WoW interpreted the decision to cooperate with the new plan as betrayal. They insist on their right to pray in the women's section of the Wall.[77] Here is another woe of WoW. They were banned from the Wall under pretext of unity but in accepting a compromise they sacrifice their own internal unity.

As this article comes to a close, WoW's leader, Anat Hoffman announced that while accepting the new plan, the members insist on their right to pray at the women's section, until the plan is materialized. No one knows if it will. One thing is clear. WoW's road has been full of thorns, a never-ending chain of woes. They are thus a splendid if sad metaphor for the status of women in Jewish culture, particularly in Israel. They courageously fight for their right to be equal under the law, Halachic and secular, and they keep being rebuffed by followers of ancient patriarchal principles and by cynical politicians who look at their struggle as a mere nuisance. Stay tuned for further developments.

Notes

* An abridged and previous version of this article appeared in the *Israel Studies Review*, *ISR* vol. 30, issue 2 (Winter 2015). Earlier drafts of this paper were written in the context of a year-long religion-fellows seminar at the Boston University School of Theology, 2010–2011. I wish to thank members of the seminar for stimulating and enriching sessions, and for their insightful comments and suggestions. A part of this paper was presented at the University of Chicago Law School's conference "What pertains to a man?". The paper was also presented as the *Diane Markowicz Memorial Lecture* on General and Human Rights, Brandeis University, the Eli Weisel Center for Judaic Studies, Boston University and at the workshop of the UCLA Law School. I am grateful to Mary Anne Case for inviting me to participate and for challenging discussion of the subject matter. I also wish to thank Leora Bilsky, Zvi Triger, Simon Rabinovitch and Michael Zank for reading a previous draft and making very valuable suggestions. My research assistants Andrew Smith and Elizabeth Nagle deserves special thanks for fine editorial work.

† Pnina Lahav is a Professor of Law and Law Alumni Scholar at the Elle Wiesel Center for Judaic Studies at Boston University Law School. Do not quote, cite, use or distribute without author's permission.

1 Eliav Shocethman, "Aliyyot for Women," in *Women and Men in Communal Prayer: Halakhic Perspectives*, ed. Rabbi Daniel Sperber et al. (New York: JOFA, 2010), 291.

2 See Ariel Hirschfeld's analysis of the Wall as Makom in *Local Notes* (Am Oved: 2002), 13.

3 Ein Makom Acher – "There is no other place" – was the title of an important book by the Israeli literary critic, Gershon Shaked. In it, he discussed the role of this particular geographic spot – Israel – in Hebrew literature and in Zionist thought.

4 This is not a comprehensive list of segregation demands put forth. Another major argument revolved around women raising their voices in song in mixed secular and religious assemblies. In the military, too, an effort is under way to ban women soldier-instructors from bases where religious men are serving.

5 Naomi Ragen v. Minister of Transportation HC 746/07 http://versa-cardozo.yu.edu/opinions/ragen-v-ministry-transport; see also report "Excluded, For God's Sake: Gender Segregation in Public Space in Israel" (2010) http://www.irac.org/userfiles/Excluded,%20For%20God's%20Sake%20-%20Report%20on%20Gender%20Segregation%20in%20the%20Public%20Sphere%20in%20Israel(1).pdf (last accessed 9 November, 2015).

6 Professor Frances Raday, who litigated the case on behalf of WoW, wrote extensively about their plight as well as about the legal status of Israeli women generally. See e.g.

"The Fight Against Being Silenced," in Chesler and Haut, infra n. 7 at 115. Raday Frances, "Claiming Equal Religious Personhood: Women of the Wall's Constitutional Saga," *Religion in the Public Sphere: A Comparative Analysis of German, Israeli, American and International Law* (Springer Berlin Heidelberg, 2007), 255–298. See most recently, Yofi Tirosh, "Abnormal Normality," *Orech Hadin*, October 2013, 83. (Hebrew).

7 See particularly Phyllis Chesler and Rivka Haut eds., *Women of the Wall: Claiming Sacred Ground at Judaism's Holy Site* (Woodstock, VT: Jewish Lights Publishing, 2003).

8 In this paper I do not elaborate on the details of the Halachic controversy about the extent to which the entire communal prayer is accessible to women's participation.

9 Judaism has at least three main schools of thought and religious practice, orthodox, conservative, and reform. The orthodox school, based on a pre-enlightenment worldview, excludes women from the public sphere and delegates to them specific roles within the family and the private sphere. However, the modern orthodox movement attempts to adjust this world-view to the modern context. The reform movement, inspired by the enlightenment, upholds gender equality, and is the most willing to adjust its practice to enhance egalitarianism. The conservative school, located between the previous two schools, has accepted gender equality, and has accelerated its commitment to egalitarianism since the 1970s. See Lahav, "Seeking Recognition: Women's Struggle for Full Citizenship in the Community of Religious Worship," in *Gendering Religion and Politics* eds. H. Herzog and A. Braude (Palgrave, 2009), 125. Coming from the strictly Orthodox milieu in New York City, Haut was a pioneer in her effort to understand the intellectual underpinnings of women's exclusion, and to sift the rules requiring exclusion that are based on divine commands (and therefore may not be amended), and rules based on cultural customs which should be open to re-assessment. Her conclusion was that the prohibition on women's communal prayer is not divinely ordained. For illuminating discussions see T. Ross, *Expanding the Palace of Torah, Orthodoxy and Feminism* (Brandeis University Press, 2004) and references there, and Sperber et al., supra n. 1. Of course, whether consciously or not, these women were influenced by the spirit of the women's rights movement then raging in the United States and sending its message to other societies, but the important point to remember is that these women were committed to a religious way of life and aspired to equality within Judaism and under Jewish law. In other words, and this is crucial, these women did not wish to exit their religious communities, build other communities, or become secular. They wanted to retain their identity and have the religious law change, by shedding the skin of patriarchy, which was not divinely required, and assume an egalitarian approach, which they argued, was perfectly coherent and compatible with the core of Jewish orthodoxy.

10 See Tova Hartman, *Feminism Encounters Traditional Judaism: Resistance and Accommodation* (Waltham, MA: Brandeis University Press, 2007).

11 In keeping with traditional orthodoxy, there was no Torah scroll at the women's section, or any furniture (such as a table) to assist in the performance of the ritual. The women's section had a few prayer books, "fit for women", the space itself is a statement that women are excluded from the religious rituals.

12 In my discussion I refer to American Judaism because it represents the largest Jewish Community outside of Israel, but the reader should keep in mind that pluralistic Judaism thrives in other parts of the Jewish Diaspora, from Canada to Europe, Australia, South Africa, and parts of Asia as well. I also emphasize that

this is modern, not traditional orthodoxy, and that the emphasis on the segregation on the basis of gender was meant to honor the orthodox canon that women and men should not perform the ritual prayer together.

13 US Constitution, First Amendment: "Congress shall make no law respecting an establishment of religion, or prohibit the free exercise thereof." Fourteenth Amendment: "No state shall …deny to any person within its jurisdiction the equal protection of the laws."

14 See Cooper v. Aaron 358 U.S.I (1958) and its aftermath.

15 Indeed, the tension between Israel's image as the state of the Jewish people (Diaspora Jewry included), and of Israel as a state whose legal apparatus applies to its citizens alone, could be raised in the form of challenging ICWoW's standing to petition before the Court, as ICWoW was an extraterritorial group, but the government, evidently mindful of this potentially explosive issue, decided not to challenge their standing. Miriam Benson, in Chesler and Haut, supra n. 7, 142.

16 Both principles appear explicitly in Israel's Declaration of dependence and have been consistently honored by the courts. See generally Amnon Rubinstein and Barak Medina, *The Constitutional Law of the State of Israel*, vol. 2. (Tel Aviv: Shocken Press, 2005). (Hebrew).

17 See generally, P. Lahav, "Israel's Supreme Court" in *Contemporary Israel*, ed. R. O. Freedman, (Boulder, CO: Westview Press, 2009), 135–158.

18 Ibid.

19 Shakdiel v. Minister of Religions HC 153/87 42(2) PD (22).1, 309. Shakdiel was thereafter admitted as a member of the religious council of her local community.

20 Patricia Woods, *Judicial Power and National Politics* (New York: State University of New York Press, 2008), 160–163.

21 Poraz v. Shlomo Lahat, Mayor of Tel Aviv HC 953/87, 42 (2) PD (1988). See generally, Ruth Halperin Kaddari, *Women in Israel, A State of Their Own* (Philadelphia: University of Pennsylvania Press, 2004). For the struggle of women to vote in community elections during the pre-state period see Margalit Shiloh, "Feminist Voices regarding Gender Equality in the Struggle for the Right to Vote in the Yishuv," in *One Law for Man and Woman*, eds. Katvan et al. (Bar Ilan University Press, 2010) 221. (Hebrew).

22 See Susan Sered, comparing these two cases to the case of WoW and concluding that WoW was qualitatively different and therefore unlikely to win. However, it appears that Sered takes the orthodox position on the question of women group prayer as static (i.e., Jewish law cannot accept it). Given recent developments in the Jewish world, it may well be that the orthodox position is dynamic and capable of change, albeit a slow change. Susan Sered, "Women and Religious Change in Israel: Rebellion or Revolution," 1 *Sociology of Religion* 58 (1997).

23 See www.phyllis-chesler.com/ for comprehensive information on Chesler. Last visited on July 19, 2011.

24 Indeed, the leaders of ICWoW dedicated their book on the subject "to the State of Israel", see Chesler and Haut, supra n. 7. Like many American Jews they were somewhat infatuated with the image of the Israeli female soldier, generally a beautiful young woman carrying an Uzi. They were probably not aware of the fact that the widely spread image was a public relations ploy by the State, trying to present itself as progressive. In reality, women in the Israeli army of the late 1980s were confined to traditional female roles and hardly treated as equal. See ibid.

25 From the feminist perspective a question should be raised whether, with all of their considerable sophistication in matters of feminist theory, members of the ICWoW were not simply conforming and adhering to the patriarchal leadership of the US Jewish Community and its judgment about the legitimate contours of criticism. The call for unity has historically been deployed in order to subordinate

women's equality to other social goals. Women were encouraged to sacrifice their interests for the purpose of pursuing "other, more pressing" social agendas.

26 See generally Aronoff, in Chesler and Haut, supra n. 7. at 187: "We were tying one hand behind our back by shunning the general media and negative publicity for Israel, but concern about damaging Israel took precedence at that time."

27 There is one bright line, which the US Jewish community is not prepared to cross, and this is the issue of conversion, also known as the question of who is a Jew. Repeated efforts by the Israeli orthodox establishment to change the law of return so that it recognizes only orthodox conversions, has consistently met with the firm opposition of the American Jewish leadership. See e.g., E. Bronner, "Israel puts off crisis over conversion law," *New York Times*, July 23, 2010, www.nytimes.com/2010/07/24/world/middleeast/24israel.html (last visited July 31, 2011).

28 I.e., they were American or Brazilian or British citizens, but also Jewish, and thus a minority within the national boundaries of their respective non-Jewish polities. See S. Rabinovitch, *Jews and Diaspora Nationalism* (Brandeis, 2012).

29 Note that American Jewish politics remain relevant, as much of the emotional and financial support for the cause depended on US good will.

30 Conservative and reform Judaism, which is the overwhelming practice of American Jews, is practiced in tiny (although presently may be growing) communities, and there is an on-going legal struggle concerning state recognition of their legitimacy. See, for example, the current debate about whether reform and conservative conversions should be recognized by state institutions: see generally Woods, supra n. 20. For the decades-long struggle about recognition of conservative and reform conversions to Judaism (qualifying the convert to citizenship under the law of return) see Bryna Bogoch and Yifat Holzman Gazit, "Clashing Over Conversion: 'Who is a Jew', and Media Representations of an Israeli Supreme Court Decision," 24 no. 4 *International Journal for the Semiotics of Law*, (2011) particularly sections 3.1 to 3.3.

31 See Jonathan Sarna, *American Judaism* (Yale University Press, 2004) for a historical analysis of the development of the distinct form of American Jewish pluralism.

32 I thank Leora Bilsky for bringing this aspect to my attention. In Israel the entire matter of marriage and divorce is under rabbinical (Halachic) jurisdiction. The issues decided by the all male and often female-biased religious judges go well beyond the issue of Agunot, so familiar to American Jewish feminists.

33 Riva Haut passed away in April, 2014. J. Mark, "Rivka Haut, 71, Champion of Agunot," *The Jewish Week*, April 1, 2014.

34 http://reformjudaismmag.org/Articles/index.cfm?id=1414 (last visited July 19, 2011). Hoffman is also president of IRAC (Israel Religious Action Center) in Israel, an NGO that aims to introduce progressive Judaism into Israeli society. See www.irac.org/ (last visited on July 19, 2011).

35 The Israeli principle of the separation of church and state co-exists with state support of religion in many forms (including religious schooling). A ministry of religions is supported by taxpayers' money.

36 Israeli orthodox women, however, are discouraged from attempting to introduce gender equality into the synagogue ritual. See T. Hartman, supra n. 10. Hartman is the founder of Shira Hadasha (Hebrew for "A new song"), a Jerusalem modern orthodox synagogue based on gender equality. The synagogue was established more than a decade after Haut first led her group to pray at the Wall.

37 But see sociologist Susan Sered's insight that the problem here lies with the "traditional Jewish conflation of women and sacred text, both of which are subject to male control and scrutiny. By holding Torah scrolls at the Wall they have changed their ontological status from that of symbol to that of agent, a transformation that cannot but evoke fury in a culture predicated upon male ownership of the symbol

system." Susan Sered, *What Makes Women Sick* (Brandeis University Press, 2000), 140. See also S. Sered, "Women and Religious Change in Israel: Rebellion or Revolution," 58 *Sociology of Religion* 1 (1997).

38 Supra n. 2.

39 The segregation between the sexes at the Wall's plaza began at this time. Historically, men and women prayed together at the Kotel. See Zvi H. Triger, "Gender Segregation as Sexual Harassment," 35 *Tel Aviv University Law Review* (2013), 703–746, Iyuney Mishpat text accompanying fn. 80–86. (Hebrew).

40 For a good discussion see Gad Barzilai, *Communities and Law: Politics and Cultures of Legal Identities* (University of Michigan Press, 2003), 209.

41 For an analysis see Leah Shakdiel, "Women of the Wall: Radical Feminism as an Opportunity for a New Discourse in Israel," *Journal of Israeli History* (2002), 126. See also Raday's critique, supra n. 6.

42 See description by one of WoW's founders, Bonna Haberman: "Soon after we began our prayers in the women's section, men began to hurl objects in our direction, over the partition. Metal chairs and even a table were flying toward us... one woman was injured. A chair had landed on her head.... The border police ... refused to even descend from their vans...Finally, the police issued instructions. Two shiny silver tear gas canisters were hurled towards the crowd at the Wall... One man wearing a black suit, with phylacteries on his arm and head, masking his face with his tallis, picked up one of the canisters and pitched it directly in our midst..." Haberman, "Drama in Jerusalem", 3 at 18, in Chesler and Haut, supra n. 7.

43 For a description see Chesler and Haut, supra n. 7, 4–6.

44 In 1981, the regulations prohibited all religious rituals not held in accordance with the "custom of the space" ("minhag hamakom") and which offend the feelings of the worshippers toward the space. Rubinstein and Medina, supra n. 16, vol. 1, 378. (In Hebrew). Note that the term "space" was cleverly chosen. The Hebrew word for space is "Makom". "The custom of 'makom' " therefore implies that the banning of women from communal prayer is the will of God. Similarly, the offense to the feelings of the worshippers is "towards the makom", i.e., towards God. See discussion supra, text accompanying n. 2.

45 See Miriam Benson, "The Lawsuit: 1989–Present," in Chesler and Haut, supra n. 7, 136.

46 Frances Raday, "The Fight Against Being Silenced," in Chesler and Haut, supra n. 7, 115. See also Ruth Halperin Kaddari, *Women in Israel* (2004), supra n. 21.

47 See generally Peter L. Berger, *The Sacred Canopy: Elements of a Sociological Theory of Religion* (Doubleday, 1967), and P. Berger et al., *The Homeless Mind* (Vintage Books, 1974).

48 Sperber et al., supra n. 1. D. Sperber is an eminent rabbi as well as a professor of Jewish Law at Bar Ilan University.

49 See Rubinstein and Medina, supra n. 16, vol. 2, 378. (In Hebrew).

50 Sered (2000), supra, n. 37 at 138.

51 For example, the Rabbi of the Wall was quoted as saying that "a woman carrying the Torah is like a pig at the Wailing Wall", Susan Sered (2000) supra n. 37, 139.

52 Hereby one confronts another woe of WoW: The willingness to compromise was interpreted by hardcore orthodox as proof that WoW was not sufficiently "Jewish".

53 For information concerning the safeguarding of antiquities in Israel see: www.antiquities.org.il/about_heb.aspx?Modul_id=103 (last visited July 16, 2015). The Robinson Arch has been officially declared an archeological park. In 1995 the Israel Antiquities Authority submitted an expert opinion to the Court stating

that "it does not appear that any prayers may be conducted at the site.". http://alt-arch.org/he/holysites_heb/ (last visited July 16, 2015).

54 But it is important to stress the difference between WoW and the reform and conservative movements. WoW includes women who are strictly (modern) orthodox. It is thus a group reflecting religious pluralism in Judaism.

55 Until 1990, the major religious parties were the national religious party (Mafdal), the sephardi party (Shas), and the ultra orthodox party (Agudat Yisrael). See www.knesset.gov.il/faction/heb/FactionListAll.asp?view=1 (last visited August 16, 2011).

56 Evidently in the beginning the ICWoW was not sufficiently tuned to the feminist aspect of the controversy and more focused on the religion/state aspects of it.

57 See R. Hirschl's theory that their marginality led to their defeat at the hands of the court, R. Hirschl, *Towards Juristocracy: The Origins and the Consequences of the New Constitutionalism* (Harvard University Press, 2004). It is important to add that women still suffer extensive gender discrimination in Israel. See generally N. Rimalt, *Legal Feminism From Theory to Practice: The Struggle for Gender Equality in Israel and the United States* (Pardes Publishing House: Haifa University Press, 2010) (Hebrew) and H. Herzog ed., *Sex Gender Politics – Women in Israel* (Tel Aviv: Hakibbutz Hameuchad, 1999) (Hebrew).

58 Hoffman v. Western Wall Commissioner (the Rabbi of the Wall) 48(2) PD 265 (1994).

59 Even though Justice Elon was a distinguished scholar of Jewish law, his opinion has not met due deference in the orthodox world. For the orthodox, Elon represented the secular establishment (by virtue of his service on a secular court) and his opinion was therefore not considered authoritative. As a learned scholar of Jewish law said to me: "Elon said it, so what? His opinion does not matter to those in authority."

60 For a chronology, see Chesler and Haut, supra n. 7, 362.

61 Hoffman v. Prime Minister Office, 2 Tak-Al 846 (2000). Quite naively and short-sightedly, I celebrated the opinion as a happy ending to the saga. P. Lahav, "Up Against the Wall," 16 *Israel Studies Bulletin* 19 (2000). One of the early predecessors, if not the first, of the technique of declaring a bold principle of law but refraining from offering a remedy is Brown v. Board of Education II, where the Supreme Court of the United States ordered segregation "with all deliberate speed". The agony of creating a social crisis is clear in both cases.

62 See Menachem Mautner, *Law and the Culture of Israel* (Oxford: Oxford University Press, 2010) discussing the nature of the tension between the religious and the secular camps and their cultural and legal ramifications. See also Rubinstein and Medina, supra n. 16, vol. 2, chapter 6. (In Hebrew). The foremost Israeli scholar studying religious society in Israel and its interaction with secular society is Menachem Friedman. Friedman has published several books and many articles about this subject, and the reader is referred to his scholarship.

63 Compare the hardships described by Tova Hartman as she went forth with her plan to establish an egalitarian synagogue in Jerusalem, supra n. 10.

64 Compare the confrontation between the pro-segregation forces in the American South and the National Guard, sent by President Eisenhower to enforce the Supreme Court's order. Eisenhower was not a supporter of desegregation, but deployed the machinery of the federal government to defend the constitution as interpreted by the Supreme Court. See T.A Freyer, *The Little Rock Crisis: A Constitutional Interpretation* (Greenwood Press, 1984).

65 Further hearing 4128/00, Director of Prime Minister's Office v. Hoffman, 47(3) PD 289.

66 Faye Lederman, "Women of the Wall", www.newday.com/films/WomenoftheWall.html (last visited on July 19, 2011), and Yael Katzir, "In Her Own Voice", http://israelfilm.blogspot.com/2009/02/women-of-wall.html (last visited on July 19, 2011). YouTube also has a number of videos on this subject.

67 See Rabbi Daniel Sperber, "Congregational Dignity and Human Dignity," in 3:2 *The Edah Journal Elul* 5763 1–14 (2002); and Rabbi Mendel Shapira, "Qeri'at ha-Torah by Women: A Halachic Analysis," in *Women and Men in Communal Prayer*, ed. Chaim Trachtman, (New York: JOFA in Association with Ktav Publishing, 2010) at 27 and 207.

68 See e.g., Leah Aharoni, "Women of the Wall: An Agent of Contention," Sh'ma, October, 2013, 5. This organization also has a website, http://womenforthewall.org/; it is interesting that the argument from "modesty" does not appear in Aharoni's column. WoW is urged to defer to the Orthorox patriarch in the name of "unity".

69 The first woman to be arrested was Nofrat Frenkel. The chilling effect of such an arrest is significant. Frenkel was a medical student, and a conviction could jeopardize her chances to get a license to practice medicine. For Ms Frenkel's description of the event see http://judaism.about.com/b/2009/11/24/in-her-own-words-nofrat-frenkel.htm (last visited July 29, 2011). Thereafter Anat Hoffman, the leader of the group was arrested as well, www.huffingtonpost.com/anat-hoffman/arrested-for-praying-at-western-wall_b_1987099.html.

70 See Daniela Dekel, "Speaking to the Wall", http://womenofthewall.org.il/wp-content/uploads/2013/05/%D7%9E%D7%93%D7%91%D7%A8%D7%95%D7%AA-%D7%90%D7%9C-%D7%94%D7%A7%D7%99%D7%A8-1.pdf, Yediot Acharonot, Shiva Yamim, 6.14.2013, p. 32 (Hebrew). This is a particularly insightful discussion of WoW from the Israeli Secular perspective.

71 "Number of Days" appeal number 23834-04. Unpublished. Author's archives.

72 Judge Sobel's opinion is quite legalistic and takes no accout of context; still one may make the following observations. First, by now WoW may be credited with a substantial body of both secular and Halachic opinions supporting its rights: the holding by Justice Elon, a scholar of Jewish law, that women do have the right to pray communally under Jewish law, and the holding of the unanimous three-judge panel that secular Israeli law and fundamental principles of civil rights support their petition, and the dissenting opinions of the four justices in the third round. These too, are well crafted and well written opinions. Other opinions by Israeli courts denouncing plans of gender segregation in the public sector fortify the principle of gender equality and further undercut the notion that there is something about women that is not modest and should therefore be confined. It should also be pointed out that Judge Sobel appears to be a religious man. His Resume discloses that he is a yeshiva graduate. Hence he must have been quite familiar with the debate about women's rights under Halacha. While he does not mention the Halachic controversy, it may well be that he thinks that Halacha is not averse to women's equal rights.

73 For my analysis of this case see Pnina Lahav, "Women of the Wall: A Temporary but Meaningful Milestone," 9 *Hamishpat online: Human rights – insight into recent judgements* 4 (June 2013) (English), www.colman.ac.il/research/research_institute/katedra_HumanRights/Psika/Documents/9/9_june_2013_3_Lahav_EN.pdf; see also Yossi Nechushtan, criticizing the methodology of Sobel's opinion (while agreeing with the result), www.colman.ac.il/research/research_institute/katedra_HumanRights/Psika/Documents/9/9_june_2013_4_nehushtan.pdf

74 The recommendations were released on May 9, 2013. http://index.justice.gov.il/Pubilcations/Articles/Pages/HadaratNasim.aspx.

75 See e.g., "Shas mobilizes seminary girls to disrupt Women of the Wall prayer service", Haaretz, October 4, 2013, www.haaretz.com/news/israel/.premium-1.550540, (last visited July 16, 2015).
76 I thank Assaf Likhovsky for pointing this important point to me.
77 www.phyllis-chesler.com/1189/drawn-to-holiness-women-of-the-wall-speak-to. Rivka Haut (who passed away since) was one of the signatories of the letter. Most of the women who signed the letter gave a US address.

8 Religious coercion and violence against women

The case of Beit Shemesh

*Sima Zalcberg Block**

Introduction

The rise of fundamentalist movements and the phenomenon of religious zealotry have been among the main characteristics of the past three decades all over the world, and they have a significant impact on contemporary society and culture (Appleby and Marty, 2002; Dawson, 1998; Litvak and Limor, 2007). This phenomenon in the modern era is mainly a counter-response to the secularization process that led to the loss of the hegemonic position of religion, to the marginalization of religion, and to a feeling of distress due to the secular lifestyle (Almond et al., 2003).

Religious zealotry is characterized by a tendency to increase the level of rigor and severity of the system of religious observance; favoring a strict interpretation of religious law (halakha); applying religious law to all areas of life; and the use of religious coercion (Liebman, 1983). The zealot is also characterized by a tendency to hold an apocalyptic worldview, which sees life as an expression of a cosmic struggle between God and Satan, between good and evil, and between the righteous and the sinners. Consistent with this, zealot groups emphasize a distinction between purity of their own community and impurity of the outside world (Almond et al., 2003; Appleby and Marty, 2002; Douglas, 1966). To do so, they create "enclave cultures" that build social and cultural barriers between themselves and the outside "sinner" world (Sivan, 1995).

The zealots believe that only they possess the divine truth and therefore they are the ones who represent the will of God on earth (Appleby and Marty, 2002; Liebman, 1983). In extreme cases, religious zealotry leads to extreme actions which end in violence toward others. The turn to violence stems from the zealot's feeling that he derives the authority for his actions from God, and that the severity of danger to the true faith justifies taking every possible measure (Litvak and Limor, 2007).

In recent years, one of the main hubs of violence based on religious zealotry and religious coercion in Israel has been located in the city of Beit Shemesh (Zalcberg, 2009). These incidents involve harsh acts of violence perpetrated by local radical haredim (ultra-Orthodox), who have made the lives of many of the city's residents so unbearable as to cause them to leave town.

Expressions of religio-ideological violence by haredi zealots are not a new development (Ben-Yehuda, 2010; Caplan, 2010; Friedman, 2002). Menachem Friedman explained that as the haredi society perceived itself through the years as being under constant threat from the surrounding secular society and engaged in an unremitting struggle to preserve its self-definition, it has conducted its wars against modernity and secularization through various forms of violence. Nachman Ben-Yehuda claimed that the culture war taking place in Israel between the secular and the haredim – as a result of the lack of legal separation between religion and state – leads to tension between the two sides, and the various expressions of violence are a central feature of this tension. Friedman as well as Ben-Yehuda stress that violence is a common phenomenon in haredi society, which derives from a theological notion that all Jews are mutually responsible, and that sins of the few are paid for by the many.

Ben-Yehuda's study (2010) showed that the violence of the haredim is not random or a result of momentary outbursts of anger, but systematic, planned, and aimed at pushing Israel toward a more theocratic society. However, as Friedman (2002) emphasized, manifestations of extreme violence and terror that risk human life or lead to serious physical injury are utterly taboo in the haredi society. Therefore, violence in this society is generally defined, circumscribed, and controlled by the religious authorities, both through education and effective social control.

Violent activity by haredi extremists aims most prominently at those who violate their norms of sexual behavior. This is expressed mainly in verbal abuse, but sometimes also in physical violence, towards women in haredi neighborhoods who have breached the locally accepted code of modesty (Friedman, 2002). Yet, in recent years, it seems that the nature of violence among certain segments of the haredi public has changed, with violence directed by extremist zealots at violators of accepted modesty norms increasing and becoming unbridled.

Evidence of this can be found in present-day events in Beit Shemesh: "lawlessness", "Wild West", "organized crime", "fear" and "It's likely to end in murder" are just some of the expressions used by residents of Beit Shemesh in an attempt to describe what has been happening in the city in recent years. Even many of the haredim, both residents of Beit Shemesh and those living in other places, have noted that slightly different rules apply in Beit Shemesh than the familiar rules of haredi society, and that here there is unprecedented religious extremism.

Public awareness of the events in Beit Shemesh increased sharply in 2011, as a result of incidents involving Na'ama Margolis. Margolis, a third grade student, from a national religious family, was perpetually being spat upon and threatened by haredi extremists while she was walking home from school, because her appearance was not modest enough for these radical zealots. Margolis' case sparked the Israeli media, and led to mass demonstrations and public battles against the haredi population in Israel.

Although Margolis' story was only exposed in 2011, it is important to emphasize that she was neither the first nor the last victim who experienced abusive behavior from the local haredim. This is a phenomenon that has lasted for more than 15 years, and many of the city's residents have complained about it.

In light of these events, the purpose of this article is to present the various arenas in which religious coercion and violence have been triggered in Beit Shemesh, to point out the characteristics of the people who commit these violent activities, and to provide insights into the processes and factors that have made Beit Shemesh into a center of religious extremist activity.

The article is based on ethnographic work (Fetterman, 1989; Atkinson and Hammersley, 1994) including lengthy tours in Beit Shemesh, especially in its haredi neighborhoods. During the field work I conducted "incidental" interviews with a variety of people I met in the various neighborhoods of Beit Shemesh. The "incidental" interviews seem like friendly casual conversation, but behind them lies a clear research agenda. They are considered particularly useful for learning about meaningful categories in the community under study, revealing the thoughts of local residents in order to examine similarities and differences in their perspectives. Thus, they can help in learning about the acceptable behavior norms in the community and identifying shared values of its members (Fetterman, 1989). In addition I conducted in-depth interviews (Reinharz, 1992; Patton, 1990) with a wide spectrum of residents who suffer from the haredi extremism, including secular, religious Zionists, and haredi population alike. Furthermore, I spoke with several members of those extremist groups, with the rabbis who direct and back them, with key people in the municipality, as well as with local health and mental health professionals who provide services to the local population.

Background of the haredi population in Beit Shemesh

Beit Shemesh is a city in Jerusalem County, Israel. It is geographically located in the center of the State of Israel, 10 minutes south of the highway connecting Tel Aviv and Jerusalem in foothills of the Judean mountains, about a forty or fifty minute drive to Jerusalem or Tel Aviv.

The haredi population of Beit Shemesh constitutes roughly half the city's population, and it includes more than 40,000 people.[1] They are concentrated mainly in three neighborhoods: HaKirya HaHaredit, Ramat Beit Shemesh (meaning Beit Shemesh Heights) A, and Ramat Beit Shemesh B (hereafter, HaKirya, Ramah A and Ramah B, respectively).

HaKirya HaHaredit (meaning the Haredi borough) was the first haredi neighborhood in the city, established in 1994. Initially, this neighborhood was populated primarily by families from the radical Toldot Aharon hasidic sect and the Yerushalmi (Jerusalemite) group who represent the radical tradition of the Ashkenazi, anti-Zionist *Old Yishuv*.[2] These families had been living in the Mea Shearim neighborhood of Jerusalem and were forced to leave because of a housing shortage. Since this population is characterized by anti-Zionist attitudes (Friedman, 1991; Caplan, 2010), and its members object to settlement beyond the Green Line, they saw Beit Shemesh as a reasonably suitable location for a new community that would be led in the spirit of their original community in Jerusalem.

It is important to note that the move to HaKirya in Beit Shemesh was not a simple matter for these people, who advocate social separation from general society and who for years had been closed off in a kind of "haredi ghetto" (Friedman, 1991), which it rarely they left. Regarding the meaning of the move and internal group tensions which accompanied it, we can learn from Moshe,[3] a member of the Toldot Aharon hasidic sect and a resident of Beit Shemesh:

> For many years our community feared crossing boundaries and the effects of the world outside, and the group members feared that the transition would lead to the influence of the secular society on our youth. Therefore the group's elite spoke out against leaving the old neighborhood. After long discussions, the decision was made to move, and when we announced that we were coming to Beit Shemesh, other haredi groups began to join us. Over time people from all the groups arrived, and now it is a mosaic of all the haredi circles.

And indeed, the three haredi neighborhoods in Beit Shemesh are populated with families from a very wide spectrum of haredi groupings, including: the *Edah Haredit*[4] (hereinafter: the *Edah*) in all its denominations (mainly in HaKirya and Ramah B); hasidim from various hasidic courts that are not part of the *Edah*, such as Ger, Vizhnits and Chabad (in HaKirya, Ramah A and Ramah B); Litvaks-Yeshivish[5] (hereinafter 'Litvaks'), mostly considered moderate and some considered radical (in HaKirya and mainly Ramah A); Haredi Sephardim (in HaKirya, Ramah A and Ramah B); and *ba'alei teshuvah* (newly observant) (mainly in Ramah B).

Ramah B is located between HaKirya and Ramah A. In its center, on Nehar HaYarden Street, live members of the "extremist group of the 'Yerushalmim'," in the language of the residents. This street is the main thoroughfare connecting Ramah B to Ramah A – which also includes non-haredi neighborhoods. This, then, is a zone that is not totally separated out, and a non-haredi population is accustomed to passing through it (Zalcberg, 2009b).

Ramah A is situated above Ramah B. Whereas HaKirya is populated only by haredi families and the vast majority of Ramah B is also haredi (with a small national-religious minority), in Ramah A only half of the families are haredi, with the other half being mostly national-religious and a minority of secular residents (Kahaner, 2009). As a result, the place is considered more religiously "open-minded" than Ramah B or HaKirya.

Another neighborhood, Ramat Beit Shemesh C (Ramah C), is a new area situated above Ramah A. Ramah C began to be developed only in 2013. During tenders marketing for the neighborhood, conflicts arose between the haredi population and other populations in the city regarding construction areas. The conflicts were severe enough that many tenders for the area were canceled (Kahaner, 2009). Currently the area is under advanced stages of construction, with apartments directed more toward modern Orthodox and moderate ultra-Orthodox families (Litvaks) who have no hand in the violence. It is the haredi residents of the first three neighborhoods (HaKirya, Ramah A, and Ramah B) that are involved in the tension that besets the city, in acts of religious coercion, and in violence. The different ways they demonstrate violent behavior against residents of the city are elaborated below.

Vandalism, graffiti and "modesty signs"

The entire length of Nehar HaYarden Street, the main road leading from Ramah A to Ramah B, is littered with destroyed remnants of park benches which are unfit for sitting. These remnants result from systematic acts of uprooting seats from benches on the street leaving only the backrests, mute testimony to deliberate vandalism. The benches were modified by a group of extremist zealots from Ramah B to prevent immodest sitting by women, or mixed seating of men and women together. Rivki, a local haredi woman, explained:

> There is a group of fanatic zealots from Ramah B, and they are the ones who tore out all of our benches here. My friend saw them doing it, and she wanted to call the police, but in the end she didn't. She was afraid that they would hurt her. They did it to prevent women from sitting on the benches because they think it is an offense to modesty. They don't want men and women – even a husband and wife – to sit on a bench together.

The story of the "modesty benches" appears with a twist in public parks of Ramah B, where signs are posted demanding women avoid sitting on benches in order to preserve their inner modesty, citing the verse from Psalms 45:14, "The daughter of the king is all glorious within."

Furthermore, guests arriving at a wedding hall in Ramah B, find fliers on their car that ask them to refrain from loitering in the neighborhood before they enter the wedding hall and when they leave it.

An example:

> Respected Guest
> You have come here to celebrate a happy event of a relative or friend. We would like to call your attention to the fact [...] that most of the residents here keep far away from the spirit of the street, including that known as 'haredi', both in the garb of the men and even more so, in the garb of the women, and other matters of holiness and modesty.
> Therefore, if you do not fit the spirit of the place, know that this makes us very unhappy and mortally wounds our most innermost feelings. We came here before they opened the wedding halls, with one sole purpose motivating us, to be separated and far from such sights, and when you come here – although this certainly was not your intention – you shoot poison arrows into our heart!
> This is not your fault [...] but because of the urgency of the situation, we appeal to you with a request [...] in order not to destroy our lives, please remain in the wedding hall from the moment of arrival until you decide to go home, and when you leave, try to do this quietly and quickly without delay [...].
> Thank you for your consideration and understanding.
> - The neighborhood residents

It is important to mention that most of the couples who are married in the wedding hall are themselves haredim, and accordingly, the vast majority of their guests are haredim or national-religious. And yet the external appearance of people from most circles in haredi society are not acceptable to the extremist residents of the neighborhood, and they mentioned this explicitly in the flier, when they say that "most of the residents here keep far away from the spirit of the street, *including that known as 'haredi'*." In this way the flier expresses the extremist residents' attempt to separate themselves from the general haredi public, as well as their being stricter in matters of modesty even in comparison to most other haredim.

In Ramah A, too, similar scenarios play out. Residents told of playground equipment for children that was removed for reasons of modesty. Representatives of one of the extremist groups in the city contacted the municipality and asked for removal of playground equipment that had been placed in the public park, close to houses of the national-religious community. The reason was a "problem of modesty" posed by girls playing in the park. According to those residents, the mayor did not stand up to the pressure of these extremists and he capitulated to their demands.

Signposts on the subject of modesty are not lacking in Ramah A either. At the entrance to the local supermarket, located in the heart of the commercial center, visitors are greeted by the following sign:

> Women walking through our neighborhood are requested to respect the residents' feelings and to come
> DRESSED IN MODEST CLOTHING ONLY
> Modest clothing includes: a buttoned-up blouse with long sleeves,
> a long skirt that is not tightly fitted
> Neighborhood Rabbis Torah and Charity Institutions The Residents

The residents of the neighborhood reported that the sign has undergone several transformations: it was first posted nine years ago, and was removed by municipal inspectors following a protest by residents belonging to the national-religious community who claimed that the sign offended them. The response of the extremist circles was not long in coming. They began violent disturbances, closing off roads, and spraying graffiti all over the streets in the spirit of "Walk here dressed modestly". It was not long before the modesty sign returned and was fixed above the entrance to the supermarket. Several residents appealed to the management of the supermarket and complained that the sign was against the law and demanded that it be removed. However, the management refused to remove the sign and explained that radical haredi residents had threatened to harm them if they removed it. And so, the sign is displayed there in all its glory to this day, and its presence outrages non-haredi residents and haredi residents who do not identify with the extremists.

The situation around the supermarket has intensified. Ilanit, a local resident who defines herself as "a religious woman" recounted:

> One day when I came to the supermarket dressed as usual in a long skirt (below the knees) and a blouse with sleeves, I saw a "modesty stand" stationed at the entrance to the store. The woman operating it handed me a long piece of cloth and asked me to cover myself.

The "modesty stand" operated for several months until it was removed under pressure from residents who objected to it.

It seems like the extremists are not satisfied with one sign at the entrance to the supermarket; in almost all shops in the commercial center, those entering are greeted with the following sign:

> Honored customers,
> We respect the feelings of the neighborhood residents.
> Accordingly, you are requested to enter dressed in modest
> and appropriate clothing only.

According to the residents, many of the business proprietors displayed these signs after radical haredim threatened them with a buyers' boycott, with smashing their shop windows, and even with physically harming them and their family members. "Many of the shop-owners here live in fear", said Yael, a local resident who belongs to the national-religious community and works for a local social service.

> I saw a gun held by one of our patrons where I work, and since I know that he doesn't live or work beyond the Green Line, I asked him why he carries a gun. He explained that he had received threats because he refused to place this sign in his store window.

And if that were not enough, residents have reported that in the commercial center, self-appointed "modesty inspectors" – male haredim – have approached women whom they regard as immodestly clad and warned them to dress more appropriately. There is a sense, said the residents, that these radicals are "lying in wait" in the commercial center, ready to pounce on their prey.

Graffiti is also frequently used by the extremists. For example, just a few moments before submitting this article, I learned that the word "woman" had been erased with black paint from the sign "Woman's Health Center" of them Leumit Health Services (HMO clinic) for women in Ramah B."Apparently, they think their women don't need any health or services," said a local resident. "It's no longer of matter of respect or modesty. It's complete exclusion" (Yanovsky, 2015).

Physical Violence

Zealous preservation of women's modesty is one of the most prominent characteristics of the extremist groups in Beit Shemesh. It manifests itself in both verbal and physical violence: from destroying street posters showing women's faces to cursing female pedestrians in the street, to spitting, throwing stones, and even striking them.

Yael, who lives close to HaKirya, remarked that "a person who destroys a woman's face on a poster is capable of destroying a woman's face in the flesh." She knows this from her personal experience: she experienced physical violence when one day she removed a sign, "Please appear in modest dress," which had been posted near her house. In response, rocks were hurled at her. Yael is not the only one: Debbie, a local resident, had to endure stones, spittle, and curses hurled at her over the course of her morning run. Michal, a young female local resident, boarded a Mehadrin (strict) bus (where men sit in front and women are required to sit at the back) without realizing the travel rules. She sat down in the front in the area designated for men, and, consequently, was beaten severely by other passengers.

Daniella, a 15-year-old girl who belongs to the national-religious community, had a particularly bad experience. One Friday night, after the Sabbath meal, Daniella and two of her friends left her house to walk towards Ramah B. On the way the girls noticed a gang of haredi men. "Those men," Daniella's mother related.

> attacked the three girls, threw eggs at them, and one man approached my daughter and kicked her hard from behind. One of the girls started to run away, another yelled at them, "I'm a Jewish girl, leave me alone", and my daughter, after being kicked and beaten, was rolling on the ground, unable to escape. At the other end of the street was a group of national-religious youth, and one of the boys who was there ran over to help, yelling at the group of haredi men "How dare you attack a Jewish girl?" He was unable to help the girls because the haredim pounced on

> him and beat him. A haredi woman from a nearby building heard the noise and opened her window to check what was happening. When she understood what was going on, she called to the girls to run quickly into her building. My daughter managed to pick herself up, and she and her friend ran into the building. The woman took the girls into her home, took care of them, and went to check what had happened to the third girl. After about an hour, when it calmed down outside, she put a robe on my daughter so she would look haredi and walked her home. That same woman told us that the situation was much worse than we think, and that they live in constant fear.

About the motive for the behavior of the assailants I heard from Yentl, a haredi woman who belongs to one of the extreme groups:

> On Friday night, when the men leave the "tish"[6], we take pains to make sure that they will not see girls on the street. After all, why should hasidim see all that garbage after all the songs and all that holiness that they absorb at the *tish*? So they made sure that some of the streets have a patrol assistant to do what has to be done.

To my query of what the patrol assistant does, Yentl replied: "He doesn't have a defined task. It's his feeling that tells him what to do. He makes sure that there are no punks or immodest women walking around."

These stories of Yael, Debbie, Michal, and Daniella are only a few examples among many that illustrate the physical violence which religious extremists in Beit Shemesh have perpetrated against women whose outward appearance was not sufficiently modest, from their perspective.

This violence does not spare haredi men either, who are seen by the local zealots as contributing in one form or another to improper and immodest behavior. Thus, a group of zealots made accusations against a haredi pizzeria owner in Ramah B, and poured gasoline and tar on the seats and floor of his establishment because the attire of some of the customers did not meet their standards.

Yoel, a haredi *ba'al teshuvah*, reported that a group of radicals dragged him and his son to a nearby forest, where they were viciously beaten with a hammer. The reason, explained Yoel, was:

> because those radicals claimed that they saw my son, who is now seventeen years old, walking around with girls in the street. My son does not walk around with girls; he walks with his sister, who is sixteen years old, but even that has now become forbidden.

These radicals did not stop at beatings, but brought a bulldozer to destroy part of the walls of Yoel's private home. This was the last straw for the family, who felt compelled to leave the city.

The significance of the stringent supervision of modesty

Friedman (2002) maintained that violence in reaction to a violation of modesty norms is not alien to Jewish tradition because of association with the biblical Pinchas, who killed Zimri for breaching morality codes of sexual behavior (Num. 25). Although this particular example is extreme, the Pinchas incident, as well as other violent activities in response to violations of sexual norms throughout Jewish history, have been role models for potential zealots (Friedman, 2002). These violent responses to violations of what zealots consider proper modest behavior raise questions about the meaning of the demands for stringent regulations of modesty.

Sexual permissiveness has always been perceived as a threat to the sanctified character of the Jewish people (Friedman, 2002), so that a supervision of sexuality has characterized all movements and groups within Orthodox Jewish society (Elior, 2001; Hartman, 2007). The haredi society in Beit Shemesh, like haredi society in general, is characterized by the strict supervision of sexuality (Aran, 2003; Zalcberg, 2009; Zalcberg and Zalcberg, 2012). One manifestation of this supervision is demanding of women an outward appearance that is in keeping with strict rules of modesty (Heilman, 1992; Zalcberg, 2007, 2011). Given this fact, it is no wonder that in "their" space, in "their" territory, the haredi public insists on certain standards of modesty both for haredi women and for non-haredi women who visit the area. Yet it seems that the issues surrounding this modesty as reflected in haredi neighborhoods in Beit Shemesh goes beyond what is accepted in most haredi circles in Jewish society, and is directed with great force inwardly, too – at the haredi public itself.

Many scholars see the strict modesty standards, in any society, as a means of concealing the woman's body and denying her rights over her own body, and they interpret these norms as an expression of discrimination, exclusion, and patriarchal silencing and oppression (Arthur, 1999; Daly, 1999; El Guindi, 1999; Elior, 2001). In Jewish tradition, there are various aspects in the religious rulings and rabbinic sayings that exclude women from the public realm and silence her. These aspects, claimed Rachel Elior (2001), are associated with a worldview known as 'modesty', which is based on forced protection that limits the woman. This view identifies the woman's honor with her modesty and her obedience, and the honor of the man with his control over woman's modesty and her obedience, while concepts, sayings, and verses that relate to women's modesty are all associated with her sexuality and control of it. Thus, at the overt level, modesty is a term used for making women disappear from view, and at the covert level, it is an expression of men's rights to control women's sexuality, which is perceived as being inherently dangerous and defiling (Elior, 2001).

Karen McCarthy-Brown (1994) claimed that severe modesty restrictions are salient characteristics of fundamentalist religious views in the modern world. According to her, fundamentalists strive to control the hidden forces of the human body and physical desires, especially sexual desire, which they consider a major threat. Since in most cultures women are seen as bearing the major portion of human physicality and sensuality, fundamentalists see them as the object onto which whatever is undesirable or threatening to human existence can be projected: sexuality, emotions, ritual impurity, sin, and death. Therefore, the fundamentalist agenda is focused on enabling men's control over women and supervising their sexuality, reflected by imposing severe modesty norms on them. In this light, one can see the strict regime of modesty in Beit Shemesh as the product of a view that sees women – by their inherent nature – as a threat to the spiritual world of men. And in order to minimize the threat they personify, to keep men from temptation, and to guarantee their moral conduct, stringent norms of modesty are imposed on women (Hartman, 2007).

It is important to note that many moderate haredi residents of Beit Shemesh have recoiled at this perception and at the extremism in matters of modesty derived from it, and they emphasize that extremism and violence are alien to the spirit of Haredi Judaism. Yosef, a local haredi, argued that

> these behaviors stem from two main sources: sexual frustrations that these haredi men must release, and cannot because of the norms of their society; and corrupt people who are themselves deviants from the religious norms regulating sexual behavior, and then exhibit extreme behavior to quiet their conscience on the subject. People with pure motives do not attack others! The more one goes among people with the more extreme behavior, the more problems one sees in the field of sexuality. In this fanatic society, there are no accepted channels for treating sexual problems. They hush up the problems, and the result is that these people become fanatic and violent in all matters relating to modesty.

Yosef's evaluation of the stringent supervision of sexuality is what we explain in Freudian terminology as the product of employing the defense mechanism of "reaction formation." In this mechanism a person expresses urges and feelings that are the opposite of his real urges and feelings, which are threatening – such as unconventional sexual drives and forbidden fantasies – with the object of curbing them so that he can live in society in accordance with its accepted norms (Hall 1999; Rycroft 1995). Thus, the use of a reaction formation mechanism – in the form of enforced modesty – is an expression of their internal conflict and a defense against instinctive reactions.

Yosef's further evaluation, of hushing up problems in sexuality within this public, is in line with the work of Sara Zalcberg (2014, 2015) and Friedman (2006), who claimed that there is a conspiracy of silence in haredi society surrounding everything that pertains to sexuality, to general problems in this area, and especially to sexual violence.

In addition, Yosef claimed that there is an inevitable connection between the exaggerated supervision of modesty exercised by the extremists in Beit

Shemesh and corrupt personal traits. According to him, the exaggerated preoccupation with modesty is, in fact, the "complete opposite of modesty." He argued:

> If you do not wish men to think bad thoughts [about women and about sex], why are you dealing with this all the time? Why are you writing about it all over? Modesty is what is hidden, not what is out in the open. These people do not understand the obvious contradiction in their behavior.

It seems that overly stringent supervision of sexuality, as it exists in Beit Shemesh, paradoxically results in extensive discourse about sex, and leads to an intensive, if not obsessive, preoccupation with sex. Michel Foucault (1980, 1984) claimed that the discourse on sexuality becomes a means of control over society, as the ramifications of such a discourse are a knowledge monopoly that defines what may and what may not be said. Consequently, one may view the discourse on sexuality that has erupted in every corner of the haredi neighborhoods of Beit Shemesh as part of the supervision and control mechanisms imposed by the radical zealots on all the residents.

Denial of "the *other*" and his lifestyle

Although the focus of this article is religious coercion regarding modesty and violence as a reaction to "lack of modesty", it is noteworthy that residents of Beit Shemesh suffer from violent harassment for other reasons as well. I will refer to these in brief because it supplies context for what is happening in the city and to sharpen insights into what characterizes these haredi zealots and the motives that drive their behavior.

The residents of Beit Shemesh suffer harassment because of "desecration of the Sabbath", as defined by the extremists. Residents who drove on the Sabbath (henceforth: Shabbat) in neighborhoods close to the haredi neighborhoods of Beit Shemesh, or on the main highway that passes through them, have been complaining for a decade and half about harassment and rock-throwing at their cars. Ronit, for example, reported that she, her husband, and son suffered a violent attack by haredi residents because they dared to drive on Shabbat on a road that passes through Ramah B:

> During the trip, a group of some 100 haredi men blocked the only means of access to our neighborhood. My husband left the car in an attempt to handle the matter, and my son drove a bit forward and parked the car on the side of the road. And then, they all jumped us, spit on us, cursed us, pushed us onto the ground, and kicked us. People around, who saw what was happening and wanted to help us, were afraid to get near because they would have received the same treatment.

These extremist haredim also do not spare ambulances that carry people on Shabbat even when required to save a life. Rivki, who is a haredi woman, as was stated, related that her husband is a volunteer paramedic and ambulance driver. He is occasionally called out on Shabbat to go to the hospital, and many times when he drives the ambulance on Shabbat, he is accompanied by disapproving shouts of "Shabbos, Shabbos."

The behavior of the haredi zealots reflects their opposition to anyone whose lifestyle and beliefs differ from theirs, and they try to impose their way on others. An additional expression of denial of the *other* may be seen in the demand by certain haredi rabbis to close a ritual bath (*mikvah*) which was built in an area of national-religious population in Ramah A. Benjamin, a haredi local resident, explained the reason was that "the *mikvah* attendant was a woman of Sephardic origin who belonged to the national-religious community, and the rabbis demanded that the mikvah be closed until the attendant was replaced by a haredi, Ashekenazi woman." For these extremists, the *other* is anyone who is not of their ethnic origin, whose lifestyle is different than theirs, and whose sexual preferences are not legitimate by their standards.

Thus, one conspicuous activity of an extremist group in Beit Shemesh, took place several years ago, when members of the group came out against the gay parade in Jerusalem. This was done despite the fact that rabbis of general haredi public asked everyone to refrain from demonstrations and provocations because the parade did not pass through haredi neighborhoods of Jerusalem. Yosef recounted:

> They actually turned Beit Shemesh upside down; they ripped out trees from the middle of the street, turned over garbage cans, and rolled them onto the highway. Garbage cans were rolled towards men, women, and children, and almost ran down baby carriages. This is unprecedented fanaticism. In Jerusalem they never reached such a level, throwing rocks that almost killed babies. They also set fire to a forest nearby.

Another expression of intolerance of the extremists is their disrespect for symbols and ceremonies of the Zionist public in the city, particularly on Memorial Day and Independence Day. These days are days of woe for non-haredi residents because their radical neighbors have anti-Zionist opinions and demonstrate them publicly. Many residents have reported that these extremists mock anyone who stands during the sounding of the siren,[7] rip the national flag off cars and private homes, and hang black flags as a sign of mourning over the establishment of the Jewish State.

The vilification and offense are not directed exclusively at the secular or national-religious public, but at anyone whose ways are different from the haredi zealots. This can be seen in the wall posters (pashquivilim) that extremists post in the city's haredi neighborhoods, which defame the local

Chabad (Lubavitch) hasidim and their yeshiva heads because they take part in the national elections.

The harassment of *others* as described above demonstrates the inability of these extremist haredim to tolerate people whose lifestyle and *weltanschauung* are different from their own, and a desire to force all the residents to adopt their ways. As Shlomo, a haredi resident observes, they "wish to show the residents who is the real boss."

Who are these extremists and how are they perceived among the local residents?

The haredi community does not constitute one uniform bloc, but has a wide spectrum of groups and denominations (Friedman, 1991). Many of the few remaining secular people in these neighborhoods, and even most of the national-religious who live there, do not distinguish among the various haredi groups when complaining that "haredim" have taken over the area and are inciting violence against its inhabitants. The haredim, for their part, are aware that they are talking about only a few extreme groups that impose a reign of terror upon haredi circles as well. Moreover, among the local haredim, there are some who are trying to battle this minority of radical zealots, because these zealots have been infringing upon their quality of life, have been intimidating the haredi "silent majority," as they put it, and have been defaming the general haredi public.

A large portion of the radical activists originate from the Mea Shearim neighborhood in Jerusalem, and belong to the "Yerushalmi" and Neturei Karta (an Aramaic phrase meaning "Guardians of the Wall") factions.[8] These factions have a rich history of violent activity spurred by religious zealotry, years before the move to Beit Shemesh (Friedman, 2002). Over time their presence has become stronger in Ramah B, and today they control extensive sections of the neighborhood.

Many of these radical zealots operate within groups that bear names like *Tiferet Yerushalaym* [glory of Jerusalem], *Anshei Yerushalayim* [people of Jerusalem], *Kehal Hasidei Yerushalayim* [Congregation of Jerusalem Hasidim], and *Mishkenot HaRo'im* [Dwellings of the Shepherds, i.e., Leaders]. By estimates of the neighborhood residents, "these groups add up to some 200 people who are the 'hard-core' and another 400 who join occasionally." In Ramah A, too, there are extremist groups. This refers mainly to groups of the Litvak-haredi movement.

Local residents, including moderate haredim and health and mental health professionals, noted that these are particularly problematic people from a low socio-economic level. Most consist of *kollel* (yeshiva for married men) students who are idle, without profession or employment, whose level of education is very low even in relation to haredim from other groups. They also include first and second generation of *ba'alei teshuvah*. This finding is not surprising because extremist religious movements tend to attract people from the fringes of society, characterized by a low socio-economic status (Appleby and Marty, 2002; Lipset, 1981). The residents, both haredi and others, explained the violent activities of the zealots as something for them to do in their spare time. Since they have nothing else with which to occupied themselves, it fulfills their quest for thrills and challenges. "After all", said Yankl, "this behavior is the result of lack of occupation. They don't go to the army and they have no other way to release their energy." Yechiel, one of the leading activists in the fight against violence in the city, joined in "They are looking for action in a religious guise – action that includes violence and spitting at women and the like. They base their fanaticism on their religion and think that being faithful to God is being extremist."

It turns out that some of the zealots of Beit Shemesh are unemployed and idle because "they don't have to work," as Benjamin explained, "they are registered at local *kollels* which are a hotbed of zealot extremists, and they receive a stipend from them. There are cover organizations that support them because they see them as soldiers in the war of modesty."

Usually these "soldiers" do not operate alone and on their own initiative but in gangs or groups. They are led by local rabbis who advocate religious coercion and extremism and they get support and backing from other rabbis. Sivan (1995) noted that growth of fanatic movements depends on the appearance of charismatic leaders. According to him, these leaders who often come out against the establishment's tendency to compromise, offer their supporters a radical vision, and succeed in motivating them to take extreme measures to realize this vision. Similarly Shaul Kimchi and Sh`muel Even (2004) ascribed the activity of extreme Islamists, who belong to terrorist groups, to a group process that they undergo, which is cynically exploited by leaders of their organizations. This process is like the group process that characterizes cults whose members carry out their leader's instructions without demur.

And indeed, moderate haredim in Beit Shemesh view some of these groups as a "cult" for all intents and purposes. "They are a cult," explained Shlomo, a local haredi resident,

> with all the characteristics of a cult, including heavy brainwashing, strong social supervision and a social managerial regime, a guru, negating the *other*, negating all others who do not adhere to their system.

How Beit Shemesh become a hotbed of haredi zealots

The picture described above shows that many parts of Beit Shemesh, a city that until a decade and a half ago had a *masorti* (traditional) and secular majority (Kahaner, 2009), have turned into a major hub for the activities of radical zealots. It appears that a number of cumulative factors led to this revolution.

First, most of the Beit Shemesh extremists are the *Edah Haharedit* people who came from the "Haredi Ghetto" of the Mea Shearim neighborhood. For these people, it was important to demonstrate that leaving their separatist origins at what used to be the very heart of haredi Jerusalem, and moving to the periphery in both senses of the word, would not cause a decline in their standards of separatism, religious punctiliousness, and zealotry. From their perspective, the best way to express this was by demonstrating behavior that was even stricter than the "original." Yentl, who herself had left Mea Shearim, expressed this aptly:

> Those who came here were afraid that the younger generation would be influenced by the secular. That is why they came here, with one purpose: "We are not yielding anything about religion and the education of our children." Everything here has to be one hundred percent – and better.

Second, in the past few decades, haredi society in Israel has been undergoing a change which can be seen in a greater openness to Israeli society, to modernity, and to Zionism (Caplan, 2003, 2007; Caplan and Stadler, 2009, 2012; Sivan, 2003). These changes are mainly the product of a selective process of "Israelization" affecting the haredi community, especially moderates, which includes internalizing the cultural values and behaviors of the surrounding Israeli society; and an influx of haredim from the US and Europe, who are considered more open-minded and more moderate. The greater openness is not in keeping with the spirit of the radical zealots, who aspire to "rectify" the situation in Beit Shemesh by building a community based on 'pure sanctity' with all possible strictures.

Third, the existence of young *kollel* students, with no education or profession, who are restless and adventure-seeking, constitutes fertile ground for the growth of violent zealous activity committed under the guise of religiosity (Appleby and Marty, 2002; Lipset, 1981), an activity that offers a goal and thrills that are not available from other sources. The pursuit of thrill-seeking among religious zealots is not exclusive to members of the violent groups in Beit Shemesh. Thus, for example, the psychiatrist Mahmad Amiralli, who analyzed the profile of Islamic extremists, asserted that it applied to the young men he investigated who were seeking thrills and adventure (Kimchi and Even, 2004).

In this context one cannot ignore a possible analogy between the characteristics of these extremist groups and classic characteristics of "street gangs" which were identified and described in the 1960s. The gang usually has a defined leadership and a tendency to demand control over a certain territory. Its members carry out criminal activities, disturb the public order, create an atmosphere of fear and menace, and harm the citizenry's sense of security. Gang members have a shared identity that is acquired through the name of the gang, a characteristic style of dress, graffiti, and other such features (Asbury and Borges, 2001: Gans, 1962; Piven and Cloward 1977) – features that are recognizable among the extremist groups in Beit Shemesh.

Fourth, we cannot ignore the presence of many *ba'alei teshuvah* in the city. *Ba'alei teshuvah* also constitute a ready platform for development of religious zealotry (Friedman, 2002; Zalcberg, 1998). Given their desire to cope with growing internal doubts (Sh'til, 1993), given their wish to be "more Catholic than the Pope" in order to be accepted as equal members of the community, and given their lack of a deep-rooted family tradition that could be a role model of moderation for them, these individuals are likely to adopt especially stringent norms that might lead them to religious zealotry. Moreover, some of the *Ba'alei teshuvah* are former criminals for whom violence was an integral part of their life, and this also seeps into authentic haredi society (Friedman, 2002; Zalcberg, 1998).

Fifth, fundamentalist Muslims and Christians, who resort to violence for ideological and religious reasons may have an influence on the extremist haredim, being a role model of sorts, both consciously and unconsciously (Friedman, 2002).

Sixth, from the accounts described here it emerges that one of the central problems in Beit Shemesh is rooted in the attempt of extremist groups to impose stringent norms on the entire population living in areas that are not part of "their" exclusive territory. Because Beit Shemesh does not have a clear policy regarding residential zones for the haredi sector, nor well-defined boundaries between haredi areas and non-haredi areas, the radical zealots have been unable to create a haredi area of concentration that is completely separate from the "outside world", i.e., general society. Consequently, the non-haredi population has to pass through areas with a high concentration of haredi population, and the different populations often have to share the same municipal services. Thus, unavoidable contact between radical extremists from the haredi community and the general population takes place, and the former try to compel the general population to adopt their lifestyles and their stringent norms. Thus, the battle surrounding various signs demanding modesty, as well as the conflict regarding use of public spaces that are open to the general population, expresses the struggle for power and control taking place between the radical haredi people and general society, and of attempts by the former to determine the rules of the game for the latter.

Seventh, haredi communities (like all religious communities) operate today in a competitive and free market, which enables individuals to choose their religious communities (Friedman, 1990b). Since there is a "market", and therefore competition for potential believers, religious leaders – in this case, the rabbis – tend to issue *halakhic* rulings in accordance with the inclinations of their members, and rule according to their tendencies whether to be lenient or strict, so that their members will continue to accept their authority and not abandon the community. Thus, in a community where most of the members tend to be over-scrupulous in their observance, the halachic decisor (*posek*, rabbi) will likely decide on more stringent halakhic norms in order to survive the "market competition" (Friedman, 1990b). This phenomenon is well-attested to in Beit Shemesh, where a number of rabbis have radicalized their positions in response to pressure exerted on them by radicals in their communities. Yechiel explained:

> There are rabbis who are forced to submit to dictates of radicals in their community because they know that if they don't, members of their community will rebel against them. We spoke with more than a few haredi rabbis who are considered relatively moderate, and they denounce this phenomenon to us in private, but they are not ready or able to act publicly to fight the problem. In many instances they are afraid to appear as someone washing their dirty laundry in public. In addition, there are some who are afraid of pressure from the haredi community, or of reactions, or of objections.

Furthermore, Beit Shemesh invites a unique encounter of groups and movements within haredi society, with aspects dividing as much as uniting them. As such, tensions and conflicts between them are inevitable. These tensions are frequently expressed in an undeclared competition among certain groups regarding the degree of stringency to be adopted. As Benjamin asserted, "The minute one group decides upon a certain stringency, or carries out radical activity, extremists from another group imitate them, so they will not be considered less radical than the first group."

And where are the law enforcement agencies?

Residents that suffer from violence and terrorism in Beit Shemesh are not sparing their criticism of the city municipality. In keeping with the examples described above, many of the residents claim that Moshe Abutbul, the mayor since 2008 and haredi himself (from Shas, a Sephardic-religious party), is not a competent leader, and therefore his ability to bring about change in the city is very limited. Yechiel noted that "For years politicians and members of the City Council referred to these problems as a passing phenomenon so there is no need to deal with it."

The residents are not the only ones who disparage the way the city leadership handled the extremists' activities in the city. The Magistrates Court of the city also recently (January 25, 2015) determined that the municipality of Beit Shemesh and the mayor did not fulfill their obligations and that they were seriously negligent in not acting for the removal of signs against the "immodest dress" in central locations in the city (Adamker, 2015).

This decision is the first such case in Israel regarding modesty signs which are directed against women. The ruling was made as a result of a lawsuit filed by the Israel Religious Action Center of the Israel Movement for Progressive Judaism, in the name of four Modern Orthodox women residents of the city. The lawsuit was against the city and the mayor, because of the refusal to remove modesty signs hanging in central locations in the city. The claim alleges that not only are the signs offensive and humiliating, but the municipality's refusal to remove the signs sets a precedent of acceptance of violence used against women by the extremists. In addition, the court ordered compensation to each of the petitioners for distress.

In his ruling, Judge David Gidoni intoned that the message conveyed by the signs is "discriminatory and abusive [...]. The signs are designed to limit the access of women – being women [...] – to the public sphere," and that they

> lead to serious and severe harm to a woman's right to equality and dignity. The signs also embody degradation. The refusal of the authorities to act to remove the sign creates the impression that the sign is placed there with their agreement.

Judge Gidoni also wrote that:

> The facts presented to the court show a bleak picture of reality [...]. The municipality and the mayor accepted the presence of the harmful signs around the city [...]. A situation where the municipality and the mayor avoid carrying out their powers and duties under the law, and do not act for the removal of the offensive and discriminatory signs, only because of fear that people who would not be pleased with this act would use violence or violate the order, raises significant difficulty and rewards violence and may encourage additional violence. (Adamker, 2015)

The Beit Shemesh municipality said in response:

> The municipality removed the private signs several times, but they were hung again within minutes and even caused riots and friction between the various sectors in the city. Coping with this complex issue is beyond the ability of the municipal inspectors, therefore we turned to the Israeli police system, asking it to come to grips and enforce the law. (Adamker, 2015)

However, many residents complain about police efficiency. According to them, the police are afraid to confront violent haredim, and the control of the city is actually in the hands of the rabbis. Yechiel explained:

> Almost all of Beit Shemesh knows who are the rabbis that support the violence, but it's difficult for the police to find evidence that would lead to conviction of the agitators, mostly because individuals are afraid to give the evidence they have. On the other hand, in many cases the police give the impression that they are hesitant or afraid to act to protect residents.

For example, Yechiel continued:

> At a public meeting that was held at the community center in the city, with hundreds of residents, the outgoing local chief of police and the former mayor, one resident complained about the refusal of police to respond to an incident she reported. In response to her complaint, the chief of police said: "I will not send my officers as sheep to the slaughter."

Similarly, said Ron, another resident:

> The police exist to guard against outlaws, but policemen here do not want to get involved. The police claim many times that they could not act because they have no evidence, but haredim who sprayed graffiti were caught on camera and the recording was given to the police, but the police still make no progress with the investigation of this issue.

The way the police treated the case of stones thrown at Yael illustrates the police dis-functionality, as she elaborated:

> When the guy started to throw stones at me I knew that if I will call the police and report on a violence of haredim, the police will not arrive. They do not arrive when there are violent incidents by haredim, because they don't want to deal with them. So, when it happened I just said, "Someone is attacking me". A few minutes later a policeman came and the guy who threw stones began running to a nearby field and escaped; And the officer, instead of running and try catching him, said to me, "Why do you tease them?" I told him I was not teasing and that what the guy did was illegal, and again, I turned to him and asked him to catch that guy. Only after a long time the policeman agreed to get into the police van and try to find the guy, but the guy already managed to escape.

Yael, who identified the guy and found his home address, gave these details to the police, but to no avail:

> They showed me pictures of suspects and the guy did not appear among them, so they told me that because I couldn't identify him in the pictures the case was closed. I went back to them and said again: "Here's his address", and the policeman said to me: "what do you want? That we will go into his house and take him out?" I told him: "Yes, you are a policeman", but nothing has been done about it, and the police commander hung up the phone on me.

Moreover, Yael emphasized, "this commander got a promotion!" Yael, a brave and stubborn woman, came to the office of the District Police Chief, but he, as she said, "threw us out of the room." She did not give in and reported this event to the office of Avi Dichter, who was at the time Minister of Domestic Security. However, continued Yael, "nothing has been done. All the policemen know, Avi Dichter knows, and the guy still lives there. They are all just organized crime, Beit Shemesh is the Wild West. If you are haredi the police would not mess with you."

Yael's story and the story of the photographed graffiti spraying are but two of many examples illustrating the impotence of the Beit Shemesh police. With such a situation, many residents feel that the police do not relate seriously to their reports and they have stopped reporting harassment and violence committed by haredim. Yael's words sum up the feelings of many of the residents:

> Someone has abandoned us, abandoned Beit Shemesh to the hands of the haredim. I'm struggling against the police. If the police will do their job it would be possible to stop the violence in Beit Shemesh. The police here do nothing for the security of the residents. What frightens me is that the policemen have no control, and that the rabbis and not the police are in control here. Everything is in the hands of these rabbis, who decide when to be quiet and when to attack.

Summary and discussion

From the facts presented here it emerges that the vast majority of violence and religious coercion in Beit Shemesh revolved around women and their bodies and around the *other*, whoever that may be. This is not surprising because in many cultures, women are perceived as *other* (de Beauvoir, 1973), and a strong connection may be found in various groups between hatred of women and hatred of the *other* (Hyman, 1995). Despite the fact that the general population of Beit Shemesh is hurt by the violence, there is no doubt that women are the chief victims. Therefore, these findings may contribute to an understanding of the phenomenon of violence against women and shed light on this specific aspect of gender-based violence (Krantz and Garcia-Moreno, 2005) in a religious context.

Religious coercion and violence in the city find their expression in various forms, beginning with the exclusion and humiliation of women in the public arena, through vandalism and verbal violence, and ending in severe physical violence. This activity is the work of local extremists who have no education, no profession, nor employment, and who see themselves as soldiers in the war of modesty and as responsible for safeguarding the purity of the community. Although these extremists sow terror throughout an entire city, it is important to remember that we are dealing with a very small minority – marginal extremists who do not represent the general haredi community.

Furthermore, it seems that a considerable percentage of moderate haredim in the city are also harmed by these extremists and they condemn their activity. Hence, these research findings may also shed light on internal wars taking place today within haredi society and tensions between various groups, tensions whose roots lie in differing perceptions of the Zionist enterprise, the Jewish population in the Land of Israel, and the State of Israel (Caplan, 2010; Friedman, 1990a, 1991).

The findings further indicate that together with a trend toward openness that has characterized some of the haredi groups in recent years, especially the moderate ones (Caplan, 2003, 2007; Caplan and Stadler, 2009, 2012), we are also witness to a process of religious radicalization among other groups. This radicalization is, paradoxically, an expression of a "deviation" from traditional norms (which had been accepted in traditional Jewish society) leaning *le-humra*, namely, towards adopting stricter halakhic norms (Friedman, 1990a). Friedman (2003) maintained that in modern society as compared with traditional society, it is easier to institutionalize stricter norms, since in the latter, adopting stricter norms was seen as threatening the integrity and solidarity of the community; therefore, the religious authorities used mechanisms to reject them. In contrast, in modern society today, with religion traded on the free market and with a large supply of religious groups to choose from, these mechanisms are almost non-existent – the power of the community does not avail to force the individual to uphold the traditional norms of life. As a result, "deviations towards stringency" not only are not rejected but they may be received warmly, as is clearly the case in Beit Shemesh. Because stringency in modesty is perceived as highly significant in haredi society (Heilman, 1992; Zalcberg 2007, 2011), because women's outward appearance is something immediately noticeable, and because women are seen as a convenient object to be dominated, their outward appearance has become the central arena for demonstrating religious stringency and violence against those failing to observe the rules.

The findings, which point to offensive behavior by extremist zealot men, raise the question of extremist zealot women in Beit Shemesh and their conduct. An oblique response may be seen in Yosef's remarks, who noted that "there is a reason 'Mother Taliban' developed here" – referring to the woman who in 2007 introduced haredi women to "Taliban fashion" – consisting of a multi-layered covering of head and body by means of shawls, including covering the head with a veil which sometimes extended to cover the face and even the eyes (Zalcberg, 2011).

Consistent with what Yosef said, several articles published in recent years confirm that in Beit Shemesh there is religious zealotry of a type that had never been seen before among women, and this too finds expression to a large extent in the area of modesty (Fisher, 2010; Zalcberg, 2011). Indeed, the prominent example for this is the group of women headed by "Mother Taliban", as she was dubbed by the Israeli media. This group has taken upon itself extreme stringencies in the area of modesty and other areas; such as *ta'anit dibur* – a pledge not to speak for an extended period of time, refraining from walking in public areas, and home schooling for girls. However, there is almost no scholarly attention to the extent to which these women exercise religious coercion and violence against the surrounding society. This issue calls for a follow-up study in the future.

Although the picture that has been presented relates to what is happening in Beit Shemesh, one may see it as a case study for a phenomenon that is universal – fundamentalism and religious zealotry in the modern age (Almond et al., 2003; Litvak and Limor, 2007). Mordechai Kedar (2011), an expert in Middle Eastern affairs, described a reality where

> one Muslim will fight another Muslim over the length of the mischievous curl that is allowed to peek out from under the hijab, or how many lashes a woman should be given if she dared to go out into the street without her husband or another man from her family. A person would call his opponent a heretic solely in order to legitimize killing him and if someone tried to promote a political or social agenda that is not in line with the opinions of people more extreme than him, he might find himself the target of jihad.

This reality, although it describes developments among Islamic nations, reflects faithfully what is happening among the zealot groups in Beit Shemesh, as among other groups of religious zealots.

One of the interesting questions that arise from the findings relates to continuity of violence in Beit Shemesh by extremist groups. The future activity of these groups depends on several key factors: the response of the haredi leadership, which until now has not acted notably to curb the phenomenon; the conduct of the police, who the residents believe to be afraid of confrontation with these extremists and act as though powerless; and the conduct of the municipality, which the residents feel capitulates to the dictates of the extremist haredim.

The last municipal elections in Beit Shemesh, about a year before writing this article (at October 2013), were fraught with controversy: Abutbul won a second term as mayor by a small margin, which was nullified by a court for voter fraud and rescheduled. Following this, tempers raged in Beit Shemesh and many of the residents participated in angry demonstrations under the slogan "We are not giving up the city."

The demonstrations had an impact, and second elections were held in the city, with Abutbul being elected again, but with greater turnout and a smaller margin. Residents with whom I spoke after the reelections reported that, paradoxically, since the reelection tensions in the city have decreased and there has been a significant reduction in the level of violence. They attribute this change to the fact that "now the extremist groups are in a position of control, as they can get from the mayor's office whatever they want, and are therefore making less troubles." Another explanation that was mentioned relates to these groups being busy with issues of resisting haredi recruitment to the Israel Defense Forces, which is not a local but a national issue, and they redirect most of their resources to this.

During the conversation with Yael, she noted that the city has often had occasional periods of relative calm, but after each calm, waves of violence are renewed. Is the relative quiet that currently prevails in Beit Shemesh a temporary wave, only to be followed again by violence? Or this time are we talking about a real trend toward change in the activity patterns of the extremist zealots? In order to answer this, events in the city will need to be followed over time, as well as the behavior of the extremist groups in the public sphere.

Notes

* This article is based in part on an article of mine that appeared in Hebrew: "The Intersection Between Religious Zealotry, Class and Gender in Beit Shemesh" (in press). In S. Fisher (Ed.), *Religion and Class in Israel*, Jerusalem: Hakibuts Hameuchad and Van Leer Institute Press [Heb].

1 In 2006, the haredi population of Beit Shemesh represented 46 percent of the city's population, with this percentage steadily increasing (Kahaner, 2009). According to the Israeli Central Bureau of Statistics (2014), in 2013 the city's population stood at 94,069. Accordingly the haredi population of the city may be estimated as at least 40,000.

2 The Jewish community in Israel that arrived before 1882.

3 This is a fictional name to preserve the privacy of this individual. Likewise, all interviewees in this article have been given fictional names.

4 The *Edah Haredit* is the framework that unites the groups that refuse to recognize the legitimacy of the State of Israel as a Jewish State. This camp adopted a hard-line anti-Zionist stance and demanded that its members isolate themselves totally from the Zionist enterprise and the State of Israel (Friedman, 1990b). Several camps and circles are identified with the *Edah*, most prominent among these are: Neturei Karta, Brisk and the Yerushalmi families of the Old Yishuv of Jerusalem, as well as other groups and hasidic courts such as Dushinsky, Munkach, Pinsk-Karlin, Spinka, Toldot Aharon, and Toldot Avraham Yitzhak (Caplan, 2010).

5 The Litvaks [Yiddish for 'Lithuanians'] see themselves as the direct continuation of the *Mitnagdim* movement that developed in Lithuania, which is characterized in particular by a culture of Torah scholarship that took shape in the yeshivot of Lithuania.

6 *Tish* in Yiddish means table. In Hasidism, this word is used to describe the custom of hasidic men crowding around the table of their rebbe (religious spiritual leader) when he eats Sabbath eve dinner in the synagogue. During the *tish*, the hasidim sing and they receive *shirayim* (small bits of food from his table) which they regard as having beneficial powers. The *tish* is a key social event in the lives of Hasidism and hasidism, and they attribute great spiritual significance to it.

7 On Memorial Day a two minutes siren sounded nation wide, marking a national moment of silence, where most of the nation comes to a complete stop and people stand in silence remembering the fallen solders.

8 Neturei Karta is a haredi sub-group characterized by strong resistance to Zionism and modernity, and by its militant activities against Sabbath violations; against conducting Biblical archaeological excavations in Israel, claiming that in these excavations there are graves of Jews; against modesty norms violators, and against other haredi denominations who think differently than them.

Part III

Religious divorce in civil courts

9 The impact of "foreign law" bans on the struggle for women's equality under Jewish law in the United States of America

Lisa Fishbayn Joffe

Introduction: the plural nature of Jewish marriage in the US

Orthodox Jewish women can have a complicated relationship to family law. Their marital lives are founded on a religious marriage contract and may be governed by daily observance of religious obligations regarding food, comportment, conduct and marital intimacy. Should the marriage end in divorce, however, all but the most traditional will turn to the civil courts to divide the family assets and determine maintenance responsibilities. Most couples that marry in a religious ceremony do so with the aid of a rabbi who is also a civil marriage officiant and register these marriages with the state.

However, the egalitarian norms that now prevail in American family law find no counterpart in the doctrines of Jewish family law. Divorce is the sole prerogative of the husband, who can withhold it out of spite or agree to grant it on almost any extortionate conditions he might wish to set.

Jewish law differs from Anglo-American civil marriage and the model of Christian religious marriage upon which it is based in two key ways. First, the marriage cannot be dissolved by religious authorities, only by the mutual consent of the parties. A divorce is achieved through the delivery of a bill of divorcement (get) in which the husband renounces the rights he had acquired over the wife and pronounces her a free woman. Second, the wife cannot end the marriage through a parallel process of renunciation. She may ask a beit din (rabbinical court) to declare that the husband may be compelled to grant her a get for a range of reasons recognized under Jewish law, but the court itself cannot dissolve the marriage. The beit din's declaratory powers have limited effect in most modern-day regimes where religious courts lack any formal enforcement power.

The wife must consent to receive the get and can prevent the dissolution of the marriage if she refuses to do so. However, the consequences for husbands and wives in this situation are very different. Even without a divorce, a husband may cohabit with a new partner and have children with her. When and if he is divorced, he can marry this new partner without any legal consequences. If his wife continues to refuse to accept the get, he may even be able to get permission to take a second wife without divorcing the first one.[1]

For a woman, however, refusal by her husband to deliver the get may have implications that last for generations. Should she have children with a new partner, they would be considered the illegitimate products of adultery (*mamzerim*, bastards) and would be ineligible to marry within the Jewish community. As a result, in ultra-Orthodox communities, women who are *agunot* are socially isolated. While the lives of their peers continue to revolve around bearing and rearing children and socializing at life cycle events, the agunot occupy a social no-man's land.

The story of *agunot*, women denied a divorce under Jewish law, or subjected to extortion in order to be granted a divorce, is a story about a distinctly Jewish form of domestic abuse. The term "agunah" derives from the term "agun" or anchor and refers to a woman who is chained to a marriage that is dead in all but name. There have always been agunot, women whose marriages are effectively over but who are unable to divorce under Jewish law and go on with their lives. The shape of this problem has, however, changed over time.

The Talmud describes the sad plight of the classical agunah whose husband could not consent to divorce. This might be because the man had disappeared while travelling to another town to trade or been lost on a ship at sea. No one could be sure whether the husband had drowned, fallen victim to bandits on the road or whether he had simply taken up with a new companion somewhere else. Perhaps he had been injured and lost his memory of where home was and of who waited there for him. In those situations, rabbis wanted certain evidence of death before allowing a woman to remarry, lest her wayward husband should someday return. Alternatively, the husband might have been physically present but unable to form the requisite intent to consent to divorce because of mental illness or a malady rendering him unconscious. In these situations, rabbis developed strategies to try to minimize the suffering of these women, through establishing grounds to presume death or to validate the consent of a mentally ill man during moments of lucidity, but, nevertheless, many, women remained agunot.

In the late 19th century, the agunah problem became one of men abandoning their families. The popular Yiddish media of the time was replete with advertisements from women trying to find their missing husbands.[2] These men had disappeared into another province, another European country or on a boat to America. With the emancipation of Jews in Europe, Jewish men could for the first time travel freely outside of Jewish ghettos and found even greater freedom in the promised land of America. They could leave behind their Jewish identities. For some, this meant leaving their Jewish wives as well.

From the late twentieth century to the present day, we have seen a new form of agunah problem emerge. We still have instances where the husband has absconded or is unable to consent, but now the most common context for the creation of an agunah is a contested civil divorce. The husband is physically present and mentally sound, but seeks to use his power to withhold a religious divorce to inflict pain on the wife or as a bargaining chip in negotiations over property, alimony and custody in the civil divorce. Often the husband may demand that the wife give up her rights to family property or make cash payments in order to be granted a divorce.

One explanation for this transformation may be the dramatic changes that have taken place in civil family law over this period. In the wake of the second wave feminist movement, states across the US rewrote their family laws to recognize the value of women's contributions to the family enterprise and award spouses equal rights to assets accumulated during the course of marriage. Some men perceive their rights to withhold divorce under Jewish law as an appropriate tool to use to claw back some of the hard-won gains of the women's movement.

A second factor is how difficult it is now to simply abscond and disappear without taking financial responsibility for one's children. Tracing missing husbands through their social security numbers, tax returns and social media identities is much easier. States now see it as in their interest to locate missing husbands so that the burden of supporting dependent children remains with the parents rather than being passed to the state. This may mean that the men who in another age would have simply disappeared are now being located and, once found, they use their power to withhold the get to resist taking financial responsibility for their families.

Various streams within Judaism have sought to develop solutions to this problem of gender inequality in Jewish divorce. The liberal Reform movement has abolished the requirement for a religious divorce, treating the Jewish marriage as terminated by the civil divorce.[3] The moderate Conservative movement has, since the 1960s, incorporated a clause into the marriage contract that requires the spouses to accept arbitration of their divorce dispute by a rabbinical court. In the twenty-first century, Modern Orthodox Jews have encouraged marrying couples to sign prenuptial agreements which name a rabbinical court as arbitrator for divorce disputes and sets out a scheme of liquidated damages if a husband refuses to grant his wife a divorce. The details of the latter two ameliorative strategies will be discussed in detail below. At this point, it is important to stress that they cannot be effective on their own, but are dependent upon the threat of implementation by the civil courts. Jewish law as practiced in North America thus incorporates resort to civil enforcement. Civil courts will enforce agreements to arbitrate before rabbinical courts and, if these arbitral awards are filed with the courts, will enforce the awards themselves. Civil courts across the US have ordered specific performance and imposed damages for failure to comply with these arbitration agreements. In some jurisdictions, the state has itself passed laws that permit civil family courts to take into account refusal to cooperate in delivery of a religious divorce when determining whether to accept a recalcitrant spouse's pleadings, to grant his petition for civil divorce, or how to equitably distribute the couples' assets.

These approaches have been effective in creating an emergent cultural norm among American Jews that rejects get-based extortion and get-refusal.

The effectiveness of these remedies and of this fragile new consensus is being jeopardized by attacks on the commingling of "foreign" religious law in American courts. While motivated by animus against Muslims, I argue that the primary impact of these new "foreign law" bans will be to undermine carefully drafted protections for women under Jewish law that have the potential to benefit Muslim women as well.

The emergence of "foreign law" bans

The role of civil courts as an enforcement mechanism for contracts that seek to alter the presumptive gender inequality in Jewish law or for civil judicial decisions that seek to compensate women for this inequality has been called into question by a recent American legislative trend. Since 2010, 34 of the 50 States in the US have introduced bills seeking to ban the use of "foreign or international law" in state courts.[4] Foreign law bans have passed into law in nine of these states: Oklahoma, Kansas, Louisiana, Tennessee, Arizona, South Dakota, North Carolina, Alabama and Florida.[5] These laws are based on a template drawn up by the anti-Muslim group, American Public Policy Alliance, through its program American Law for American Courts (ALAC). The template redefines the public policy of the drafting state to include a duty:

> To protect its citizens from the application of *foreign laws* when the application of a foreign law will result in the violation of a right guaranteed by the constitution of this state or of the United States, including but not limited to due process, freedom of religion, speech, or press, and any right of privacy or marriage as specifically defined by the constitution of this state.

When actually enacted at the state level, the term "*foreign laws*" has been defined in different ways. Some formulations prohibit state courts or agencies from enforcing "*any provisions of a religious code*".[6] Others forbid state courts and arbitrators from enforcing "*any law, rule or legal code or system established and used or applied in a jurisdiction outside of the states or territories of the United States*".[7] Some are merely declarative, such as a resolution of the Idaho state legislature calling upon the United States Congress to pass a foreign law ban and bar foreign entities like the United Nations from exercising authority in the US.[8]

The explicit objective of these laws is to prevent the enforcement of what anti-Muslim activists describe as "creeping Shariah law" in the United States.[9] They believe that Muslim Americans have an agenda to re-create America as an Islamic law compliant country and that they seek to use the courts to do so. They caution that Islamic law discriminates against women and warn that its recognition in American courts puts the rights of Muslim women at risk. This picture both exaggerates the extent to which Islamic law is applied in the US and ignores the ways in which Jewish law presents many of the same challenges. Paradoxically, this anti-Muslim discourse cloaks itself as the defender of religious women, when a complete break of the nexus between religious and civil laws around divorce may harm the women it purports to defend.[10]

The first laws based on the ALAC template focused solely on Sharia. The Oklahoma effort, for example, was the product of a referendum in which 70 percent of voters approved an amendment to the state constitution that explicitly forbade courts from referring to Sharia Law in making judicial decisions.[11] The initiative was entitled the "Save our State Amendment". It enumerated the laws that could be enforced by the courts, but then stated:

> The courts shall not look to the legal precepts of other nations or cultures. Specifically, the court shall not consider international law or Sharia law.[12]

This law was immediately struck down as invalid by a federal appellate court on First Amendment grounds as explicitly and intentionally discriminatory against Muslims who would be subjected to stigma and unable to fully practise their faith.[13] A law that discriminates among religions can only be sustained if it is closely fitted to achieving some compelling governmental objective. The appellate court noted that the state could not point to one Oklahoma case in which Sharia had been applied at all, let alone in a problematic manner.

Tennessee passed a law that criminalized Sharia organizations and made it an offence to conspire with others "in support of Sharia".[14] The Act sought to delegitimize Islam as a sham religion and purported to define Sharia as "a legal-political-military doctrinal system combined with certain religious beliefs" which required adherents to overthrow the governments of the state of Tennessee and the United States and then replace it with a government based on Sharia law. This account defined all Islam based on an interpretation of the extremist views of groups like the fundamentalist Islamic State in Syria.[15] After robust criticism, this bill was later amended, to excise every single reference to Sharia, and was passed as a bill barring support of terrorism.[16] Later versions of anti-Sharia laws do not explicitly refer to Sharia but use the religiously neutral term "foreign law".

However it is phrased, this form of legislation is largely a solution seeking a problem, as American courts routinely decline to follow foreign law when the provision in question conflicts with American conceptions of women's rights.[17] Indeed, even the illustrative cases cited by ALAC on its website, dealing with custody disputes, pre-marital *mahr* (dower) contracts, divorce and marriage, are ones in which the trial court refused to grant comity (recognize and apply the relevant foreign law), where the trial court was reversed on appeal or where religious law was not key to the finding in the case.

The potential impact of these foreign law bans on Jewish women is particularly odd given that ALAC is led by Brooklyn lawyer, David Yerushalmi, a self-described Orthodox Jew and anti-Muslim activist. In an interview with the *New York Times*, Yerushalmi acknowledged that these laws would have little practical effect on cases before US courts. Rather, the primary and intended effect of such legislation is to demonize Muslims and Sharia law by erroneously suggesting that its doctrines are frequently in conflict with American civil rights norms, more than those of other religious groups:

> For Mr. Yerushalmi, the statutes themselves are a secondary concern. "If this thing passed in every state without any friction, it would have not served its purpose," he said in one of several extensive interviews. "The purpose was heuristic – to get people asking this question, 'What is Shariah?' "[18]

A secondary, perhaps unintended, effect of these laws may be to undermine religious feminists' attempts to use the civil courts to ameliorate women's inequality under religious family law regimes. It may be that Yerushalmi and his colleagues were aware of but indifferent to this effect.[19] It may be that they believe that while Islam is a proselytizing faith, there is no risk that Jewish authorities might seek to impose halakhah on non-Jews. In a letter to the Florida legislature encouraging passage of its draft foreign law ban, Yerushalmi's colleague, Rabbi Jonathan Hausman, dismissed concerns about the impact of the law on Florida's large Orthodox community. He claimed that halakhah is only for voluntary adherents while adherents to Sharia are obligated to impose it on others and that Jewish law will always give way to US law, in accordance with the doctrine of ***dina d'malchuta dina*** (the law of the king is the law).[20] Yerushalmi told the *New York Times* he did not believe that court cases involving Jewish or canon law would be affected by the statutes because they were unlikely to involve violations of constitutional rights.[21]

This rosy picture underestimates the extent to which women's substantive rights to divorce under Jewish law and procedural rights to invoke remedies before rabbinical courts often deviate from American norms. In the rest of this chapter I will describe the ways in which civil courts have engaged with Jewish law to provide remedies that level the playing field between Jewish spouses. I also describe the ways in which rabbinical courts can collaborate with civil courts to aid this process, by testifying as expert witnesses and drafting religious prenuptial agreements that carve out a role for civil court enforcement.

Civil remedies for gender inequality under Jewish law

Experts on the operation of Jewish law in the United States have made the point that Islamic religious arbitration can learn from the instructive experience of Jewish law arbitration.[22] There are important areas of overlap. Both Jewish and Islamic law purport to provide religious/ethical norms that govern all areas of life. Both establish religious law tribunals to resolve disputes that arise between adherents based on these norms. Both express a preference for adherents to take cases to religious courts where available rather than to civil courts.[23] Jewish law requires that, where possible, Jews take disputes with other Jews to Jewish courts.[24] Use of rabbinical courts is both a religious obligation to understand and apply God's laws and seen as prudent in societies where the claims of Jews might not be treated fairly by intolerant majorities.

However, there may be some important differences between the Islamic and Jewish law in diasporic communities like the US. Islamic legal authorities have produced a well-developed doctrine for dealing with religious minorities within their midst.[25] Conversely, Jewish courts have for centuries operated as the institutional expression of a tolerated minority in lands governed by religious majorities of another faith, be they Christian or Muslim. Islamic law theorists did not develop a similarly elaborate jurisprudence providing guidance about how conflicts between Sharia and the laws of the land should be dealt with.[26]

Both regimes may also be in a period of transition. The creation of the state of Israel has created opportunities for rabbinical courts to re-assert their authority in ways not possible in the diasporic communities of Europe or North America.[27] Many recent cases in Israel reflect the desire of rabbinical courts to take back jurisdiction over a broader swathe of Jewish citizens' lives.[28] Conversely, adherent immigrant Muslim populations face the challenge of adjusting some of their doctrines to societies in which they are now in the minority.

One thing these regimes share in common in this time of transition is a particular interest in the regulation of family law. Even in those jurisdictions where religious authorities have been largely stripped of authority over most of public life, they remain empowered to control marriage and divorce and associated claims. Even in diasporic nations, observant Jews and Muslims believe that they need a religious divorce in order to continue their lives and remarry. The regulation of the family, and the interests of women and children so closely implicated by it, have become a locus for the affirmation of religious identity and the exercise of religious power, often to the detriment of women trying to straddle their identities as citizens and adherents to religious traditions.[29]

A significant proportion of the work of American rabbinical courts is devoted to family law matters.[30] The best known, the Beit Din of America, devotes the majority of its docket to divorce cases, dealing with 400 cases per year.[31] Divorce makes up a smaller proportion of the workload of ultra-Orthodox courts, which also deal with many employment, commercial and contract issues.[32]

As will be described below, a range of civil remedies have been developed which support resolution of Jewish divorce disputes precisely by having civil courts take notice of, respond to and even enforce elements of Jewish law and decisions of rabbinical courts. While some foreign law bans, like the Florida one, may seek to shelter rabbinical court proceedings by designing acceptable procedures with them in mind, other legislatures attack Jewish law directly. Draft versions of the Arizona law explicitly envisioned prohibiting the application of halakhah along with Sharia law, canon law and karma. In pleadings defending the explicit ban on Sharia in the *Awad* case, the attorney general for Oklahoma suggested that it was not discriminatory against Muslims because Sharia was mentioned only for illustrative purposes and the law could also be used to bar the application of other religious laws.[33] The next section describes the ways in which Jewish law might be implicated by application of these prohibitions.

The New York State "get" laws

In 1983, New York, the state where 20 percent of the seven million Jewish population in the US lives,[34] passed a law that allows courts to withhold a civil divorce decree, unless and until the husband removes all barriers to the wife's religious remarriage.[35] Similar provisions were passed in South Africa in 1995 and the United Kingdom in 2002.[36] Unfortunately, the provision is phrased to allow withholding of the civil decree only where the husband is the plaintiff, so is of no assistance to a woman who applies for the civil divorce herself.[37]

New York State passed another "get" law in 1992 which allowed get refusal to be taken into account when determining a fair and equitable division of the couple's assets on divorce.[38] In most cases, consideration of this factor has only contributed to a small increase in the wife's share of the family property, but in some egregious cases, the courts have used it as the basis to give the wife 100 percent of the shared assets. In *Giahn v. Giahn*,[39] the judge held that eight years of get-based extortion which had not resulted in delivery of the get justified completely extinguishing the husband's rights in the remaining family property.

Agreements to arbitrate disputes before a rabbinical court

In the US, Jewish law courts have no statutory jurisdiction. They operate as arbitrators selected by the parties and are thus subject to ordinary principles of administrative law. These are found in both the common law and state statutes based on the Revised Uniform Arbitration Act (RUAA) of 2000. Courts have consistently held that judicial review of beit din decisions does not entail the interpretation of religious law in order to answer religious questions, but can be conducted based on "neutral principles of law".[40]

The enforceability of arbitration agreements to appear before a beit din depends upon the language in which they are expressed. Those married by Conservative movement rabbis have a clause in the marriage contract itself through which the parties agree to the jurisdiction of the Conservative movement rabbinical courts as arbitrator, to abide by its advice on dissolving the marital relationship and to allow the rabbinical court to impose financial and other penalties.

The Orthodox community has only recently begun to accept and promote the use of prenuptial contracts that grant arbitral authority to an Orthodox beit din. Current divorce cases, involving Orthodox parties who married without benefit of these innovations, therefore contain no explicit agreement to arbitrate in the marriage contract or an ancillary prenuptial contract, but must rely on interpretation of the marriage vows. In an Orthodox marriage ceremony, a husband says to the wife: "Behold, by this ring you are consecrated to me as my wife according to the laws of Moses and Israel". The ketubah records this declaration.[41]

In the key case of *Avitzur v. Avitzur*, the parties had undergone a Conservative Jewish marriage ceremony. In it, they authorized the Conservative beit din to summon them to appear "in order to enable the party so requesting to live in accordance with the standards of the Jewish law of marriage throughout his lifetime", a euphemism for cooperating in terminating the Jewish marriage if the parties become civilly divorced.[42] When the husband refused to attend before the beit din, the wife sought a declaration that the ketubah was a valid "marital contract" and an order of specific performance for her husband to appear before the beit din:

> It should be noted that the plaintiff is not attempting to compel defendant to obtain a Get or to enforce a religious practice arising solely out of principles of religious law. She merely seeks to enforce an agreement made by defendant to appear before and accept the decision of a designated tribunal.[43]

The court found that it could interpret the obligations under the contract relying "solely upon the application of neutral principles of contract law, without reference to any religious principle".[44]

Avitzur has been relied on in a long line of cases establishing that agreements to appear before rabbinical courts to arbitrate divorce disputes are enforceable. US civil courts have been willing to back up these orders with findings of contempt and even orders for incarceration.[45]

The courts have been more ambivalent when the parties married in an Orthodox ceremony, which until recently, contained no agreement to arbitrate. In *Mayer-Kolker v. Kolker*, the court declined to enforce an Orthodox ketubah. The court found, in the absence of explicit reference to an obligation to cooperate in the delivery of the get and expert testimony regarding whether Mosaic law required the husband to appear and give the get, it could not enforce the contract.[46] However, where Orthodox ketubot have been supported by appropriate expert evidence, courts have been willing to enforce them. In *Minkin*, the parties married with an Orthodox ketubah. The court heard four Orthodox rabbis testifiy that the husband was obligated, under the laws of Moses and Israel, to give a get when he alleged adultery of his wife in the civil divorce petition and the court therefore ordered him to do so.[47] In *In re Goldman*,[48] the couple had used an Orthodox ketubah even though they married in a Reconstructionist ceremony. Upon divorce, the husband told the wife he would withhold the divorce to punish her for the rest of her life, but later offered to grant it in exchange for her agreement to join custody of the children. The court heard testimony from Rabbi Gedalia Schwartz and Rabbi Emmanuel Rackman, two very well-respected Orthodox authorities on Jewish family law, that the marriage contract could be dissolved "without any profession of religious belief or act of worship" by the husband. The husband, however, argued that he had signed the ketubah without realizing it was a legally binding document under Jewish law:

> Kenneth Goldman testified that he considered the ketubah to be poetry or art rather than a contract. In an evidence deposition [Reconstructionist] Rabbi Rachlis, who officiated at the marriage ceremony, stated that from his perspective as a liberal Jew, he viewed the ketubah in a symbolic rather than a literal sense. Kenneth testified that he could not read the Aramaic text and the English translation did not contain any reference to divorce or a get.... Kenneth then testified at great length as to his dislike for Orthodox Judaism. He stated that Orthodox Jews discriminate against women, and characterized Orthodox Jews as "anti-modern" and repulsive.[49]

Nevertheless, the appellate court found that contempt for Orthodox Jews was a preference, not a religious belief protected by the First Amendment's Free Exercise clause. He was ordered to cooperate with the Chicago Rabbinical Council in delivering the get.[50]

The advice of rabbinical authorities on the significance of the get ritual is important for validity under both systems. Rabbinical court authorities have sought to protect the limits of their jurisdiction for centuries, cautious to discourage parties from turning to secular courts for the resolution of their disputes. In the context of Jewish divorce, this concern plays out in several ways. As Rabbi Klapper notes in Chapter 10,[51] parties should seek permission to go to the secular courts with their disputes and may be denied the full panoply of remedies available under Jewish law if they fail to secure it.

On a substantive level, Jewish law requires that a man grant a divorce of his own free will, without (inappropriate) coercion. A coerced divorce is invalid and does not dissolve the marriage. Coercion can only be authorized by a competent beit din which determines that there are grounds to encourage or compel a man to free his wife. This compulsion once took the form of physical as well as financial inducements, but in the modern day is limited to exhortations, shunning, fines, and in the state of Israel, the revocation of licenses, freezing of bank accounts and, rarely, imprisonment.[52] A rabbinical court can also authorize coercion implemented by civil authorities if the message sent by such enforcement is essentially "Do what the Jewish court asks of you".[53] An order from a civil court to grant a get rather than to accept the jurisdiction or ruling of a beit din would therefore be inappropriate and would produce an invalid divorce under Jewish law.

American secular courts will take issues of validity under Jewish law into account when fashioning their remedies. In *Burns v. Burns*, the parties were already civilly divorced but the husband refused to grant the get, saying that he no longer viewed it as necessary to dissolve the marriage (presumably because he now followed the tenets of Reform Judaism). He did offer to give the get if the wife made a "gift" of $25,000 in the name of their minor daughter. The judge acknowledged the fact that only a beit din can make a valid finding that a get ought to be delivered under such circumstances and ordered that the husband submit to the jurisdiction of the beit din.[54]

In *In re Scholl*[55], the couple was Orthodox but the husband refused to attend before the local Orthodox rabbinical court, instead giving a get under the auspices of a Conservative beit din. This court was not recognized by Orthodox authorities and its get would not be accepted for purposes of remarriage by Orthodox clergy. The court found him in breach of the settlement order and ordered him to go to the beit din that could issue a valid divorce.

In *Aflalo v. Aflalo*, the parties were married in Israel, which only permits Orthodox rabbis to solemnize marriage. The husband refused to grant the get unless the wife agreed to appear before the beit din and attempt reconciliation. The wife refused to proceed with the civil divorce until the get had been delivered. She asked that the court order him to cooperate with the Jewish divorce, but the court found that he was already offering to appear before the beit din and agreed to follow its advice if they ordered him to give the divorce.[56] They concluded that her petition was unwise because any action on the part of the civil court in this context would produce an invalid get.[57] The wife's petition was rejected.

These cases demonstrate that American courts will uphold pre-marital agreements to appear before a rabbinical court to give a Jewish divorce whether these are part of civil or religious contracts. They draw the line, however, at ordering husbands to actually deliver the divorce.

Undertakings in separation and divorce agreements

Jewish law can also enter into civil proceedings when the husband makes an explicit commitment to appear before a beit din in order to grant a divorce as part of a separation or divorce agreement.[58] Many courts have thus far been willing to hold men to these obligations.[59] *Waxstein v. Waxtstein*, provides an example of how Jewish law and civil law can be commingled in processing the divorce of Jewish people in these cases. The couple signed a separation agreement in which the husband undertook to give the get if the wife arranged and paid for it, but he later refused to comply. The court ordered him to:

> Take whatever steps are necessary to secure a "Get" for the plaintiff, be it by his own commencement of and appearance and participation in such a religious proceeding or his consent, appearance and participation in a proceeding begun by the plaintiff (see *Matter of "Rubin" v "Rubin"*, 75 Misc 2d 776, 778–781). This court may also condition enforcement of other provisions in the separation agreement upon the defendant's co-operation in securing the "Get" (*Matter of "Rubin" v "Rubin", supra*, pp 782–784). Accordingly, the court further holds that the stock and the deed to the marital residence now being held by the plaintiff's attorneys shall not be turned over to the defendant until he has obtained a "Get".[60]

These provisions may be enforced through setting aside petitions, withholding property awards, financial penalties or civil commitment until the get is delivered. Courts are also willing to compel women to cooperate in acceptance of the get.[61]

Enforcement of the prohibition on dealing with foreign religious law would also make it difficult for American judges dealing with cases connected to Israel. The state of Israel has no civil law of marriage and divorce. Jurisdiction over the solemnization of marriage and its dissolution is reserved for the confessional regime of the parties. Jews must marry and divorce under the auspices of the rabbinate, Muslims under Shariah and Christians in accordance with the doctrines of the various recognized churches. Israeli women sometimes resort to American courts to deal with husbands who have absconded here without granting them a divorce. In *Shapiro v. Shapiro*, the Israeli husband had abandoned the wife for 19 years. When she finally located him in the US, she sought to have the Israeli rabbinical court order that he grant the get enforced in New York State. The court agreed, ordering him to appear before the Rabbinical Council of America and "to perform all ritual acts of the "get" ceremony in accordance with the directions of the Rabbinical Court".[62] The order in this case also demonstrates the extent to which religious authorities in Israel and America may cooperate in setting policy and settling disputes.

The emergence of the halachic prenuptial agreement as the preferred solution to the agunah problem

The success of *Avitzur*, combined with growing awareness of the problem of get-based extortion and get refusal, has given rise to adoption of prenuptial contracts in the Orthodox community. In *Avitzur*, Judge Wachtler made clear:

> Thus, the contractual obligation the plaintiff seeks to enforce is closely analogous to an ante-nuptial agreement to arbitrate a dispute in accordance with the law and tradition chosen by the parties. There can be little doubt that a duly executed ante-nuptial agreement by which the parties agree in advance of the marriage to the resolution of disputes that may arise after its termination, is valid and enforceable.[63]

Shifts in the attitudes of Orthodox authorities towards prenuptial agreements have tracked those of American courts. It was considered unseemly in the former and against public policy in the latter to enter into contracts that anticipated the eventuality of divorce.[64] Orthodox rabbis in the United States have been urging the adoption of prenuptial agreements as a mechanism to head off get refusal for the last decade. In 1993, the Rabbinical Council of America (RCA), the main professional association of Orthodox ordained rabbis, passed a resolution calling on members to ask marrying couples to sign its version of the prenuptial agreement. In 1999, leaders of the RCA were among the signatories to a joint letter addressed "to our rabbinic colleagues and students" at Yeshiva University (the leading seminary ordaining modern Orthodox rabbis in the US), "strongly urging all officiating rabbis to counsel and encourage marrying couples to sign such an agreement".[65] In the new millennium, their position became more emphatic. In 2006 and 2015, the RCA passed resolutions declaring that "no rabbi should officiate at a wedding where a proper prenuptial agreement on get has not been executed". In a recent survey conducted by the RCA of its members who officiate at weddings, 33 percent said they refused to perform the marriage unless a prenup was signed, 37 percent encourage signing a prenup but do not require it. Amongst the 40 percent who neither advocate nor require it, the reasons varied from distaste at discussing divorce with a couple about to marry (12 percent), specific objections to certain of its provisions on Jewish law grounds (2 percent), the fact that it has not received approval from rabbinic organizations whose opinion he valued (12 percent), and uncertainty about its effectiveness in preventing agunah cases (14 percent). The majority of those who had not adopted it (60 percent) had no objections or gave no reasons.[66] Since 2012, the International Rabbinic Fellowship, (an alternative modern Orthodox rabbinical association more sympathetic to gender equality claims) has required its member rabbis to use prenuptial agreements. It also requires its own members to sign postnuptial agreements with their wives if they hadn't previously signed a prenuptial one.[67]

The Rabbinical Council of America prenuptial agreement is an agreement to accept binding arbitration of the divorce issue by its rabbinical court, the Beit Din of America. In it, the husband assumes liability for support payments (*parnasah*) to the wife from the date of separation until termination of the marriage through delivery of the get. The wife loses her right to this maintenance if she fails to appear when summoned to the BDA or if she refuses to receive a get issued under their supervision. The current version is calculated at $150 per day (this would amount to $55,000 per annum). This payment cannot be offset by her assets or earnings. The agreement gives spouses the option of also granting the beit din the power to decide questions of property division and maintenance, child support and custody and to consider issues of fault in determining entitlements with regard to those things.

The RCA prenuptial agreement was held to be enforceable in a case of first impression in Connecticut Superior Court in 2012. The wife did not ask that the court compel her husband to grant the get, or even to appear before the beit din. She asked only for the daily damages set out in the agreement of $100 per day from the date they ceased to live together as husband and wife. The husband objected, arguing that enforcing the contract would violate the First Amendment prohibition against judicial entanglement in religion, in violation of the Establishment clause. The court disagreed, finding that the contract could be enforced through the application of neutral principles of Connecticut contract law, which required no understanding of or position on the merits of Jewish law. It required no profession of belief or religious act from the husband. Enforcing the contract would only incidentally provide support to the Jewish religion, because the parties had elected to use it to trigger the contract. Moreover, the state had a legitimate interest in enforcing premarital contracts.[68]

The RCA prenuptial agreement has been enthusiastically adopted by many young American Orthodox couples. There are attempts to legitimate the practice of signing prenups by clergy and community. The practice is emerging of signing the prenup as part of the marriage ceremony in order to celebrate the husband for demonstrating concern for the wife.[69] While this may normalize the practice in popular Jewish culture, it may pose problems with enforcement. If the prenup is understood to be a premarital agreement, the law in some states requires that it be signed well in advance of the wedding ceremony in order to avoid the possibility of spouses being coerced to sign prenups at the last moment.[70]

Conclusion: potential impact of foreign law bans on remedies for gender inequality under Jewish law

Until passage of the Florida law in May of 2014, the impact of these foreign law bans on Jewish law practices was somewhat speculative, as the states in which they were passed did not have large observant Jewish communities. Florida is different. There are approximately 640,000 Jewish Floridians, constituting just over 3 percent of the state population[71] and 9 percent of Jews in the US.[72] The effect of the new law is to require a court to reject contractual provisions selecting a forum that will apply foreign law to family law disputes involving divorce, alimony, division of marital assets, child support and child custody[73] if this alternate legal regime does not guarantee the rights the parties would enjoy under Florida law.[74] Parties can waive these rights under contract, but these waivers should be narrowly construed.[75]

The Florida legislature clearly attempts to calm fears that this will disable Jewish law practices, by suggesting that Jewish law as administered by mainstream rabbinical courts in America would likely be in compliance with the procedural protections required by the new law. See, for example, the laudatory reference to the Beit Din of America in the report of the State Judiciary Committee:

The BDA established itself as a limited court alternative to civil disputes. Functioning primarily as a court of arbitration, BDA has undergone significant changes since its inception 50 years ago. Present-day proceedings include:

- A detailed and standardized rules of procedure.
- An internal appellate process.
- Consideration of choice of law.
- Testimony from experts on secular law and commercial practice.
- Recognition of common commercial custom.
- Belief in communal governance, as reflected in multiple individual arbitration.

As noted, the BDA incorporated these features over time. "Recognizing this secular focus on procedure and procedural fairness, the BDA adopted detailed rules and procedures that contributed tremendously to the eventual secular acceptance of BDA decisions".[76]

This characterization of the best practices observed in this rabbinical court makes no mention of the extent to which the substantive law administered there might respect the rights of Americans. The prenuptial agreement's protections for women have been watered down since the first models were promulgated. Some rabbinical authorities expressed concerns that this arrangement might be abused by wives who would fail to request the get in a timely fashion after separation or to schedule an appointment to receive it, while accruing maintenance entitlements. Worries were also expressed that the husband might be improperly penalized for delays in delivery of the get that flowed from reasonable logistical challenges. The model agreement was amended in 2008 to require that the wife's right to support only accrues from the date upon which she serves her husband with written notice of her intent to collect on it.

The Beit Din of America has also published an opinion finding that a husband who acts in good faith can be exempted from the obligation where this appears to the beit din to be equitable, where the wife has implicitly waived this right by leaving the marriage or where the wife has brought a claim for support in civil court. It is hard to imagine what proportion of cases might be left over after the contract has been gutted in this way.[77]

Lang v. Levi[78] gives a sense of the scope of the rabbinical courts' discretion in these cases. The couple separated in 2005 and the husband offered to give the get in 2006. The wife refused to accept the get.[79] The get was not actually delivered and accepted until 2008. At that time, the wife sought daily damages from the date of separation until actual delivery of the get (over $100,000). The beit din disagreed with this interpretation, awarding her damages only from the date of separation until his first offer to deliver the get in 2006 ($10,000). Both spouses were unhappy with this interpretation and applied for review by the beit din. Rabbi Mordechai Willig, *Segan Av*

(Deputy Chair) of beit din, reversed the beit din's award, ordering that the wife was not entitled to any damages under the contract. Jewish law entitled him to interpret the terms of the contract in light of the underlying intent. This was to punish unreasonable withholding of the get and that the husband had offered the get within a reasonable time. Willig also found the wife had implicitly waived her right to support under the contract by failing to seek to enforce it in a timely manner and that she was barred from bringing a claim for financial relief in the rabbinical court when she had already pursued these matters fully in civil court.

The wife sought judicial review of the beit din's arbitration decision with the Circuit Court of Montgomery County, but the case was dismissed on the basis that the arbitration agreement gave the beit din the sole power to interpret the contract in accordance with Jewish law. The wife appealed again, and lost again. The Court of Special Appeals held that Rabbi Willig's decisions were reasonable. Even if they disagreed, the First Amendment prevented them from second guessing the rabbinical court's interpretations of its powers under Jewish law, as to do so would involve the state in interpreting religious doctrine.

Some feminist commentators may welcome the role foreign law bans may play in weakening the authority of rabbinical courts in America. Susan Weiss cautions that rabbinical courts are not committed to preserving the rights of women and that the primary effect of these prenuptial contracts is to bring people to accept the jurisdiction of rabbinical courts.[80] Indeed, some ultra-Orthodox rabbinical courts have drafted their own versions of the prenuptial agreement which arrogate much more power to the beit din, for example, dealing with all aspects of finance, property and custody and forbidding the parties to resort to the civil court.[81]

I am more conflicted, noting the educational role that signing prenuptial agreements, even if they are never acted upon, can play in creating a culture within the Jewish community that delegitimizes get-based extortion and get refusal. The loss of the possibility of civil enforcement may discourage people from signing prenuptial agreements in the first place. When the province of Ontario barred faith-based arbitration in family law after a similar moral panic about Sharia law in 2006,[82] many rabbis across Canada stopped using the RCA prenuptial agreement. The practice is only now re-emerging in Quebec, where the law is more amenable.[83] Canadian Jewish feminists give the Ontario ban on faith-based arbitration mixed reviews. They were actually pleased with some of its implications. It makes it much easier to resist a husband's demands that he wants the rabbinical courts to decide all issues in the divorce, including property and maintenance. Such orders, unless based on Ontario law, would be moot. Moreover, it does not preclude the beit din from ruling on issues that are not covered by Ontario law, like the supervision of a get and whether the husband is in contempt for failing to appear before them. Conversely, Yael Machtinger's chapter in this volume demonstrates the negative impact loss of the remedy of the halachic prenuptial agreement to arbitrate has had on processing Jewish divorce disputes in Canada.[84]

A case decided under the Kansas foreign law ban suggests the potential these laws have for undoing strategies developed to protect women disadvantaged under religious laws, both Muslim and Jewish. In *Soleimani v. Soleimani*, the parties had been married under Sharia law in Iran and then moved to the US. They had signed a prenuptial contract in which the husband promised to pay the wife *maher* (deferred dower) of $700,000 which would become payable only upon divorce. They separated after two years. The husband argued that the maher payment was an unenforceable foreign law obligation.

The wife brought evidence that maher is intended as a disincentive to divorce and to provide financial compensation for the wife should the marriage fail, in lieu of property division or maintenance which are not available under Islamic law. The Kansas court could merely have declined to enforce the maher agreement based on evidence grounds, for it was not provided with a proper translation of the document. However, the judge went on to say that the claim should also be rejected because the foreign law ban now made enforcement of such contractual terms contrary to the public policy of Kansas.

While accepting that the maher provision was meant to ameliorate women's disadvantage under Muslim laws of divorce, the judge found that it could not be enforced because it could not be severed from the overall patriarchal tone of Islamic divorce.[85] Such analysis could clearly also bar enforcement of ameliorative provisions in Jewish prenuptial agreements as well. Indeed, the *Soleimani* court opined that it would be equally reluctant to enforce Jewish ketubot, characterizing both species of contracts as "products of a legal system which is obnoxious to equal rights based on gender".[86] The *Soleimani* court refused to enforce elements of a legal system that "embeds discrimination through religious doctrine. Rather the protection of Kansas law, applicable to the parties here, requires an equitable division of property in a secular system that is not controlled by the dictates of religious authorities or even a society dominated by men who place value on women in medieval terms".[87]

Activists on behalf of divorcing Jewish women have sought to create a nexus between the disadvantages women experience under Jewish divorce law and the more egalitarian norms of civil family law. Civil law is used both to counter-balance the unfair bargaining power conferred on men by Jewish law and to put pressure on Jewish law authorities to find solutions within Jewish law for this disadvantage. It is a mistake to understand the relation between Jewish law and civil law in this area as binary. Religious women's lives overflow these demarcations. Both religious authorities and parties to disputes seek to manage the relationship between the two regimes to their best advantage. Men may seek to use their power under Jewish law to claw back awards women have received under civil law. Women may use the civil law to undermine these male prerogatives. Rabbinical court judges, at least those who serve a modern constituency, seek to harmonize the two systems and welcome the assistance of civil law in appropriate cases.

Thus, the notion promulgated in *Soleimani* and the foreign law ban that gave rise to it, that all aspects of a "system" of foreign religious law should be banned to protect women fails to understand that even the "system" of Jewish law does not speak with a uniform voice. Rather there are competing conceptions and Jewish law in particular cases may be egalitarian. The job of feminist law reform is to identify and enhance these elements. Civil law can and has helped to do this in the US and Canada. Foreign law bans, a bad faith effort to demonize Sharia law under cover of protecting women, put these careful connections between civil and religious law in jeopardy. They undermine an important source of protection for religious women and an incentive to transformation of discriminatory religious family laws.

Notes

1 In a notorious 2014 case, Israel Meir Kin, who is alleged to have withheld a divorce from his wife Lonna, for 10 years, seeking money and sole custody, claimed to have received a *heter mea rabbanim* (permission of 100 rabbis) to take a second wife because his first wife was unable or unreasonably unwilling to receive a divorce at the beit din he had selected. She refused to appear there because she believed it to be corrupt and feared she would be coerced into acceding to his demands. The Organization for the Resolution of Agunot, an activist group, organized a rally outside this second wedding, calling for him to free his first wife. Ryan Torok, "Till Get Do Us Part", March 27, 2014, *The Jewish Journal*. www.jewishjournal.com/cover_story/article/till_get_do_us_part_israel_meir_kins_las_vegas_wedding. For analysis, see Rabbi Aryeh Klapper, "Why We Have the Lonna Kin Situation", May 9, 2014, *Fresh Ideas from the HBI: The HBI Blog*. https://blogs.brandeis.edu/freshideasfromhbi/why-we-have-the-lonna-kin-situation/.

2 See, for example, the excerpts from the "Gallery of Missing Husbands" section of the *Jewish Forward* in Isaac Metzker (ed), *A Bintel Brief: Sixty Years of Letters From The Lower East Side To The Jewish Daily Forward* (New York: Schocken Books, 1971).

3 Rabbi Simeon J. Maslin, *Yes, There is a Reform Divorce Document, But Don't Call it a Get*. www.reformjudaism.org/yes-there-reform-divorce-document. Maslin notes that some Reform rabbis nevertheless advise couples to get a Conservative or Orthodox Jewish divorce if they wish to ensure that they can remarry in a Jewish ceremony and that any future children will be considered legitimate under Jewish law. The Reform movement does conduct a Ritual of Release to provide a sense of closure for the parties after a civil divorce, but they make clear that this has no legal effect under Jewish law.

4 Faiza Patel, Matthew Duss and Amos Toh, *Foreign Law Bans: Legal Uncertainties and Practical Problems*, 1 (New York: Brennan Center for Justice/Center for American Progress, May 2013).

5 The most recent instances were Alabama's *Foreign Laws in Court, Amendment 1* (2014) and Florida SB 386 *Application of Foreign Law in Courts* (2014). Legislation was passed in Missouri in 2013 but vetoed by the governor. Legislation was introduced but failed to pass in Alaska, Utah, Wyoming, New Mexico, Nebraska, Texas, Minnesota, Iowa, Missouri, Arkansas, Michigan, Indiana, Kentucky, Mississippi, Georgia, Florida, South Carolina, Virginia, West Virginia, Pennsylvania, New Jersey, New Hampshire and Maine. *State Legislation Restricting Use of Foreign or Religious Law*, Pew Research, Religion and Public Life Project.

6 South Dakota HB 1253, signed into law March 19, 2012. 19-8-7.
7 Louisiana Act no. 886, July 2, 2010.
8 Idaho House Concurrent Resolution 44, passed March 25, 2010. Congress has not seen fit to act on this suggestion.
9 See, for example, *Atlas Shrugged*, the un-ironically named website of Pamela Geller who runs Stop Islamization of America. She was instrumental in the successful campaign to stop the construction of a mosque near ground zero of the September 11, 2001 attacks in New York City. For a description of links between Geller and ALAC, see the Anti-Defamation League account at www.adl.org/civil-rights/discrimination/c/stop-islamization-of-america.html.
10 For a detailed discussion of how white supremacist discourse has adopted the notion of protecting vulnerable minority women, see Sherene Razack, *Casting Out: The Eviction of Muslims from Western Law and Politics* (Toronto: University of Toronto Press, 2008) and Lila Abu-Lughod, *Do Muslim Women Need Saving?* (Cambridge, MA: Harvard University Press, 2013).
11 Patel et al., *Foreign Law Bans*, at 7.
12 Oklahoma State Question Number 755, received May 25, 2010.
13 *Awad v. Ziriax*, 670 F. 3d 1111, 1130 (10th Circ. 2012).
14 Tennessee, *Material Support to Designated Entities Act of 2011*, P.C. no. 497.
15 Igor Volsky and Jack Jenkins, "Why Isis is not, in fact, Islamic", *Think Progress*, September 11, 2014.
16 *Material Support to Designated Entities Act 2011.*
17 For example, a Maryland court refused to recognize a talaq divorce purportedly delivered at the US embassy in Washington DC by a Pakistani husband now domiciled in the US. He had rushed to the embassy after his wife sued for civil divorce and support in Maryland state court, *Aleem v. Aleem*, 931 A. 2d1123 (Md Spec. App. 2007), affirmed 947 A. 2d. 489 (Md. 2008) (cited as a worrying Sharia law case on the ALAC website *Ten American Families and Shariah Law*).
18 Andrea Eiliott,"David Yerushalmi, The Man Behind the Anti-Shariah Movement", *New York Times*, July 30, 2011.
19 Southern Poverty Law Centre, *Extremist File: David Yerushalmi.*' www.splcenter.org/get-informed/intelligence-files/profiles/david-yerushalmi.
20 Jerry Gordon, "Massachusetts Rabbi Sends Letter To Florida Legislature On American Law For American Courts Bills" *Watchdogwire* March 29, 2013. http://watchdogwire.com/florida/2013/03/29/new-jersey-rabbi-sends-letter-to-florida-legislature-on-american-law-for-american-courts-bills/.
21 Andrea Eiliott, "David Yerushalmi".
22 See, for example, Lee Ann Bambach, "The Enforceability of Arbitration Decisions Made by Muslim Religious Tribunals: Examining the *Beth Din* Precedent" 25, 2 *Journal of Law and Religion* 379–414 (2009–10); Cristina Puglia, "Will Parties Take to Takhim? The Use of Islamic Law and Arbitration in the United States" *Chicago-Kent Journal of International and Comparative Law* 13 (2013) 151, 173. Michael J. Broyde, "The Pillars of Successful Religious Arbitration: Models for American Islamic Arbitration Based on the Beth Din of America and Muslim Arbitration Tribunal Experience" *Harvard Journal of Racial and Ethnic Justice* 30 (2014) 33; Michael J. Broyde, "Sharia and Halakha in North America: Faith Based Arbitration as a Model for Preserving Rights and Values in a Pluralistic Society" *Chicago-Kent Law Review* 90 (2015) 111.
23 David Masci and Elizabeth Lawton, *Applying God's Law: Religious Courts and Mediation in the U.S.*, April 8, 2013. (Pew Research Centre, Forum on Religion and Public Life.) www.pewforum.org/2013/04/08/applying-gods-law-religious-courts-and-mediation-in-the-us/.
24 Yaacov Feit, "The Prohibition on Litigating in Secular Courts" 1:1 *Journal of the Beit Din of America* 30–47 (2012). Simcha Krauss, "Litigation in Secular Courts" 2:1 *Journal of Halacha and Contemporary Society* 35, 48 (1982).

25 See Anver M. Emon, *Religious Pluralism and Islamic Law: Dhmimmis and Others in the Empire of Law* (Oxford: Oxford University Press, 2012).

26 Lee Ann Bambach, "The Enforceability of Arbitration Decisions Made by Muslim Religious Tribunals", 25:2 *Journal of Law and Religion* 385 (2009–10).

27 See supra, Chapter 7 by Lahav and Chapter 8 by Zalcberg Block.

28 See Susan Weiss and Netty C. Gross-Horowitz, *Marriage and Divorce in the Jewish State: Israel's Civil War* (Waltham: Brandeis University Press, 2012); Elana Sztokman, *The War on Women in Israel: A Story of Religious Radicalism and the Ravaging of Freedom* (Naperville, IL: Sourcebooks, 2014).

29 See, for example, Samia Bano, *Muslim Women and Shari'ah Councils: Transcending the Boundaries of Community and Law* (Basingstoke: Palgrave, 2012) and Samia Bano and Jennifer Pierce, *Gender Equality and Justice in Family Law Disputes: Women, Mediation, and Religious Arbitration* (forthcoming, Brandeis University Press, 2016).

30 See infra, Chapter 10 by Klapper.

31 David Masci and Elizabeth Lawton, *Applying Gods Law: Religious Courts and Mediation in the US*, April 8, 2013. www.pewforum.org/2013/04/08/applying-gods-law-religious-courts-and-mediation-in-the-us/.

32 Ibid.

33 *Awad*, supra 13.

34 Elizabeth Tighe et al., *American Jewish Population Estimates* (Waltham: Brandeis University, Cohen Center for Modern Jewish Studies, 2013).

35 *New York Domestic Relations Law* s 253 (McKinney 1986 and Supp. 1997).

36 S 10A *Matrimonial Causes Act 1973* as amended by the *Divorce (Religious Marriages Act) 2002.* In South Africa, a 1997 amendment added s 5A of the *Divorce Act of 1979.* Similar legislation was recommended in 1992 by the Australian Law Reform Commission, but this proposal has not been adopted. Melinda Jones and Peta Jones-Pellach, "Jewish Women & Religious Freedom" *in Australia Status Report* (2011).

37 *Schwartz v. Schwartz*, 153 Misc 2d789 (1992).

38 *New York Domestic Relations Law* s. 236(b) (McKinney 1986 and Supp. 1997). This codified the ruling in *Schwartz v. Schwartz* that "the misuse of a power differential between the parties be it a monetary differential or otherwise (i.e., the withholding of a Get or withholding one's appearance before a Beit Din) can be taken into account by a court in equity." Thus, such misuse of a power differential *may* be a factor in determining equitable distribution under the catch-all clause (13) of *Domestic Relations Law* § 236 (B) (5) (d). 153 Misc 2d 789 (1992).

39 *Giahn v. Giahn*, *New York Law Journal* 25 (April 13, 2000).

40 Bambach notes that most cases do not even bother to raise the issue in order to dismiss it. Bambach, "The Enforceability of Arbitration Decisions Made by Muslim Religious Tribunals" 25:2 *Journal of Law and Religion* 389 (2009–10).

41 Danial Gordis, *Erusin: The First of the Two Ceremonies.* www.myjewishlearning.com/article/erusin-the-first-of-the-two-ceremonies/2/.

42 For a detailed account of how the English translation of the Conservative ketubah was altered to obscure references to unhappy prospects of divorce while the Aramaic version retained them, see Ben Steiner, "Readings of the 'Lieberman Clause': Development, Translation and Interpretation", MA. Thesis, Jewish Theological Seminary, 2014 (on file with the author) and Ben Steiner, "The Lieberman Clause Revisited" (forthcoming 31 *Nashim*: Special issue on "New Historical and Socio-Legal Perspectives on Jewish Divorce", Lisa Fishbayn Joffe and Haim Sperber, eds.).

43 *Avitzur v. Avitzur*, 58 NY 2d 113 (1983).

44 Ibid. at 115.

45 *Margulies v. Marguilies*, 42 A.D.2d 517; 344 N.Y.S.2d 482; 1973 NY App. Div. LEXIS 3798. An appellate court struck down a further order for incarceration for contempt because such coercion might render any get given invalid. They upheld the contempt finding and related fines because the husband's later behavior was clearly contumacious. He never intended to grant the get despite having since remarried and was clearly using the civil court to serve his own motives in freeing himself. *Kaplinsky v. Kaplinsky*, 198 A.D.2d 212; 603 N.Y.S.2d 574; 1993 N.Y. App. Div. LEXIS 10208. The Supreme Court of New York, Appellate division, upheld an order of contempt and ordered an uneven distribution of the couple's assets under s. 253 of New York's *Domestic Relations Law* (the get law) giving the wife 75% of the family assets.
46 *Mayer-Kolker v. Kolker*, 359 N.J. Super. 98; 819 A.2d 17; 2003 NJ Super. LEXIS 116.
47 *Minkin v. Minkin*, 180 NJ Super. 260; 434 A.2d 665; 1981 NJ Super. LEXIS 653. The court does not say whether a rabbinical court had made a compulsory order against the husband, but given that the Orthodox rabbis agreed to testify that he was obligated, such an order may have been in place. In this situation, the get issued subsequent to the civil court intervention may have been valid under Jewish law because its effect was to order him to do what the Jewish court was already ordering him to do.
48 *In re Goldman*, 196 Ill. App. 3d 785 (1990).
49 Ibid. at 790.
50 Ibid. at 797.
51 See supra Klapper in Chapter 10.
52 There are exceptions to this rule. Convictions were handed down in 2014 of a group of Rabbis who, for $50,000, would kidnap a recalcitrant husband and induce him to grant the divorce with a cattle prod. William Sokolic, "Three New Jersey Rabbis Convicted in Forced Divorce Scheme", *Reuters*, April 21, 2015. www.reuters.com/article/2015/04/22/us-usa-new-jersey-rabbis-idUSKBN0NC2LJ20150422.
53 *Babylonian Talmud*, *Gittin* 9:8, as translated in Judith Hauptman, *Rereading the Rabbis: A Woman's Voice*, 114 (Boulder, CO: Westview Press, 1998).
54 *Burns v. Burns*, 223 NJ Super. 219 (1987) at 225.
55 *In re Scholl*, 621 A.2d 808 (1992) Family Court of Delaware.
56 *Aflalo v. Aflalo*, 295 NJ Super. 527, 525 (1996).
57 "If the get is something which can be coerced then it should be the Beth Din which does the coercing. In coercing the husband, the civil court is, in essence, overruling or superseding any judgment which the Beth Din can or will enter, contrary to accepted First Amendment principles," *Aflalo*, para 19.
58 For a powerful statement from the Supreme Court of Canada, see *Bruker v. Marcovitz*, [2007] 3 S.C.R. 607; 2007 SCC 54.
59 *Koeppel v. Koeppel*, 138 NY S 2d 366 (1954). The husband refused to comply with undertaking in separation agreement to give the get, even when the rabbis and scribes showed up at his place of work to make it easy for him. His appearance before the Rabbinate to answer questions and give evidence needed by them to make a decision is not a profession of faith. "Specific performance herein would merely require the defendant to do what he voluntarily agreed to do. Defendant's statement that the ceremony before the Rabbinate takes from two to two and one-half hours is not worthy of discussion. That is not much out of a lifetime, especially if it will bring peace of mind and conscience to one whom defendant must at one time have loved." 373. But also see *Steinberg v. Steinberg*, 1982 Ohio App. LEXIS 12314, in which 8th Circuit Court of Appeals declares reciprocal undertakings to cooperate in Jewish divorce unenforceable because it constitutes enforcement of a religious practice.

60 *Waxstein v. Waxstein*, 90 Misc.2d 784 (1976).

61 *Rubin v. Rubin*, 75 Misc. 2d 776 (1973). The wife sought enforcement of a newly negotiated support agreement granting her increased support. The agreement required the wife to consent to receive the get which she did not do. In a judgment carefully parsing Jewish law sources, Judge Gartenstein refused her petition and ordered her to accept the get.

62 *Shapiro v. Shapiro*, 110 Misc 2d, 726 (1981).

63 *Avitzur v. Avitzur*, 114.

64 Linda Kahan, "Jewish Divorce and Secular Courts: The Promise of Avitzur" 73 *Georgetown Law Journal* 193–225 (1984) at 221–2. In *In Marriage of Noghrey*, 169 Cal App 3d 326, 332 n2 (CT App 1985), a ketubah which granted wife liquidated damages of 500k or half of the husband's property was declared invalid because it provided an incentive for her to seek divorce to gain a windfall. California passed legislation the following year which permits prenuptial agreements dealing with financial issues so this may no longer be good law. Christopher C. Melcher, "Evaluating the Enforceabilty of a Premarital Agreement" 31:1 *Family Law News* (2009).

65 Rachel Levmore, "Rabbinic Responses in Favor of Prenuptial Agreements" 42:1 *Tradition* 29–49 (2009).

66 Rabbi Shlomo Weissmann, Director of the Beit Din of America, personal communication, May 3, 2012.

67 "International Rabbinic Fellowship Takes Historic Step to Prevent Future Agunot", *International Rabbinic Fellowship* website, May 24, 2012.

68 *Light v. Light*, 55 Conn L. Rptr 145 (2012).

69 There is also a movement to get people to sign post-nuptial agreements. Happily married couples are encouraged to renew their vows by committing to treat each other fairly in the case of divorce. In one such ceremony, 32 couples, some of whom had been married for almost 50 years, came together at Bais Abraham Synagogue in St. Louis to celebrate their post-nuptial contracts with dinner and dancing. The event, called "Untying the Knot", was meant to educate the community about the importance of signing prenups as a solution to the agunah problem and to provide protection for the generations of couples who married without them before they began to come into favor. Rori Picker Neiss, a maharat (ordained female clergy) student working at the synagogue, explained that without retroactive signing of these documents it would take 50 to 60 years for the process of insisting on prenuptial agreements to stamp out the problem. Hody Nemes, "Postnup Parties Get Happily Married Orthodox Couples To Plan for Divorce", *The Jewish Forward*, February 9, 2014. Read more: http://forward.com/articles/192443/postnup-parties-get-happily-married-orthodox-coupl/?p=all#ixzz2swsr8ZDT.

70 Esther Macner, *Jewish Prenuptial Agreements: The Promises and the Pitfalls*, paper delivered at the Seminar on New Approaches to the Agunah Problem, HBI Project on Gender, Culture, Religion and the Law, April 15, 2015 (on file with the author). There is a separate RCA model prenuptial agreement for California which aims to comply with that state's rules regarding full financial disclosure, independent legal advice and completion of the agreement at least seven days before the wedding. All versions are downloadable from the BDA website at: www.bethdin.org/forms-publications.asp. After signing, the document is sent to the BDA in New York City where it is registered. The couple later receives a copy.

71 Ira M. Sheskin and Arnold Dashefsky (eds). "Jewish Population in the United States, 2012" *American Jewish Year Book* (Dordrecht: Springer, 2012) 143–211.

72 American Jewish Population Estimates.

73 The Florida Senate Committee on the Judiciary, Bill Analysis and Fiscal Impact Statement, SB 386, March 24, 2014.
74 Florida SB 386 *Application of Foreign Law in Courts.*
75 Bill Analysis, ibid.
76 Bill Analysis, quoting Michael J. Broyde, "Jewish Law Courts in America: Lessons Offered to Sharia Courts by the Beth Din of American Precedent" 57 *New York Law School Review*, 287, 303 (2012–13).
77 Rabbi Mordechai Willig, "The Prenuptial Agreement: Recent Developments" 12 *The Journal of the Beit Din of America* (Spring 2012).
78 *Lang v. Levi*, 16 A. 3d 980 (2011) Court of Special Appeals of Maryland.
79 This decision gives no reason for her refusal. Another decision of the Special Court of Appeals relating to these parties discusses the ongoing disputes they engaged in over child support, alimony and attorneys' fees that were note settled until 2008. See *Julie Levi v. Zion Levi*, 8 MFLM Supp 101 (2009).
80 Susan Weiss, "Sign At Your Own Risk: The RCA Prenuptial May Prejudice The Fairness Of Your Future Divorce Agreement" *Cardozo Women's Law Journal* 6, no. 49 (1999).
81 Esther Macner, *Jewish Prenuptial Agreements*, supra.
82 S 2.2 *Arbitration Act of Ontario* 1991.
83 Janice Arnold, "Prenups Now Required at Two Orthodox Shuls" *Canadian Jewish News*, June 4, 2012.
84 See Yael Machtinger, infra Chapter 11 in this book.
85 *Soleimani v. Soleimani*, Kansas District Court, Johnson City, (no. 11cv 4668, August 28, 2012).
86 "Similar to the traditional Jewish law discussed in *Noghrey*, which allows men to unilaterally declare a divorce, under Islamic law, a husband enjoys similar unilateral rights and the maher obligation is viewed as a means of tempering the inequities of traditional religious law", para 24.
87 "If this Court had been presented with expert testimony and an accurate translation of the contract at issue, it might have the ability to separate religious doctrine from that which is obnoxious to our public policy", para 31. The court appeared reluctant to recognize the Maher agreement in any event. The case dealt with a very short "temporary marriage" and would have obligated the husband to pay maher in the amount of $677,000.

10 Systemic misunderstanding between rabbinical courts and civil courts

The perspective of an American rabbinical court judge

Rabbi Aryeh Klapper

Introduction

American religious communities are fundamentally voluntaristic, and the Constitution is understood as denying all coercive authority to religion. This does not prevent religions from claiming universal jurisdiction, however, only from enforcing it. They are permitted no tools other than persuasion to change others' offending behaviors and beliefs.

In stark contrast, the Torah[1] assumes throughout that the Jewish people are a political community bound and constituted by enforceable religious law. Its legislation relates comprehensively to the human condition rather than only to matters ecclesiastical, including for example laws regarding torts, employment, and manslaughter as well as animal sacrifice, holidays, and circumcision. The extensive set of laws regulating sexuality include prohibitions against particular couplings, obligations within marriage, and a divorce process.

Rabbinic legal tradition, known as Halakhah, self-understands as an organic outgrowth of Torah whose existence and authority are recognized by Torah. However, that tradition developed for more than a millennium in conditions of political subordination. Its legal system was compelled to negotiate questions of authority and jurisdiction with the non-halakhic state.

Until the Emancipation, Jews were treated by almost all states as a separate political community within the non-Jewish state rather than as part of a politically undifferentiated citizenry. Negotiating jurisdiction generally involved carving out spheres where the state would support the autonomous operation of Jewish law. Endogamous Jewish marriage generally fell within those autonomous spheres. That is to say, the state would recognize marriages of Jews to other Jews only if they were recognized by halakhic authorities. For women in polygamous societies, and for both men and women in monogamous societies, remarriage in the lifetime of an initial spouse required obtaining a religious divorce. This is the law in the contemporary State of Israel, for better or for worse.

Post-Emancipation, Western states relate to their Jewish citizens exclusively as individual members of their national political communities. They on principle deny Halakhah all secular authority. Jewish citizens can therefore remarry after obtaining only a civil divorce, even if they were previously married in a manner recognized by *both* civil and halakhic authorities and their earlier spouse is still alive. They can also resolve all ancillary issues, such as asset division and child custody, through the state's legal system without reference to Halakhah or halakhic authorities.

The democratic secular state's regulations regarding those ancillary issues tend to track the changing ethical and practical opinions of secular society. Halakhah does not necessarily develop in tandem, although, as we will see below, its practice also does not develop in hermetic isolation. The current American and Jewish systems for divorce recognize and require very different grounds and procedures for divorce, and impose very different consequences for the failure to obtain divorce. Their default settings on issues such as property division may also differ significantly.

Many American Jews have little awareness of the Jewish system, and do not consider themselves subject to its jurisdiction. Nonetheless, Jewish law sees all Jews as subject to its jurisdiction in this area, and applies its consequences whether not they recognize its jurisdiction.

As a judge on an Orthodox Jewish religious court (the Beit Din of Boston), my task in the area of divorce is to navigate this contrast in a fashion that preserves the integrity of both Jewish law and the Jewish community to the extent possible. Our court sees itself as responsible for and accountable to the entire Jewish community, and not just to those who see themselves as bound by Jewish law. This is particularly true with regard to those non-Orthodox Jews who voluntarily seek Orthodox halakhic divorces. It is our obligation and aspiration to ensure that their experience of Jewish law is positive, and certainly to ensure that Jewish law is not seen as generating or complicit in extortion or cruelty.

This is not the case everywhere. The phenomenon of the "*modern agunah*",[2] of women who are trapped in Jewish marriages involuntarily despite having completed their civil divorce, represents the most egregious failure of halakhic leadership in this regard. Furthermore, during secular divorce negotiations many Jewish women in Israel and the West experience religious law as enabling the implicit or explicit extortionist threat of being trapped as an agunah.

There is no reliable assessment of how many women in the United States fall into the modern agunah category, or of how widespread and effective the threat is. But there is no question that the phenomenon exists and constitutes an ongoing desecration of G-d's Name.

The Beit Din of Boston is justly proud of its record in this area. In my dozen years of service, we have had only two agunah situations extend for any length of time after civil divorce, and we have never permitted a husband to demand payment in exchange for agreeing to the Jewish divorce. Nonetheless, we cannot be certain that there are no "silent agunot", i.e.

women trapped in marriages who for reasons of misinformation or hopelessness have not sought our help. Nor do we know whether or to what extent the implicit threat colors property and custody negotiations, although it seems intuitive that the power of the threat is related to the frequency and effectiveness with which it is carried out.

In this article I hope to offer a perhaps somewhat original account of why the phenomenon exists. *Specifically, I argue that modern agunah situations are better understood as resulting from the interaction between legal systems than from the internal dynamics of Halakhah.*

My hope and belief is that this analysis, and the resulting strategies and tactics recommended – many of which are in place at the Beit Din of America, the Beit Din of the Chicago Rabbinical Council, and/or the Beit Din of Boston – can enable women in the process of divorce, their attorneys and advocates, and effective batei din to work together to significantly diminish both the frequency and effectiveness of attempts to create agunot. I must emphasize at the outset that signing a prenuptial agreement that binds the couple to arbitrate any issues of religious divorce in the Beit Din of America is the single most effective method currently available for preventing subsequent injustice. The standard such agreement, which is secularly enforceable and includes a financial agreement which in practice strongly discourages get-refusal, is known as "The RCA Prenup" and can be downloaded free of charge from www.rabbis.org.

I must also stress that my analysis is not intended to address injustices or gender inequities, real or alleged, that arise purely from considerations internal to Jewish law, Jewish legal interpretation, or Jewish jurisprudence. Such issues require separate treatment.

Interaction and injustice

The existence of parallel legal systems always carries the risk that they can be leveraged or arbitraged to create injustice, and that risk is exacerbated when the outcome of a particular system matters more to one party than the other. For example, the Boston Beit Din sees cases in which only one party regards themselves as sexually restricted by the absence of the Jewish divorce, or *get*. In such cases, the Jewish divorce is clearly worth more to the party which already regards itself as unrestricted, and he or she may seek to use the threat of withholding the get as a negotiating tactic in settlement negotiations. In other cases, a party that cares only about the Jewish divorce threatens to leave the country as soon as the get is completed, even though the civil process is ongoing.

There are at least four ways in which interaction between the American and Jewish divorce systems can lead to injustices intended by neither:

1) Lack of enforceability: Halakhah (Jewish law) recognizes only its own divorces, and requires the consent of both parties for divorce. It also recognizes that the withholding of consent can become an illegitimate

weapon of control or blackmail, and permits a beit din to coerce consent in order to prevent injustice. However, rabbinic courts in the US have no secular enforcement capacity and no mandatory personal jurisdiction even under Jewish law. The requirement for consent remains in force, but the capacity to coerce is greatly limited by the lack of mandatory jurisdiction and capacity for enforcement. What remains is social pressure, and to be effective that requires a communal cohesion that is largely absent.

2) Two bites at the apple: Because Halakhah cannot enforce its rulings, parties who lose a case in beit din have the practical option of rejecting that ruling and suing afterward in secular court, essentially restarting the case from scratch. Similarly, parties dissatisfied with a civil settlement may suddenly "get religion" and seek to relitigate the case in a beit din. This will often be accompanied by a claim that they went to secular court only in response to a summons from the other side.
3) Use of one system precludes proper use of the other: Halakhah provides for the issuance of a *seruv* (contempt citation), which enables the use of coercion even if a party has not appeared to plead their case. However, standard practice is not to issue a *seruv* on behalf of a party who is themselves rejecting the jurisdiction of the beit din on any other issue. If one spouse files first for divorce in a secular court, a rabbinic court may see them as rejecting its jurisdiction over property issues, and therefore decline to issue a *seruv* against their spouse who is refusing to participate in a Jewish divorce.
4) Use of one system undoes the other: A Jewish divorce which a husband issues under coercion is completely invalid unless that coercion has been directly and properly authorized by a beit din. For example, if a secular court orders the husband to issue a Jewish divorce, any divorce he issues will likely be considered invalid under Jewish law[3].

Below I seek to identify and clarify the jurisdictional issues arising from the interaction of the halakhic and secular systems of divorce law in the United States, and to provide some guidance as to the best ways of negotiating them in the interest of justice.

However, it is necessary to emphasize at the outset that there is no formal system linking Jewish divorce courts in America. Different courts may therefore legitimately have very different procedural and substantive approaches to crucial issues.

The lack of institutional accountability also makes it difficult to combat corruption. Parties and lawyers must research the reputation and positions of any beit din before appearing before it. Yet since there is so little information in the public record about most batei din, such research is likely to be based on unreliable rumor and hearsay. It is therefore best practice to:

a) Move cases whenever possible to a beit din which does have a strong public record, such as the Beit Din of America.

b) When issues beyond the issuing of a get, such as custody and asset division, will be litigated in beit din, write a detailed arbitration agreement specifying the procedures and legal framework the beit din should follow.

Of course, in a contested divorce these issues themselves will be subject to negotiation, as will be discussed below.

The need for Jewish divorce

Under Halakhah, valid marriages between living Jews can only be dissolved through the divorce procedure of Jewish law (*get*). Neither party to a marriage may remarry until such a divorce has been obtained. However, the consequences of formal adultery fall more heavily on wives than on husbands, in two ways:

1. Sex between a married woman and a man other than her husband violates a Biblical prohibition, whereas sex between a married man and a woman other than his wife violates a Rabbinic prohibition. In a variety of ways the social and religious implications of violating Biblical prohibitions are generally more severe than those for violating Rabbinic prohibitions.
2. The child of a married woman and a man other than her husband is a *mamzer or mamzeret (bastard)*, who has severely limited marital options within the Jewish community. This status will be transmitted to their children as well. The child of a married man and a woman other than his wife does not face any unique barriers to marriage.

Jewish divorce generally takes place only with the consent of both parties. In a limited set of cases, Halakhah permits batei din to obtain consent via coercion in order to prevent women from being trapped in dead marriages. However, Halakhah expressly invalidates consent obtained by coercion via non-Jewish courts or private Jewish parties, even in circumstances where coercion by rabbinic courts would be legitimate and effective. Divorce formally requires the husband or his appointed agent to prepare and deliver a *get* (bill of divorce) which cannot cannot take place without the participation of the husband at least to the extent of appointing an agent.

It should be noted that divorce is not the only way to enable a presumptively married woman to remarry under Halakhah. A beit din may challenge the presumption and declare that the couple was in fact never married. This can happen in two basic ways. a) The beit din can find that the initial marriage ceremony was flawed. There are three kinds of marriage flaws:

1) Flaws in the substance of the marriage ceremony. For example, marriage is affected by the symbolic transfer of an object worth at least a

perutah[4] from the possession of the husband to the possession of the wife. (It is necessary to note that the object, generally a ring, is purely symbolic – it is not a purchase price, and the husband does not afterward own the wife. The simplest demonstration of this is that the husband cannot transfer possession of the wife to anyone else. Rather, the formal making of a *kinyan*[5] is the way in which halakhah gives obligations legal force.) An example of a flaw might be discovering that the husband was not the owner of the ring used at the ceremony.

2) Flaws in the witnessing of the marriage ceremony. A marriage that was not witnessed is not valid, even if there is incontrovertible evidence that it occurred. The witnesses serve a ritual purpose – they make the wedding a public affair – rather than an evidentiary purpose. For example, close relatives, women, and flagrant Shabbat violators are invalid witnesses for this purpose, as they are for the purposes of witnessing and signing the get, even though batei din will accept their testimony as evidence where the goal is to establish the facts.
3) Flaws in the eligibility of the parties to marry. For example, a marriage is invalid if at the time of marriage the wife had previously married another man who was still alive and had not given her a get, or if either party was not then halakhically Jewish, or if the marriage was incestuous.
4) The beit din may determine that the marriage took place under a fundamental misconception.
   The standard here is the following: The husband must have had a condition at the time of marriage which the wife was unaware of and which, had she been aware of it, would have caused her to refuse to marry him.

To the best of my knowledge, the default setting of most batei din is to write a get for any monogamously committed heterosexual Jewish couple that requests one, even if a legal argument could be constructed to invalidate their marriage. This is especially the case when a beit din, such as the Boston Beit Din, explicitly sees its constituency as including the nonobservant and/or non-Orthodox Jewish communities. For example, such a beit din will write a get for a couple that includes a convert who was converted by a non-Orthodox beit din and has never been observant, even though it would certainly refuse to recognize the conversion in question[6]. For this reason a divorce receipt is not per se sufficient evidence of Jewishness in a beit din.

However, when the husband refuses to give a get, or demands money in exchange for his permission, the beit din will revisit each of these issues. In an uncontested divorce, for example, the beit din will not ordinarily enquire as to the Shabbat-observance of the witnesses to the parties' marriage. But if the husband refuses the get, or uses the possibility of refusal as a negotiating tactic, the beit din will ask such questions as part of its efforts to prevent extortion or cruelty.

The key challenge to understanding here is that Halakhah does not see legal arguments as subject to the true/false binary. Rather, Halakhah assigns legal arguments a probability, and then consults formal decision procedures to determine what level of probability is necessary to make an argument probative in a particular case. This means that a beit din can make apparently contradictory rulings, e.g. that one couple requires a divorce and another does not, even though the only legally relevant distinction between the cases is that the husband sought to use the get as a blackmail tool.

For example: Halakhah invalidates certain kinds of gamblers as witnesses, but there is much dispute as to the boundaries of that rule. A beit din might rule generally that betting on fantasy sports leagues does not invalidate witnesses, and nonetheless cite the involvement of a witness in such leagues as among the grounds for invalidating a wedding in an agunah situation. If the husband subsequently agrees to participate in a Jewish divorce procedure, the beit din will write and deliver the get[7].

This can be very confusing to both wives and lawyers. Best practice is to go for the get in all circumstances, and to act as if the get is necessary in all cases, but if there is recalcitrance, to ask the beit din to investigate the possibility of retroactive invalidation.

Another case in which the beit din should be proactive is if a previously married woman has children or is pregnant by another man, and now comes to be divorced from the first husband. In such a case, granting the get would likely be seen as recognizing that the first marriage was valid, and therefore that the children are mamzerim and legally unmarriageable within the Jewish fold. The beit din will therefore seek ways to invalidate the marriage, although such ways cannot always be found[8].

It is important to understand that different courts will have different standards and positions as to which arguments suffice to invalidate a marriage under what circumstances. For example: Some batei din will rule that a marriage at which a non-Orthodox rabbi officiated is presumed to have been invalidly witnessed and can be invalidated on that ground alone. Other batei din may seek to investigate the guest list or watch the wedding video to determine whether any valid witnesses were present, even if the groom or officiant specifically designated invalid witnesses. Batei din will disagree as to whether Jews who have never been openmindedly exposed to fully halakhic Judaism are considered flagrant Sabbath violators and therefore invalid wedding witnesses.

Bottom line: Women should never assume that their marriage will be invalidated, but they should also not surrender hope because one rabbi or beit din failed to find an argument to free them[9].

Issues of administrative jurisdiction

The halakhic system as described in the Mishnah[10] and Talmud[11] assumes:

a) that batei din have the power to physically and financially coerce obedience to their decisions, and

b) that they have mandatory and exclusive jurisdiction over Jews with regard to all areas of divorce, including child custody and the disposition of assets, and
c) the existence of an effective system for resolving jurisdictional issues among batei din. These include mandatory personal jurisdiction for an established local beit din, rules for assigning jurisdiction in cases involving parties from different localities, and the ZABLA mechanism for resolving any remaining jurisdictional disputes. Under ZABLA, which is a Hebrew acronym for "this litigant chooses one for himself", each party appoints one judge, and the two judges thus selected combine to choose a third. Rabbinic courts generally consist of panels of at least three judges.

None of these conditions (a–c) currently holds true in the United States:

a) Batei din have no power beyond the purely social, and in a voluntary and fragmented community, the majority of which does not see Jewish law as binding, their social power is severely limited.
b) Secular courts claim jurisdiction over all financial and custody issues, and even couples who seek a Jewish divorce generally litigate all such issues in the secular courts. Even when a couple signs a secularly enforceable agreement to arbitrate finances and custody in a beit din, secular courts will not give great deference to the beit din's custody rulings.
c) There is controversy as to whether any batei din in the US are considered suffciently "established" under Jewish law to have mandatory jurisdiction in their locality. This means that in the absence of a prior agreement to arbitrate in a specific beit din, either spouse can reject the authority of any particular beit din and demand ZABLA. In the absence of effective oversight, the ZABLA system has become an ethical swamp, owing to a combination of genuine corruption and a fundamental disagreement as to whether the judges chosen directly by the parties are intended to serve as their advocates. ZABLA should be considered only when a reputable beit din is given the power to reject proposed arbiters from either side.

The upshot is that all contemporary Jewish divorces involve both the rabbinic and the secular courts, whether directly or by implication. For example, secular negotiations and proceedings regarding custody may take place under the threat by one or both parties that they will refuse to give or accept a get unless they are satisfied with the custody outcome. Negotiations in beit din on any issue other than religious divorce take place under the threat that a dissatisfied party will ignore the outcome in beit din and file suit in secular court. Even parties with a strong preference for using the rabbinic court system must use the secular system to enforce any beit din verdict. Even sincere efforts to use batei din exclusively may be frustrated by issues of forum shopping, jurisdictional standoffs, or vulnerability to biased or corrupt tribunals.

In practice, even in divorce cases where both parties have been and remain[12] observant Jews, one party or the other generally insists on litigating issues of custody or finances in secular court. There are a variety of reasons for this, including:

a) a broadly held view that women do better in both areas in secular court than they do in rabbinic court. I think that this is an overgeneralization, but it is certainly true on some issues in some courts. This perception can lead husbands to see themselves as victims if their wife files in civil court,
b) a popular lack of confidence even among religiously observant Jews in the competence and incorruptibility of rabbinic courts,
c) a sense that a large advantage in financial resources translates more effectively into power in the secular courts than it does in rabbinic court. For example, the sheer expense of responding to motions in secular court can bring a party to the brink of financial ruin and beyond.

Default settings for administrative jurisdiction

Different legal systems can be leveraged only where they infringe on each other's spheres of operation. To understand how Halakhah and American law can be leveraged to create injustice, and what we can do to prevent such injustices, we need to explore the ways in which these systems naturally tend to infringe on each other's spheres, and then find ways to prevent or manage such infringements.

Secular courts

The Establishment clause of the Constitution prevents the US government from treating any person as involuntarily subject to the jurisdiction of any religious court on any matter. The secular legal system therefore claims primary jurisdiction over any matter of divorce that it is not precluded from, without regard to the jurisdictional claims of the Jewish legal system.

However, the secular courts may disclaim jurisdiction on the grounds of:

a) "excessive entanglement" with religion –

   For example: There are many disputes among classical, medieval, or contemporary Jewish legal authorities and texts that affect whether a woman in a particular case is considered married under Jewish law, or whether a husband in a particular case is obligated to divorce his wife. Secular courts will generally not see it as their job to make such decisions.

b) freedom of religion –

   For example: Secular courts generally cannot require someone to engage in a religious ritual, even if their participation in that ritual is in the interest of another party[13].

Neither of these principles is absolute, and they can be overridden on grounds such as compelling public interest or the best interests of a child. New York State, for example, has several laws intended to prevent a party from withholding a religious divorce while pursuing a secular divorce, on the argument that the State has a compelling interest in preventing its citizens from being trapped in dead marriages.

Final divorce decrees will often include a commitment by each party to remove all barriers to the remarriage of the other. We will address below the halakhic issues these raise. From a constitutional perspective, there are two challenges to such commitments:

1) Can the courts enforce a commitment to perform a religious act? (As noted above, Rabbi Bleich argues that no religious act is involved in divorcing Jewishly.)
2) Can the courts effectively decide whether all halakhic barriers to remarriage have been removed? For example, I was involved in a case where, to fulfill such a commitment, the husband arranged for the Jewish divorce under the auspices of a Conservative Rabbinic court, which would not be recognized by most or all Orthodox Rabbinic courts. The wife insisted that an Orthodox divorce was required. Could the courts have held the husband in contempt under those circumstances?

Rabbinic courts

Jewish law gives rabbinic courts primary jurisdiction in all cases where both parties are Jewish, regardless of the civil or political setting. The Biblical verse "These are the law-matters that you will place before **them**"[14] is understood as a formal prohibition against bringing a dispute with another Jew into the secular courts.

Even if one party has already filed in the civil courts, batei din may assume jurisdiction if the other party requests this. However, batei din may refuse jurisdiction over a case if the party making the request has previously refused their jurisdiction on this matter or is currently refusing their jurisdiction on another matter, especially if the matters are substantively related.

Furthermore, a rabbinic court may provide one or both parties with a *heter arkaot*, a religious dispensation to use the secular courts, if:

a) the other party has already filed in secular court, and is presumed unwilling to drop their case and litigate in beit din instead.
b) there is no realistic prospect of a beit din's ruling being followed by the other side. For example, in many batei din the refusal to sign a binding arbitration agreement at the outset of the divorce process is prima facie evidence of unwillingness to follow an eventual ruling.

As well, for some issues there is little or no possibility that the beit din's ruling will be secularly enforceable, and in cases of abuse or violence there may be a need for the threat of coercion by the police.

c) it is clear for other reasons that the rabbinic court system cannot provide justice. For example, some batei din see a party's insistence on using ZABLA rather than an existing court as prima facie evidence that the process will be corrupt, especially if that party also refuses to give an established beit din the power to veto potential arbiters.

As well, few if any batei din have the infrastructure and resources to deal with complicated discovery issues, abuse allegations, et al. Rabbinic divorce courts in the United States are funded mostly by direct fees, in some cases supplemented by funds obtained through other activities such as kashrut supervision. As a result, understaffing is endemic, and service on such courts is generally a third or even fourth job for judges. For example, the Boston Beit Din has no full-time employees, no support staff, meets at most once weekly, and pays judges a minimal per diem for their service. It is funded largely by a flat $550 fee for divorces, which must cover the fee for a scribe, three judges, and two witnesses, as well as all overhead, and the expenses of most non-divorce cases. The Boston Beit Din does not charge for any stage of the conversion process, or for certificates of Jewishness or singleness, both of which are required for Jewish marriage in the State of Israel. The absence of a broad community funding mechanism also means that the judges and courts are often not directly accountable to the lay communities they serve, and often they are not accountable to any local rabbinic community either.

Interaction of administrative jurisdictions: problems and approaches

Filing first in beit din has little or no impact on secular proceedings. However, filing first in secular court can have significant impact on rabbinic proceedings, in the following ways:

a) The party which files first in secular proceedings, in the absence of rabbinic permission or post facto justification, may be seen as having illegitimately rejected the jurisdiction of beit din. This is true even if that party now agrees to remove all matters to the rabbinic courts, on a logic of equity that they are forum shopping after a negative assessment of the likely outcome in secular court rather than genuinely accepting rabbinic jurisdiction.

It is therefore recommended that a party obtain explicit and specific written halakhic permission, preferably from a broadly recognized rabbinic court (or from the rabbinic court that will have jurisdiction over the Jewish divorce case as the result of a binding arbitration agreement: see below), rather than from a private rabbi, before filing any divorce-related matters in secular court. As the criteria for authorizing such filings differ from beit din to beit din, it is best to ask in advance specifically what grounds any particular beit din would consider sufficient to authorize such a removal. Better practice would be for batei din to post their criteria publicly, as the Beit Din of America has done.

b) Responding to an opposing party's filing in secular court generally does not create difficulties. However, if new issues are raised, and counterclaims, a rabbinic court may choose to regard this as a first filing. In such cases ongoing communication with a rabbinic court is desirable.

Regarding both a and b: it is important, for both practical and equity reasons, to distinguish between cases in which the husband and wife have a substantive dispute about jurisdiction, and those in which one party is using the jurisdictional issue purely as a tactic. In other words:

a) In some cases, one spouse genuinely wished to have property and/or custody issues in beit din, and the other genuinely refused to do so and filed in secular court against the other spouse's will.
b) But in other cases, neither the husband nor the wife ever intended to submit property or custody issues in beit din rather than in secular court. Whichever spouse filed first for divorce would file in secular court – in our case, it is the wife. When she subsequently asks beit din to compel her husband's appearance, or his giving the get, the husband claims that the wife forfeited the beit din's protection by filing in secular court rather than in beit din.

In the latter set of cases, most batei din, and I believe strongly that this is the correct and equitable policy, will rule that the wife is still entitled to their assistance. The formal logic behind this policy is as follows: the default setting is that every member of the community is entitled to the full efforts of the beit din. This right is forfeited only when a person is declared in contempt of the beit din. To be in contempt of beit din, it is not sufficient for a person to have chosen to utilize the secular courts rather than the rabbinic courts. Rather, a person must have:

a) Failed to obey the summons or order of a particular beit din which possessed mandatory jurisdiction over the question at issue.
b) Responded to the formal summons (*hazmanah)* or order of a particular beit din by refusing to allow the case to be decided before any reputable beit din. (Note: with regard to property issues, I believe the correct and equitable policy is to regard someone as refusing to appear unless they sign a binding arbitration agreement. Otherwise, their agreement may be a sham. See "two bites at the apple" above. This is the policy of the Boston Beit Din and of the Beit Din of America.)

c) Acted in a manner that convinced a reputable beit din to issue a heter arkaot to their opposing party.
This however is a potentially dangerous loophole, since a beit din with poor judgment could issue a heter arkaot to a husband who was merely bluffing and had no intention of going to beit din, especially if they issue the heter without requiring the husband to sign a binding arbitration agreement. The better policy, as per above, is for a beit din to issue the heter only after the moving party has signed a binding arbitration agreement.

The former set of cases requires its own division, into cases where:

a) The husband wishes to adjudicate issues in beit din out of genuine religious principle.
b) The husband seeks to adjudicate issues in beit din because he believes that forum will be more advantageous to his interests than the secular courts.

Let us discuss b) first.

On a formal level, in such a case a beit din is entitled to issue a summons to the wife, and declare her in contempt if she refuses to appear. Furthermore, it is not easy for a beit din to establish a husband's motives if he chooses to dissemble.

Nonetheless, there is an issue of equity here, as the husband is not actually in a different abstract relationship to the authority of beit din than the wife – he will submit to it only when doing so serves his own interests.

The possibility of such cases is created when there is a large gap between the expected outcomes of the two systems. This is the first of several reasons that I will adduce in support of the position that it is in the interests of batei din to narrow that gap.

As a matter of practice, in cases where the wife receives a summons from a beit din whose positions on such issues are unknown, or whose positions are known to diverge negatively from those of the secular court with regard to her interests, she should counterfile in a beit din with known and more favorable positions. However, as I point out below, the goal has to be to find an acceptable tribunal, not an ideal one. ZABLA under the auspices of an acceptable beit din may be the best available outcome.

My policy argument, however, is that while a beit din *need* not issue a summons on behalf of someone who is themselves in contempt, it is not forbidden to do so. In cases such as these the beit din should pursue the get as if there were no other issues, and pursue those other issues as if there were no get.

However, I would be open – as I am not in other cases – to beit din considering the equities of individual cases.

Let's move on to a), cases where the husband wishes to adjudicate issues in beit din out of genuine religious principle.

In such cases, it is very difficult for a beit din to issue a summons on behalf of the wife. Certainly it cannot do so before the completion of the civil divorce, as the husband, from the perspective of Halakhah, is only demanding his just due.

However, it is vital again to note that there is no mandatory jurisdiction without a prenup. If the husband refuses to go to an equitable court, or to agree to equitable arbitrators, the beit din is entitled to say that the wife has done all she could.

Moreover, once the civil divorce is complete, the beit din is entitled to say that the husband has suffered a past *process* wrong in being forced to litigate in secular court, but that he has suffered no *substantive* harm[15], and thus has no valid grounds for withholding a get and can be ordered to do so.

It should be clear, however, that a beit din will in practice only adopt these policies if it sees the secular courts as presumptively equitable. If it does not, the mere plea of inequity on the husband will suffice to have the wife declared in contempt.

We will discuss below why batei din might or might not think secular courts are presumptively equitable.

There is a strong temptation for a spouse to forum-shop among rabbinic courts when deciding where to file. However, in the absence of compulsory jurisdiction, the other spouse will respond by filing in a rabbinic court with a record of favoring their own gender or circumstances. The result is a jurisdictional standoff which prevents anything constructive from happening, and the secular courts will not interfere on the ground of excessive entanglement.

It is therefore best practice for the lawyer for one spouse to file from the beginning in the beit din whose jurisdiction is most likely to be accepted by the other spouse, so long as that court is known to be procedurally just and honest and to issue decisions that fall within the range of equity, *even if a different court might rule more in accordance with their client's interests.* It is vital to research the reputation and policies of a rabbinic court before filing.

Unfortunately, there is not yet a reliable online or other formal source for such research. A reasonable approach for now is to ask the Beit Din of America, the Beit Din of Boston, or the Beit Din of the Chicago Rabbinical Council whether they are confident that a particular beit din will be just, honest, and equitable, and whether any divorce it produces will be accepted by other batei din. If no local beit din meets that standard, one should file in the Beit Din of America.

A party will often seek, for reasons good or ill, to postpone the Jewish divorce until after the financial and custody issues have been resolved in secular court. When this happens, lawyers often put in the final divorce decree a requirement that each party do all they can to remove any religious or other barriers to the other party's remarriage. As noted above, such requirements can be difficult to enforce secularly on freedom of religion grounds, and counterproductive Jewishly in that the threat of contempt may constitute coercion. It is therefore best practice in such cases to insist that the Jewish divorce be completed immediately *before* the final decree is signed. This can be done in the secular courtroom itself if necessary. In cases where the agreement has already been signed, but one party is obstructing the Jewish divorce, it is essential to receive expert rabbinic advice as to how to proceed.

The best solution to the potential problem of conflicting jurisdictions among batei din is a prior arbitration agreement binding the parties to a specific beit din on all issues related to the Jewish divorce. This should ideally have been done premaritally, but failing that should be arranged at the very outset of divorce proceedings. (Note: The secular courts will likely not enforce a beit din's order to deliver a get, even if that order results from a binding arbitration agreement. However, such an agreement will make it more difficult for the husband to file in a different beit din. Furthermore, the beit din may award additional support until the Jewish marriage is ended, and such as award will likely be enforced by the secular court.)

The question of whether and how to sign agreements binding the parties to arbitrate custody and financial issues in a specific beit din will be addressed below.

Content jurisdiction

Issues of jurisdiction arise with regard to the content as well as the administration of the law. Jewish law recognizes the legitimacy of secular law and courts in particular circumstances. A beit din may decide that the Jewishly proper basis for decision in a case is secular law. It may also decide that a particular party is properly pursuing his or her case in secular courts, but that he or she may nonetheless not take advantage of any decisions in those courts that substantively conflicts with Jewish law.

At the outset of any divorce case in which at least one party seeks to be divorced under Jewish law, both Jewish and US law will claim jurisdiction over all issues other than the issuance of the Jewish divorce, and US law will have some claims to jurisdiction over that issue as well. However, ultimately only Jewish law can determine the validity of the Jewish divorce, and a divorce that is ruled to have been coerced by the civil court will be deemed invalid. Similarly, any custody arrangements ordered by a religious court will be reviewed by the secular court, or an appointed guardian ad litem, to ensure that they are compatible with the best interests of the child. For example, custody decisions based on purely religious grounds will likely be viewed skeptically.

With regard to financial issues, matters are more complex, and it is best to prevent any daylight from opening between the secular and religious systems. Each system has a method for allowing itself to legitimate the content of the other. Specifically:

a) Secular law generally recognizes binding arbitration agreements that allow or mandate that the chosen arbitrator use a system of religious law.
b) Halakhah generally grants parties the capacity to stipulate the rules which an arbitrator should use.

> However, the stipulation should be to a static set of rules, not a grant of authority to a non-halakhic system which can then evolve during the years of marriage into something utterly different. The rules can leave much room for the arbitrator to exercise discretion in the application of standards, for example New York State law as of the date of agreement. However, there is controversy as to the halakhic validity of an agreement to arbitrate under whatever New York State law will be at the time a dispute arises.

The interests of justice, and generally of any party desiring a Jewish divorce, are to prevent any conflicts of either administrative or content jurisdiction. Both parties are best off when they have signed a binding arbitration agreement that commits them to a specific beit din with transparent procedures and policies.

The prenuptial agreement endorsed by the Rabbinic Council of America offers parties the option of stipulating that finances will be resolved in accordance with principles of equitable distribution endorsed by the state in which the marriage takes place at that time. This option is intended to account for women's concerns that they will do less well under Halakhah than under secular law. To some extent this is built off procedural concerns that are largely mythical with regard to mainstream batei din, such as a belief that the courts will not directly engage with women but only with their male representatives. Similarly, the supposition that women will do substantially less well under Halakhah is not necessarily true. To understand why, we need first to distinguish between the law concretized in the texts of the halakhic tradition and the law as practiced by batei din, in both areas.

Property

Under the law of the Mishnah, the husband agrees to support the wife (beyond feeding and clothing her, which may be mandates preceding this bargain) in exchange for her ordinary earnings. The wife keeps the principal of any property which she brings into the marriage, but has no presumptive share in any capital accrued by the couple subsequently. She is entitled to collect the ketubah, which is a flat sum determined prenuptially. (For Ashkenazi Jews, this is either a fairly small amount of silver or else a sum of not more than a year's support at a middle-class level[16]. For Sefardic Jews, the amount is negotiated prenuptially, but sometimes exorbitant sums negotiated in that form are disregarded by batei din as emotional expressions rather than financial commitments.)

Husbands are exclusively responsible for the support of minor children. If there is a nursing child, the wife can demand the going rate for nursemaids in exchange for suckling the child.

In comparison to the standard default legal frameworks in the US, community property and equitable distribution, it seems clear that the default halakhic framework gives the wife less in cases where the couple has amassed significant assets during the marriage, even and especially in cases where she has been the major earner. The presumption or fear that a beit din will rule on the basis of this framework drives many women to avoid beit din even at the risk of becoming an agunah. It should also be clear that the halakhic framework may be advantageous to the wife when the marital assets are minimal, or if the expenses of child support are great, but this is little-known or understood.

However, there are at least four halakhic principles that can sideline or overcome this default framework:

1) The law of the Mishnah is understood as applying to "ordinary" earnings of the wife, as opposed to earnings obtained through "extra effort".
2) "All conditions in financial matters are binding" is a general principle of financial Halakhah. This means that almost all default conditions can be set aside by the explicit agreement of the parties.
3) "The law of the land is the land" may be taken as incorporating civil law defaults into Halakhah. In other words, according to many authorities Halakhah allows civil law to override its default settings if the civil legislation is understood to be serving a legitimate neutral civil purpose.
4) "The custom of the land" may be taken as a presumptive default even when it differs from the default halakhic framework. In other words, Halakhah acknowledges that justice in contracts is related to the expectations of the parties, and sometimes acknowledges that the expectations of the parties are shaped by civil rather than religious law. In such cases the interests of justice may require incorporating civil law into Halakhah even where their defaults contradict.

How might these principles play out in contemporary beit din jurisprudence?

1) A beit din might rule that all of a wife's earnings at a job outside the home are considered to be obtained through "extra effort". They might similarly rule this about earnings at any job that occupies a significant amount of her time. On this argument the husband would in practice have no right to almost any of the wife's earnings.
2) Placing assets in a joint account, or in the wife's name, may be regarded by a beit din as a waiver of the husband's rights to such assets.
3) If the state's default framework is understood as serving a compelling state interest, e.g. discouraging divorce, or preventing divorcees from becoming wards of the state, a beit din may rule that it overrides the halakhic default.
4) A beit din may rule that, for good or for ill, most couples marry with the expectation that the civil default framework will govern asset division if they divorce. That expectation will function in the same way as an explicit condition.

In addition, explicit prenuptial or arbitration agreements will be taken as overriding the default.

For all these reasons, it is entirely possible that a beit din's legal framework for asset distribution will be neutral relative to that of the civil courts.

The problem is that because:

a) the virtue of transparency is not widely recognized by rabbinic courts,
b) batei din operate under the presumption that divorce settlements should be private,
c) batei din generally lack even minimal administrative resources, and
d) very few batei din deal with the financial outcome of more than a few divorces each year

it is very difficult for a woman to know in advance how a beit din will rule in her particular circumstances.

The Beit Din of America has published its guidelines on most of these issues, but otherwise women can rely only on word of mouth or the personalities of the judges.

It is therefore best practice for lawyers, in a case where the wife chooses for reasons of conscience or pragmatism to litigate in beit din, to reach an arbitration agreement with the other side that specifies the legal framework for the arbitration in as much detail as possible.

Custody

There may be concern that a beit din will mechanically apply the rule found in Shulchan Arukh Even HaEzer 82:7 that awards custody of all children to the wife until the age of six; all boys over six to the father; and all girls over six to the mother. There may also be concern that a beit din will consider the religious interests of the child, as it understands them, to be dispositive. Finally, there may be concern that a beit din is simply not competent to determine issues where complicated psychological issues are involved, let alone where there are charges of abuse.

On the other hand, a beit din may well be more culturally sensitive in significant ways. The Boston Beit Din has seen cases in which issues that may not be on the radar of secular courts became major irritants, deliberately or not, between the divorced parties. These include the timing of transferring children on Fridays, which can make observance of the Jewish Sabbath[17] difficult for both child and parent, and the halakhic prohibition against ex-spouses being secluded together, which can complicate pickup and dropoff.

My impression is that most batei din in North America adopt a "best interests of the child" standard substantively indistinguishable from that used by the secular courts[18]. The better batei din will call in psychological advice and/or appoint the equivalent of a guardian ad litem. Here too the lack of transparency and of actual precedent makes this difficult to know with confidence in advance. However, the civil court will in any case overrule any beit din ruling that it perceives as being against the best interests of the child.

Conclusion

Very few husbands begin the divorce process with the intent of withholding a get simply to torment their wives. Agunah situations generally develop out of attempts to use the get as leverage to obtain more favorable terms for asset distribution and custody. This is among the reasons why the RCA Prenuptial Agreement has been so effective at preventing such situations; it creates an upfront cost for withholding a get that makes the tactic prudentially unwise.

Use of that agreement has become widespread only recently, however, and even then only within the Modern Orthodox community. This means that the vast majority of Jewish divorces in North America today and for at least some years will take place without the protections afforded by that agreement, and therefore in the shadow of or under the actual threat of get refusal.

This threat and shadow are created and fostered by the perception that the outcomes of Jewish and secular law in such cases diverge widely, with secular law strongly tending to favor women. This perception enables husbands to justify get refusal as an effort to obtain justice and redress their wives' illegitimate gains in secular court. Furthermore, this perception drives women to insist on litigating such issues in secular court even when this risks depriving them of the protections of Jewish law against get refusal.

This perception is not necessarily unfair or unjust. Outcomes in some rabbinic courts do in fact diverge widely from those of secular court, and do so consistently in favor of husbands' interests. Since few batei din have published their guidelines, or handle, let alone publish, enough cases for a clear trail of precedent to be found, women are reasonably concerned about this.

My argument here has been that this concern can be substantively alleviated in three intertwined ways:

a) by seeking to locate arbitration in batei din that have clear published guidelines,
b) by specifying the rules that a beit din will use in any particular arbitration,
c) by properly understanding the ways in which a beit din will relate to litigation in secular court, and where possible obtaining explicit religious permission for using the secular courts.

My hope is that this article will enable women to protect themselves against the threat and reality of get-refusal, and at the same time increase the viability of arbitration in batei din as the forum of choice for resolving all such issues.

Notes

1 "The Torah" is how Jews refer to the Pentateuch in English.
2 The "classical agunah" was a woman whose husband had disappeared and there was insufficient evidence to declare him dead.

3 This can sometimes be seen in reverse, as beit din undermining the civil process. If the civil authorities pass a law intended to protect a wife during the divorce process, and the beit din declares that by invoking the law the wife will make it impossible for the husband to divorce her, the beit din effectively undoes the law.
4 A copper coin which served as the penny, or lowest value coin, of the Talmudic era.
5 A *kinyan* can involve either the transfer of property or else the assumption of an obligation. In either case it may be effected by the symbolic transfer of an object owned by one party to the other.
6 Among American Jewish denominations, only the Orthodox and Conservative claim to see Halakhah as binding. The exact boundaries between the denominations are always in dispute. As a general rule, however, Orthodox halakhists do not give faith and credit to the acts of Conservative rabbinic courts, for a variety of reasons ranging from specific substantive disagreements about the conversion and divorce processes to suspicions about the academic and religious qualifications of their judges. Conservative halakhists generally do recognize the acts of Orthodox rabbinic courts. With regard to the specific issue of agunot, Conservative rabbinic courts use a variety of mechanisms to dissolve the marriage without a consensual get, but a woman who remarried on the basis of such a ruling would be considered an adulteress by essentially all Orthodox batei din.
7 Unless the wife has already remarried, so as not to cast aspersions on the legitimacy of her second marriage, and a fortiori if she is pregnant or has children from a relationship subsequent to the beit din's declaring her free to marry.
8 Should they not be found, the beit din will investigate alternate ways of declaring that the children are not mamzerim. Again, however, there is no guarantee that such ways will be found.
9 The question of whether a marriage is invalid is not treated as part of a dispute between parties, and therefore can be submitted by one party to their preferred beit din without the consent of the other party. Furthermore, it is not really subject to jurisdiction at all, but can be submitted to whatever rabbinic authority one chooses. In practice, batei din do not always react well to having one aspect of a case that is before them taken elsewhere, especially if the other court is not generally seen as superbly qualified in this area. Since the goal must always be to release the woman from the marriage in a manner that is noncontroversial, so that she can remarry as freely as possible, it is generally best to submit the issue first to the court that has been handling the case, and to seek their permission or encourage them to ask advice and counsel from other batei din if they cannot themselves devise a solution. However, if the first beit din adopts a stringent position on a relevant issue – for example if it is unwilling to presume that the witnesses at a ceremony with a non-Orthodox officiant were invalid – and the woman knows that other broadly accepted batei din adopt a more lenient position, and the first beit din is unwilling to refer her case to that court, she may have no alternative but to bring it there herself. However, batei din need each other's recognition and goodwill to be effective, and so are loathe to intrude into each other's cases. Such transfers should therefore be handled with great delicacy.
10 The anthology of Jewish law compiled by Rabbi Judah the Prince circa 220 CE. There is much debate as to whether he intended it as a code or rather as a textbook.
11 The authoritative anthology of pre-Medieval Jewish tradition, arranged around the Mishnah. The precise date of the Talmud's compilation is a matter of great debate, but it certainly reached a form resembling that of today's text well before the millennium, and perhaps as early as the fifth century.
12 Talmud Gittin 88b.
13 My teacher Rabbi J. David Bleich has argued that Jewish divorce is not a religious ritual for the purposes of American law, since it does not require belief and the document of divorce itself is almost universally not regarded as holy by Jewish

legal authorities. See Lisa Fishbayn Joffe's chapter in this volume, for a survey of cases testing this argument.

14 Exodus 21:1, emphasis added.

15 Having been compelled to litigate in the wrong court is a non-redressable wrong. If the wife is not in illegitimate possession of the husband's money or goods, i.e. if she derived no quantifiable financial benefit from going to secular court rather than beit din, he has no cause of action against her.

16 See generally "The Ketubah in America", by Michael Broyde and Jonathan Reiss, *Journal of Halacha and Contemporary Society* (2004), available at www.jlaw.com/Articles/KETUBAH.pdf.

17 Which begins before sundown on Friday.

18 For a broad theory and some analysis of Israeli practice, see "Child Custody in Jewish Law: A Pure Law Analysis" by Michael J. Broyde, available at www.jlaw.com/Articles/childcus1.html.

11 Socio-legal gendered remedies to *get* refusal

Top down, bottom up

*Yael Machtinger**

Introduction

The purpose of this chapter is to examine (and advocate for) socio-legal gendered remedies to *get* refusal. Focusing on Toronto, I will argue that legal pluralist solutions and gendered storytelling are remedies that simultaneously negotiate between Jewish women's right to religion and their claims for equality in their right to divorce. I will begin by briefly describing the phenomenon of *siruv get*, or *get* refusal, followed by a discussion about the persistence and viability of religion in modern, public life in the twenty-first century. This discussion will establish that *siruv get* is not a problem with religion's mere existence in the secular sphere, nor a problem with Judaism or religious observance in and of itself. I will also introduce legal pluralism as a viable gendered remedy incorporating religious and secular legal orders. I will then investigate three aspects of inequality that women face in navigating both their right to religion and their right to divorce when seeking a *get*: access, impact and silencing. Examples include: access to a timely and consistent *beit din* (rabbinic court of law) in Toronto, the disproportionate impact of *get* refusal, and (re) silencing by the non-rabbinic experts/advocates who ignore women's desires for inclusion and self-narration. Finally, I argue for classic 'top down' legally implemented, and 'bottom up' grassroots socio-legal remedies. Legal pluralism, dealing explicitly with the interactions between religious law and civil courts, and gendered storytelling, empowering women by their self-narration, are remedies to *get* refusal which allow women to actively negotiate between their right to religion and their right to divorce.

Feminist sociologist, Ruth Frankenberg noted in a chapter, *On Unsteady Ground*, that researchers ought to account for their positionality.[1] As a knowledge producer and feminist researcher in socio-legal studies, it is important to be reflexive, especially in the context of this edited collection, *Women's Rights and Religious Law*. Inclusion of a diversity of positionalities in a collection like this, on the convergence of gender, religion, law, and culture, produces a rich and multifaceted study of religion and equality in public life in the twenty-first century. Consequently, it is vital as researchers to acknowledge our own particular positionalities in order to recognize that they impact the research we choose, or choose not to do and the perspectives from which we write. In other words, our positionality impacts the way we produce knowledge.[2] In that vein, my positionality, as an observant, not-yet-married, Orthodox Jewish woman, in Toronto, undoubtedly plays a central role in my research on *siruv get* generally, and my suggestions of gendered socio-legal remedies for women navigating *get* refusal in particular. I come to my research on *siruv get* with those identities in tow – observant Jew, woman, and researcher.

This chapter is part of a larger project on *get* refusal focusing on tracing gaps between law reform and social behaviour with a concentration on gendered storytelling and the complexities that surround religion, culture and identity in a particular socio-legal context. In this project, I explore to what degree Toronto is distinct from other legally plural Jewish communities, such as New York, regarding *get* refusal.[3] I hope to contribute to women's historiography of marriage, and I am inspired by the method of legal pluralism. Focusing on women's storytelling, the project also demonstrates that *get* refusal is indiscriminate and interdenominational; impacting all types of women at all levels of (non) observance, and that *get* refusal is a form of domestic abuse women endure in a pattern of other abuses. I interviewed 36 participants over the course of just under a year, from roughly early fall 2013 through late summer 2014 – beginning with expert interviews, followed by interviews with women refused a *get* in the past and present. The in-depth interviews ranged in length, typically lasting about an hour and a half to two hours. While *get* refusal falls completely within the 'classic' socio-legal sites for analysis, and is an ideal case study to examine gender, religion and equality in public life and the ways in which religious laws interact with civil courts, there have been few socio-legal scholars who have taken it up,[4] and none from a religious feminist approach or methodology. In this chapter and my larger project, I seek to ground my analysis in fieldwork, place women at the centre of analysis and write from an "insider's" perspective without abandoning Jewish precepts altogether. In the next section, I will explore *halakhic* marriage and divorce and ascertain how an asymmetry in law can lead to *get* refusal in abusive instances.

Ascertaining the asymmetry

Jewish weddings entail a religious ceremony that has its own set of laws and rituals. A Jewish wedding is sealed with a *ketuba*, a marriage contract, ensuring protection for the woman in case of mistreatment, neglect, or refusal of rights, such as the right to adequate sustenance and the right to be sexually satisfied by her husband. Judaism was the first religion to produce a document (thousands of years ago) that held the woman's rights in any esteem. The other component of a *halakhic* wedding ritual is *kiddushin*, which reserves the woman's sexual (and other) capacities for her husband alone.

A *get* is the legal way of releasing the husband from his *ketuba* contract and *kiddushin* entitlements. A *get* is a written document that has to be composed by a *sofer* (scribe) in the presence of a *beit din* (court of Jewish law). A civil divorce alone is immaterial if individuals choose to remarry within their faith and remain in their communities. Husbands are the ones who must grant a *get* by physically placing the document in the wife's waiting, open hands even if the woman is the one who initiates the proceedings. Thus, men do have the absolute right in divorce, a distinct and gendered asymmetry. At first glance, it might seem as though their positions are equivalent. The *get* must be given of his free will and must be accepted of her free will; he cannot be compelled to execute a divorce and reciprocally, she cannot be compelled to accept one. This process has the guise of equality. However, in practice, the position of the husband and wife are different in a crucial way. "The necessity for the man's consent to give the *get*, the Jewish writ of divorce, is biblically ordained, while the woman's consent is necessary by rabbinic decree. This difference facilitates resolving of the situation when a man is a victim of *get* refusal"[5] more easily, while a woman remains without the same opportunity for dissolution.[6]

Another reason that men are not often "chained" by their wives is because there are occasions where a proxy may be appointed to accept the *get* on her behalf, with her consent "presumed", yet this option is not available to women. This has led to a phenomenon whereby women (disproportionately) become *agunot* or "chained women" or more accurately, *mesuravot get*, women refused a *get*. They are unable to be released from their marital contracts and thus unable in many (religious) circles to remarry or have children without their children being deemed illegitimate or *mamzerim*. To clarify, the *get* terminates the husband's obligation to provide sustenance as per the *ketuba*, and nullifies his *kiddushin* entitlements from her (including her sexual capacity) allowing her to move on with her life freely. Hence *get* refusal has a disproportionate impact on women's lives (in a way that is unequal to men). She remains bound literally, figuratively and sexually. Consequently, it is predominantly husbands who trap their wives without issuing *gittin* (rather than the reverse)[7] making it "primarily a disability women face."[8] There is frequently *get* extortion as well, when women are compelled to forgo financial payments, custody or access in exchange for a *get* because their husbands are using the religious divorce as leverage to exact greater civil rewards.

In the vast majority of divorce cases, the legal asymmetry in *halakha* is simply a processual and banal legal step, and women are granted a *get*. Consequently, and notwithstanding, the abuse that individual men might perpetrate by taking advantage of the asymmetry, all rabbis, individual men, and particularly all of Orthodox Judaism and *Halakha* must not be branded as misogynist, discriminatory or segregationist, as some critics have said.[9] Many *mesuravot get* (women refused a *get*), who have been at the mercy of their recalcitrant husbands with the absolute right in divorce, oppose the characterization. The labels are egregious overstatements and inaccurate generalizations, despite those individual recalcitrant men, rabbis, *batei din*, and communities who do support a husband's *get* refusal. Interviews with women refused a *get* have shown that Judaism and *halakha*, in and of themselves are not 'bad', but there are Jewish men who do bad things in the name of religion.[10]

Two more points to note for clarity: first, while not all Jews feel these religious divorce proceedings are necessary, a significant number *do* – no matter to which sector of Judaism they adhere. Second, the *get* consists of roughly twelve lines wherein there is no mention of rabbis or G-d and did not use to require rabbinic supervision.[11] It was simply a legal exchange. Thus, it is noteworthy that the issue is one with interpretation or manipulation of Jewish law, not with Jewish law or Judaism writ large, and it is one that may affect Jewish women (and men) of various and *all* observance levels, *not* only Ultra or Modern Orthodox.[12] To be clear, my discussion is situated within the religious spectrum of Judaism pertaining predominantly to the Orthodox and Conservative. There are, however, a range of Jewish denominations and practices. The Conservative movement has its own set of responses on divorce, its own *batei din* and *poskim*, or rabbinical arbiters, some of whom are women (which is not yet true of Orthodox Judaism). Reform Judaism has its own practices and ideas about what constitutes a religiously binding or sanctioned marriage and divorce. For example, Reform responses believe a civil divorce suffices to undo a religious marriage. That said, the vital point to elucidate is that many Jewish women who do *not* self-define as Orthodox (or even observant in any capacity, falling within any denomination) may well want, and even feel they deserve or are owed as a right, an Orthodox *get* and wish to satisfy Orthodox *halakhic* requirements[13] and as such, *siruv get* definitively has an inter-denominational impact. I will now turn to our analysis of religion's persistence in public life.

Feasible faith: religion in modern public life in the twenty-first century

Religion is feasible in modern public life despite tendencies of the state to force religious norms and practices to the private sphere. Though there is a perception that public life in the twenty-first century ought to ideally be secular, and that religion is incongruous with secular, democratic principles of neutrality, rule of law, or democracy, it is a narrow approach not taken seriously in academic writing, or indeed in the Canadian courts.[14] This anthology shows that simply relegating religion to the private sphere does not effectively preclude it from entering the public sphere. Indeed, religious law enters civil domains in every legally plural society, including Toronto.

In socio-legal studies, case studies such as this one, about *get* refusal, are often characterized by or framed as issues of religious law or religious diversity. The secular state in the twenty-first century deals with them through tools or techniques of religious isolation.[15] In other words, the 'problem' is often framed as one with religion, rather than embracing a deeper analytical structure which would seek legal pluralist remedies[16] and the understanding that *get* refusal stems from a particular legal asymmetry, often banal, and those individuals who take advantage of them.

Though multicultural approaches, like the ones we have in Canada, ideally embrace diversity and suggest accommodation, in reality they only 'regulate' the 'others' insofar as they do not come to threaten the secular ideal. Once there is a perceived threat, or trope about the Other as 'primitive' or 'barbaric' the idealist multicultural policies quickly fade.[17] A prime example from recent Canadian memory is the banning of all religious arbitration of family disputes in Ontario in 2005 largely due to tropes about 'honour killings' in the media at the time, and a moral panic around Sharia law generally.[18] Despite Marion Boyd's recommendation *not* to ban religious arbitration for numerous reasons, including protecting women from inequalities they may face in navigating conflicting rights, like their right to divorce and right of religion, the ban went ahead to contain the threat of religion.[19] Similar tropes have recently been in the media due to the arrest of a group of 'uncivilized, barbaric' rabbis. Most recently even a sensationalized piece in *Gentleman's Quarterly* reported an FBI sting operation that sent a group of rabbis or "vigilantes", "violent crime gangs", to jail for kidnapping and using cattle prods to 'convince' husbands to grant their wives a *get* for a nominal fee of $10,000–$60,000 with inaccurate and damaging contextualizing.[20] Though I do not condone violence, the article did not explore the circumstances leading to such extreme cases in order to secure a *get*. There was no mention of the fact that to the women they helped, some of whom I interviewed, these men were heroes and by arresting them, some women were stripped of their hope for freedom.

In Canada, multiculturalist approaches to religious socio-legal issues have proven to be insufficient and inadequate. They reinforce existing hegemonic hierarchies regarding idyllic dominance of 'Christo-secularism/neutrality' in law rather than a non-essentialist dialogic approach that might actually embrace religion. Multiculturalism has served as the state's cultural regulation "tool" tolerating religion only on condition that it is private and not troubling law.[21]

Consequently these approaches change the secular legal reality, but not the social reality law on the books, not on the ground. As such, the persistence of *siruv get* despite such multiculturalist, 'tolerating' approaches, must *not* enable the secularist myth[22] that religion itself and Judaism in particular, are barbaric, primitive and must be contained – yet this is precisely the risk, the dangerous trope that emerges and which threatens religion in public life.[23]

The contention that we ought to get rid of religion altogether to correct bad behaviours done in the name of religion[24] is similar to the contention that we ought to get rid of *halakhic* marriages altogether, by jettisoning *kinyan* and *kiddushin*.[25] Just like religion persists in public life, so too will *halakhic* marriages. Similar to failures to secularize public life because large segments of the population continue to express their religion in public and interact with civil courts, there will be failures to secularize Jewish marriage because large segments of the Jewish population will continue to view *kinyan* and *kiddushin* as legal requirements to *halakhic* marriage.[26] For some, abandoning religion or relegating it to the private sphere is not a viable solution; nor should it be[27] and this conflict goes to the core of our discussion regarding women navigating between their right to religion and their right to divorce. Abandonment is not a realistic or practical remedy. My fieldwork has shown that women of all levels of observance do not want, nor should they be compelled, to sacrifice their faith for their freedom; they should not be forced to choose (a stalwart principle of feminism, by the way). By advocating for solutions that portray the religion or the rabbinic legal system themselves as the flaws, we are in reality jettisoning large segments of the Jewish community and a sacred feminist principle, thereby making Ultra-Orthodox women perhaps even more vulnerable, knowing that they would still follow the legal/*halakhic* ritual. And so we must embrace religion, even Orthodoxy and its viability, even in public life in the twenty-first century.

The tension of how to manage religion and religious marriage/divorce in secular law and society,[28] and the critique, that some aspects of religious law may be viewed as human rights violations by Canadian law, have led to a variety of failed approaches to 'manage' difference and perpetuate inequalities rather than the embrace of legal pluralist solutions which would seek a more holistic and integrative approach and which would potentially give women both a voice and a remedy to *get* refusal. This next section will consider three aspects of inequality women face in navigating both their right to religion and their right to divorce when seeking a *get*.

Examining (un)expected inequalities

Women refused a *get* suffer inequality in their right to divorce in a multitude of ways, three of which I examine here. Firstly, women lack access to *beit din* and *beit din* protocol/mechanisms of support, like *hazmanot and seiruvim*, in Toronto specifically. Secondly, *get* refusal disproportionately and detrimentally impacts women due to troubling normative cultural assumptions around get-extortion and lack of rabbinic will. Finally, widespread silencing of women's experiences persists at the hands of rabbis, advocates, and scholars alike.

While in theory, *batei din* or rabbinic courts are a community service organization that work with and for the community, unfortunately, there is unequal access to the *beit din*, especially in Toronto. Since my Masters in 2009,[29] women experiencing *get* refusal in Toronto, have continuously reiterated the difficulties they faced in simply accessing the Toronto *beit din*. From Torontonian women who got their *gets* from American *batei din*, after lengthy waits to no avail in Toronto, I repeatedly heard things like, "*I would still be an aguna all these years later if I had waited for the beit din in this community to help*" and "*the way it is handled in Toronto and New York is like night and day."*[30] Women expressed that *"it was like pulling teeth to get the secretary of the beit din to even write a letter..."* and that *"the leaders of Toronto are not being leaders."*[31] Others told me, *"I was very disappointed in the beit din of Toronto...they don't even talk to you..."* and, *"my own rabbi said 'call me when it's over & we'll drink a l'chaim'... he used to also call me on his way to New York asking me if there was anybody I would like him to call to help me convince my husband to give me a get ... Can you imagine? I told him that I do my own calls...."*[32]

Already in 2009, *mesuravot get* of Toronto taught me about the suppression they experienced in trying to access the *beit din* and enlist the *beit din*'s action and support. Women asserted their agency and took their cases into their own hands instead of relying solely on the Toronto rabbis and *beit din*. Multiple women described that the Toronto *beit din* did not return their incessant phone calls, but more disturbingly, took liberties regarding the 'standard protocol' generally implemented by *batei din* when one initiates a *get*.[33]

In instances where a spouse (the husband more commonly) refuses to appear at the *beit din* in order to begin the *get* process, there is a protocol that *batei din* must follow (although the workings of each *beit din* differ slightly according to the nuances of the community and the rabbis who serve as *dayanim*, or judges). Initially the *beit din* will call or send a *hazmana*, a letter or summons, via regular and certified mail asking the reluctant spouse to contact the *beit din* for an appointment within fourteen days. Should there be no response, the *beit din* will send a second *hazmana*, and if necessary, a third *hazmana* as well. After three summonses have been issued without appropriate response from the reluctant spouse, the *beit din* will issue a *hatra'at seiruv*, a letter of warning of the forthcoming issuance of a contempt order. If a satisfactory response is still not received from the spouse, the *beit din* may issue a *seiruv*, a contempt order, which declares the spouse to be (officially) 'recalcitrant', in contempt of rabbinic court, and subject to *kherem*, or public ostracism and condemnation, calling upon the community to take appropriate action.[34]

I was told by a number of *mesuravot get* and attorney, Sharon Shore,[35] that the Toronto *beit din* does *not* follow its own protocol, and does not issue *hazmanot*. Often, rather than send a *hazmana*, the *beit din* is more likely to issue one *only* if they are confident that the husband will actually show up, largely defeating the utility of the entire protocol of summonses and contempt orders, tools instituted to aid in prompt and fair adjudication. Of course, if they are not issuing summonses to appear, they are by default not issuing *seiruvim* and not finding would-be recalcitrant husbands in contempt of court. The Toronto *beit din* rarely (if at all) issues *seiruvim* and if they do, though not one woman reported it to me in dozens of interviews both in 2009 and 2013/14, the community is not made aware. Thus, through their reluctance to follow customary protocol or the guidelines of the Rabbinic Council of America/Beth Din of America, RCA or BDA, the *beit din* is depriving *mesuravot get* access to their day in court, and equally as disturbing, preventing them from making use of a long-standing, traditional, and uncontroversial tool often useful in convincing husbands to grant *gets*, timely *hazmanot* followed by a *seiruv* and then a *kherem*.[36]

Compounding the inequality regarding access to the *beit din* and its adjudicating mechanisms, is that the *beit din* seems to use a narrow definition to determine who is 'officially' an *aguna*, or woman chained to her marriage due to *get refusal* and will only give this classification to a woman who had been refused a *get* over an extended period of time. This is significant in that only after a woman is classified 'officially' as an *aguna* may certain remedying approaches be legitimate.

At a panel held at BAYT, the largest Orthodox synagogue in Canada, on "The Plight of the Aguna in Our Community" on April 29, 2012,[37] the Director of the Beis Din of the Vaad Harabonim of Toronto himself established that there certainly *is* breach of protocol regarding access to the rabbinical court. He confirmed that there are instances where the *beit din* will not issue a *hazmana* if they suspect a not-yet-officially-recalcitrant-husband will not show up, and he also elucidated the reason for their resistance. A *hazmana* will not be issued when the *beit din* suspects a not-yet-officially-recalcitrant-husband will not show up because that would be "disrespectful to the beit din and we cannot allow for such disrespect to occur",[38] despite the fact that this avoidance of potential disrespect comes not only at the expense of the *beit din*, but also at the expense of the *mesurevet get*. By not issuing *hazmanot* and *seiruvim*, the Toronto *beit din* is sadly delegitimizing itself and allowing the not-yet-officially-recalcitrant-husband to be more powerful not only than his wife, but also than the *beit din* (which is somehow not considered disrespectful to the *beit din* according to their own logic). Should women know that the Toronto *beit din* will take whatever action is necessary, in line with *halakha*, to help them get their *get* perhaps the gendered access to the *beit din* might be alleviated.[39]

A second aspect of inequality that occurs around the phenomenon of *siruv get* is its gendered impact. In other words, although there have been claims made to the contrary,[40] there is widespread acknowledgment that the phenomenon of *siruv get* by men overwhelmingly and indubitably impacts women disproportionately which highlights the struggle between Jewish women's right to religion and their claims for equality in their right to divorce.

There are contentions that because Orthodox *batei din* are by and large unwilling to embrace bygone Talmudic solutions to the asymmetry which leads to *siruv get*, some of which are viewed as radical and no longer appropriate for our socio-legal context, this has reinforced the husband's "absolute right in divorce".[41] These historic remedies may be viewed as inappropriate or inadequate for a number of reasons. For example, and as I noted above, women at all levels of religious (non) observance believe it is their right to get the (Orthodox) *get*[42] and not accept an 'alternate' remedy or "alleviation",[43] and because various rabbis do not view themselves as authoritative enough to reinstitute remedies that have fallen into disuse over the centuries, despite early, rabbinic-legal precedent. Indeed, perhaps if rabbis had the will to creatively embrace Talmudic solutions like *hafka'ot*, *kiddushei ta'ut*, or *get al t'nai* (annulments, mistaken or fraudulent marriage, or conditional divorce) – to name a few – there would be less of an impact on women, or at least a more equal 'playing field'. These Talmudic mitigations would, in practice, obviate the need of a husband's unconditional and uncoerced delivery of the *get* into his wife's hand because they would remove his absolute right. While that is true, I would argue that it is not enough to place blame solely on the rabbis' unwillingness to accept the alleviations. I would further reason that we not be so narrow-minded as to segregate women to an alternate or independent *beit din* that would be willing to (re)introduce alleviations like *hafka'ot, kiddushei ta'ut, get al t'nai*, or *get zikui* and tout them as 'solutions', when my fieldwork shows that women feel adamant about wanting a *get* and not an alternative. Multiple women commented, "*I'm not religious but it became so important to me.*"[44]

Women are overwhelmingly and disproportionately impacted by *get* refusal due to the uninterrogated, normative cultural assumption that a husband's refusal is his prerogative, his bargaining chip, and not a gross domestic abuse violation. The disproportionate impact on women is not (only) due to *batei dins*' reluctance or 'unwillingness' to embrace the largely defunct 'alleviations' or 'remedies'[45] like *kiddushei ta'ut* and *hafka'ot* but because communities perpetuate the norm that a *get* can be leveraged. In reality, should communities shift their normative thinking, the disproportionate impact on women when faced with *get* refusal would begin to alleviate. It is untenable and morally reprehensible that there exists a notion that a *get* must come at a price, that it can be negotiated, or that it ought to be used as a bargaining chip. The dominant discourse about '*get*-giving' must change. I would argue that in the interest of gender equality, it must become normative that the *get* is unconditional and that it is given and accepted first, before and separate from civil bargaining. It should not come during civil negotiations and thus (perhaps inevitably) be used as leverage for more favourable concessions. A cultural norm has somehow developed that a *get* is negotiable, that a husband may wait and negotiate all other matters such as custody, access, alimony and division of assets before granting a *get*, resulting in a disproportionate gendered impact to the detriment of women. Waiting until after the negotiation of the terms opens the door for *get* extortion; implying that if a woman grants her husband favourable terms, he will grant her a *get*. The *get* must be given and accepted unconditionally, and swiftly.

Moreover, as the Organization for the Resolution for Agunot (ORA) has been trying to encourage in New York, the default normative principle must emerge that any delay caused by the withholding of a *get* for any reason is tantamount to severe domestic abuse. I would argue that to alleviate some of the gendered impact of *get* refusal, Jewish communities must create a new hegemonic discourse which would frame *get* refusal as the ultimate form of abuse and control. Doing this would demonstrate that the abuse women experience by being refused a *get* impacts them disproportionately.[46] If a woman (of any level of observance), is refused a *get*, her husband has the power and control to turn her into a persona non grata; no man concerned with *halakha* will date her, and she becomes segregated from her community, unable to move on with her life and freely exit her dead marriage. *Get* refusal is a form of domestic abuse that a woman does not have the ability to escape from; it follows the *mesurevet* wherever she may go.

Perhaps the unequal impact women face would diminish if there was a concerted effort to rid our communities of the notion that "inducements" or even "bribery" are acceptable requirements in exchange for a *get*, a notion whose origins can be traced back to the twelfth century[47] (and if communities are using the *get* as a bargaining chip by relying on the twelfth century precedent, perhaps the alternate remedies which also date back ought to be equally embraced). This effort to rid the *get* of its bargaining power ought not to be taken lightly. We cannot and should not rely only on the rabbinic will to embrace old *halakhic* solutions that had once been viable; women are also impacted disproportionately because of our problematic, gendered, normative cultural ideas about '*get*-giving'. This struggle is a perfect example of juggling between Jewish women's right to religion and their claims for equality in their right to divorce. "*The bottom line is, when communities cease to tolerate wives being extorted, the problem will cease to exist.*"[48]

To reiterate, changing the cultural norm about *get*-giving *could* alleviate the gendered impact of *siruv get* for *all* women, whereas the rabbinic will to embrace alternative remedies could always only alleviate the gendered impact of *siruv get* for *some* women – those who feel a *get* is not required. There will always be some women who will hold out for a *get* because it is their will and right. Thus I contend that changing the conception of a *get's* bargaining power must thus be a part of the methods to alleviate the gendered impact of *siruv get* and not overlooked in favour of a solitary, narrow approach which seeks only to admonish the lack of rabbinic will.

The third aspect of inequality that occurs around the phenomenon of *siruv get* is silencing. There are numerous ways women are silenced while navigating the *siruv get* process, particularly in Toronto. Individual pulpit rabbis are unwilling to speak up in public in support of particular *mesuravot get* who are part of their own congregations or community at large (though they often profess their support and dismay in one-on-one meetings). Furthermore, in not speaking up, they themselves are silencing and isolating the women. The rabbis' lack of public outrage and lack of enforcing ostracism of recalcitrant husbands (or in one Toronto case, a recalcitrant brother-in-law who is refusing to perform *khalitza*[49]), creates and perpetuates indefensible passivity and ignorance about *siruv get* and places the onus solely on the unsupported women, whose plights have been silenced. One woman explained, "*When I was going through it I had nowhere to turn. I suffered in silence. [...] There is no support here in Toronto, not legal, nor rabbinical and so there is nothing to give hope*,"[50] and this excerpt reflects dozens of similar narratives. The silent acquiescence enables the persistence of this unique form of abuse – *get* refusal. Particularly in Toronto, where *seiruvim* are not issued, and rabbis are often complacent, the silencing that *mesuravot* face is especially salient.

Women working with and for *mesuravot get* have also been silenced by *batei din* to some degree. The rabbis of the Beth Din of America have ruled that *toanot* (female rabbinic court advocates) cannot be trained in America nor can they accept them in the courts as advocates.[51] There have not been any *toanot* in the Beis Din of the Vaad Harabonim of Toronto either.[52] Although these are two of many examples of silencing as a result of segregationist behaviour which women experience in light of *siruv get*, I would like to focus on one, perhaps unexpected, gendered exclusion.

No one has worked as selflessly and tirelessly for *mesuravot get* than the advocates (women and men) from a diverse body of support organizations.[53] Nonetheless, insensitive segregation of *mesuravot get* from within the field itself, and on the part of experts who work on their behalf, is frequent. First in the Mellman group survey, attempting to quantify *agunot*,[54] then at the historic 'Aguna Summit' cosponsored by JOFA – Jewish Orthodox Feminist Alliance and New York University School of Law's Tikvah Center for Law and Jewish Civilization, at each *aguna* panel or symposium held in Toronto, and in the literature, *mesuravot get* have been ignored at best, and purposefully excluded and silenced at worst.

In 2010, an attempt to quantify *agunot* began in the United States with the distribution of an *aguna* survey to secondary support organizations in the United States and Canada, such as women's domestic violence shelters that may have dealt with *agunot* who had been chained to their marriages.[55] *Agunot* themselves, however, were not personally interviewed. In designing the research, the goal was explicitly *not* to sample *agunot* or to attempt to quantify them by interacting with the women themselves, the primary source. Rather, the goal was simply to conduct a census based on secondary sources solely to quantify exactly how many cases of *iggun* existed in 2010 and had existed in the previous two and five years. The census identified 462 *agunot*.[56]

The census did not acknowledge limitations of the methods employed, and after close examination, it had methodological flaws. The main shortcoming in the context of silencing *agunot* was an unchallenged and unacknowledged presupposition that quantifying *agunot* could be achieved through simply asking support organizations, rather than, at least attempting to track the women themselves.[57] In using secondary support organizations as the sole source of data *only* case files that had been opened or reported to support organizations could have been counted in the census. Thus, there was an unacknowledged presumption of and need for the self-identification of the *agunot* to one of the polled support groups in order to be counted in the statistic. The study could not possibly have been aware of (nor did it seem to be concerned with counting or including) women who had *not* opened case files or sought support from the polled organizations. Consequently, and as with any type of domestic abuse, many *agunot* would have lived quietly, too frightened, too ashamed, or too proud to turn to support organizations for relief and thus they did not exist (statistically) in the census' point of view. The *agunot* themselves were silenced.

I would argue, that in the interest of avoiding the gender inequality of silencing, it would be more useful to actually use the *agunot*'s voices to tell the story of *iggun*'s persistence, significance, and inequalities rather than relying only on the questionable statistic that emerged from attempting to quantify *agunot* through a census whose goal was explicitly not to talk to the *agunot* themselves. Listening to women's stories in in-depth interviews made possible by trusting relationships and rapport as an insider within communities achieves a threefold goal: *mesuravot get* are heard and empowered, both social and legal change may ensue from the powerful narratives that emerge, and the method leads to much richer and impactful data.[58] This method, using women's narratives, giving sounds to the silences, rather than quantifying, would have accurately portrayed Jewish women as active agents navigating and negotiating their way through *iggun*, rather than suppressing them due to the presumption of self-identification to particular support organizations.

In June 2013, a historic 'Aguna Summit' cosponsored by Jewish Orthodox Feminist Alliance (JOFA) and New York University School of Law's Tikvah Center for Law and Jewish Civilization took place.[59] The by-invitation-only 'Agunah Summit' brought together some 200 international experts. Noted speakers included Israeli Justice Minister Tzipi Livni, Israeli Supreme Court Justice Dorit Beinisch, Professor Alan Dershowitz, Ruth Halperin-Kaddari former Vice President of the UN Expert Committee of CEDAW, and a significant group of rabbis, activists, and scholars. "The purpose of the Agunah Summit was twofold: to demonstrate the existence of systemic solutions already existing within legal systems that can resolve current agunah cases and prevent future ones and to commit as a community to their broader application."[60] At the conference, at least eight solutions or remedies were suggested.[61] The proposed remedies ranged from the Talmudic (annulments), to the modern-legal (suing for damages in civil court) and from creative (disbar lawyers aiding in extortion) to extreme (get rid of *halakhic* marriage altogether and just use civil). An outcome that seemed to gain much traction was the (re)establishment of an independent (Orthodox) *beit din* that would more readily embrace historic Talmudic alleviations, "the Rackman court revisited,"[62] the 'IBD', International Beit Din.

As the day went on, it seemed glaringly incongruous to me that the 'by-invitation-only experts' were privy to this historic day while *mesuravot get*, if present, were completely silent. Although the room was full of advocates working for justice for *mesuravot get*, some of them for over forty years, they were now also speaking on their behalf, silencing the women, preventing them from sharing their experiences and expertize at this historic Summit. The *mesuravot* were silenced. Moreover, when I asked a few organizers why there seemed to be silencing of *mesuravot get* I was told that there was concern about the Summit getting "too emotional" had the *mesuravot get* been invited to speak; a gendered cliché at its worst.[63]

Over the last five years that I have spent 'in the field', interviewing scores of *mesuravot get*, I have discovered that they are more than eager to speak out, to share their experiences, and that many actually have a burning desire to be heard. Rather than sending the message that the experts at the Summit know best which solutions *mesuravot get* ought to embrace, there could have been empowerment of women and true dialogue encouraging participants to (re) consider proposed remedies that the *mesuravot get* themselves may feel quite resistant to embracing. There was room for press, multiple panels, plenty of pastries, but no platform for the *mesuravot get* themselves.

There has also been silencing of *mesuravot get* at panels in Toronto, not surprisingly. Since I began researching *siruv get*, there has been about one event per year on the subject of *get* refusal, beginning in summer 2009. But again, what each panel or symposium had in common is that they silenced *mesuravot get*, by ignoring them at best, and/or purposefully suppressing them, at worst.[64] *Mesuravot get* are simply left out of conversations that are happening about and for them. Women constantly tell me that they want to be heard, saying things like, "*Whatever I had to say would not be heard.*"[65] After a symposium at BAYT, the largest Orthodox congregation in Toronto, a former *mesurevet get* told me how offended she was that no *mesuravot get* were included on the panel. She understood firsthand the impact a story may have; the compassion, rage, and action that a first-hand, experiential account may elicit when a woman's story is forced on the dead ears of a passive community like Toronto. A panel, a symposium, or a Summit, are often just performative compassion (lip service). Individuals come out to events with righteous indignation, talk about it, and then go home to their lives. Giving voice, giving sound to the silences of *mesuravot get* would not only empower them, and potentially elicit positive action and dialogue, particularly in Toronto, but would alleviate an often ignored and unexpected manifestation of gendered inequality that results from *siruv get*: silencing.

Much of the existing literature on *get* refusal both the more traditional, rabbinic strands, such as those by Bleich, Breitowitz, Riskin, and others, as well as the more contemporary, legal or socio-legal strands such as those by Broyde, Fishbayn Joffe, Fournier, Levmore, Weiss, and others have chosen to focus elsewhere. Their collective work is crucial to the body of literature and to movements and solutions yet the narratives of the *mesuravot get* have been left out of the debates in the literature as well.[66]

These few examples demonstrate the systemic exclusion of *mesuravot get* within the field itself and not only on the part of rabbis or *batei din*.[67] I use the word 'systemic' because the unequal silencing within the field is overlooked, unacknowledged, and yet, so deeply embedded that it is covert. Allowing the individual experiences and narratives of the *mesuravot get* to be at the centre of the 'expert' discourse creates a uniquely inclusive method that gives a voice to those who are too often silenced and marginalized.[68] In the next section, I explore gendered socio-legal remedies that address the three types of inequality discussed, and alleviate the tensions between women's inequality in their right to divorce and their right to religion.

Socio-legal remedies: top down, bottom up

Based on three types of inequality which manifest as a result of *siruv get* explored above, I will examine and advocate for legally implemented (top down) and grassroots (bottom up) socio-legal remedies which would offset each of the three gendered aspects of inequality, and which ought to be embraced simultaneously. The remedies are legal pluralist approaches[69] and gendered, socio-legal storytelling,[70] both of which are often employed in contexts where religious law and civil courts meet or where secular legislation has attempted to alter normative religious behaviour.[71] I am not advocating for one particular solution, nor am I advocating for an altogether new solution.[72]

I would describe top down approaches as all those made by any legal system, legal player, or court – secular or Jewish – regardless of religious affiliation, that attempt to change realities through legal decisions, case precedents, amendments, or any other legal innovation. The bottom up approach invoked here is the self-narration of *mesuravot get*, whose stories not only empower themselves and others, but also evoke powerful transformations of the social and legal realities ('in the field').[73]

Top down

Contrary to the multicultural approaches, in the tradition of classic legal pluralist approaches which seek to embrace a plurality or multiplicity of legal orders, there need not be an eviction of religion from secular society altogether. A legal pluralist approach is one where the method of inquiry and analysis are focused on overlapping normative orders in specific social fields,[74] in the case of *siruv get* those would be the secular and religious legal systems. Framing *siruv get* from a legal pluralist perspective would enable a cross-cultural encounter with a diversity of remedies at hand to alleviate abusive instances that take advantage of a *halakhic* asymmetry.

Legal pluralism does not restrain religion in an effort to separate law and religion and the approach allows space for religion to be taken seriously *both* as a valid iteration of identity *and* as a legal system. William Connolly contends "deep pluralism" is the solution for religion in the secular sphere, enabling layered practices of connection to coexist in the public realm[75] and Bender and Klassen contend that pluralism is about hybridity and encounter[76] which would also see religion as an integral part of modern public life in the twenty-first century. Moreover, Benjamin Berger notes in Bender and Klassen that (multiculturalist) legal tools coming to manage diversity, distort the fact that law and religion meeting is not necessarily a crisis, or a culture clash, but rather a "cross-cultural encounter" which could alleviate emerging tensions, like *get* refusal and the inequalities women face as a result.[77] The most productive form of law's pluralism is when "the nature of the cross-cultural encounter between law and religion becomes transparent – an understanding cross-cultural experience."[78] Understanding the diversity of remedies available to *siruv get* in this way, may enable communities to embrace the multiple remedies available that are at times ignored or even resisted, particularly in Toronto.

Recognizing and embracing legal pluralist solutions enables the existence of religion in the public sphere and allows for the recognition of religions as complex networks of affiliations rather than an altogether narrow and simplistic view of religions or religious leaders as necessarily misogynist.[79] Moreover, embracing legal pluralist solutions allows plural legal systems to respectfully, mutually coexist with the ability for Jewish law in this case, to invoke the power of the state in instances where there is abuse of the internal religious order (*halakha*) or conflicting rights for women, in this case the right to religion and the right of equality in divorce.[80] There are many top down, legal pluralist solutions available. They include remedies made by any legal system, legal player, or court, secular or Jewish, regardless of religious affiliation, that attempt to change realities through legal decisions, case precedents, amendments, or any other legal innovation. Some examples include:

Scholars and activists have suggested that *siruv get* be framed as a human rights issue both internally[81] and/or externally.[82] Framing it as an internal human rights violation would establish *get* refusal as a "violation of every woman faithful to tradition", according to Greenberg.[83] This is similar to viewing *get* refusal as a type of domestic abuse but this type of internal human rights framing would *not* include a public forum, like the UN, that would review legal cases, individually. As Kaddari contended, framing *iggun* as an external human rights issue *should* include the UN because women are not autonomous over their marital status.[84] According to Dershowitz, "let us not mince words, *agunot* are modern day slaves" in fact the word *agun* literally translates from Hebrew to 'anchor' so an *aguna* is anchored, or shackled to an unwanted marriage.[85] Dershowitz added that this is a human rights concern, "her plight is the responsibility not only of every Jew in the world, but of every human being that cares about equality and dignity" no matter the scope of the problem (which speaks to the contentions I have made about the insignificance and harm of quantification).[86]

A number of other religious commentators suggested that an independent (alternative) international *beit din*, IBD, be (re) established.[87] As previously discussed, this court would supervise divorces using historic rabbinic mechanisms, some established up to 3000 years ago (controversial to some, in that they have been unused for years by Orthodox Judaism). These solutions include but are not limited to: *hafka'ot*, *kiddushei ta'ut*, *get al t'nai*, or *get zikui* (annulments, mistaken or fraudulent marriage which are transactions entered into with a flawed understanding/without full disclosure, conditional marriage, or *get* with the presumption of consent).[88] This *beit din* would then also officiate at the remarriages of these women. Since 2013, the IBD was established, headed by Rabbis Simcha Krauss, Ronald Warburg, and Yosef Blau along with support from Blu Greenberg and others, and has started adjudicating difficult cases. They have ensured transparency to ensure that *gittin* granted will be *halakhic* but their rulings have not yet been made public as of winter 2015.

Alan Dershowitz suggested, in his keynote address, that lawyers aiding and abetting *get* refusal and extortion must face disbarment.[89] This innovative approach did not garner much reaction at the Summit nor has it been tested in New York or Toronto to my knowledge, although it is a creative, pluralist remedy that ought to be tested. Using disbarment as a threat, is another way of employing a civil, secular mechanism to undercut the support a recalcitrant husband has in his *get* refusal; support which enables his abuse.

Probably, the most popular suggestion to date has been the use of pre- and postnuptial agreements.[90] There are a variety of prenuptial agreements available, from a variety of denominations including the *halakhic* prenuptial agreement endorsed by the Rabbinic Council of America/Beth Din of America–RCA or BDA respectively, which has been upheld in court as justiciable[91] (related to the next solution, below). This approach would include communal involvement such as not going to weddings where no prenuptial agreement is used, insisting the agreement be read or displayed at weddings – like the *ketuba*, and most significantly, rabbis not officiating at weddings where couples refuse to sign a prenuptial agreement.

In Toronto, the utility of the existing prenuptial agreements is precluded due to legal and *hashkafic* (religious-*halakhic* worldview) reasons. The agreements are not viable because they necessitate arbitration and, due to the removal of religious arbitration of family law matters in Ontario, the prenuptial agreements are impracticable. Additionally, (and even if the matter of arbitration was moot) the rabbis and *beit din* of Toronto would have to support the initiative *hashkafically*. Currently, some of the rabbis and the *beit din* do not, in principle, support prenuptial agreements, viewing them as a coercive tool and a subject inappropriate at a time of marriage (planning for divorce before marriage),[92] despite the fact that leading rabbinic figures in New York and Israel have supported prenuptial agreements. Thus, for prenuptial agreements to be a viable solution in Toronto, the *beit din* would have to change their stance and support this remedy, and individual rabbis would have to encourage couples to sign prenuptial agreements in each wedding over which they preside.

Some lawyers and advocates have recommended suing for damages in civil court, which has worked in a variety of jurisdictions. In the Canadian Supreme Court Case, *Bruker v. Marcovitz*, in 2007, Justice Rosalie Abella for the majority insisted the Court was *not* wading into in the "religious thicket" in their decision to award Stephanie Bruker $47,500 in damages for her husband's breach of contract in which he had agreed to give his wife a *get* upon their civil divorce.[93] More recently, in the *Light v. Light* case, in 2012, a Connecticut ruling affirmed the constitutionality of the RCA prenuptial agreement enabling Rachel Light to demand more than $100,000 under the terms of the agreement which had stipulated Eben Light was to pay $100 (maintenance) for each day the couple remained married.[94] In 2001, Susan Weiss of the Center for Women's Justice began suing husbands in civil courts for damages in tort suits in Israel. In 2004, she won her first award for approximately $125,000, "reflecting that *get* withholding constitutes actual damages."[95]

Some commentators also advised that secular *get* laws be used more willingly and more creatively where they exist.[96] In the 1980s and 1990s, amendments were made to the *Family Law Act* provincially, in Ontario, and the *Divorce Act* federally in Canada, (and twice to the *Domestic Relations Law* in New York). These amendments were secular legal changes that, although state enacted, directly impacted and attempted to remedy *siruv get* by lessening a recalcitrant husband's bargaining power when refusing to grant a wife her *get*. There are cases where invoking the amendments in order to aid in the giving of a *get* may be viewed as coercive, and thus invalid by a *beit din*, known as a *get meuseh*, a coerced *get*. This is especially true in Toronto, where the amendments were initially supported by *beit din*, but are now most often resisted by them.[97] Nonetheless, willingness to use these legal pluralist *get* laws would support *mesuravot get*.

Bottom up

There are a few bottom up remedies available that include communal *kherem*, as well as other tactics that are community organized through grassroots initiatives. They include, but are not limited to rallies, support groups, and educational initiatives in schools and synagogues (in line with my earlier contention about changing the normative cultural perception about *get*-giving). However, the bottom up, grassroots approach invoked here, and one which is too often ignored despite its immense potential, is the self-narration of *mesuravot get*, whose stories empower themselves and others while simultaneously evoking powerful transformations of the social and legal realities 'in the field'.

The classic feminist method of gendered storytelling is not only a means of 'talking back', where marginalized women move from the margins to the main stage. Gendered storytelling is also a method, and in this case a remedy, which allows women to transform their silence where there had previously been segregation and void, into language and then action in order to resolve inequalities women face in navigating their right to divorce.

Gendered socio-legal storytelling allows us "to create knowledge that challenges rather than supports ruling regimes, by constantly being attentive to histories, experiences and perspectives that are unnoticed, unfamiliar, or too easily neglected or misrepresented."[98] Furthermore, 'stories from the bottom' or the margins are particularly valuable to socio-legal research[99] being that they may 'cure' problems in law such as gender discrimination,[100] leading to social and legal change. Carol Weisbrod notes, "The power of narrative lies in its capacity to awaken us, and then changes us. They challenge or trouble the status quo. Often, we want to say that the narrative shapes attitudes that shape the law"; they are emotive and so they have transformative power.[101] Gendered storytelling in law is thus a deconstructive step[102] that marginalized groups can use to challenge and unsettle the legal status quo because stories give uniquely vivid representation to particular voices, perspectives and experiences of victimization, subjugation, and discrimination. These types of stories are traditionally left out of legal scholarship and ignored when shaping law, which has been the case with *mesuravot get*, whose stories and voices are segregated in a multiplicity of ways, as discussed and revealed earlier.[103] Shulamit Reinharz articulates that individual storytelling may reframe previously held biased views and that consequently, injustices can be remedied as a result of storytelling, which is precisely the goal of *mesuravot get* sharing their narratives.[104] Heinzleman and Wiseman, who explicitly write on the nexus of gender, law, and storytelling,[105] view storytelling as "one strategy that has become increasingly important to women in the face of deep conflicts,"[106] like *get* refusal. They argue that normative legal scholarship must stretch to include feminine narrative or rather, it must stretch its understanding that feminine narratives *are* equal to law because in reality " 'excluded voices' *can* effect legal change by correcting partial representations."[107] Bottom up, gendered storytelling is an act of power or even resistance that may elicit transformation, both social and legal, and in that way is an effective remedy for *siruv get* and the manifestations of inequality that often ensue.

In fact, there are examples of gendered storytelling by *mesuravot get* that demonstrate the effectiveness of this powerful remedy. Examples include (but are not limited to) *Bintl Briv* letters in response to *A Galeriye Fun Farshvundene Mener*, Gital Dodelson's first-person narrative in *The New York Post* and the public self-narration of other *mesuravot get*, such as Tamar Epstein, as well as the self-narration of Torontonian women during my fieldwork.

Translated as 'bundle of letters', *Bintl Briv* was a popular 'Dear Abbey'-type column introduced in 1906 to *Der Forverts* or *The Jewish Daily Forward* by Abraham Cahan[108] and was published in both the United States and Canada. The *Bintl Brivs* are letters that were written to the paper as a response and resistance to *A Galeriye Fun Farshvundene Mener*, or gallery of vanished husbands that featured men who had disappeared leaving their wives without a *get*. The *Bintl Brivs* are an example of bottom up, gendered storytelling as an impactful remedy to *get* refusal and are fascinating in that they brought the issue and the faces of deserters "compellingly into the broad public arena."[109] In these letters women demanded that their voices and stories be heard and that *their* needs and experiences be known by the community; they shared their narratives. The *Bintl Brivs* reflect the powerful remedy, seldom invoked, giving sounds to the silences and voicing the voids of the marginalized.

Gital Dodelson married Avrohom Meir Weiss in 2009. Ten months later, Dodelson took their newborn son and left. Weiss initially filed for full custody in New Jersey civil court in 2010, circumventing the tradition, particularly of the Ultra-Orthodox (which the couple was), to go first to *beit din* to resolve legal issues. The couple civilly divorced in 2012. Weiss was unhappy with the conditions of the civil court, and used the *get* as leverage in the *beit din*, attempting to renegotiate terms in his favour, in exchange for the *get*. Among his new demands was shared custody, as well as $350,000, yet he was also ignoring several *seiruvim* from *batei din* and rabbis in the Ultra-Orthodox community.

Unable to convince Weiss to give a *get* and "after more than three years… she has gone public with her story."[110] Dodelson wrote a first-person narrative in the *New York Post* on November 4, 2012, reverting back to the potent, yet overlooked remedy of the self-narration of women seen in *Der Forverts* 107 years prior. A conflagration erupted since sounding her silence. Through speaking out, and resisting the silencing, communities were forced to take heed and listen to Dodelson's story, proving the effectiveness of gendered storytelling in light of *siruv get*, creating a movement of ostracism of a *get*-refuser, support of the *mesurevet get*, and greater awareness of the issue of *get* refusal generally. The case of Tamar Epstein as well, saw improvements when she went public about her husband's *get* refusal in 2012. Her husband, Aharon Freidman was an aide to Congressman David Camp, House Chair of the Ways and Means Committee.[111]

Although these are well-known American cases, we nonetheless should use them as prototypes and inspiration for storytelling as an effective gendered remedy to the inequalities women face in their right to divorce, particularly in Toronto, a close-knit community. Both Epstein and Weiss were able to rely on the reputations of their husbands and their families in order to elicit response and action by going public. That said, this remedy ought to be embraced more widely by all *mesuravot get*. I am not suggesting necessarily, that each woman go to the *New York Post*. I am, however, advocating for giving *mesuravot get* a safe, welcoming and encouraging platform from which to tell their stories, within communities, at panels and conferences, in synagogues and schools. There is strong evidence, both historical and current, that gendered storytelling by *mesuravot get* does have a positive impact, and may remedy the abusive instances that result from the legal-*halakhic* asymmetry as well as the unequal fallouts that women experience in navigating their right to religion and their right to divorce.

Consequently, as a third example, I will include excerpts from Torontonian *mesuravot get*. Communities have not as yet heard these examples of narratives. However, the excerpts highlight the utility of the powerful, compelling gendered remedy of storytelling being that they enrich your understanding of the issue and compel you to act after reading.

"During the 25 years we were mostly happily married, there were at times red flags, a couple of uncontrolled rages before our daughter's wedding, and before each wedding things got bad, crazy fights about money; there was a choking incident and I knew then I would have to leave but I didn't know how & who do you ask? I had nowhere to turn for help. It just kept getting worse, and in 2000 I went to get the get. He had the pen in his hand to sign it and said 'I changed my mind' he felt I was his property [...] From 1997 to 2007–10 years, I lived knowing I had to get out and for 1 ½ years I lived in fear for my life, I didn't sleep at night. [...] He was so defiant of Beit Din he treated them terribly despite the fact that it came up he was living with a woman... When I was going through it I had nowhere to turn. I suffered in silence. [...] There is no support here in Toronto, not legal, nor rabbinic and so there is nothing to give hope. I had to get a job at my age... [...] I sought out Yad L'Isha in Israel myself and worked with an advocate there. I know I couldn't have gotten the get if he hadn't moved to Israel. There is no way I would have my get even today, if I was depending on or waiting for the actions of the Toronto Beit Din."[112]

"He had put me down, told me he hadn't loved me in 10 years, told me I was too frumpy and not good in bed. I changed plenty for him. [...] You feel stuck, like a chain on your leg and you can't really move. I felt stuck. It's the worst feeling I've ever had in my life & no one in the community helped. I had called Rabbi O 20x; he never called me back and never once called my hubby. He just said, 'when he's ready he'll come'; Rabbi S too just said 'hatzlocha raba'."[113]

"If the rabbis would stand up against domestic abuse, women wouldn't have to live in fear; they wouldn't have to go back into abusive marriages because they are left no other choice, without a get!"[114]

"I was vulnerable and emotionally dependent. He was 10 years older than me and I was 20. We were married for 2 years during which time he had threatened and mostly succeeded to cut me off from my family. After 2.5 months I was pregnant and 'clued in' and realized his control [...] At the time, I felt they were abusing their authority, that they shouldn't have authority, but really–if people cared, we would have another beit din. But if no one cares, if the community is silent, complacent, why should rabbis care?"[115]

"There had been verbal, emotional and then a couple of incidents of physical abuse. There were threats and fear. I had a restraining order against him in place [...] I got divorced because of abuse – and this–[get refusal] was just another form of abuse–another form of control. The communal silence is a whole other level. [...] We all agree the halakha is archaic but a true believer will be okay with archaic halakhic principles. The issue is the leaders must step up and must acknowledge that get refusal is a form of domestic abuse, that abuse exists within our communities altogether, and about how individual men can abuse halakha [...] The Toronto Beit Din are scared of the secular legal system encroaching on their turf and the women are the

> *collateral damage. [...] Leaves me questioning. I don't know if I'd ever get married again, and if I do, maybe only civilly."*[116]

The narrative excerpts of Toronto's *mesuravot get* call for contextualizing and analysis, particularly on the issues of domestic abuse and the status of the Toronto *beit din*.[117] But for the purposes of this chapter, simply a space and an audience for the narratives of the women are all that is required. To hear their narratives serves as an example of the powerful potential of women's storytelling to elicit changes to both law and society, particularly as *mesuravot get* are forced to navigate their way between their right to religion and inequalities they face in their right to divorce. Each example of gendered, socio-legal storytelling had the power to unsettle the socio-legal status quo. The *Bintl Brivs*, demanding acknowledgement of women's experiences of abandonment, and the strategic storytelling by women change not only the individual women's social and legal realities, but also challenge widespread misconceptions about the power of *mesuravot get*, who are so often silenced.

The top down, legally implemented and bottom up, grassroots approaches of legal pluralist remedies and gendered storytelling should be used simultaneously. The legal pluralist approaches would alleviate unequal access to *batei din* and other communal services as well as influence the disproportionately gendered impact of the phenomenon, while gendered storytelling would further relieve the unequal impact and would certainly remedy the silencing *mesuravot get* face both by individual rabbis and *batei din*, but within their own communities and among advocates as well. Used in conjunction, not only are these approaches reactive to the three types of inequality explored here: access, impact, and silencing, but in tandem, these socio-legal tools or methods – the legal pluralist approaches *and* gendered storytelling – may actually remedy abusive instances resulting from the legal-*halakhic* asymmetry causing *siruv get*.

Conclusion

Because *siruv get is* a socio-legal phenomenon, caused by and impacting law and society simultaneously, it needs simultaneous legal and social solutions, *both* grassroots, bottom up *and* legally implemented, top down remedies. Advocating for just one remedy, whatever that remedy may be (getting rid of kiddushin *altogether*, or believing prenuptial agreements are the answer, or relying only on traditional *kherem*) is inadequate. The top down approaches, alone, will always be only partial: both imperfect *and* incomplete, never dependable to *all* Jewish women impacted by *siruv get*. The dual approach, of both top down *and* bottom up approaches, which seek not only a diversity of creative solutions to the abuse resulting from legal-*halakhic* asymmetry, but also to empower and listen to the gendered experiences and narratives of *mesuravot get*, is the valuable socio-legal approach that ought to be fully embraced in light of *siruv get* and the inequalities that emerge as a result.

In conclusion, I have examined and advocated for socio-legal gendered remedies to *get* refusal which simultaneously negotiate between women's right to religion and their claims for equality in their right to divorce. I began by briefly describing the phenomenon of *siruv get* followed by a discussion about the persistence and viability of religion in modern, public life in the twenty-first century. Consequently I established that *siruv get* is *not* a problem with religion's existence in the secular sphere generally, and it is *not* a problem with Judaism in and of itself. I then investigated three aspects of inequality that occur as a result of the phenomenon of *siruv get*, including but not limited to access to a timely and consistent *beit din* in Toronto especially, but I also suggested that silencing occurs by the 'experts' who often exclude the *mesuravot get* whose desires to self-narrate are most often ignored. Finally, I advocated for both classic 'top down' and 'bottom up' socio-legal remedies regarding the issue of *siruv get* in the twenty-first century, the unabashed embrace of legal pluralism and gendered storytelling.

*Acknowledgments

I would like to thank the editors for inviting me to participate in this collection, particularly Lisa Fishbayn Joffe, whom I met at the Aguna Summit in June 2013. This chapter benefitted from thoughtful comments and valued guidance from Annie M. Bunting, as well as Benjamin L. Berger and Sara R. Horowitz. I thank them for their continued support, encouragement and inspiration. This chapter forms a part of my Doctoral Dissertation that uses a socio-legal analysis to compare *siruv get* in Toronto and New York, supported by the Social Sciences and Humanities Research Council of Canada and the Religion and Diversity Project.

Notes

1 Ruth Frankenberg, "On Unsteady Ground: Crafting and Engaging in the Critical Study of Whiteness," in *Researching Race and Racism*, eds. Martin Blumer and John Solomos (London: Routledge, 2004), 104–118. She is one of many key feminist scholars who writes on methodologies and advocates for reflexivity or, to be more precise, "recursivity".
2 Frankenberg, "On Unsteady Ground," 107.
3 Though I focus on Toronto in this chapter, where I use US, International, and Canadian examples, it is more for a sense of a loose but broad holistic picture of *get* refusal in our time and I avoid, for the sake of brevity exploring in depth how the contexts differ and affect each other. I engage with, analyze, and unpack the differences between Toronto and New York and what makes Toronto distinct in my Dissertation. These explorations are merely touched on in this chapter and would benefit from greater discussion but they are beyond the scope of this chapter.
4 Perhaps Michael Broyde, Pascale Fournier, or Susan Weiss, though likely only Fournier would self-ascribe as a socio-legal scholar.
5 Rachel Levmore, "A Coalition to Solve the Agunah Problem," *The Jerusalem Post*, February 23, 2013, www.jpost.com/Opinion/Op-Ed-Contributors/A-coalition-to-solve-the-agunah-problem.

6 This is known as *heter mea rabbanim* or permission by one hundred rabbis domiciled in at least three different jurisdictions to allow the husband to remarry without the wife's acceptance of the *get* in particular situations warranting an exemption.

7 I have had no first-hand examples or interactions of men refused a *get* in my research in Toronto and New York, since 2009. ORA has said they have seen a couple of cases in New York amongst their 220 cases to date. Private conversations with Rabbi Jeremy Stern.

8 Rabbi Yitzchak/Irving A. Breitowitz, Lunch Talk at Linden & Associates, Toronto, February 23, 2015.

9 I am engaging in this paper implicitly with the threads of three scholarly discourses:
   a) Wherein some feminist theologians say that any patriarchy in Christianity or Western culture is a legacy of Judaism. Judith Plaskow and Susannah Heschel have written on the anti-Judaic thrust. Judith Plaskow, "Blaming the Jews for the Birth of Patriarchy," in *Nice Jewish Girls*, ed. Evelyn T. Beck (Watertown, MA: Persephone, 1982), 250–254; Susannah Heschel, "Anti-Judaism in Christian Feminist Theology," *Tikkun* Vol. 5 (3) (1990): 25–28, 95–97.
   b) Wherein some Jewish feminists argue that Jewish marriage (and hence divorce) is inherently anti-woman, relegating women to the position of chattel, for example, Rachel Adler, *Engendering Judaism: An Inclusive Theology and Ethics* (Boston, MA: Beacon Press, 1999).
   c) Wherein some argue that Judaism or Jewish marriage is *not* systematically anti-woman. Among others, Judith Hauptman and Avraham Grossman have written on this. Judith Hauptman, *Rereading the Rabbis: A Woman's Voice* (Boulder CO: Westview Press, 1998); Avraham Grossman, *Pious and Rebellious: Jewish Women in Medieval Europe* (Waltham, MA: Brandeis University Press, 2004).

   In the context of our particular case study, on *get* refusal, these critiques have been made to some degree by Susan M. Weiss and Netty C. Gross-Horowitz, *Marriage and Divorce in the Jewish State: Israel's Civil War* (Waltham MA: Brandeis University Press, 2012).

10 Men of all religions have historically used this approach, doing something 'bad' and even contrary to the principles of their own religions and/or contrary to equality in democracy, in the name of religion. Ibid. See supra note 9 for the threads of discourse with which I am engaging.

11 John Syrtash, *Religion and Culture in Family Law* (Toronto: Butterworths Canada Ltd., 1992), 119.

12 This is confirmed by my interviews with participants in Toronto and with New York participants referred to me by ORA, Organization for the Resolution of Agunot, a non-profit organization that advocates for the unconditional giving of the *get*. They have helped hundreds of women, have approximately 50 active cases at any time, and have a constant list of women wait-listed.
   a) Often, (Conservative & Orthodox) women who have been *mesuravot get* find their belief in G-d and faith in Judaism is strengthened during their plight (despite the length of refusal). They would often refuse to blame individual rabbis or *batei din* and insist the blame should be on the individual recalcitrant husband and his defenders. Often too, they would agree that it is the recalcitrant husband or 'rabbinic will' and interpretation that were the foes, not the *halakha* or religion itself.
   b) Women self-identified with all types of denominations, including non-denominational and/or unaffiliated yet were still impacted by *get* refusal, some of whom insisted it is their "right" to get their *get* despite the assortment of alternative remedies available to them which are embraced by the *batei din*

and rabbinates that are non-Orthodox, including but not limited to *hafka'ot*, or annulments.

13 Yael Machtinger, upcoming Dissertation in fulfillment of PhD requirements in Socio-legal Studies at York University, and "Sounds of Silence: A Socio-Legal Exploration of *Siruv Get* and *Iggun* in Toronto" (Major Research Paper, York University, Toronto, 2009).

14 There is a rich literature on this debate, a debate that is beyond the scope of this chapter. The following authors speak to these debates: Jacques Derrida and Gil Anidjar, *Acts of Religion* (Routledge, 2001); Jürgen Habermas, "Religion in the Public Sphere," *European Journal of Philosophy* Vol. 14 (1) (2006): 1–25; Emmanuel Melissaris, *Ubiquitous Law: Legal Theory and the Space for Legal Pluralism* (Ashgate Pub Co, 2009); Charles Taylor, *A Secular Age* (Harvard University Press, 2007).

15 Wendy Brown, *Regulating Aversion: Tolerance in the Age of Identity and Empire* (Princeton, NJ: Princeton University Press, 2006); Seyla Benhabib, *The Claims of Culture: Equality and Diversity in the Global Era* (Princeton, NJ: Princeton University Press, 2002); Avigail Eisenberg, *Reasons of Identity: A Normative Guide to the Political and Legal Assessment of Identity Claims* (New York: Oxford University Press, 2011). Will Kymlicka, *Multicultural Citizenship: A Liberal Theory of Minority Rights* (Oxford: Clarendon Press, 1995); Sherene Razack, *Casting Out: Eviction of Muslims from Western Law and Politics* (Toronto: University of Toronto Press, 2008).

16 Courtney Bender and Pamela E. Klassen, *After Pluralism: Reimagining Religious Engagement (Religion, Culture, and Public Life)* (Columbia University Press, 2010).

17 Ibid. Particularly Kymlicka and Razack. Solange Lefebre and Lori G. Beaman, *Religion in the Public Sphere: Canadian Case Studies* (University of Toronto Press, 2014); Richard J. Moon, *Law and Religious Pluralism in Canada* (UBC Press, 2009); Ayelet Shachar, *Multicultural Jurisdictions: Cultural Differences and Women's Rights* (Cambridge University Press, 2001); Ayelet Shachar, "Privatizing Diversity: A Cautionary Tale from Religious Arbitration in Family Law," *Theoretical Inquiries in Law* Vol. 9 (2) (2008): 573–607. Timothy Fitzgerald, *Discourse on Civility and Barbarity: A Critical History of Religion and Related Categories* (Oxford: Oxford University Press, 2007).

18 Anna C. Korteweg, "The Sharia Debate in Ontario: Gender, Islam, and Representations of Muslim Women's Agency," *Gender & Society* Vol. 22 (4) (2008): 434–54; Anna C. Korteweg and Jennifer A. Selby, *Debating Sharia: Islam, Gender Politics, and Family Law Arbitration* (University of Toronto Press, 2012); Anver E. Emon, "Islamic Law and the Canadian Mosaic: Politics, Jurisprudence and Multicultural Accommodation," *The Canadian Bar Review* Vol. 87 (2) (2009) 391–425.

19 *Arbitration Act*, 1991 S.O. 1991, c.18 amended; "McGuinty to Ban Religious Tribunals," *Kitchener Record*, September 12, 2005; Lorraine E. Weinrib, "Ontario's Sharia Law Debate: Law and Politics Under the Charter," in *Law and Religious Pluralism in Canada*, ed. Richard Moon (Vancouver: University of British Columbia Press, 2008), 239–263.

20 Ken Serrano, "Rabbis in Divorce-Gang Sting Could be Out on Bail Soon," *USA Today*, October 16, 2013, www.usatoday.com/story/news/nation/2013/10/16/rabbis-fbi-divorce-sting-hearing/2996211/; Laurel Babcock and Bruce Golding, "New Accusers in Rabbi 'Torture' Ring," *New York Post*, October 17, 2013, http://nypost.com/2013/10/17/new-accusers-in-rabbi-torture-ring/; "Mendel Epstein and Martin Wolmark 'Plotted to Torture Husband'," October 10, 2013, www.bbc.co.uk/news/world-us-canada-24485128; Matthew Shaer,

"The Orthodox Hit Squad," *Gentleman's Quarterly*, September 2014, www.gq.com/news-politics/newsmakers/201409/epstein-orthodox-hit-squad?printable=true.

21 Brown, *Regulating Aversion* (Princeton, NJ: Princeton University Press, 2006).

22 Peter Fitzpatrick, *The Mythology of Modern Law (Sociology of Law and Crime)* (New York: Routledge, 1992); Emmanuel Melissaris, *Ubiquitous Law: Legal Theory and the Space for Legal Pluralism* (Surrey, England: Ashgate Publishing Company, 2009).

23 Anna C. Korteweg, "The Sharia Debate in Ontario," *Gender & Society* Vol. 22 (4) (2008): 434–54; Anna C. Korteweg and Jennifer A. Selby, *Debating Sharia* (University of Toronto Press, 2012). Anver E. Emon, "Islamic Law and the Canadian Mosaic," *The Canadian Bar Review* Vol. 87 (2) (2009): 391–425.

24 As I noted earlier, this contention is not taken seriously in academic writing, or indeed the Canadian courts.

25 Alexandra Leichter, Susan Aranoff, Susan Weiss, and others, *The Agunah Summit* (Conference by The NYU Tikvah Center for Law and Jewish Civilization and JOFA-Jewish Orthodox Feminist Alliance Lecture, New York University School of Law, New York, June 24, 2013).

26 "The Necessity of the Property Component in Halakhic Marriage" (Conference by Rackman Center for the Advancement of the Status of Women, Bar-Ilan University, Israel, June 12, 2013).

27 This has some grounding in Supreme Court of Canada decisions. We can look to *Bruker* for some of the debates about religious marriage and divorce in public life, and also to recent rulings on veiling and education. But, two classic cases about religious practices persisting in public life include: *Syndicat Northcrest v. Amselem* [2004] 2 S.C.R. 551; *Multani v. Commission Scolaire Marguerite-Bourgeoys*, [2006] 1 S.C.R. 256, 2006 SCC 6.

28 Ayelet Shachar, *Multicultural Jurisdictions* (Cambridge University Press, 2001); Ayelet Shachar, "Privatizing Diversity," *Theoretical Inquiries in Law* Vol. 9(2) (2008): 573–607.

29 Machtinger, "Sounds of Silence," 2009.

30 Interviews with author, July 5 and July 14, 2009, Toronto.

31 Ibid.

32 Ibid. "*L'chaim*" is translated as "to life"; it is a congratulatory toast.

33 These acts, or inaction I should say more accurately, create the false perception that the problem of *Iggun* does not exist in Toronto altogether, a troubling misconception I discussed in my Masters (see supra note 13).

34 *Beth Din* of America webpage – www.bethdin.org/docs/FAQ_d.pdf. *Kherem*, or ostracism, shunning, or excommunication, has been used as a tool by Jewish communities since the Talmudic times, for a variety of offences, historically and socially relevant. An essential caveat however, is that while the recalcitrant may be 'subject' to such sanctions, the sanctions are not necessarily arranged by the *beit din*. Often the sanctions are the responsibility of the community and local rabbis and are thus largely case and community specific.

35 Sharon Shore is a partner at Epstein Cole, a Toronto firm, with a focus on family law and is an Executive Member of a new-found organization (2012), TASC – Toronto Agunah Support Coalition.

36 See supra note 34.

37 Panel discussion on *The Plight of the Agunah in Our Community: Bridging Gaps Between Rabbinate, Academy, & Community*, Beth Avraham Yoseph of Toronto Congregation, Thornhill, Ontario, April 29, 2012. Also available at: http://koshertube.com/videos/index.php?option=com_seyret&task=videodirectlink&Itemid=4&id=11072.

38 Ibid.
39 The Director also noted that evening that the *halakhic* Prenuptial Agreement, an accepted and widely supported remedy, is "One of the solutions we don't use in Toronto for technical reasons as well as certain *hashkafic* reasons according to some rabbis" (*hashkafa* means worldview or belief). I should note that the prenuptial agreements that are slowly becoming recognized as a significant, viable *halakhic* remedy around the world, are not viable in Toronto not only due to certain rabbis' beliefs that they may be coercive (although leading rabbis in New York and Israel disagree) but also due to secular, legal preclusions (one of which is the removal of religious arbitration, which the prenuptial agreement necessitates).
40 Hillel Fendel, "Rabbinate Stats: 180 Women, 185 Men 'Chained' by Spouses," *Israel National News*, August 23, 2007, www.israelnationalnews.com/News/News.aspx/123472.
41 Blu Greenberg, "Where There is a Rabbinic Will, There is a Halakhic Way: A Defense and Critique" (The Tikvah Center's Twelfth Annual Caroline and Joseph S. Gruss Lecture at New York University School of Law, New York, October 21, 2013).
42 See supra note 12.
43 Bernard Jackson et al., "Agunah: A Manchester Analysis: Draft Final report of the Agunah Research Unit, University of Manchester" (Manchester, 2009), 1–211.
44 Interview with author, October 23, 2013, New York.
45 I say "defunct" not because of my own personal contention that the alternative, creative solutions ought not to be embraced (since that is not my contention), but rather simply because the individuals and movements which have sought for them to be embraced were either rejected outright (such as Rabbi Emmanuel Rackman's *Beit Din L'Ba'ayot Agunot* which was quickly criticized even by Rackman's rabbinic mentors as a rogue court and not *halakhic)*, or virtually ignored (like Professor Bernard Jackson and his team's Agunah Research Unit, out of Manchester University). Even recent attempts at creative remedies by the IBD and a recent case in Tzfat, in spring 2014, where a *beit din* invoked *get zikui* have come under scrutiny. Per Rabbi Yitzchak/Irving A. Breitowitz, Lunch Talk at Linden & Associates, Toronto, February 23, 2015.
46 Concurrently, I acknowledge that even if there are cultural shifts that lead to behavioural change, domestic violence and *get* refusal may persist. As students of gender violence we know all too well about the persistence of abuse.
47 Bernard Jackson et al., "Agunah: A Manchester Analysis," 12–13.
48 Interview with author, May 26, 2014, New York.
49 The Torah dictates that if a married man dies childless, the widow is to marry her dead husband's brother, known as *yibbum* or levirate marriage. If the dead man's brother does not wish to marry the widow, or she does not want to marry him, they perform a procedure known as *khalitza*, which means removal; in this case, the removal of the brother-in-law's shoe. Some suggest that the removal of his shoe serves to symbolize that he has no claim to his brother's inheritance. Only after the *khalitza* ceremony has been completed is the widow free to marry someone else. There is currently a case in Toronto where a recalcitrant brother-in-law, who has his own wife and children, is refusing to perform the *khalitza* ceremony to free his sister-in-law until his sister-in-law grants him her husband's inheritance (since there was no heir).
50 Interview with author, August 17, 2014, Toronto.
51 Blu Greenberg, "Halakhic Justice for the Agunah: A 40 Year Retrospective" (JOFA International Conference on Feminism and Orthodoxy, New York, 2010), 1–12.
52 Sharon Shore, an orthodox attorney has appeared before The Toronto *beit din* only in her capacity as a civil attorney, when the two jurisdictions – religious and

secular/civil – are converging. Shore has not appeared in a 'toenet' capacity and would not be permitted to appear in front of *beit din* in cases not involving the secular, civil legal system.

53 These include, but are not limited to: JOFA, *Mavoi Satum*, *Yad L'Isha*, Centre for Women's Justice, GETTLINK, Aguna Inc., ICAR, ICJW, ORA. This is far from an exhaustive list and includes American and Israeli organizations as well as organizations that work transnationally.

54 Ruth Halperin-Kaddari has also done extensive work on quantifying agunot in the Israeli context, which she presented at the 2013 Agunah Summit.

55 Barbara Zakheim, "Results from a Survey of *Agunot*" (Washington, DC: The Mellman Group Inc. *Research Based Strategy* October 10, 2011), 1–6.

56 Ibid.

57 Let me be explicitly clear, I do not advocate for attempting to count *agunot* themselves. I have presented multiple times on the shortcomings of quantifying in social science research generally, and quantifying these women particularly. Ultimately, an accurate statistic can never be achieved, and obsessions about quantifying cloud the issues themselves. As I have said in previous presentations, "The mantra ought to be: 'one *aguna* is too many, NOT how many *agunot* are there." Yael Machtinger, "To Count or not to Count? Examining the Quantifying Quandary Regarding the Prevalence of Jewish Divorce Refusal (In Defense of a New Method of Analysis)," paper presented at *Women, the Charter, and CEDAW in the 21st Century: Taking Stock and Moving Forward* (Queen's Feminist Legal Symposium, Queen's University, Kingston, Ontario, March 2–3, 2012); paper presented at panel discussion on *The Plight of the Agunah in Our Community: Bridging Gaps Between Rabbinate, Academy, & Community* (Beth Avraham Yoseph of Toronto Congregation, Thornhill, Ontario, April 29, 2012). Also available at: http://koshertube.com/videos/index.php?option=com_seyret&task=videodirectlink&Itemid=4&id=11072. This builds on Rachel Levmore's article, "The Aguna: a Statistic or a Real Problem?" *The Jerusalem Post*, August 31, 2009.

58 This is the method I used in my doctoral fieldwork. The question of 'how to find the women' deserves more discussion and analysis, but it is beyond the scope of this chapter. I will say that in the interest of academic integrity, one must not act as though they are a part of a community to simply 'access' or 'extract' data or 'find' women. I believe that this type of (feminist) research is more ethically achieved when the researcher is already a part of communities with trusting relationships and contacts. It is through my status as "insider" and my well-established relationships that women, advocates, and rabbis were willing to speak with me and organizations were willing to help me in this endeavor. Marjorie L. DeVault and Glenda Gross, "Feminist Interviewing: Experience, Talk and Knowledge," in *Handbook of Feminist Research: Theory and Praxis*, ed. Sharlene Nagy Hesse-Biber (Thousand Oaks CA: Sage Publications Inc., 2007), 173–198; Clifford Geertz, *The Interpretation of Cultures: Selected Essays* (New York: Basic Books, 1973); Sharlene Nagy Hesse-Biber, and Patricia Lina Leavy, *Qualitative Research* (New York: Oxford University Press, 2004); Ann Oakley, "Interviewing Women: A Contradiction in Terms?" in *Doing Feminist Research*, eds. Helen Roberts and Paul Kegan (London: Routledge, 1988), 30–61.

59 *The Agunah Summit* (Conference by The NYU Tikvah Center for Law and Jewish Civilization and JOFA-Jewish Orthodox Feminist Alliance Lecture, New York University School of Law, New York, June 24, 2013).

60 New York University's School of Law calendar page, https://its.law.nyu.edu/eventcalendar/index.cfm?fuseaction=main.detail&id=25378

61 I discussed all eight in detail in my talk, "On the 'Edge' of the 'Religious Thicket' Using *Bruker v. Marcovitz* to Explore Other Creative Ways to get One's '*Get*')," paper presented at *Law on the Edge* (Canadian Law and Society Association's Annual Meeting, Vancouver, British Columbia, July 2, 2013).

62 Rabbi Asher Lopatin, Rabbi Shlomo Riskin, Rabbi David Bigman, presented on the panel "Discussion of Halakhic Solutions"; and Blu Greenberg at *The Agunah Summit* (Conference by The NYU Tikvah Center for Law and Jewish Civilization and JOFA-Jewish Orthodox Feminist Alliance Lecture, New York University School of Law, New York, June 24, 2013).

63 Appropriation of voice and this type of gender stereotype is a common discussion in feminist literature. Lorraine B. Code, *What Can She Know? Feminist Theory and the Construction of Knowledge* (Ithaca NY: Cornell University Press, 1991); Margaret Eichler, *Nonsexist Research Methods: A Practical Guide* (Boston: Allen & Unwin, 1988); Michelle Fine, *Disruptive Voices: The Possibilities of Feminist Research* (Ann Arbor: University of Michigan Press, 1992); Ann Oakley, "Interviewing Women" in *Doing Feminist Research*, ed. Helen Roberts (London: Routledge & Kegan Paul, 1981), 30–61.

64 ORA, Organization for Resolution of Agunot, in New York, has at times included *mesuravot get* on panels they have initiated and/or organized, to their great credit. For example: "YU Agunah Panel 2012" Featuring Rabbi Hershel Shachter, Dr. David Pelcovitz, Rabbi Jeremy Stern, and Tamar Epstein, Yeshiva University, New York, March 29, 2012.

65 Interview with author, August 17, 2014, Toronto.

66 David J. Bleich, "A Suggested Antenuptial Agreement: A Proposal in Wake of Avitzur," *Journal of Halakha and Contemporary Society* 7 (1984): 25–41; David J. Bleich, "Jewish Divorce: Judicial Misconceptions and Possible Means of Civil Enforcement," *Connecticut Law Review* 16 (2) (1984): 201–290; Irving A. Breitowitz, *Between Civil and Religious Law: The Plight of the Agunah in American Society* (Westport CT: Greenwood Press, 1993); Michael J. Broyde, *Marriage, Divorce and the Abandoned Wife in Jewish Law: A Conceptual Approach to the Agunah Problems in America* (Hoboken NJ: Ktav, 2001); Lisa Fishbayn Joffe and Sylvia Neil, eds., *Gender, Religion, and Family Law: Theorizing Conflicts between Women's Rights and Cultural Traditions* (Waltham MA: Brandeis University Press, 2012); Lisa Fishbayn Joffe, "Gender, Multiculturalism and Dialogue: The Case of Jewish Divorce," *Canadian Journal of Law & Jurisprudence* 21 (2008): 71–96; Pascale Fournier, "*Halakha*, the 'Jewish State' and the Canadian Agunah: Comparative Law at the Intersection of Religious and Secular Orders," *Journal of Legal Pluralism and Unofficial Law* 65 (2012): 165–204; Rachel Levmore, *Spare your Eyes Tears "Min'ee Eiynayich Me'Dimah": Complete Guide to Orthodox Jewish Pre-Nuptial Agreements-The Halakhic Prenuptial Agreement for Mutual Respect and Prenuptial Agreements for the Prevention of Get-Refusal* (Israel: Millennium Publishing, 2009); Shlomo Riskin, *A Jewish Woman's Right to Divorce: A Halakhic History and a Solution for the Agunah* (Hoboken NJ: Ktav Publishing, 2006); Susan M. Weiss, and Netty C. Gross-Horowitz, *Marriage and Divorce in the Jewish State: Israel's Civil War* (Waltham MA: Brandeis University Press, 2012).

67 Another example of suppression/silencing that occurs within the field itself, particularly in Toronto, comes unfortunately at the hands of TASC – Toronto Agunah Support Coalition. Various women in the community have shared with me that TASC has ignored their emails and attempts to volunteer, get updates on the current *siruv get* situation in Toronto, and help establish a (sub) *aguna* support group just for these women to have an understanding community where they can talk openly. One woman, a previous *mesurevet get*, even noted that

after attending an event where the TASC executive had sent around a volunteer request form, she had been emailing one of the executive members once a month for over a year, and still had not heard back. The *mesurevet get* felt that TASC is falling short. Further, this woman expressed her frustration to me about a Toronto panel event where not only were there no *mesuravot get* on the panel, but only one Canadian, an executive member of TASC. She said, "What can possibly come from yet another event like this!" (Private conversation, November 18, 2013).

68 Socio-legal examples include: Patricia Ewick and Susan Silbey, *The Common Place of Law: Stories From Everyday Life* (Chicago: University of Chicago Press, 1998); David M. Engel and Frank W. Munger, *Rights of Inclusion: Law and Identity in the Life Stories of Americans with Disabilities* (Chicago: University of Chicago Press, 2003); Sally Engle Merry, *Getting Justice and Getting Even: Legal Consciousness among Working Class Americans* (Chicago: University of Chicago Press, 1990); Rae Anderson, "Engendering the Mask: Three Voices," in *Ethnographic Feminisms: Essay in Anthropology*, eds. Rae Anderson and Lynne Phillips (Ottawa: Carleton University Press, 1995), 207–231.

69 Harry W. Arthurs, *'Without the Law': Administrative Justice and Legal Pluralism in Nineteenth Century England* (Toronto: University of Toronto Press, 1985); John Griffiths, "What is Legal Pluralism?" *Journal of Legal Pluralism*, 24 (1986): 1–56; Sally Engle Merry, "Legal Pluralism," *Law and Society Review* 22 (1988): 869–896; Sally Falk Moore, "Law and Social Change: The Semi-Autonomous Social Field as an Appropriate Subject of Study," *Law and Society Review* 7(1973): 719–750; and others.

70 Peter Brooks and Paul Gewirtz, eds., *Law's Stories: Narrative and Rhetoric in the Law* (Yale University Press, 1998); Susan Sage Heinzelman and Zipporah Batshaw Wiseman, *Representing Women: Law, Literature, and Feminism* (Duke University Press, 1994); Carol Weisbrod, *Butterfly, The Bride: Essays on Law, Narrative, and the Family* (University of Michigan Press, 2004).

71 Annie Bunting and Shadi Mokhtari, "Migrant Muslim Women's Interests and the case of 'Shari'a Tribunals' in Ontario," in *Racialized Migrant Women in Canada: Essays on Health, Violence and Equity*, ed. Vijay Agnew (Toronto: University of Toronto Press, 2009); Ginnine Fried, "The Collision of Church and State: A Primer to *Beth Din* Arbitration and the New York Secular Courts," *Fordham Urban Law Journal*, 31 (2) (2004): 633–655; Susan Hirsch, *Pronouncing and Persevering: Gender and the Discourses of Disputing in an African Islamic Court* (Chicago: University of Chicago Press, 1998); Suzanne Last Stone, "The Intervention of American Law in Jewish Divorce: A Pluralist Analysis," *Israel Law Review*, 34 (2) (2000): 170–210.

72 I stand humbly on the shoulders of the tremendous women and men who have come before me and advocated innovative approaches or solutions; noting in particular the recent work of Rabbi Jeremy Stern and ORA, Dr. Rachel Levmore, Blu Greenberg, and others.

73 Other bottom up approaches may include community organized initiatives that serve to impact the realities ('in the field') through grassroots campaigns in synagogues, schools, rallies, support groups and the like, however, these initiatives are beyond the scope of this analysis.

74 Arthurs, '*Without the Law*'; Griffiths, "What is Legal Pluralism?" 1–56; Merry, "Legal Pluralism," 869–896; Moore, "Law and Social Change," 719–750.

75 William E. Connolly, *Pluralism* (Durham, NC: Duke University Press, 2005).

76 Courtney Bender and Pamela E. Klassen, *After Pluralism: Reimagining Religious Engagement (Religion, Culture, and Public Life)* (New York: Columbia University Press, 2010).

77 Benjamin L. Berger, "The Cultural Limits of Legal Tolerance," in *After Pluralism: Reimagining Religious Engagement (Religion, Culture, and Public Life)*, eds. Courtney Bender and Pamela E. Klassen (New York: Columbia University Press, 2010), 98–126.

78 Bender and Klassen, *After Pluralism*, 20.

79 Despite my respect for Susan Weiss, and her work on behalf of *mesuravot get* in Israel, she seems to hold this belief when referring to rabbis of the *beit din* in Israel as "short-sighted, arbitrary, patriarchal and not concerned with justice" presented on the panel "Lessons from the Front" at *The Agunah Summit* (Conference by The NYU Tikvah Center for Law and Jewish Civilization and JOFA-Jewish Orthodox Feminist Alliance Lecture, New York University School of Law, New York, June 24, 2013).

80 Of course, there are also instances where the state centralist/secular legal order, may step in to alleviate, what it perceives as human rights or other violations of law which are said to be in the name of religion or religious practices. Consequently, there is a complexity to the cross cultural exchange, when one of the cultures – law, is always superior to the other – religion, in the eyes of the state. Nonetheless, I would strongly encourage legal pluralist approaches, wherever possible.

81 Blu Greenberg, *The Agunah Summit*, New York (June 24, 2013).

82 Ruth Halperin-Kaddari; Joseph Weiler; Alan Dershowitz, *The Agunah Summit*, New York (June 24, 2013).

83 Blu Greenberg, *The Agunah Summit*, New York (June 24, 2013).

84 Ruth Halperin-Kaddari, *The Agunah Summit*, New York (June 24, 2013).

85 Alan Dershowitz, *The Agunah Summit*, New York (June 24, 2013).

86 Ibid.

87 Rabbi Asher Lopatin, Rabbi Shlomo Riskin, Rabbi David Bigman, *The Agunah Summit*, New York (June 24, 2013).

88 Each of these alleviation mechanisms is complex and intricate. I have truncated definitions for purposes of brevity here.

89 Alan Dershowitz, *The Agunah Summit*, New York (June 24, 2013).

90 Rabbi Jeremy Stern; Dr. Rachel Levmore, *The Agunah Summit*, New York (June 24, 2013). Stern and Levmore are celebrated advocates for prenuptial agreements. Jeremy Stern advocates for the RCA prenuptial agreement in North America and Rachel Levmore advocates for the Young Israel Agreement for Mutual Respect in Israel. Rabbi Michael J. Broyde has authored the Tripartite Prenuptial Agreement, although he states, it is "*shelo l'halakha*" not to be taken as *halakha* or *halakhically permissible*. Michael J. Broyde, "A Proposed Tripartite Agreement To Solve Some Of The Agunah Problems: A Solution Without Any Innovation" (online document), 1–15. Abridged version *JOFA Journal* 5 (4) (Summer 2005): 1–24. http://cslr.law.emory.edu/fileadmin/media/PDFs/Lectures/Broyde_Solutions_Agunah_Problem.pdf Most recently, Tzhohar, a movement of "moderate Orthodox" rabbis, proposed a new prenuptial agreement in Israel in conjunction with the Israel Bar Association, meeting both rabbinical requirements and demands of the Israeli court system. As of this writing, they are still waiting for official support from the Israeli Rabbinate. www.tzohar.org.il/English/in-the-press/. Although the remedy of prenuptial agreements is likely the most effective to date, and has gained much traction and many significant endorsements from various leaders and a variety of denominations, it is undoubtedly a 'band -aid' solution. In other words, it is not effective in all cases. It can only be effective where it has been signed, and in a jurisdiction (both secular and rabbinic) wherein it will be viewed as justiciable (not encroaching on religious freedoms, and not viewed as coercive, respectively).

91 *Light v. Light* [2012] Conn. Superior Ct. 55 Conn. L. Rptr. 145. Docket No. NNHFA124051863S.
92 The Director of the *Beis Din of the Vaad Harabonim* of Toronto, Panel discussion on *The Plight of the Agunah in Our Community: Bridging Gaps Between Rabbinate, Academy, & Community* (Beth Avraham Yoseph of Toronto Congregation, Thornhill, Ontario, April 29, 2012). Also available at: http://koshertube.com/videos/index.php?option=com_seyret&task=videodirectlink&Itemid=4&id=11072.
93 *Bruker v. Marcovitz* [2007] SCC 54. Docket No. 31212.
94 *Light v. Light* [2012] Conn. Superior Ct. 55 Conn. L. Rptr. 145. Docket No. NNHFA124051863S.
95 Batya Ungar-Sargon, "Israel Has a Marriage Problem. One American-Born Lawyer is Trying to Solve it," *Tablet Magazine*, October 9, 2013. www.tabletmag.com/jewish-news-and-politics/148148/susan-weiss-american-agunah-warrior; Susan M. Weiss and Netty C. Gross-Horowitz, *Marriage and Divorce in the Jewish State: Israel's Civil War* (Waltham MA: Brandeis University Press, 2012).
96 *Family Law Act*, R.S.O. 1990. C.f. 3 *Divorce Act*, R.S.C. 1985, c. 3 (2nd Supp.) sec. 21.1. *Domestic Relations Law* 253 (First New York Get Law), 1983; *Domestic Relations Law* 236 (B) (5) (h), 236 (B) (6) (d) (Second N.Y. Get Law), 1992.
97 Sharon Shore, Panel discussion on *The Plight of the Agunah in Our Community: Bridging Gaps Between Rabbinate, Academy, & Community* (Beth Avraham Yoseph of Toronto Congregation, Thornhill, Ontario, April 29, 2012). Also available at: http://koshertube.com/videos/index.php?option=com_seyret&task=videodirectlink&Itemid=4&id=11072.
98 Marjorie L. DeVault and Glenda Gross, *Feminist Interviewing*, (Thousand Oaks CA: Sage Publications Inc., 2007), 182.
99 Daniel A. Farber and Suzanna Sherry, "Telling Stories Out of School: An Essay on Legal Narratives," *Stanford Law Review* 45 (1992–1993): 807–855.
100 Kim Lane Scheppele, "Telling Stories," *Michigan Law Review*, 87 (1988–1989): 2073–2098.
101 Weisbrod, *Butterfly, The Bride: Essays on Law, Narrative, and the Family* (Ann Arbor: University of Michigan Press, 2004), 17.
102 Jaques Derrida and Gil Anidjar, *Acts of Religion* (London: Routledge, 2001).
103 Brooks and Gewirtz eds., *Law's Stories: Narrative and Rhetoric in the Law* (New Haven: Yale University Press, 1998), 5.
104 Shulamit Reinharz, *Feminist Methods in Social Research* (New York: Oxford University Press, 1992).
105 Susan Sage Heinzelman and Zipporah Batshaw Wiseman, eds., *Representing Women: Law, Literature, and Feminism* (Durham: Duke University Press, 1994), 109.
106 Ibid., 4.
107 Judy Scales Trent in *Representing Women: Law, Literature, and Feminism*, ed. Susan Sage Heinzelman and Zipporah Batshaw Wiseman (Durham: Duke University Press, 1994), 5.
108 Bluma Goldstein, *Enforced Marginality: Jewish Narratives on Abandoned Wives* (California: University of California Press, 2007).
109 Goldstein, *Enforced Marginality*, 92–93.
110 Doree Lewak, "An Orthodox Woman's Three-Year Divorce Fight," *New York Post*, November 4, 2013. http://nypost.com/2013/11/04/orthodox-jewish-womans-plea-for-a-divorce/.

111 Eventually, both Dodelson and Epstein received *gets*, after each spent several years as a *mesurevet get*. The circumstances and conditions of each *get* remains ambiguous and private.
112 Interview with author, August 17, 2014, Toronto.
113 Interview with author, June 14, 2014, Toronto.
114 Interview with author, August 22, 2014, Toronto.
115 Interview with author, June 16, 2014, Toronto.
116 Interview with author, August 13, 2014, Toronto.
117 These discussions will be included in my upcoming Dissertation.

12 Challenging stereotypes

Gender-sensitive imams and the resolution of family disputes in Montreal

*Anne Saris**

Important changes were introduced into Quebec law when the Code of Civil Procedure was reformed; these changes will come into force in the autumn of 2016.[1]

In an attempt to reduce the delays and costs associated with the court system, a new section of the Code states that 'parties must consider private prevention and resolution processes before referring their dispute to the courts'. This change will not only call upon mediations before formally trained mediators, but may also allow for more informal private dispute prevention and resolution processes, such as those conducted by religious authorities. Imams may notably be called upon more frequently. In an effort to assess the potential impact of these changes, this chapter revisits a qualitative research study completed during the last decade.[2] In that study, we decided to focus on women, in part, to explore their experiences of informal dispute processing using religious frameworks. We were conscious of the research which seemed to indicate that women experience gender-based discrimination in religious and other informal processes.[3] There was, of course, the added dimension of the socio-legal interaction of communities belonging to minority groups[4] who had immigrated to Canada.[5]

A thumbnail sketch on method and the data set

In 2005, the National Assembly passed a motion prohibiting the creation of 'Islamic tribunals' in Quebec.[6]

Did such Islamic tribunals exist? If not, how did Canadian Muslim women manage their family conflicts?

In order to answer these questions, we interviewed a total of 37 persons including: 24 Canadian Muslim women (W), five community workers (ComWork), four social workers (SocWork), six accredited family mediators (AccMed), one lay mediator, two judges, six lawyers (L), and 13 Muslim religious counsellors (RC – imams and others[7]).

The sample of women was representative of a variety of geographic and ethnic origins and immigration histories and who also reflected different relationships to Islam as a religion. Eighteen of the 24 women had had direct experience of negotiating family conflicts while six gave their opinions on the issues. Regarding the marriage situation of the participants, two were single but 19 out of 24 had a religious marriage in their country of origin. Three married in Montreal in front of an imam who presided over both the religious and civil marriages. Eight had family-arranged marriages and one said she had been forced to marry. With regards to their children's religious education, 14 out of the 15 participants who expressed their views on the matter said they valued the transmission of Islamic values to their children. Amongst the 18 (of 24) women interviewed who had experienced family conflict, five consulted with both a religious counsellor and a lawyer, while one woman consulted solely with a religious counsellor. Amongst the women interviewed most had used the services of a social worker or community worker and some had consulted lawyers, mainly from legal aid clinics. None of them had seen an accredited family mediator. Two reasons would appear to account for this: on the one hand accredited mediators did not speak their mother tongue or come from their ethno-cultural community and on the hand other women wrongly associated accredited mediation with the informal mediations they experienced with religious counsellors, social workers or community workers and therefore did not see the use of it.

Among the 13 religious counsellors interviewed, there were 12 men and one woman. There were five full-time imams of mosques, six part-time or occasional imams, and two non-imams. Furthermore, it must be noted that the functions and roles of the imam are different in the Twelver Shi'i and Sunni traditions. There is a form of clerical hierarchy in the former composed of scholars ('ulama') who designate the imams of Shi'i mosques, often from the countries of origin. The Lebanese, Iraqi and Iranian Shi'ites have their own associations connected to particular high-ranking scholars (ayatollahs). While in the case of Sunnis, in principle any believer who is recognized as having sufficient knowledge of Islam can lead the prayer. They had been working in the field of prevention and resolution of family conflicts for a number of years: 21–35 years (six), 16–20 years (four), 10–15 years (two), 8 years (two); they came from: Levant (six: Lebanon four, Lebanon-Palestine one, Palestine one), Maghreb (three: Tunisia two, Morocco one), South Asia (Indo-Pakistanis one, Bengali one), West Africa (Mali one), Irak (one whose clientele was partly Iranian). Most of them were Sunni (ten) while the other three were twelve Shi'ites; the schools of thought they mentioned were 'conservative' (eight), amongst which three Hanafites, two Shafi'ites, three Ja'farites; two reformist / Muslim brotherhood, one Sufi, one Tablighi, the last one was a Sunni who did not mention a specific school of thought. Their working languages were primarily Arabic (eight), French (two), English (two), and Urdu (one).[8]

This chapter will on the one hand outline the role of these religious counsellors, examine how they view their work and describe on the other hand their know-how regarding the imbalance of power within a couple as well as the determination of the child best interest.

The roles of religious counsellors and the possible overlap with the legal system

The religious counsellors we interviewed revealed themselves to be well connected to other religious actors, as well as to lay actors. Indeed, we found that some religious counsellors work with other religious counsellors. For instance, RC4, from Morocco, said he worked with Pakistani muftis since according to him they have a better knowledge of local customs. Religious counsellors are moreover regularly consulted by lawyers (RC4); and they even work, albeit rarely, with them on specific issues (RC12 recalls three times in his whole practice). They are also sometimes contacted by social workers (RC10 especially when children are at stake). Some social workers refuse to contact the RC themselves, but have no objection if a woman wants to contact an imam herself (SocWork3). In that respect, social and community workers mentioned that a woman would approach the imam for the religious divorce and they would have to negotiate with him (SocWork1) or in cases of spousal abuse (ComWork5).[9]

Some give public presentations on Islam for the police (RC9),[10] act as expert witnesses in court proceedings (RC9[11], RC7[12], RC12[13]) and cooperate with youth protection services, acting as 'guarantors' that parents will not mistreat their child again (RC2).

Numerous religious counsellors will get in contact with lawyers. RC6 stated that lawyers will advise him on a family matter while RC3 regularly consults a lawyer who helps him find information on specific legal questions. They also work in collaboration with consulates, as well as with officials from the Canadian government in cases of child abduction (RC5).

Most religious counsellors are thus well connected with lay interveners as well as state legal actors.

But is there in the Montreal Muslim communities a parallel justice system for the resolution of family disputes?

If one understands the role of a tribunal as that of deciding between two conflicting claims (adjudication) and of being able to enforce its decision, then the empirical research revealed without a doubt that religious counsellors, who are before and above anything else leaders of prayers (i.e. Imams *stricto sensu*), acted as persons with knowledge of religious norms, and possibly as counsellors, but definitively not as adjudicators. For instance, RC1 stated that: 'I never impose any decision on them, I only bring forward the viewpoint of Islam from Qur'an and Sunna and I want them to arrive at a decision. When they say "you decide", most of the time I decline to take on that role.' W11, a woman divorced religiously (talâq) and separated from bed and board confirmed that description of the counsellor's role: 'with the law, it is the judge who decides. There is no agreement. Each spouse presents whatever their viewpoint is but it is the judge who takes the final decision. In front of the imam, both spouses have to make an effort to get along. It is as if you were in front of a mediator' (loose translation).

Religious counsellors are well aware of the limits of their power, since all of them explained that both parties (man and woman) were often consulting them as part of forum shopping for the solution that would best suits their needs. For instance, RC9 recalled: 'when it comes to divorce and when it comes to heritage, they go and see the Imam. And when an Imam says something and they don't accept it, they go and ask another Imam. They go in circles until they find someone who will give them what they want. Sometimes they come and they don't ask you the question, but they say, please tell us that this is true, or this opinion we want to take and we will agree.' RC1 confirmed the process of forum shopping and mentioned that: 'men. (…) All the time they are testing the waters. Do we get more from Islamic jurisprudence, or do we get more from this society? The party gravitates to the system where they benefit more. So fathers, mostly the husbands, they will come to Islam, and mostly the ladies, the women or mothers, they go to the Canadian legal system. So both of them are looking for convenience.'[14]

Furthermore, regarding their authority, religious counsellors mentioned that decisions reached under their guidance were not binding, albeit they could be morally binding, as RC10 mentioned unequivocally.[15] The mutual agreement of the parties on the content of the settlement was always necessary according to them.

However, even the moral weight of their decision seems to be doubtful to them, since most of the religious counsellors indicated that the parties were in the process of shopping for the solution best suited to their needs (shopping between different actors, be they religious counsellors or civil law actors), and sometimes did not respect their expertize on religious norms. For instance, RC1 remembered a case in which the wife had contacted him, and then the husband had called him: 'The guy thinks that he is very educated and doesn't have to listen to religious thoughts. That he's not living in a religious context of society and he doesn't want to know about it.'

This was confirmed by the other actors interviewed. As a matter of fact, most of the Canadian Muslim women we interviewed were motivated by the results they wanted to achieve. In that perspective a few envisioned no hierarchy between the state tribunals and the religious counsellors (only one did put above all the religious normative systems), while others (Quebec-born converts, second-generation immigrants, or immigrants who had arrived in Quebec at a very young age) had internalized the idea that the state legal system is the prominent system while comparing it to other legal systems (religious or state). They criticized the state forum for not taking their (religious) needs into account and demanded that such accommodation be made.

Finally other women clearly perceived the state legislation as hermetical and not allowing for the importation of foreign norms.

Who consults religious counsellors and why?

Canadian Muslim women and various actors in the field quote the following difficulties as lying behind marital problems (18 of the 24 women interviewed had encountered severe spousal difficulties): changing roles in the couple following the arrival in Canada, the question of children's education (RC6 was once consulted by a woman who wanted to put her children in the Koranic school on Sunday, against the advice of her husband), the fear of a new culture's impact on children and the crisis of adolescence (RC10, ComWork2), as well as disagreement concerning religious practices.

The interviews revealed that cultural shifts occasioned by immigration can result in changes in immigrant women's behaviour (e.g. wanting more freedom, being less compliant, wanting to manage their personal assets[16]) as well as men's behaviour (e.g. taking up drinking or gambling – SocWork3, W11) and even children's behavior (e.g. wanting to have girl- and boyfriends, to drink or to stay out later).

In the vast majority of cases under review, women initiated the *de facto* separation, as well as the legal proceedings towards separation of bed and board, or divorce. They were also the ones who reached out to seek reconciliation (RC10, RC7, RC9 and RC12[17]). According to RC7: 'Men tend to feel it's no problem; I can have another wife if this one doesn't work out. But women tend to try to stick to their marriage.'

According to religious counsellors and women interviewed, trust in the 'father-figure' authority of a disinterested person, as well as confidentiality, geographical proximity, and the fact that the assistance is free are the main factors that motivated the women to seek the help of religious counsellors. The issue of trust is of great importance and may distinguish the religious process from the legal one. As RC12 put it: 'They think that this man – the scholar – hasn't got any other interests except to put people's lives in order. They trust us. I don't think that they put the same degree of trust in an attorney or a civil judge, because they think that the attorney will only look out for his or her own interests, because they like to charge people. And the judge will decide the cases according to what they have on hand only.' RC5 concurred: 'finding an amicable solution with the help of lawyers costs a lot of money. Moreover in this process one tends to forget the point of view of the couple' (loose translation).

The father figure is also one of authority as pointed out by social and community workers. According to them, some Canadian Muslim women are looking for an authority figure that could sit down with the husband and tell him that what he is doing is wrong. This figure does not have to be a religious counsellor (ComWork1), and according to a social worker, religious counsels act as psychologists, just like Catholic priests used to do traditionally in Quebec (SocWork3).

For most of the 13 religious counsellors, their role consists in enabling the couple to salvage their marriage, and this is why most women will contact them. Their role is to provide religious guidance concerning past or future behavior, to reconcile the couple's views ('as a pacifier, conciliating and deterring many cases of divorce'– RC11; 'For that reason, as a conciliator I always make my effort that the family should not break up' – RC1), to exercise moral influence on the spouse, and give an Islamic divorce; 'The importance of that role is in keeping families together' (RC8).

Most religious counsellors thought that doing everything in their capacity to reconcile the couple was one of their specific functions, as compared to other interveners. RC10 mentioned that women 'think that tribunals do not make any effort towards reconciliation, because they leave the choice to the members of the couple to divorce if they want. On the contrary, we try everything to solve the issue. These two approaches are somewhat different' (loose translation). Additionally, RC11 put forward the idea that counsellors may even prevent many divorces.

When reconciliation is impossible, religious counsellors will tell the spouses to go to court. For instance RC1 declared that: 'Where there is completely no choice left between husband and the wife and the children, at that time I tell them again that, because these things cannot be reconciled, and since I cannot give legal support to either of the parties in conflict, they should go to the government of Quebec, and get legal counsel.' RC6 stated that: 'I have tried to find a solution to the spouses' problems, but regarding the kids, money, expenses, I tell them right away that is the law of the government. I tried, if I can, to solve the problem … otherwise I send them to court. But we do not give an Islamic divorce without first a civil divorce. We have to abide by the law' (loose translation).

This leads us to one specificity of the religious counsellor's jurisdiction, i.e. the issue of unilateral religious divorce, or Tâlaq.[18] Four out of the thirteen religious counsellors (RC1, RC6, RC7 and RC12) stated that they automatically referred the spouse to the civil court. Most of the religious counsellors acted as a witness in divorce proceedings. Some give the religious divorce according to criteria that depend on the school of thought followed by the imam (for instance when the husband has abandoned his wife, when he does not pay spousal support, or when he abuses her). Finally two religious counsellors considered that a civil divorce has the same effect as a religious one. According to RC9: 'when the Quebec court grants a divorce, the husband has to sign the papers. So his signature is his acceptance that he is divorcing, so I take it for granted that the Islamic divorce is there. Other imams, they don't and they won't let the woman get married again unless they have a written paper from that husband that he did the divorce Islamically.' However this is not always true, especially in a context of private international law. Acknowledging this situation, RC6[19] and RC12 produced religious divorce documents that were, according to them, officially recognized in Lebanon.[20] A lawyer (L6) recalled a case where his counterpart in Lebanon refused to acknowledge the Quebec justice decision of divorce. Only RC9 mentioned explicitly that he gave khul: 'if this were in Lebanon, I would tell her to fill out an application in the courts. It takes three hearings. We send a note to the husband. If he doesn't appear before three hearings, it's a khul[21]. It's easy .... But here, I'm not in a position of doing that because I'm not a Qadi and I'm not a judge. I can do it as an Imam. I can do it as a Shiite.... I'm contacting him; I'm contacting his friends. If I don't get any news from his family or from him, I will call him in Syria. If I don't get any news I'll send .... for the divorce. She is a life! I'm looking at her as a life! She's surviving, so why will I oppress her just because her husband ran away?'[22]

The reason why women are so adamant about getting a religious divorce is because they are afraid that, if they are still considered married in their country of origin, they might not be able to return to Canada, or they might lose the custody of their children, if they go back, for instance, to visit their parents (W5, W20). SocWork1 confirms this: 'there are two divorces when things happen here in Canada, in Montreal: a civil divorce and a religious divorce. It is necessary because Iranian women cannot go back to their country if they do not have the Iranian divorce... because the right to leave the country is up to the man in Iran. Hence for a woman who is civilly divorced in Canada and who does not have her Iranian or religious divorce, it is possible that the husband will retaliate and prohibit her from leaving' (loose translation).

Possible overlap with the legal system

Regarding the possible overlap between religious norms and legal norms, a majority of religious counsellors (seven) have never had cases dealing with alimony, dower and family asset division and custody, or else they systematically referred such matters to the civil justice system, while the rest of them (six) oversaw such matters to a varying degrees (2–30 percent of cases). Only one, RC5, mentioned that he had the skills to prepare a draft of the agreement in a case of joint application for divorce based on an agreement between the spouses. He added that this agreement was shown to a lawyer and that, once accepted by the parties, it was 'automatically accepted by the judges'.

According to the religious counsellors, while the mahr[23] usually amounted to a symbolic dollar for women from the Maghreb, in the case of Middle Eastern persons the amount could go up to '$100 000: $10 000 comptant et $90 000 au futur' (RC10). A community worker mentioned that the mahr could amount to one year of the husband's salary (ComWork3). When there is no major disagreement, some religious counsellors will make a decision on the mahr. According to RC5: 'it is a very simple agreement...divorce with mahr.... We cite the mahr that was on the document' (loose translation). All of the religiously married Canadian Muslim women that we interviewed had a mention of the mahr in their marriage contract. Two of them received the mahr during the marriage. Only one asked for it in civil court, without success (W21). The reason why women will not ask for the payment of the mahr is that most of the time it is a negligible amount.

In some cases, religious counsellors will ask a husband to give ongoing financial support to his ex-wife after the divorce, through alimony especially when the ex-husband is well off (RC12, RC5) or when the ex-wife is poor (RC10). This is an interesting example of the cross-pollination of normative frameworks, for usually a woman would be confined to three months' maintenance following divorce (the *idaat).*

Regarding the division of family assets, some religious counsellors justify not dividing the family assets equally by referring to the different responsibilities of spouses. Since women are exempted from providing for the household and day-to-day expenses, they cannot, according to certain counsellors, expect to receive an equal portion of the family assets. Other religious counsellors nuanced those positions in cases of inequality, for instance when the husband did not provide financially for the family, or when the wife assumed extra responsibilities such as housework, or the education of the children. In such cases, wives were considered to deserve a portion of the family assets. This reasoning echoed the concept of family patrimony in Quebec law. RC9 asked spouses in some specific cases to share their assets: 'when they are separating there are assets, a house, etc. Sometimes I take a decision to give something's to the wife – based on the situation. (...) Especially if she's abused' or 'when he's working and she's working at home raising the children, cooking, cleaning, and yet she doesn't feel like she's the wife. He doesn't sometimes buy her makeup, clothes, give her pocket money. He's not fulfilling his responsibilities so sometimes I decide. (...) Ok you have part of the house, part of his assets. Because in Islam she is not asked to help the husband unless she wants to.' Two religious counsellors (RC4, RC5) gave complete freedom to the spouses in the negotiation of the division of their assets.

The know-how of religious counsellors compared to the one of lay interveners

In this section, I will examine how these religious actors view their work in this area, and the impact of this vision on the rights of women and children.

Most of the religious counsellors align themselves with a specific school of thought (Madhhab) and will try to adapt their answer to the profile of the participant according to their madhhab (RC9[24]), or consult with persons specialized in the madhhab of the participants (RC4). Although they strictly distinguish between religious norms and cultural norms[25], most religious counsellors find that knowing the culture of origin of the parties helps them understand the issues at stake (typical spousal relationships, relations with extended family).

Spousal relationship

Balancing the powers in the couple[26]

Some religious counsellors acknowledged that Islamic norms do not favor women (for instance RC3). This is especially true with religious divorce. RC4 for instance mentioned that if a husband refuses to sign civil divorce papers, the wife will not be considered religiously divorced. Others will interpret Islamic norms in such a way as to be less prejudicial to women. Two religious counsellors will give a religious divorce without the husband's consent in cases where the latter has not paid alimonies (RC3, RC9) or in cases of abuse (RC9). Others (RC1, RC7) have told Canadian Muslim women that they can consider themselves both religiously and civilly divorced when they obtain their divorce in a Quebec court of law. Indeed according to RC7: 'a civil divorce is procedural, and the way they process it is similar to Islamic ways'.

Regarding the different processes put into place to ensure that the balance of power between members of the couple is maintained, we found that religious counsellors and lay counsellors use a number of similar practices, especially in relation to issues of pressuring and influencing the parties. Both developed similar techniques, such as allowing equal time for both parties to speak (e.g. speaking separately with each party), and ensuring that they were informed of their rights or of the relevant applicable norms. We also found that religious counsellors, depending how they frame their mission (e.g. reconcile or facilitate negotiation between spouses) will act differently, for instance by giving information in both cases but helping one party to argue his or her case.

For instance RC12 said: 'First I give them a chance to explain their problem. I stay silent and I only listen. I advise them to not challenge each other during the explanation of the problem. I will hear the woman first and then the man. When the woman speaks about her problem, or her view, I don't accept it for the man to interrupt her, nor vice-versa.' When the balance of powers seems upset, some religious counsellors will speak to the husband, and even to the in-laws, in order to explain to him the rights and freedom that a woman should have in Canada (RC7).[27]

However, if it does not work, some religious counsellors will use third parties, such as the family or a person in charge of protecting the woman, or a lawyer. This recourse to third parties might be one major difference with the practice of the relevant actors in the legal system (i.e. accredited mediators, judges). Depending on the religious counsellor, the family can play the role of a simple observer or even give some feedback. In his practice, RC1 makes sure that during the session the members of the family 'are not allowed to speak. If they have some information to the situation, yes. Otherwise they can sit there as an observer, and tell (him) afterwards where and what has gone wrong.' RC5 said that he favors sessions in which each member of the couple comes with a family member called a hakam. This happens in 40 percent of cases. According to him, this helps with the process of conciliation since both hakams do listen carefully to each spouse's claims. RC12 mentioned the fact that a family friend, 'someone who has power over the man or the woman' can help him or her make sure that they will listen to the counsellor.

However, other religious counsellors (in line with most lay actors) will highlight the negative impact of involving family members, either because the extended family is one possible cause of spousal conflict or because family members opposed the religious counsellor's decision. RC7 mentioned a case in which the 'husband's mother, father, everybody tries to dominate her ...and ... pressures the husband to divorce her, or do this and that, etc.' A Canadian Muslim woman (W7) recounted that her husband's family argued against the payment of the sadâq.[28] In response to this undue pressure, some religious counsellors will ask spouses to put some distance between themselves and their family (RC4) or even live in a different home than the extended family's home (RC7).

As already noted, a number of religious counsellors take a more proactive approach and make sure that both parties are made well aware of their rights and entitlements. According to RC3, if this preliminary work is not done, the negotiation will be unbalanced. Therefore, in order to address this situation he will typically tell the woman ahead of time what she can legitimately demand. As for RC5, he will give the parties, and especially the more vulnerable one, arguments and information that will help him/her in the negotiation, while RC10 admits to helping women who do not want a divorce to counter-argue with her husband. Neutrality of religious counsellors does not seem to be a strong feature of these processes, which distinguishes their type of intervention from the work of accredited mediators.

Giving up/forfeiting/relinquishing one's rights

Once they have made sure that the relevant information has been given and that powers within the negotiation process are balanced, religious counsellors tend to grant parties a great margin of appreciation. A central question is the problem of a vulnerable party possibly renouncing her rights. Women are known to voluntarily surrender different entitlements: their right to the mahr, to spousal support, to child alimony, to their share in the division of family assets, and to the custody of their child. The factors gearing toward this renunciation are multiple and not necessarily connected to a lack of religious or legal information.

Numerous women forfeit their rights with full knowledge of the facts. In their view, they do so in order to obtain their freedom; to escape swiftly from an abusive relationship, as a bargaining chip in exchange for a religious divorce that will allow them to remarry or in exchange for the custody of the children; or in order to deserve the respect of her children and of her family. Financial questions are thus often quite secondary in importance and influence.

According to lay interveners, women will forfeit their share in family assets in exchange for custody of their child or children. A lawyer recalled cases in which ex-wives did not claim shares in the amount of 100 000 to 200 000 dollars (L4). This situation was confirmed by a social worker who reported having seen numerous cases in which women, in exchange for custody or access rights, did not claim their share in the family assets. In one case the ex-wife did not ask for the custody of her child, in order to obtain the religious divorce (SocWork 1) or because she was getting remarried (AccMed1).

Regarding the former situation, RC2 and RC8 mentioned situations in which the ex-husband would ask, in accordance with the rules, for the custody of the kids because their wife has remarried.[29]

Religious counsellors are well aware that various reasons can lead a spouse not to claim such rights: generosity, fatigue, avoiding additional bargaining, or cost-benefit analysis (RC3, RC5, RC12). While RC5 identified spousal abuse as the major reason why women would not want to claim their rights, according to RC12 it is the husband's pugnaciousness that will lead the wife to relinquish her rights: 'he will challenge her to the point where she says, just give me the divorce and I will take nothing'.

Two among the Canadian Muslim women that we interviewed explained that they deliberately did not ask for any spousal alimony or share in the family assets, in order to sever any relationship with a difficult, if not abusive, spouse and regain their freedom (W12, W22). This motive is also mentioned by lawyers (L1[30], L2[31]) as well as a social worker (SocWork1). Other women mentioned that they will not ask for the mahr/sadâq in order to keep the respect of their family (W10, W7). The impact of family pressure is regularly observed by the lawyers. One attorney remembered that the husband's family would call the wife's family in their country of origin in order to pressure her to drop her claim for alimony (L2).

Faced with such renunciation/forgoing, some of the religious counsellors, acting similarly to some accredited mediators, will then try to establish the extent of the loss incurred, what the renouncing party will be getting out of it, and what ultimately motivates them to do it (AccMed1, RC3, RC5).

For RC2, giving up one's dowry in order to keep the respect of their family is acceptable, because one provides 'a higher reason, more important than your right'. Others will find it reasonable that the wife, in order to escape an abusive relationship, decides to abandon her mahr (RC5). An accredited mediator found it acceptable to negotiate custody by decreasing the amount of spousal alimony (AccMed2 mentioned that 'you're negotiating. And sometimes you have to help him in this case, to save face').

While some religious counsellors will deem acceptable that the wife decides to give up her rights, and will thus respect that decision (RC10 – mahr, RC9), others will argue against giving up rights as 'it will give the wrong message to the other party. That you can do whatever you want without being held responsible for anything (...) Sometimes yeah I will encourage. Especially the women, when they fail to ask for their rights. I will tell them that these are your rights. You can leave the rights at the end, but this is your right, you can ask for it' (RC2), or even act as 'her lawyer' in order to help her get the maximum she can out of the settlement (RC5). Unlike some lawyers and accredited mediators interviewed, none of the religious counsellors opposed the decision of a woman to forfeit her rights when it was final.

In summary, it is worth noting that religious counsellors in their interaction with the parties fit nicely into the three categories developed by Simon Roberts to describe family mediation: directive mediation, minimal intervention, and therapeutic intervention.[32] While in minimal intervention, the religious counsellors will focus on maintaining the communication between the members of the couple, in the directive approach, he will provide additional information, therefore influencing the content of the decision that will be reached by the parties (through: 1) the assessment of information relating to the parties and their quarrel, 2) the evaluation of their option and 3) persuading the parties to take the course of action he thinks most suited for them). Finally, the therapeutic intervention implies postponing joint decision making in order to heal the relationship and reconcile the couple.

Children caught in the middle

While all thirteen religious counsellors had dealt with custody and access issues, nine had experience in child abduction, as well as in problems regarding out-of-country vacation periods, ten with child support, seven with religious education and issues related to the 'crisis of adolescence'.

The birth of the first child can trigger disagreements, due in particular to different attitudes towards religious education. In mixed marriages religious differences between partners become more important after children are born. Religious difference can also become a source of conflict in couples, whether religiously mixed or not, where one partner becomes more observant and the other does not follow suit. A power struggle can then develop with children caught in middle. Mediator 5 remembered a case in which a Quebec convert woman became very observant and her Muslim husband did not agree with her approach. Some Muslim couples' experience also conflicts around the 'crisis of adolescence' when they are not equipped to handle the challenges posed by this period in their children's lives. They also have fears about the dangers of the surrounding dominant culture and may not agree on the appropriate ways to handle this (e.g. one parent tries to seek a measure of accommodation, while the other tries to enforce strict norms from the home country). Fathers may blame mothers for failing to keep children in line, and mothers may feel that fathers are not present enough in their children's life, especially in the case of the boys. For all these reasons, parents will sometimes reach out to a religious counsellor in order to find a solution to their emerging conflict. Although these issues are quite important for Canadian

Muslim women, I focus the remainder of my analysis on issues that reveal a clear interface between the work and norms of religious counselling, on the one hand, and the work performed by actors within the judicial system, on the other hand. Typical illustrations are found in the issues of custody, access and abduction.

Issues faced by women: obtaining the custody of their children and fearing international abduction

Obtaining the custody of children is of paramount importance to Canadian Muslim women involved in separation proceedings. Among the 11 of the 24 women interviewed whose custody issues had been dealt with in front of the civil courts, all but one obtained custody. Lay interveners that we interviewed also mentioned that, based on their experience, women in that type of situation are granted custody in Quebec courts in a high percentage of cases. A social worker suggested that this trend revealed an inaptitude of fathers to offer a stable environment to their child (SocWork2). According to both lay and religious participants in the research, many Muslim men are resentful and frustrated because they come from a cultural and religious context where they would be generally favoured in terms of custody. Some may have expected to be granted custody, until they find out about Canadian laws relating to divorce and custody. Some religious counsellors feel that men are discriminated against by the courts. RC5 referred to the *Fathers for Justice* campaign as providing a credible point of view in that matter. The sense of injustice is clearly a major factor in child abduction scenarios.

According to the vast majority of the participants interviewed, Canadian Muslim mothers are fearful of the abduction scenario, in particular those women with husbands coming from non-Hague Convention countries.[33] This issue was raised by almost all the women and social interveners interviewed. According to RC9, abductions might be more prevalent or plausible in mixed marriages. In those cases, fathers may feel more sidelined and fearful in divorce proceedings because the child might not be raised in a Muslim environment as a result of the outcome of the proceedings. It was also indicated that abduction was sometimes a way for fathers to avoid paying both spousal and child support. Participants raised also the problem faced by Canadian Muslim women who could not take their children to the country of origin because the former husband could then prevent her and her children from returning to Canada, even though they are Canadian citizens.

Although all religious counsellors spoke about the Canadian Muslim women's fear of abduction of their children by the father, only three of them had had first-hand experience (RC5[34], RC3[35], RC12[36]). RC1 was asked by a man about the Islamic viewpoint on the matter, and he responded that 'no… you cannot do that'.[37] RC2 and RC12 confirm that according to Islamic norms there is no Islamic right for the father to take the children out of the country, and especially not if the child is under 7 years of age.[38] RC12 highlighted the difficulty of dealing with countries, such as Lebanon, that had not ratified the *Hague Convention on the Civil Aspects of International Child Abduction*, or bilateral agreement on such matters, with Canada.

Religious counsellor's positions regarding the best interest of the child in case of separation of the parents

Best interest of the child and role of parents towards children

In Quebec, the best interest of the child is a standard that 'encompasses a myriad of considerations. Courts must attempt to balance such considerations as the age, physical and emotional constitution and psychology of both the child and his or her parents and the particular milieu in which the child will live.'[39]

The interviews revealed a general consensus amongst the participants that Muslim norms require obedience and respect from children towards parents, and that Muslim parental authority is generally stricter or more severe than the Canadian norms would dictate. A Community Worker (ComWork2) said that the parental authority of Arab fathers is supposed to be overriding.

All religious counsellors knew of the concept of the best interest of the child, and thought that Islamic norms provided guidance in matters involving children in a similar way. All religious counsellors thought that children should be protected in the divorce process, and that family was a primordial necessity for children and existed to care for them.

While all religious counsellors mentioned the need to respect an agreement reached between the parents regarding the custody of children (be it in court or outside the court system), there were considerable variations regarding their opinion on custodial norms in cases where the spouses thereafter disagreed on the issue and turned to the religious counsellors for advice. According to some, children should be with their mother unless she remarries or is incompetent (RC6, RC4, RC10), others considered that children should be with their mother until age 7 (RC5, RC11, RC4), 9 (RC9) or 14/15 (RC8, RC12), after which they can choose where to live (RC4, RC7). Others suggested that the competence of each parent should be reconsidered, or they should go live with their father (RC2, RC4).

A number of criteria besides age will be taken into consideration by religious counsellors in determining parental capacity, such as physical security (RC9), education (RC9), 'spending of money in an inappropriate way' (RC9), psychological/emotional balance (RC3, RC10), ability to take care of the child (RC12), economic criteria (RC3, RC5), ability to give good support for a Muslim religious education (RC6, RC7, RC5[40]).

The positions of religious counsellors varied regarding the custody of children in the case of mixed marriage: RC2 and RC4 advised the Muslim parent to apply for single custody in case of marriage with a non-Muslim, while RC8[41] was adamantly opposed to joint custody (two lawyers were incidentally of the same opinion when young children were concerned – L4 and L5), while RC5 advised the Muslim parent in a mixed marriage to compromise with joint custody, so that the child can be exposed to both religions.

In comparison, all seven mediators interviewed tend to see their job as that of promoting an outcome that is the most beneficial for the children, to be achieved through the parents learning communication and negotiation skills along the way. For one mediator, the best interest of the child is constituted by what serves the children best, which means before anything an absence of conflict and pressure tactics.

All mediators were proactive on behalf of children's interests and were not neutral in these instances. One mediator even makes an explicit mention of this point in the mediation contract.

How do religious counsellors take account of children's needs/ wishes? The child's participation to the alternative dispute resolution processes

Conscious of the rights of the children, four out of six accredited mediators (the seventh is not accredited) met with the children as way to help ensure that their voices were part of the process. Among them, two accredited mediators met with children as a matter of course, while the other two only met them when required by specific circumstances (i.e. conflicting information from parents). One accredited mediator and lawyer (AccMed5) collaborated where necessary with a mediator psychologist who was experienced in working with children.

Each mediator was found to work in distinct ways. Two of them involved children systematically and the third on an ad hoc basis. AccMed1 brought children into a session once the agreement was nearly complete, as their input was considered to help finalize the agreement (regarding most notably the issue of time to be spent with each parent). AccMed3 said that he might bring children in at any point to help the parents get through roadblocks and develop a more open dialogue. AccMed2 involved children age 12+ if necessary, e.g. if parents had conflicting stories about what children wanted. AccMed2 and 3 did not involve children in decision making, e.g. regarding time to be spent with each parent. AccMed6 met with children as a last resort when it would be impossible to get a clear picture of the children's desires from the parents (i.e. where parents differed drastically on what children wanted). The information that the mediator received from children was then kept confidential.

Children were generally not involved in decision making itself, except with one mediator, who encouraged children to help decide about time spent with each parent.

In contrast, seven out of the thirteen religious counsellors involved children in alternative dispute resolution processes directly. Seven met with children during the process, either separately on in the presence of parents. Some religious counsellors met with children to gain information/insight about the family conflict (RC9[42], RC7), to make sure that children would not be harmed by certain decisions (RC3[43], RC12), or to help find better solutions with the help of information provided by children, rather than to ask children's views per se. Some consulted children directly about their wishes (RC5[44], RC4[45], RC7 and RC12). One, however, met with children and admitted to encouraging them to convince parents not to separate (RC10).

Usually religious counsellors only met with older children (i.e. 7 or 9 years and more – RC3, RC5, RC12). RC10 met them in the presence of their parents, while RC7, after having requested the parents' permission, will speak privately and in confidentiality with children, and RC12 saw them both alone and with their parents: 'Because I want to be sure that this child isn't under pressure from either of his parents.'

RC8 and RC9 mentioned that after a certain age, it is up to the child to decide where he/she wants to live, but it is unclear whether these religious counsellors met directly with such children in order to be informed of the children's own decision.

Although religious counsellors do not seem to have given as much thought as mediators to the issue of involvement of children in the resolution of spousal conflict, many of their practices are similar to the ones used by mediators.

Conclusion

It seems that the main functions that both Montreal Muslim women and religious counsellors attribute to Muslim dispute resolution processes are, first, that of religious advice, second, that of conciliation (divorce prevention), and, third, various kinds of support in the amicable settlement of the religious divorce. The last two types of practices are known in the Islamic legal tradition as *sulh*. Indeed, recent research shows that *sulh* has historically been a key institutional method of dispute resolution in the Muslim world alongside adjudication (*qad{a'*) and arbitration (*tah{kim*), and that it is still highly esteemed in Muslim minority communities such as in the United States.[46]

The practice of religious counsellors, as conveyed through their discourse, presents a mixed picture. First, with regards to process, less than half of them grant religious divorces in a manner completely disconnected from the civil legal system, while more than half of them see the civil legal system as serving a complementary role to theirs, based on the better recognition and enforcement of civil decisions.

In addition, and even if it accounts for only a smaller part of their practice (2 to 30 percent of their cases), more than half of them deal also with matters involving payment of the mahr, of spousal or child support, custody and access issues as well as the rarer abduction cases.

This potential complementarity of roles is enhanced by the fact that by far the most prominent functions of religious counsellors consist in advice and conciliation, followed by mediation of divorce. Approximately half of surveyed religious counsellors help spouses reach an informal agreement that they will be able to shape into a divorce agreement, which will then be submitted to the Quebec court of justice – with two religious counsellors thus actually helping in the process of drafting such an agreement and sometimes accompanying the parties throughout the judicial process.

Second, concerning the norms that the religious counsellors refer to in their practice, in most cases, the use of Muslim norms shows no signs of obvious influence from Quebec law, which highlights an insular trend in dispute resolution based on religious norms. Nevertheless, a minority of religious counsellors refer to *shari'a* norms as more compatible, or overlapping, with Quebec legal norms, or let the parties negotiate on the basis of such norms (e.g. best interest of the child, consent to divorce, vision of marriage as an economic partnership) whether explicitly or not. In some cases, a cross-pollination of legal, social, and cultural concepts are at stake. For instance RC compensate the wife for domestic labour, while the legal norm of best interest of the child is revisited with the help of religious norms.

Here, the internal diversity of Muslim norms, the flexibility of certain *shari'a* principles and the potential influence of historical dynamics of reform inherent to the Islamic legal tradition are factors as important to the understanding of this phenomenon of compatibility and overlap, as is the influence of Quebec socio-legal factors.

Regarding more specifically the process of dispute resolution, both when addressing unbalanced power distribution within the couple and the best interest of the children involved, religious counsellors tend to use similar techniques as accredited mediators would in similar situations, such as for instance meeting the persons separately in addition to meeting them jointly as part of the negotiation.

Their practice differs however from that of mediators on two key aspects: 1) some religious counsellors will include third parties in the negotiation between spouses; 2) some will not be neutral between the spouses during the dispute resolution process, and will take a proactive stance in order to defend the woman's interests, while not habitually taking a similarly interventionist role for the children's best interest.

Finally, on balance, the interviews showed that, far from discriminating against women, the religious counsellors showed great gender sensitivity and tried to ensure that justice was done.

Notes

* Anne Saris, Law Professor, Université du Québec à Montréal: Special thanks to Alejandro Escorihuela Lorite for his suggestions and careful editing.

1 Art 1: 'Parties must consider private prevention and resolution processes before referring their dispute to the courts,' Bill n 28: An Act to establish the new Code of Civil Procedure. It is important to note here that the participation in these processes is voluntary. It is the consideration of their possibility that is mandatory. Out of

court negotiation would thus become a compulsory step to consider before initiating legal proceedings, a duty that would be placed on the parties and not on their lawyers. This negotiation can be attained through various private resolution and prevention processes. Usually private resolution processes refers to mediation and arbitration, while private prevention refers to conciliation as well as mediation. (See legislative debates, 8 October 2013, Justice Minister St-Arnaud: 'Ces modes privés sont principalement la négociation entre les parties au différend de même que la médiation ou l'arbitrage dans lesquels les parties font appel à l'assistance d'un tiers. Les parties peuvent aussi recourir à tout autre mode qui leur convient et qu'elles considèrent adéquat, qu'il emprunte ou non à ces modes.') In Quebec, family issues cannot be adjudicated by an arbitrator and family mediation paid by the state is done by accredited mediators (lawyers, notaries, psychologists, etc.). While the use of the verb 'must' leads us to think that these pre-court processes, or at least the fact of considering them, is compulsory, nothing is said about who and how one checks that this prerequirement has been fulfilled. It is unclear whether these processes need to be accredited by the state (with potentially part of it financed). Finally there are no clear guidelines as to the penalties one will be subject to if he or she refuses to abide by section 1 of the new Code. Some speculate that this will have an impact on how costs are to be awarded (Luc Chamberland, *Le nouveau code de procedure civile commenté*, Cowansville, Yvon Blais, 2014, p. 3). During the legislative debates, the Minister of Justice mentioned the possibility of adding to the content of the summons 'avis d'assignation' the obligation to document the steps both parties would have taken to consider private prevention and resolution processes. However, it was also clear from the discussions in the national assembly that it was not the intent of the legislator to create a pre-trial protocol prescribing the manner in which the parties should act that would have to be verified by the judge during the trial.

2 See Anne Saris, Jean-Mathieu Potvin, Naima Bendriss, Wendy Ayotte and Samia Amor, 'Étude de Cas auprès de Canadiennes Musulmanes et d'intervenants Civils et Religieux en Résolution de Conflits Familiaux – une Recherche Exploratoire menée à Montréal en 2005–2007', Montréal, 2007, (final report), http://edoc.bibliothek.uni-halle.de/servlets/MCRFileNodeServlet/HALCoRe_derivate_00002510/%C3%89tude%20de%20cas%20aupr%C3%A8s%20de%20Canadiennes%20musulmanes.pdf;jsessionid=jnax53qhqih?hosts=, and Anne Saris and Jean-Mathieu Potvin, 'Canadian Muslim Women and Resolution of Family Conflicts: an Empirical Qualitative Study (2005–2007)', in *Law and Religion in the 21st Century: Relations between States and Religious Communities*, ed. Silvio Ferrari and Rinaldo Cristofori (Burlington: Ashgate, 2010).

3 See Lisa Fishbayn Joffe's Chapter 9 in this volume. At the time of the research (empirical research 2005–2006, report 2007), see Natasha Bakht, 'Religious Arbitration in Canada: Protecting Women by Protecting Them from Religion', *Canadian Journal of Women & the Law* 19 (2007): 119; Jean-François Gaudreault-DesBiens, 'The Limits of Private Justice: The Problems of the State Recognition of Arbitral Awards in Family and Personal Status Disputes in Ontario', *World Arbitration and Mediation Reports* 16.1 (2005): 18–32. See since then also Samia Bano, *Muslim Women and Shari'ah Councils: Transcending the Boundaries of Community and Law* (Basingstoke: Palgrave Macmillan, 2012).

4 In 2001, there were 579,640 Muslims out of the 29,639,030 Canadians; 61 percent lived in Ontario, while 19 percent lived in Quebec (with a majority of Sunni while Shiites represent 23 percent of the Muslim Quebec population).

5 This is another topic that is receiving increasing attention. See Ayelet Shachar, *Multicultural Jurisdictions: Cultural Differences and Women's Rights* (Cambridge: Cambridge University Press, 2001); Pascale Fournier, *Muslim Marriage in Western Courts: Lost in Transplantation* (Surrey: Ashgate, 2010); Mavis Maclean and John Eekelaar, eds., *Managing Family Justice in Diverse Societies* (Oxford: Hart, 2013);

Maleiha Malik, 'Family Law in Diverse Societies', in *Routledge Handbook of Family Law and Policy*, ed. John Eekelaar and Rob George (Abingdon: Routledge, 2014), 424–438.

6 While in Ontario, faith-based arbitration was recognized by the state until 2005, in the province of Quebec arbitration of family disputes was and is still prohibited in general (art 2039 al 1 of the Quebec Civil Code: 'Disputes over the status and capacity of persons, family matters or other matters of public order may not be submitted to arbitration'). For the debates regarding the May 26th motion, see www.assnat.qc.ca/fra/37legislature1/Debats/journal/ch/050526.htm. There was no proof of such Islamic tribunals in Quebec at the time of the motion. Our research clearly demonstrated that such tribunals did not exist and that religious counsellors did not have the legal nor religious authority to arbitrate family matters, since even when they played an adjudicator role, the result was never considered obligatory or final by either the counsellor or the parties, and the mutual consent of the parties had to be obtained regarding the content of the agreement itself.

7 I am using the term counsellors to distinguish the imams and other religious actors from accredited mediators and, to make clear that they were not seeking to claim for themselves legal authority on par with the state judicial apparatus. In practice, the imams fulfilled the role of advice givers and mediators and, rarely, the one of adjudicator.

8 The profile of the religious counsellors is detailed as follows: country of origin, sex, age, school of thought, years spent in Canada, years of experience, accredited by the Quebec administration to celebrate marriage (that are both religiously and civilly valid) and working language. Some of them were accredited by the Quebec civil status administration to celebrate marriages which were therefore recognized both by the Quebec legal system and the religious system, some others not (and consequently the religious marriages they celebrated were only valid in the religious sphere). Quebec does not seem to keep statistics of legal and religiously valid Islamic marriage. It only keeps track of civil and religious marriages that are celebrated by an accredited actor and hence legally valid. See www.stat.gouv.qc.ca/docs-hmi/statistiques/population-demographie/mariages-divorces/513.htm. RC1_Ind/Pakistan_M_60+_Hanafi_36_35_Eng/UrRC2_Lebanon_M_35/40_Shi'i/Ja'farite_19_10_AccM_Ar/EngRC3_Mali_M_30/35_Hanafi/Sufi_10/15_8_AccM_Fr/EnlRC4_Morocco_M_45/50_Sunni/Tabligh_15/20_15_Ar/FrRC5_Lebanon_M_40/45_Shafi'I_19_23_AccM_Fr/ArRC6_Lebanon_M_50/60_Hanafi_24_31_AccM_Ar/Fr/EngRC7_Bengladesh_M_45/50_Hanafi_23_23_AccM_Ur/Ben/Hin/Ar/Eng/FrRC8_Palestine_M_50/60_Sunni_10_20_Ar/EnglRC9_Pales/Leb_M_Shafi'i_9_8_Eng/ArRC10_Tunis_M_40/45_Sunni/Reform_16_16_AccM_Ar/FrRC11_Tunis_F_40/45_Sunni/SalafMuslimbrotherhood_7/11_20_Ar/EngRC12_Lebanon_M_45/50_Shi'I_16_25_AccM_Ar/Eng/FrRC13_Irak_M_60+_ Shi'I_18_36_AccM_Ar/Pers/Eng

9 ComWork5: 'In the case of Egyptian couple, she came to the shelter with two children and she went back to the husband within the second night of being at the shelter, and the husband is sort of accusing her of being mentally imbalanced and not getting adjusted… So then only would we be able to intervene or the imam and say: there's a woman and she is in an abusive relationship, can you help her? This was the latest case that we dealt with, younger one, so we go and speak to them and support them with our volunteers.'

10 According to RC9, the goal was 'so they wouldn't hurt their feelings or go against their religion. So we were doing a sort of one-on-one, sometimes at the Mosque, sometimes at the Police station.'

11 RC9 on custody.

12 RC7 mentions three times dealing with issues such as mahr, or division of family assets.

13 RC12 on custody, mahr: 'Four years ago, for ex., I counselled a couple – a Lebanese gentleman and an Iranian lady. They'd been married for two or two-and-a-half years only, and they had a child. Unfortunately they couldn't continue their life and they got divorced. But, the Iranian <had> her rights in front of the Canadian law. She took half of his money, the value of his house, 1 of the 2 cars that he owned. After she took all of this to a value of $80. – $85,000. CAD. She claimed in the court here about her right to take the second part of the mahr – $30,000. USD. She claimed she had an agreement with him according to the Shari'a. He registered this paper that if he should divorce her he will give her $30,000. USD as the final dowry. Ok the judge heard her, but the gentlemen he showed me and he told me what happened to him. I asked him if I could see his lawyer… I spoke with the lawyer and he asked me that if the judge were to ask me about this case, how can this resolve the problem for the client? I told him, very easily. I told him that according to our Shari'a the lady has the right to take the dowry one time. When she took from him half of his own, according to the Canadian Law, the value was $85,000. CAD, which is approximately three times the final dowry for her. She doesn't have anything more because she took three times the dowry. How can she now claim the dowry again? The lawyer said it was a wonderful idea and he arranged a meeting at City Hall, that I attended, at the Palais de Justice, with him and with the gentlemen. And I sat with the General Attorney. We sat with her and she asked me questions – she had an assistant.' (Note: RC12 when referring to General Attorney was actually referring to the judge.)

14 See on forum shopping, Pascale Fournier, *Muslim marriage in Western Courts: Lost in Transplantation* (Surrey: Ashgate, 2010).

15 RC10 clearly states that he does not have the authority to force people to do something.

16 RC7: 'The fact was at the time his wife was working. The husband was sending all the money to Bangladesh to his family. At one point he was sending all his money to Bangladesh and using his wife's money for living; in house and all those things. At one point his wife said no. You cannot take your money and my money so you can send to Bangladesh. So that's the sort of thing where a fight incurs, separation, divorce. The wife claimed he took her money.'

17 RC12: 'I can tell you honestly that I played the role of divorcer between 5 & 10% only. Between 90 & 95% I play the role of mediator. Because I registered the situation. Since I arrived here, around the end of 1990, until now, I saw more than 1,300 cases. But we had less than 80 cases of divorce. Maybe 76 or 77, in fifteen years.'

18 The tâlaq refers in this chapter to the unilateral divorce by the husband given in front of the religious counsellor. It is to be distinguished from the khul which is the divorce a woman obtains while forfeiting her mahr. The mahr is a dower, a lump sum that is owed to the wife by the husband as per the religious marriage contract. It can be paid partially at the wedding and in full at the end of the marital union.

19 RC6 mentions what he calls 'Islamic divorce certificates' specifying that his signature is accepted at the Algerian, Egyptian, Lebanese, Moroccan and Tunisian consulates.

20 RC12: 'I will give her a letter to the great Marja in Najaf or to Ja'fari court in Lebanon and they will judge him, and she will arrive at the divorce without his permission. But we will check this case and honestly – and between me and my god – to decide that this woman really needs to divorce… It's not necessary for

her to travel. She will give the authority for any lawyer there to represent her in the court in front of the judge, or, she will write a letter for a Marja and she can send it by email or fax. They will follow-up and they will ask me my opinion. They will trust my opinion. This is one example of practicing as wakil for a Marja. Because when they receive a letter from any woman or man here, they will check about the wakil in this area and they will ask him about what happened in this situation – because they are not here – they are not present here, but they trust the wakils. They depend on his opinion about 70–80%, in which he judges the situation; in how the result is affected.'

21 The Khul is the divorce a woman obtains while forfeiting her mahr. See note 18.

22 RC9: 'If this was in Lebanon, I would tell her to fill out an application in the courts. It takes three hearings. We send a note to the husband. If he doesn't appear before three hearings, it's a khul. It's easy if it's proven that in a year there is no contact and nothing is financially paid by that person. So it's easy. But here, I'm not in a position of doing that because I'm not a Oadi and I'm not a judge. I can do it as an Imam. I can do it as a Shiite. I can do it because I have the knowledge and I used to be in the courts in Lebanon working with the judges. The only thing is I don't want to go to that extent because they will say that I am rebelling because it's not according to what the Imams here do. This is something that Imams aren't taking initiative in and aren't taking responsibility to do something about it. They should do it and to be honest I asked for the phone number of that person. I'm contacting him; I'm contacting his friends. If I don't get any news from his family or from him, I'm calling him in Syria. If I don't get any news I'll send ....for the divorce. She's a life! I'm looking at her as a life! She's surviving, so why will I oppress her just because her husband ran away?'

23 The mahr is a dower, a lump sum that is owed to the wife by the husband as per the religious marriage contract. It can be paid partially at the wedding and in full at the end of the marital union.

24 RC9: 'Yeah. Especially North Africans they are more Mâlikite. The thing is they don't really know their madhhab, so when they come my opinions will always be Shâfi´ite.'

25 RC1: 'No. Never cultural consideration. When I sit with them, talk to them, it's always Islamic viewpoint, never cultural. Because if you bring culture into it then religion goes out the window. Because cultural demands are different. Most of the time it has nothing to do with Islam.'

26 I will not address the issue of violence in this chapter. For further information on this topic, see Saris et al., 'Étude de Cas auprès de Canadiennes Musulmanes,' final report, http://edoc.bibliothek.uni-halle.de:8080/servlets/MCRFileNodeServlet/HALCoRe_derivate_00002510/%C3%89tude%20de%20cas%20aupr%C3%A8s%20de%20Canadiennes%20musulmanes.pdf;jsessionid=1A2D38DB88B07B6385C1E91A3840EE66.

27 RC7: 'When the husband/wife comes here, the husband says that his wife has to stay home and do all the service of him. He did not see the right of the woman. What kind of freedom she should have. What she has a right and what he has right. (...) I go to the family and talk to the husband. I just explain what her Islamic rights are. When I say Islamic rights, we found that the Quebec rights are almost the same thing. .... Yes sometimes I have to intervene and I have to explain some things to the in-laws about the situation here and it's not the same as back home; how they have to change their mentality here because it's a new situation.'

28 The sadâq in this text is used as a synonym to mahr. Francophone Canadian Muslim Women interviewed referred to that term (W7 who actually renounced its payment).

29 RC2: '(…) For example. The time of having the kids with the mom – from day 1 until 6 years for example. If the man would say that he would take the kids back when she gets married – because this is the Islamic ruling. When she gets re-married he has the right to ask for their kids not to live with another strange man. Here I would say, yeah, you are right. But isn't it better for the well-being of the kids to be with their mom…'

30 L1 mentions 'peace, independence.'

31 L2 recalls a case in which the woman refused that her husband be questioned.

32 Simon Roberts, 'Three Models of Family Mediation', in *Divorce Mediation and the Legal Process*, ed. Robert Dingwall and John Eekelaar (Oxford: Oxford University Press, 1988), 145.

33 The Hague Convention on the Civil Aspects of International Child Abduction is a multilateral treaty that provides an expeditious method to return a child who was wrongfully removed by a non-custodial parent. The Hague Convention on the Civil Aspects of International Child Abduction, October 25, 1980, T.I.A.S. No. 11670, 1343 U.N.T.S. 22514.

34 RC5 mentions that it is difficult to kidnap a child since after the divorce one can inform immigration authorities that the child should not leave the country. He informs the couple that it is against criminal law that children travel without the consent of both parents.

35 RC3 recalled a case in which the mother was able with his help to travel to Senegal to bring back her children that had been taken there by her ex-husband.

36 RC12: 'Yes this happened only 2 or 3 times in the past sixteen years. I remember a man who took his family – two boys – and he promised his wife to live in Lebanon in a good situation. They travelled to Lebanon and after she lived with the family for four or five months only, he pushed her out and took the children from her. She returned here without the two boys and after the man travelled to Brazil and married another woman and took the boys to another family. I know well this woman here and she has a bad situation about this…. She asked me to do something but I told her that the problem is there is not judiciary agreement between Canada and Lebanon. You know there are countries that have judicial agreements with each other where they can speak with the authorities of the other country to do something. For example, for her as a Canadian woman, but her first nature was Lebanese; she cannot do anything because Canada and Lebanon don't have this agreement. We cannot say to the Lebanese authorities that we as Canadian authorities would like the Lebanese authorities to arrest this man and force him to give the children back to their mother. This is the problem. I told her that she could go to Lebanon and judge him in Lebanon.'

37 RC1: 'No this has never come up because Islamically it is wrong to kidnap. In some cases it has happened that the father wanted Islamic viewpoint and asked that if I kidnapped my child would that be fine. And I said no. You cannot do that.'

38 RC2: 'I would say, no you're not supposed to go and take your final decision from another system that's not Islamic, just to prove your own agenda.'

39 Young v Young [1993] 4 SCR 3.

40 RC5 mentions financial capacity, religiosity, being strict with children.

41 RC8: 'No. This life for the children is very bad. They see another woman with the father; they don't like this, that, etc. it's not good.'

42 Q.: 'Does that mean that you ask for witnesses from the people who know what they are saying?' RC9: 'Yes. Especially if she accuses him of hitting her and not treating her well. Ok, I'll take all this information and begin my investigation. (…) Sometimes I try to see the children separately. I know the kids and I'll try to talk to them. You know especially for khul when the wife comes and asks for khul it's a responsibility. If I'm giving that to her it has to be based on reliable information. Because I'm going to die one day and be asked why I gave that judgment.'

43 RC3 consults the children in order to better understand the family dynamic, to make sure that the children were not disadvantaged, and gather information that could be useful in helping conciliation within the couple, and give adequate advice.

44 According to RC5 at 9, 10 years old children are able to give their advice. While they do not participate per se to the negotiation of the agreement on custody, he meets with them before and during such process and sometimes can find solution through them (he mentions here that sometimes the wife will not want to speak of something but the children will).

45 RC4 takes into consideration the children point of view. According to him at 6, 7 years old, children start to understand what is going on and want to stay with their mother. He mentions that according to Islamic laws, the father has the right at that age to get the custody of the child and that often the women will not refuse.

46 See Aida Othman, 'And Sulh is Best: Amicable Settlement and Dispute Resolution in Islamic Law', *Arab Law Quarterly* 21 (2007): 64–90; See also Bogaç A. Ergene, *Local Court, Provincial Society and Justice in the Ottoman Empire: Legal Practice and Dispute Resolution in Çankiri and Kastamonu (1652–1744)* (Leiden; Boston: Brill, 2003).

Select bibliography

Abu-Lughod, Lila. *Do Muslim Women Need Saving?* Cambridge, MA: Harvard University Press, 2013.

Adamker, Y. "The Court: Beit Shemesh municipality humiliated women." 2015. Retrieved from http://judaism.walla.co.il/item/2823017.

Adams, Tim. "Binyavanga Wainaina interview: coming out in Kenya." *The Observer*, February 16, 2014. www.theguardian.com/books/2014/feb/16/binyavanga-wainaina-gay-rights-kenya-africa.

Adichie, Chimamanda Ngozi. *Purple Hibiscus*. New York: Fourth Estate, 2003.

Adichie, Chimamanda Ngozi. *We Should All Be Feminists*. London: Harper Collins, 2014.

Adler, Rachel. *Engendering Judaism: An Inclusive Theology and Ethics*. Boston: Beacon Press, 1999.

Afkhami, Mahnaz. "Rights of Passage: Women Shaping the Twenty-First Century." In *The Future of Women's Rights: Global Visions and Strategies*, edited by Joanna Kerr, *et al.*, 56–68. London: Zed Books, 2004.

Afro-Arab Expert Consultation on Legal Tools for the Prevention of Female Genital Mutilation." www.npwj.org/FGM/Afro-Arab-Expert-Consultation-Legal- Tools-PREVENTION-FEMALE-GENITAL-MUTILATION.html.

Agunah Summit. Conference by The NYU Tikvah Center for Law and Jewish Civilization and JOFA-Jewish Orthodox Feminist Alliance Lecture. New York University School of Law, New York, June 24, 2013.

Aharoni, Leah. "Women of the Wall: An Agent of Contention." *Sh'ma* (October 2013).

Ahmadu Bello University, Centre for Islamic Legal Studies, Great Britain. Department for International Development and British Council. *Promoting Women's Rights through Sharia in Northern Nigeria*. Zaria, Nigeria: Ahmadu Bello University, 2005. http://trove.nla.gov.au/work/21036862?q&versionId=25028503.

Al-Hibiri, Azizah. "An Islamic Perspective on Domestic Violence." *Fordham International Law Journal* 27, no. 1 (2003): 195–224.

Al-Matalka, Faisal. "Physical Violence Against Women in Jordan: Evaluation of Women Assaulted by Husbands." *Journal of Epidemiology and Community Health* 59 (2014): 818–821.

Ali, Kecia. "'A Beautiful Example': The Prophet Muḥammad as a Model for Muslim Husbands." *Islamic Studies* 43, no. 2 (2004): 273–291.

Ali, Kecia. *Marriage and Slavery in Early Islam*. Cambridge, MA: Harvard University Press, 2010.

Ali, Kecia. "Obedience and Disobedience in Islamic Discourses." *Encyclopedia of Women in Islamic Cultures,* edited by Suad Joseph. Leiden; Boston: Brill, 2007.

Ali, Kecia. *Sexual Ethics in Islam: Feminist Reflections on Qur'an, Hadīth and Jurisprudence.* Oxford: Oneworld, 2006.

Allen, John L. Jr. "Francis shoots down women cardinals." *NCR Today,* December 15, 2013. http://ncronline.org/blogs/ncr-today/francis-shoots-down-women-cardinals.

Allen, John. "Pope on Homosexuals: Who am I to Judge?" *National Catholic Reporter,* July 29, 2013. http://ncronline.org/blogs/ncr-today/pope-homosexuals-who- am-i-judge.

Allen, Prudence. "Man-Woman Complementarity: The Catholic Inspiration." *Logos* 9, no. 3 (2006): 87–108.

Allen, Prudence. *The Concept of Woman, Vol. 1: The Aristotelian Revolution, 750 B.C.-A.D. 1250.* Grand Rapids: Eerdmans Publishing Company, 1997.

Allot, A. *The Limits of Law.* London: Butterworth, 1980.

Almond, G.A., R.S. Appleby, and E. Sivan. *Strong Religion: The Rise of Fundamentalisms around the World.* Chicago: University Press, 2003.

Alwani, Zainab. *Al-Usra fī maqāṣid al-sharī'a: qirā'a fī qadāiyā wa-l-ṭalāq fī amrī kā.* Herndon, VA: The International Institute of Islamic Thought, 2012.

Alwani, Zainab. "Religion, Gender, and Family Law: Critical Perspectives on Integration for European Muslims." In *Applying Sharia in the West: Facts, Fears and the Future of Islamic Rules on Family Relations in the West,* edited by Maurits S. Berger, 227–240. Leiden, Boston: Brill, 2013.

Alwani, Zainab. "The Qur'ānic Model on Social Change: Family Structure as a Method of Social Reform." *Islam and Civilisational Renewal* 3, no. 1 (2008).

Amadi, Sam. "Religion and Secular Constitution: Human Rights and the Challenge of Sharī'ah." Carr Center for Human Rights Policy, 2003. www.hks.harvard.edu/cchrp/pdf/Amadi.pdf.

Amadiume, Ifi. *African Matriarchal Foundations: The Case of Igbo Societies.* London: Martins, 1987.

Amadiume, Ifi. *Male Daughters, Female Husbands: Gender and Sex in African Society.* London: Zed Press, 1987.

Amnesty International Sudan. "Abolish the Flogging of Women." (2010) AFR 54/005/2010.

Amoah, Jewel and Tom Bennett. "The Freedoms of Religion and Culture under the South African Constitution." *African Human Rights Law Journal* 8, no. 2 (2008): 357–375.

Arnfred, Signe. "Introduction." In *Re-thinking Sexualities in Africa,* edited by Signe Arnfred. Uppsala: Nordic Africa Institute, 2004.

Amoah, Jewel, and Tom Bennett. "The Freedoms of Religion and Culture under the South African Constitution." *African Human Rights Law Journal* 8, no. 2 (2008): 357–375.

Anderson, Rae. "Engendering the Mask: Three Voices." In *Ethnographic Feminisms: Essay in Anthropology,* edited by Rae Anderson and Lynne Phillips, 207–231. Ottawa: Carleton University Press, 1995.

Appiah, Kwame Anthony. *The Honor Code: How Moral Revolutions Happen.* New York: Norton, 2011.

Appleby, R.S and M.E. Marty. "Fundamentalism." *Foreign Policy* 128 (2002): 6–22.

Aran, G. "The Haredi's Body: Chapters of Ethnography in Process." In *Israeli Hareidim, Integration without Assimilation*, edited by E. Sivan and K. Caplan, 99–133. Jerusalem: Van Leer Institute (Hebrew), 2003.

Arieli, Yehoshua. "The Theory of Human Rights, its Origin and its Impact on Modern Society." In *Mishpat ve-Hisroryah [Law and History]*, edited by Daniel Gutwein and Menachem Mautner, 25. Jerusalem: Merkaz Zalman Shazar le-Toldot Yisra'el (Hebrew), 1999.

Arnold, Janice. "Prenups Now Required at Two Orthodox Shuls." *Canadian Jewish News*, June 4, 2012.

Arthur, L.B. "Dress and the Social Control of the Body." In *Religion, Dress and the Body*, edited by L. B. Arthur, 1–8. Oxford, UK: Berg, 1999.

Arthurs, Harry W. *'Without the Law': Administrative Justice and Legal Pluralism in Nineteenth Century England*. Toronto: University of Toronto Press, 1985.

Asbury, H. and Borges, J.L. *Gangs of New York: An Informal History of the Underworld*. New York: Thunder's Mouth Press, 2001.

Atkinson, P. and H. Martyn. "Ethnography and Participant Observation." In *Handbook of Qualitative Research*, edited by N.K. Denzin and Y.S. Lincoln, 248–261. Thousand Oaks, CA: Sage Publications, 1994.

Attia, Gamal Eldin. *Towards Realisation of the Higher Intents of Islamic Law, Maqasid Al Shari'ah: A Functional Approach* (*Naḥwa taf'īl maqāṣid al-sharīʿa*). Translated by Nancy Roberts. London; Washington: International Institute of Islamic Thought, 2008.

Auda, Jasser. *Maqāṣid al-Shariʿah as Philosophy of Islamic Law: A Systems Approach*. London; Washington: International Institute of Islamic Thought, 2008.

Ba, Mariama. *So Long a Letter*. London: Heinemann, 2008.

Babcock, Laurel, and Bruce Golding. "New Accusers in Rabbi 'Torture' Ring." *New York Post*, October 17, 2013. http://nypost.com/2013/10/17/new-accusers-in-rabbi-torture-ring/.

Baden, S. and A.M. Goetz. "Who Needs Sex When You Can Have Gender? Conflicting Discourses on Gender in Beijing." In *Feminist Visions of Development: Gender Analysis and Policy*, edited by C. Jackson and R. Pearson London: Routledge, 1998.

Bakht, Natasha. "Religious Arbitration in Canada: Protecting Women by Protecting Them from Religion." *Canadian Journal of Women & the Law* 19 (2007): 119.

Bambach, Lee Ann. "The Enforceability of Arbitration Decisions Made by Muslim Religious Tribunals: Examining the *Beth Din* Precedent." *Journal of Law and Religion* 25, no. 2 (2009–10): 379–414.

Bano, Samia. *Muslim Women and Shari'ah Councils: Transcending the Boundaries of Community and Law*. Basingstoke: Palgrave, 2012.

Bano, Samia, and Jennifer Pierce. *Gender Equality and Justice in Family Law Disputes: Women, Mediation, and Religious Arbitration*. Forthcoming. Waltham MA: Brandeis University Press, 2016.

Barzilai, Gad. *Communities and Law: Politics and Cultures of Legal Identities*. Ann Arbor: University of Michigan Press, 2003.

Bauer, Karen. "The Male is Not Like the Female (Q 3:36): The Question of Gender Egalitarianism in the Qur'an." *Religion Compass* ¾. (2009): 637–654.

Becker, Heike. "A Concise History of Gender, 'Tradition' and the State in Namibia." In *State, Society and Democracy*. Konrad Adenaur Foundation, 2010. www.kas.de/upload/auslandshomepages/namibia/State_Society_Democracy/chapter6.pdf.

Bender, Courtney and Pamela E. Klassen. *After Pluralism: Reimagining Religious Engagement (Religion, Culture, and Public Life)*. New York: Columbia University Press, 2010.

Benedict XVI. "Address of His Holiness Benedict XVI to the Members of the Roman Curia for the Traditional Exchange of Christmas Greetings." *Libreria Editrice Vaticana*, December 22, 2008. www.vatican.va/holy_father/benedict_xvi/speeches/2008/december/documents/hf_ben-xvi_spe_20081222_curia-romana_en.html.

Benhabib, Seyla. *The Claims of Culture: Equality and Diversity in the Global Era*. Princeton, NJ: Princeton University Press, 2002.

Benson, Miriam. "The Lawsuit: 1989–Present." In *Women of the Wall: Claiming Sacred Ground at Judaism's Holy Site*, edited by Phyllis Chesler and Rivka Haut. Woodstock, VT: Jewish Light Publishing, 2003.

Benson, O. and J. Stangroom. *Does God Hate Women?* London: Continuum, 2009.

Ben-Yehuda, N. *Theocratic Democracy*. New York: Oxford University Press, 2010.

Berger, Benjamin L. "The Cultural Limits of Legal Tolerance," in *After Pluralism: Reimagining Religious Engagement (Religion, Culture, and Public Life)*, edited by Courtney Bender and Pamela E. Klassen, 198–226. New York: Columbia University Press, 2010.

Berger, Peter L. *The Sacred Canopy: Elements of Sociological Theory of Religion*. New York: Doubleday, 1967.

Berger, Peter L., *et al. The Homeless Mind*. New York: Vintage Books, 1974.

Bielefeldt, Heiner. "Freedom of Religion or Belief: Thematic Reports of the UN Special Rapporteur 2010–2013." In *Religious Freedom Series (IIRF)*, Vol 3. Germany: Culture and Science Publications, 2014. www.bucer.org/uploads/tx_org/Heiner_Bielefeldt_-_Freedom_of_Religion_or_Belief.pdf.

Bielefeldt, Heiner. *Interim Report of the Special Rapporteur on Freedom of Religion or Belief*. UN Doc., A/68/290. August 7, 2013. www.ohchr.org/Documents/Issues/Religion/A.68.290.pdf.

Bielefeldt, Heiner. *Report of the Special Rapporteur on Freedom of Religion or Belief on violence committed in the name of religion*. A/HRC/28/66. December 29, 2014.

Bleich, David J. "A Suggested Antenuptial Agreement: A Proposal in Wake of Avitzur." *Journal of Halakha and Contemporary Society* 7 (1984): 25–41.

Bleich, David J. "Jewish Divorce: Judicial Misconceptions and Possible Means of Civil Enforcement." *Connecticut Law Review* 16, no. 2 (1984): 201–290.

Bogoch, Bryna and Yifat Holzman Gazit. "Clashing Over Conversion: 'Who is a Jew', and Media Representations of an Israeli Supreme Court Decision." *International Journal for the Semiotics of Law* 24, no. 4 (2011): 423–445.

Bond, Johanna. "CEDAW in Sub-Saharan Africa: Lessons on Implementation." *Michigan State Law Review* 2014: 241–263.

Bourdillon, M. *Where are the Ancestors? Changing Culture in Zimbabwe*. Harare: University of Zimbabwe Press, 1993.

Breitowitz, Irving A. *Between Civil and Religious Law: The Plight of the Agunah in American Society*. Westport CT: Greenwood Press, 1993.

Bronner, Ethan. "Israel Puts Off Crisis Over Conversion Law." *The New York Times*, July 23, 2010. www.nytimes.com/2010/07/24/world/middleeast/24israel.html.

Brooks, Peter and Paul Gewirtz, eds. *Law's Stories: Narrative and Rhetoric in the Law*. New Haven: Yale University Press, 1998.

Brown, Wendy. *Regulating Aversion: Tolerance in the Age of Identity and Empire.* Princeton, NJ: Princeton University Press, 2006.

Broyde, Michael J. "A Proposed Tripartite Agreement to Solve Some Of The Agunah Problems: A Solution Without Any Innovation." Online document, 1–15. Abridged version *JOFA Journal* 5, no. 4 (Summer 2005): 1–24. http://cslr.law.emory.edu/fileadmin/media/PDFs/Lectures/Broyde_Solutions_Agunah_Problem.pdf.

Broyde, Michael J. "Child Custody in Jewish Law: A Pure Law Analysis." www.jlaw.com/Articles/childcus1.html.

Broyde, Michael J. *Marriage, Divorce and the Abandoned Wife in Jewish Law: A Conceptual Approach to the Agunah Problems in America.* Hoboken NJ: Ktav, 2001.

Broyde, Michael J. "Sharia and Halakha in North America: Faith Based Arbitration as a Model for Preserving Rights and Values in a Pluralistic Society." *Chicago-Kent Law Review* 90, no. 111 (2015).

Broyde, Michael J. "The Pillars of Successful Religious Arbitration: Models for American Islamic Arbitration Based on the Beth Din of America and Muslim Arbitration Tribunal Experience." *Harvard Journal of Racial and Ethnic Justice* 30, no. 33 (2014).

Broyde, Michael J. and Jonathan Reiss. "The Ketubah in America." *Journal of Halacha and Contemporary Society* (2004). www.jlaw.com/Articles/KETUBAH.pdf.

Brzezinski, Zbigniew. *The Grand Failure: the Birth and Death of Communism in the Twentieth Century.* New York: Macmillan Publishers, 1989.

Bunting, Annie and Shadi Mokhtari. "Migrant Muslim Women's Interests and the Case of 'Shari'a Tribunals' in Ontario." In *Racialized Migrant Women in Canada: Essays on Health, Violence and Equity*, edited by Vijay Agnew. Toronto: University of Toronto Press, 2009.

Buss, Doris E. "Robes, Relics and Rights: the Vatican and the Beijing Conference On Women." *Social and Legal Studies* 7 (1998): 339–347.

Caldwell, P. "A Hair-Piece: Perspectives on the Intersection of Race and Gender." *Duke Law Journal* 2 (1991): 365–396.

Campbell, Colin. The Secret Religion of the Educated Classes. *Sociological Analysis* 39 (1978): 146–156.

Caplan, K. "Cheeky Dirty Convert: The Marriage of Amram Blau and Ruth Ben-David." *Iyunim Bitkumat Yisrael* 20 (2010): 300–337 (Hebrew).

Caplan, K. "Studying Israeli Hareidi Society: Characteristics, Achievements and Challenges." In *Israeli Hareidim, Integration without Assimilation*, edited by E. Sivan and K. Caplan, 224–78. Jerusalem: Van Leer Institute (Hebrew), 2003.

Caplan, K. *The Secret Hareidi Discourse.* Jerusalem: Zalman Shazar Center for Jewish History (Hebrew), 2007.

Caplan, K. and N. Stadler, eds. *From Survival to Consolidation: Changes in Israeli Haredi Society and Its Scholarly Study.* Jerusalem: The Van Leer Jerusalem Institute and Hakibbutz Hameuchad (Hebrew), 2012.

Caplan, K. and N. Stadler, eds. *Leadership and Authority in Israeli Haredi Society.* Tel-Aviv: H'akibutz H'ameuhad and the Van Leer Institute (Hebrew), 2009.

Case, Mary Anne. "After Gender The Destruction of Man? The Vatican's Nightmare Vision of the Gender Agenda for Law." *Pace Law Review* 31 (2012): 802.

Case, Mary Anne. "Does Complimentary Entail Parity?" Forthcoming in *LAWS* (2016).

Case, Mary Anne. "The Ladies? Forget About Them. A Feminist Perspective on the Limits of Originalism." *Constitutional Commentary* 29, no. 3 (2014) 431.

Case, Mary Anne. "The Role of the Popes in the Invention of Sexual Complementarity and the Anathematization of Gender." *Religion & Gender, Habemus Gender* special issue (2015).

Case, Mary Anne. "'The Very Stereotype the Law Condemns': Constitutional Sex Discrimination Law as a Quest for Perfect Proxies." *Cornell Law Review* 85 (2000): 1447–1473.

Chanock, Martin. *Law, Custom and Social Order: The Colonial Experience in Malawi and Zambia.* Portsmouth: Heinemann, 1998.

Chanock, Martin. "'Neither Customary, Nor Legal: African Customary Law in an Era of Family Law Reform." *International Journal of Law, Family and Policy* 3 (1989): 72.

Charrad, Mounira M. "Gender in the Middle East: Islam, State, Agency." *Annual Review of Sociology* 37 (2011): 417–437.

Chesler, Phyllis. "Drawn to Holiness: Women of the Wall Speak to the President of the Jewish Federations of North America." www.phyllis-chesler.com/1189/drawn-to-holiness-women-of-the-wall-speak-to.

Chesler, Phyllis and Rivka Haut, eds. *Women of the Wall: Claiming Sacred Ground at Judaism's Holy Site.* Woodstock, Vermont: Jewish Light Publishing, 2003.

Choudhary, Amit. "Polygamy not integral part of Islam: SC." *The Times of India,* February 10, 2015. http://timesofindia.indiatimes.com/india/Polygamy-not-integral-part-of-Islam-SC/articleshow/46180105.cms.

Christiansen, Lene Bull. "In our Culture – How Debates about Zimbabwe's Domestic Violence Law became a 'Culture Struggle'." *Nordic Journal of Feminist and Gender Research* 17, no. 2 (2009): 175–191.

Cimpric, A. *Children Accused of Witchcraft: An Anthropological Study of Contemporary Practices in Africa.* Dakar, UNICEF, WCARO, 2010.

Cismas, Ioana. *Religious Actors and International Law.* Oxford: Oxford University Press, 2014.

Code, Lorraine B. *What Can She Know? Feminist Theory and the Construction of Knowledge.* Ithaca NY: Cornell University Press, 1991.

Congregation for the Doctrine of the Faith. "Doctrinal Assessment of the Leadership Conference of Women Religious." www.usccb.org/upload/Doctrinal_Assessment_Leadership_Conference_Women_Religious.pdf.

Connell, Raewyn. "Rethinking Gender from the South." *Feminist Studies* 40, no. 3, (2014): 518–539.

Connolly, William E. *Pluralism.* Durham, NC: Duke University Press, 2005.

Connors, J. "Article 28: Reservations." In *CEDAW: A Commentary,* edited by M. Freeman, C. Chinkin and B. Rudolph, 565–595. Oxford University Press, 2012.

Cook, Rebecca and Simone Cusack. *Gender Stereotyping.* Philadelphia: University of Pennsylvania Press, 2010.

Coomaraswamy, Radhika. *Report of the Special Rapporteur on Violence Against Women, its Causes and Consequences.* UN Doc. E/CN.4/1999/68/Add.4. January 21, 1999.

Copnall, James. "Lubna Hussein: 'I'm not afraid of being flogged. It doesn't hurt. But it is insulting.'" *The Observer,* August 2, 2009. www.theguardian.com/world/2009/aug/02/sudan-women-dress-code.

Cornwall, Andrea, ed. *Readings in Gender in Africa.* Oxford: James Currey, 2005.

Costman, Carol, trans. *The Elementary Forms of Religious Life.* New York: Oxford University Press, 2001.

Cox, Neville. "The Class of Unprovable Universalisms: International Human Rights and Islamic Law." *Oxford Journal of Law & Religion* 2, no. 2 (2013): 307–329.

Cretney, Stephen. *Family Law in the Twentieth Century: A History*. New York: Oxford University Press, 2003.

Daly, C.M. "The 'Paarada' Expression of Hejaab among Afghan Women in a Non Muslim Community." In *Religion, Dress and the Body*, edited by L.B. Arthur, 147–162. Oxford: Berg, 1999.

Davison, Jean. *Gender, Lineage and Ethnicity in Southern Africa*. Boulder, CO: Westview Press, 1997.

Dawson, L.L. "Anti-Modernism, Modernism, and Postmodernism: Struggling with the Cultural Significance of New Religious Movements." *Sociology of Religion* 59, no. 2, (1998): 131–156.

De Beauvoir, Simone. *The Second Sex*. New York: Vintage Books, 1973.

Dekel, Daniela. "Speaking to the Wall." http://womenofthewall.org.il/.

Derrida, Jaques and Gil Anidjar. *Acts of Religion*. London: Routledge, 2001.

DeVault, Marjorie L. and Glenda Gross. "Feminist Interviewing: Experience, Talk and Knowledge." In *Handbook of Feminist Research: Theory and Praxis,* Sharlene Nagy Hesse-Biber, 173–198. Thousand Oaks, CA: Sage Publications Inc., 2007.

Dickens, Bernard. "The Rights to Conscience." In *Abortion Law in Transnational Perspective,* Rebecca Crook, Joanna Erdman, and Bernard Dickens. Philadelphia: University of Pennsylvania Press, 2014.

Donders, Dirkje. "The Tenacious Voice of Women." Rie Vendrik and the Pontifical Commission On Women in Society and in the Church, Utrecht 2002.

Donnelly, Jack. *Universal Human Rights in Theory and Practice*. 2nd ed. Ithaca and London: Cornell University Press, 2003.

Douglas, M. *Purity and Danger: An Analysis of Concepts of Pollution and Taboo*. London: Routledge and Kegan Paul, 1966.

Duffy, H. "Hadijatou Mani Koroua v Niger: Slavery Unveiled by the ECOWAS Court." *Human Rights Law Review* 9, no. 1 (2009): 151.

Dujerija, Adis. "A Case Study of Patriarchy and Slavery: The Hermeneutical Importance of Qurānic Assumptions in the Development of a Values-Based and Purposive Oriented Qurān-sunna Hermeneutic." *HAWWA Journal of Women in the Middle East and the Muslim World* 11, no. 1 (2013): 58–87.

Duodu, C. "One in the Eye for West African Slaves." *New African*, November 23, 2008. http://newafricanmagazine.com/one-in-the-eye-for-west-african-slavers/.

Dworkin, Ronald. *Religion Without God*. Cambridge MA: Harvard University Press, 2013.

Eekelaar, John. "Evaluating Legal Regulation of Family Behaviour." *International Journal of Jurisprudence of the Family* 1 (2011): 17–34. http://heinonline.org/HOL/Page?handle=hein.journals/ijjfl&id=1&collection=journals.

Eekelaar, John and Mavis Maclean. "Marriage and the Moral Basis of Personal Relationships." *Journal of Law and Society* 31 (2004): 510–38.

Eichler, Margaret. *Nonsexist Research Methods: A Practical Guide*. Boston: Allen & Unwin, 1988.

Eiliott, Andrea. "David Yerushalmi, The Man Behind the Anti-Shariah Movement." *New York Times,* July 30, 2011.

Eisenberg, Avigail. *Reasons of Identity: A Normative Guide to the Political and Legal Assessment of Identity Claims*. New York: Oxford University Press, 2011.

Eisgruber, Christopher and Lawrence Sager. *Religious Freedom and the Constitution*. Cambridge, MA: Harvard University Press, 2010.

El Feki, Shareen. *Sex and the Citadel: Intimate Life in a Changing Arab World.* London: Vintage Books, 2014.

El Guindi, F. *Veil: Modesty, Privacy and Resistance.* Oxford: Berg, 1999.

Elior, R. "Attendance Absentees: 'Still Life' and a 'Beautiful Young Woman without Eyes'." In *Will You Hear My Voice?* edited by Y. Atzmon. Jerusalem: Van Leer Publishers (Hebrew), 2001.

Elkay am-Levy, C. "Women's Rights and Religion: The Missing Element in the Jurisprudence of the European Court of Human Rights." *University of Pennsylvania Journal of International Law* 35, no.4 (2014): 1175–1222.

Elor, T. "2007/8: The Winter of the Veiled Women." *Theory and Criticism* 37 (Fall 2010).

Eltantawi, Sarah. "Stoning in the Islamic Tradition: The Case of Northern Nigeria." Dissertation, Harvard University, 2012.

Emek, Shaveh. "Archaeology is Key to Holy Sites in the Old City." http://alt-arch.org/he/holysites_heb/.

Emon, Anver E. "Islamic Law and the Canadian Mosaic: Politics, Jurisprudence and Multicultural Accommodation." *The Canadian Bar Review* 87, no. 2 (2009): 391–425.

Emon, Anver M. *Religious Pluralism and Islamic Law: Dhmimmis and Others in the Empire of Law.* Oxford: Oxford University Press, 2012.

Engel, David M. and Frank W. Munger. *Rights of Inclusion: Law and Identity in the Life Stories of Americans with Disabilities.* Chicago: University of Chicago Press, 2003.

Epprecht, Marc. *Heterosexual Africa? The History of an Idea from the Age of Exploration to the Age of AIDS.* Athens, OH: Ohio University Press, 2008.

Epprecht, Marc. *Hungochani: The History of a Dissident Sexuality in Southern Africa.* Montreal: McGill-Queens University Press, 2004.

Epprecht, Marc. *Sexuality and Social Justice in Africa: Rethinking Homophobia and Forging Resistance.* London: Zed Press, 2013.

Ergene, Bogaç A. *Local Court, Provincial Society and Justice in the Ottoman Empire: Legal Practice and Dispute Resolution in Çankiri and Kastamonu (1652–1744).* Leiden; Boston: Brill, 2003.

Eurostat. *European Social Statistics* 2013 edition.

Ewick, Patricia and Susan Silbey. *The Common Place of Law: Stories From Everyday Life.* Chicago: University of Chicago Press, 1998.

Fadel, Mohammad. "Two Women, One Man: Knowledge, Power and Gender in Medieval Sunni Legal Thought." *International Journal of Middle East Studies* 29 (1997): 185–204.

Farber, Daniel A. and Suzanna Sherry. "Telling Stories Out of School: An Essay on Legal Narratives." *Stanford Law Review* 45 (1992–1993): 807–855.

Farrago, Jason. "Pope: Save Rainforest and Heterosexuality, Too: Benedict's Christmas Message Decries Erosion of 'Traditional' Gender Roles." *Newser*, December 23, 2008. www.newser.com/story/46091/pope-save-rainforest-and-heterosexuality-too.html.

Federation of Muslim Women's Association. "Is Stoning to Death Penalty for Adultery?" *The Muslim Woman* 6 (2006): 25.

Feit, Yaacov. "The Prohibition on Litigating in Secular Courts." *Journal of the Beit Din of America* 1, no. 1 (2012): 30–47.

Fendel, Hillel. "Rabbinate Stats: 180 Women, 185 Men 'Chained' by Spouses." *Israel National News*, August 23, 2007. www.israelnationalnews.com/News/News.aspx/123472.

Fenn, Richard. *Toward a Theory of Secularization*. Storrs, CT: Society for the Scientific Study of Religion, 1978.

Fetterman, D.M. *Ethnography: Step by Step*. Thousand Oaks, CA: Sage, 1989.

Fine, Michelle. *Disruptive Voices: The Possibilities of Feminist Research*. Ann Arbor: University of Michigan Press, 1992.

Fineman, Martha Albertson. "The Meaning of Marriage." In *Marriage Proposals: Questioning a Legal Status*, edited by Anita Bernstein. New York and London: New York University Press, 2006.

Fiorenza, Elisabeth Schuessler. "We are Church – A Kingdom of Priests." Keynote Address for Women's Ordination Worldwide (WOW) Second International Conference Breaking Silence, Breaking Bread: Christ Calls Women to Lead Ottawa, Canada, July 22–24, 2005. http://womensordinationworldwide.org/ottawa-2005/2014/2/2/elizabeth-schussler-fiorenza-we-are-a-church-a-kingdom-of-priests.

Fishbayn Joffe, Lisa. "Gender, Multiculturalism and Dialogue: The Case of Jewish Divorce." *Canadian Journal of Law & Jurisprudence* 21 (2008): 71–96.

Fishbayn Joffe, Lisa and Sylvia Neil, eds. *Gender, Religion, and Family Law: Theorizing Conflicts between Women's Rights and Cultural Traditions*. Waltham MA: Brandeis University Press, 2012.

Fisher, S. "Judaism and Global Religious Trends: Some Contemporary Developments." In *World Religions and Multiculturalism – A Dialectic Relation*, edited by E. Ben-Rafael and Y.Sternberg, 315–350. Leiden: Brill Academic Publishers, 2010.

Fitzgerald, Timothy. *Discourse on Civility and Barbarity: A Critical History of Religion and Related Categories*. Oxford: Oxford University Press, 2007.

Fitzpatrick, Peter. *The Mythology of Modern Law* (Sociology of Law and Crime). New York: Routledge, 1992.

Florida Senate Committee Application of Foreign Law in Courts, 2014. Florida Senate Committee on the Judiciary, Bill Analysis and Fiscal Impact Statement, SB 386.

FOMWAN *20 Years of Service to Islam*. 20th, Anniversary edition (1985–2005), 2005.

Foreign Staff. "Pope: Saving world from homosexuality like saving rainforests." *Telegraph*, December 22, 2008. www.telegraph.co.uk/news/worldnews/europe/italy/3902931/Pope-Saving-world-from-homosexuality-like-saving-rainforests.html.

Foucault, M. "The Repressive Hypothesis." In *The Foucault Reader*, edited by P. Rabinow, 301–30. New York: Pantheon Books, 1984.

Foucault, M. "Truth and Power." In *Power/Knowledge*, edited by C. Gordon, 51–75. New York: Pantheon Books, 1980.

Fournier, Pascale. "*Halakha*, the 'Jewish State' and the Canadian Agunah: Comparative Law at the Intersection of Religious and Secular Orders." *Journal of Legal Pluralism and Unofficial Law* 65 (2012): 165–204.

Fournier, Pascale. *Muslim Marriage in Western Courts: Lost in Transplantation*. Surrey: Ashgate, 2010.

Francis. "Apostolic Journey of His Holiness Pope Francis To Sri Lanka And The Philippines (12-19 January 2015) In-Flight Press Conference Of His Holiness Pope Francis From The Philippines To Rome Papal Flight." *Libreria Editrice Vaticana*, January 19, 2015. http://w2.vatican.va/content/francesco/en/speeches/2015/january/documents/papa-francesco_20150119_srilanka-filippine-conferenza-stampa.html.

Francis. "Apostolic Journey to Rio de Janeiro on the Occasion of the XXVIII World Youth Day. Press Conference of Pope Francis during the Return Flight." *Libreria Editrice Vaticana*, July 28, 2013. http://w2.vatican.va/content/francesco/en/speeches/2013/july/documents/papa-francesco_20130728_gmg-conferenza-stampa.html.

Francis. "Not Just Good, but Beautiful." *Humanum*. http://humanum.it/talks/pope-francis-opening-address-humanum-conference/.

Francis. The Family - 10. Male and Female (I). General Audience, Wednesday, April 15, 2015.

Frankenburg, Ruth. "On Unsteady Ground: Crafting and Engaging in the Critical Study of Whiteness." In *Researching Race and Racism*, edited by Martin Blumer and John Solomos, 104–118. London: Routledge, 2004.

Frenkel, Norfrat. http://judaism.about.com/b/2009/11/24/in-her-own-words-nofrat-frenkel.htm.

"Frequently Asked Questions Regarding Jewish Divorce." *Beth Din of America*. www.bethdin.org/docs/FAQ_d.pdf.

Freyer, T.A. *The Little Rock Crisis: A Constitutional Interpretation*. Santa Barbara: Greenwood Press, 1984.

Fried, Ginnine. "The Collision of Church and State: A Primer to *Beth Din* Arbitration and the New York Secular Courts." *Fordham Urban Law Journal* 31, no. 2, (2004): 633–655.

Friedan, Betty. *It Changed My Life: Writings on the Women's Movement*. Cambridge, MA: Harvard University Press, 1998.

Friedman, M. "Haredi violence in contemporary Israeli society," *Studies in Contemporary Jewry* 18 (2002): 186–197.

Friedman, M. "'Silence' and 'Sayings' in the Haredi Society." In *Knowledge and Silence: On Mechanisms of Denial and Repression in Israeli Society*, edited by H. Herzog and K. Lahad, 113–119. Jerusalem: Van Leer Institute/Hakibbutz Hameuchad Publishing House (Hebrew), 2006.

Friedman, M. "The Lost of Tradition: The Shi'urim [Measures] Controversy." In *The Quest for Halakha: Interdisciplinary Perspectives on Jewish Law*, edited by A. Berholz, 196–218. Jerusalem: Beit Morasha - yediot aharonot (Hebrew), 2003.

Friedman, M. "The State of Israel as a Theological Dilemma." *Alpayim. A Multidisciplinary Publication for Contemporary Thought and Literature* 3, (1990a): 24–68 (Hebrew).

Friedman, M. "The Market Model and Religious Radicalism." *In the Throes of Tradition and Change: A Collection of Papers in Memory of Arye Lang*, edited by M. Kahane, 262–77. Rehovot: Kivunim Pub (Hebrew), 1990b.

Friedman, M. *Ultra-Orthodox Society: Sources Trends and Processes*. Jerusalem: Jerusalem Institute for Israel Studies (Hebrew), 1991.

Fullam, Lisa. " 'Gender Theory', Nuclear War, and the Nazis." *Commonweal*, February, 23 2015. www.commonwealmagazine.org/blog/gender-theory-nuclear-war-and-nazis-0.

Gaidzanwa, Rudo. "Bourgeois Theories of Gender and Feminism and their Shortcomings with Reference to Southern African Countries." In *Gender in Southern Africa: Conceptual and Theoretical Issues*, edited by Ruth Meena. Harare: SAPES Books, 1992.

Gans, H.J. *The Urban Villagers*. New York: The Free Press, 1962.

Garner, Rebecca L.R. and Elisabeth Goessman. "Overcoming Obstacles." In *Women Medievalists and the Academy*, edited by Jane Chance. Madison: University of Wisconsin Press, 2005.

Gaudreault-DesBiens, Jean-François. "The Limits of Private Justice: The Problems of the State Recognition of Arbitral Awards in Family and Personal Status Disputes in Ontario." *World Arbitration and Mediation Reports* 16, no. 1 (2005): 18–32.

Geertz, Clifford. *The Interpretation of Cultures: Selected Essays.* New York: Basic Books, 1973.

Gilligan, Carol. *In a Different Voice: Psychological Theory and Women's Development.* Cambridge, MA: Harvard University Press, 1993.

Ginsburg Ruth Bader. "Gender in the Supreme Court: The 1973 and 1974 Terms." *The Supreme Court Review* (1975): 1–24.

Glick, Peter and Susan T. Fiske. "The Ambivalent Sexism Inventory: Differentiating Hostile and Benevolent Sexism." *Journal of Personality and Social Psychology* 70, no. 3 (1996): 491–512.

Goldstein, Bluma. *Enforced Marginality: Jewish Narratives on Abandoned Wives.* California: University of California Press, 2007.

Gomma, Ali. "Gender Equality in Islam." *The Washington Post*, July 21, 2007.

Gordis, Danial. "Erusin: The First of the Two Ceremonies." www.myjewishlearning.com/article/erusin-the-first-of-the-two-ceremonies/2/.

Gordon, Jerry. "Massachusetts Rabbi Sends Letter To Florida Legislature On American Law For American Courts Bills." *Watchdogwire*, March 29, 2013. http://watchdogwire.com/florida/2013/03/29/new-jersey-rabbi-sends-letter-to-florida-legislature-on-american-law-for-american-courts-bills/.

Greenberg, Blu. "Halakhic Justice for the Agunah: A 40 Year Retrospective." JOFA International Conference on Feminism and Orthodoxy, New York, 2010, 1–12.

Greenberg, Blu. "Where There is a Rabbinic Will, There is a Halakhic Way: A Defense and Critique." The Tikvah Center's Twelfth Annual Caroline and Joseph S. Gruss Lecture at New York University School of Law, New York, October 21, 2013.

Griffiths, John. "What is Legal Pluralism?" *Journal of Legal Pluralism* 24 (1986): 1–56.

Grosfoguel, Ramon, Laura Oso and Anastasia Christou. "Racism, Intersectionality and Migration Studies: Framing Some Theoretical Reflections." *Identities: Global Studies in Culture and Power* (2014): 1–18.

Grossman, Avraham. *Pious and Rebellious: Jewish Women in Medieval Europe.* Waltham, MA: Brandeis University Press, 2004.

Grover, Anand. *Interim Report of the Special Rapporteur on the Right of Everyone.* UN Doc. A/66/254. 3 August, 2011.

Habermas, Jürgen. "Religion in the Public Sphere." *European Journal of Philosophy* 14, no. 1 (2006): 1–25.

Hall, C.S. *A Primer of Freudian Psychology.* New York: Penguin Books, 1999.

Hallaq, Wael B. *A History of Islamic Legal Theories: An Introduction to Sunni Usul al-Fiqh.* Cambridge: Cambridge University Press, 1997.

Hallaq, Wael B. *Sharī'a: Theory, Practice, Transformations.* Cambridge: Cambridge University Press, 2009.

Halley, Janet, Prbaha Kotiswaran, Hila Shamir and Chantal Thomas. "From the International to the Local in Feminist Legal Responses to Rape, Prostitution/Sex Work and Sex Trafficking: Four Studies in Contemporary Governance Feminism." *Harvard Journal of Law and Gender* 29 (2006): 336–360.

Haneef, Sayed Sikandar. "Treatment of Recalcitrant Wife in Islamic Law: The Need for a Purposive Juridical Construct." *Global Jurist* 12, no. 2 (2012).

Harris, Colette "Masculinities and Religion in Kaduna, Nigeria: A Struggle for Continuity at a Time of Change." *Religion and Gender* 2, no. 2 (2012): 207–230.

Hartman, Tov. *Feminism Encounters Traditional Judaism: Resistance and Accommodation.* Waltham, MA: Brandeis University Press, 2007.

Hauptman, Judith. *Rereading the Rabbis: A Woman's Voice.* Boulder, CO: Westview Press, 1998.

Hawthorne, Sian Melvill and Adriaan S. van Klinken. "Catachresis: Religion, Gender and Postcoloniality." *Religion and Gender* 3, no 2 (2013): 159–167.

Heilman, S. *Defenders of the Faith: Inside Ultra-Orthodox Jewry.* New York: Schocken, 1992.

Heinzelman, Susan Sage and Zipporah Batshaw Wiseman. *Representing Women: Law, Literature, and Feminism.* Durham: Duke University Press, 1994.

Hélie, Anissa. "Risky Rights? Gender Equality and Sexual Diversity in Muslim Contexts." In *Sexuality in Muslim Contexts*, edited by Anissa Hélie and Homa Hoodfar. London: Zed Books, 2012.

Herzog, H. *Sex Gender Politics — Women in Israel.* Tel Aviv: Hakibbutz Hameuchad, 1999.

Heschel, Susannah. "Anti-Judaism in Christian Feminist Theology." *Tikkun* 5, no. 3 (1990).

Hesse-Biber, Sharlene Nagy and Patricia Lina Leavy. *Qualitative Research.* New York: Oxford University Press, 2004.

Hidayatullah, Aysha A. *Feminist Edges of the Qur'an.* Oxford: Oxford University Press, 2014.

Hirsch, Susan. *Pronouncing and Persevering: Gender and the Discourses of Disputing in an African Islamic Court.* Chicago: University of Chicago Press, 1998.

Hirshfeld, Ariel. *Local Notes.* Tel Aviv: Am Oved, 2002.

Hirschl, Ran. *Towards Juristocracy: The Origins and the Consequences of the New Constitutionalism.* Cambridge, MA: Harvard University Press, 2004.

Hoffman, Anat. www.huffingtonpost.com/anat-hoffman/arrested-for-praying-at-western-wall_b_1987099.html.

Hoffman, Valerie. "An Islamic Activist: Zaynab Al-Ghazali." In *Women and the Family in the Middle East*, edited by Elizabeth Fernea, 233–254. Austin: University of Texas Press, 1985.

Holy See. "Statement of the Holy See in Explanation of Position on the Agreed Conclusions." The Permanent Observer Mission Of The Holy See To The United Nations. www. holyseemission.org/statements/statement.aspx?id=73.

Hooper, John. "Pope Francis jokes 'woman was from a rib' as he avoids vow to reform church." *The Guardian,* June 29, 2014. www.theguardian.com/world/2014/jun/03/pope-tells-couples-have-children-not-pets.

House of Commons. Written Statement (HCWS152), Ministry of Justice, Written Statement made by The Minister of State for Justice and Civil Liberties (Simon Hughes) on December 18, 2014.

Hyman, P. *Gender and Assimilation in Modern Jewish History: The Roles and Representation of Women.* Washington: University of Washington Press, 1995.

Institut de la Statistique Quebec. www.stat.gouv.qc.ca/docs-hmi/statistiques/population-demographie/mariages-divorces/513.html.

"International Rabbinic Fellowship Takes Historic Step to Prevent Future Agunot." May 24, 2012.

Israel Antiques Authority. www.antiquities.org.il/about_heb.aspx?Modul_id=103.

Israel Religious Action Center. www.irac.org/.

Iwobi, Andrew Ubaka. "Tiptoeing through a Constitutional Minefield: the Great Sharia Controversy in Nigeria." *Journal of African Law* 48 (2004): 111–164.

Izugbara, Chimroaoke O. and Alex C. Ezeh. "Women and High Fertility in Islamic Northern Nigeria." *Studies in Family Planning* 41, no. 3 (2010): 193–204.

Jackson, Bernard, *et al.* "Agunah: A Manchester Analysis: Draft Final report of the Agunah Research Unit, University of Manchester." Manchester, 2009, 1–211.

Jahangir, Asma. Speech given at The Parliamentary Assembly of the Council of Europe. Available at http://assembly.coe.int/Main.asp?link=/Documents/Records/2005/E/0510041000E.htm#5t.

John Paul II. "Apostolic Letter on the Dignity and Vocation of Women." *Libreria Editrice Vaticana*, August 15, 1988. http://w2.vatican.va/content/john-paul-ii/en/apost_letters/1988/documents/hf_jp-ii_apl_19880815_mulieris-dignitatem.html.

John Paul II. "Family, Marriage, and 'De Facto' Unions." *Libreria Editrice Vaticana*, July 26, 2000. www.vatican.va/roman_curia/pontifical_councils/family/documents/rc_pc_family_doc_20001109_de-facto-unions_en.html.

John Paul II. "Letter of Pope John Paul II to Women." *Libreria Editrice Vaticana*, June 29, 1995. http://w2.vatican.va/content/john-paul-ii/en/letters/1995/documents/hf_jp-ii_let_29061995_women.html.

John Paul II. "Letter to the Bishops of the Catholic Church on the Collaboration of Men and Women in the Church and in the World." *Libreria Editrice Vaticana*, May 31, 2004. www.vatican.va/roman_curia/congregations/cfaith/documents/rc_con_cfaith_doc_20040731_collaboration_en.html.

John XXIII. "Address of Pope John XXIII to the Study 'The Woman and the Profession'." *Libreria Editrice Vaticana*, September 6, 1961. http://w2.vatican.va/content/john-xxiii/it/speeches/1961/documents/hf_j-xxiii_spe_19610906_donna-professione.html.

Jones, Melinda and Peta Jones-Pellach. *Jewish Women & Religious Freedom In Australia: Status Report* (2011). Available online. http://www.academia.edu/11483799/JEWISH_WOMEN_and_RELIGIOUS_FREEDOM_IN_AUSTRALIA_STATUS_REPORT.

Jordan, Mark D. *The Invention of Sodomy in Christian Theology*. Chicago: University of Chicago Press, 1997.

Kaddari, Ruth Halperin. *Women in Israel, A State of Their Own*. Philadelphia: University of Pennsylvania Press, 2004.

Kahan, Linda. "Jewish Divorce and Secular Courts: The Promise of Avitzur." *Georgetown Law Journal* 73 (1984): 193–225.

Kahaner, L. "The Development of the Spatial and Hierarchic Structure of the Ultra-Orthodox Jewish Population in Israel." PhD dissertation, Haifa University (Hebrew), 2009.

Kamali, Mohammad Hashim. "Islamic Family Law Reform: Problems and Prospects." *Islam and Civilisational Renewal* 3, no. 1 (2011): 37–52.

Karibi-Whyte, A.G. *History and Sources of Nigerian Criminal Law*. Ibadan: Spectrum, 1993.

Katzir, Yael. "In Her Own Voice." http://israelfilm.blogspot.com/2009/02/women-of-wall.html.

Kedar, M. "Israel in a Middle East that is becoming Islamic." *Makor Rishom* (2011), 20 (Hebrew).

Keddie, Nikki R. *Women in the Middle East: Past and Present*. Princeton: Princeton University Press, 2007.

Kimchi, S. and Even, S. "Who are the Palestinian Terrorist Suiciders?" *Mizcar* 73. Tel Aviv: The Jaffee Center for Strategic Studies, Tel Aviv University (Hebrew), 2004.

Klapper, Aryeh. "Why We Have the Lonna Kin Situation." Fresh Ideas from the HBI: The HBI Blog, May 9, 2014. https://blogs.brandeis.edu/freshideasfromhbi/why-we-have-the-lonna-kin-situation/.

Knesset. "The Names of the Parties." www.knesset.gov.il/faction/heb/FactionListAll.asp?view=1.

Kolawole, Mary. "Re-Conceptualizing African Gender Theory: Feminism, Womanism and the *Arere* Metaphor." In *Re-thinking Sexualities in Africa*, edited by Signe Arnfred. Uppsala: Nordic Africa Institute, 2004.

Korteweg, Anna C. "The Sharia Debate in Ontario: Gender, Islam, and Representations of Muslim Women's Agency." *Gender & Society* 22, no. 4 (2008): 434–54.

Korteweg, Anna C. and Jennifer A. Selby. *Debating Sharia: Islam, Gender Politics, and Family Law Arbitration*. Toronto: University of Toronto Press, 2012.

Krantz, G. and Garcia-Moreno, C. "Violence Against Women", *Journal of Claudia Garcia-Moreno* (2005).

Krauss, Simcha. "Litigation in Secular Courts." *Journal of Halacha and Contemporary Society* 2, no.1 (Spring 1982).

Kuby, Gabriele. "Gender Mainstreaming: The Secret Revolution." *Vatican Magazine*, November 6, 2008.

Kuovo, S. "The United Nations and Gender Mainstreaming: Limits and Possibilities." In *International Law: Modern Feminist Approaches*, edited by D. Buss and A. Manji, 673–682. Oxford: Hart, 2005.

Kymlicka, Will. *Multicultural Citizenship: A Liberal Theory of Minority Rights*. Oxford: Clarendon Press, 1995.

Lahav, Pnina. "Israel's Rosit The Riveter: Between Secular Law and Jewish Law." *Boston University Law Review* 93 (2013): 1063.

Lahav, Pnina. "Israel's Supreme Court." In *Contemporary Israel*, edited by R.O. Freedman. Boulder, CO: Westview, 2009.

Lahav, Pnina. "Seeking Recognition: Women's Struggle for Full Citizenship in the Community of Religious Worship." In *Gendering Religion and Politics*, edited by H. Herzog and A. Bradue. London: Palgrave Macmillan, 2009.

Lahav, Pnina. "Women of the Wall: A Temporary but Meaningful Milestone." *Hampishpat Online: Human Rights: Insight into Recent Judgments* 9, no. 4 (2013). www.colman.ac.il/research/research_institute/katedra_HumanRights/Psika/Documents/9/9_june_2013_3_Lahav_EN.pdf.

Lahav, Pnina. *Women of the Wall*. Woodstock, VT: Jewish Lights Publishing, 2003.

Laquer, Thomas. *Making Sex: Body and Gender from the Greeks to Freud*. Cambridge, MA: Harvard University Press, 1992.

Lederman, Faye. "Women of the Wall." http://www.newday.com/films/WomenoftheWall.html.

Lefebre, Solange and Lori G. Beaman. *Religion in the Public Sphere: Canadian Case Studies*. Toronto: University of Toronto Press, 2014.

Legal Assistance Center. *Guide to the Married Person's Equality Act*. Windhoek: Legal Assistance Center, 2009.

Leichter, Alexandra, Susan Aranoff, Susan Weiss, *et al*. The Agunah Summit. Conference by The NYU Tikvah Center for Law and Jewish Civilization and JOFA-Jewish Orthodox Feminist Alliance Lecture, New York University School of Law, New York, June 24, 2013.

Lemaitre, J. "Catholic Constitutionalism on Sex, Women and the Beginning of Life." In *Abortion Law in Transnational Perspective,* edited by Rebecca Crook, Joanna Erdman, and Bernard Dickens. Philadelphia: University of Pennsylvania Press, 2014.

Lessing, Doris. *African Laughter: Four Visits to Zimbabwe.* London: Harper Collins, 1993.

Levmore, Rachel. "A Coalition to Solve the Agunah Problem." *The Jerusalem Post,* February 23, 2013. www.jpost.com/Opinion/Op-Ed-Contributors/A-coalition-to-solve-the-agunah-problem.

Levmore, Rachel. "Rabbinic Responses in Favor of Prenuptial Agreements." *Tradition* 42, no. 1 (2009): 24–49.

Levmore, Rachel. "The Agunah: a Statistic or a Real Problem?" *The Jerusalem Post,* August 31, 2009.

Levmore, Rachel. *Spare your Eyes Tears "Min'ee Eiynayich Me'Dimah": Complete Guide to Orthodox Jewish Pre-Nuptial Agreements The Halakhic Prenuptial Agreement for Mutual Respect and Prenuptial Agreements for the Prevention of Get-Refusal.* Israel: Millennium Publishing, 2009.

Lewak, Doree. "An Orthodox Woman's Three-Year Divorce Fight." *New York Post,* November 4, 2013. http://nypost.com/2013/11/04/orthodox-jewish-womans-plea-for-a-divorce/.

Liebman, C.S. "Extremism as a Religious Norm." *Journal for the Scientific Study of Religion* 22, no. 1 (1983): 75–86.

Lipset, S.M. *Political Man: The Social Bases of Politics* (expanded edition). Baltimore, MD: The Johns Hopkins University Press, 1981.

Litvak, M. and O. Limor. "Introduction." *Religious Fanaticism* , edited by M. Litvak and O. Limor, 11–25. Jerusalem: Zalman Shazar Center (Hebrew), 2007.

Lizzio, Celene Ayat. "Continuing Momentum in Muslim Critical Gender Scholarship." *Journal of Muslim World Affairs* 1, no. 1 (2013). www.muslimworldaffairs.com/2013/09/continuing-momentum-in-muslim-critical.html.

Lopatin, Asher, Schlomo Riskin and David Bigman. Panel on the "Discussion of Halakhic Solutions"; and Blu Greenberg. The Agunah Summit. Conference by The NYU Tikvah Center for Law and Jewish Civilization and JOFA-Jewish Orthodox Feminist Alliance Lecture, New York University School of Law, New York, June 24, 2013.

Løvdal, Lene. "*Mahr* and Gender Equality in Private International Law: The Adjudication of *Mahr* in England, France, Norway and Sweden." In *Embedding Mahr in the European Legal System,* edited by Rubya Mehdi and Jaargen S. Nielsen, 77–112. Copenhagen: Djoef Publishing, 2011.

Lugard, Frederick. "Native Courts Proclamation." Kaduna National Archives (1900).

Machtinger, Yael. "On the 'Edge' of the 'Religious Thicket' Using *Bruker v. Marcovitz* to Explore Other Creative Ways to get One's '*Get*')." Paper presented at Law on the Edge, Canadian Law and Society Association's Annual Meeting, Vancouver, British Columbia, July 2, 2013.

Machtinger, Yael. "Sounds of Silence: A Socio-Legal Exploration of *Siruv Get* and *Iggun* in Toronto." PhD dissertation, York University, 2009.

Machtinger, Yael. "To Count or not to Count? Examining the Quantifying Quandary Regarding the Prevalence of Jewish Divorce Refusal (In Defense of a New Method of Analysis)." Paper presented at Women, the Charter, and CEDAW in the 21st Century: Taking Stock and Moving Forward, Queen's Feminist Legal Symposium, Queen's University, Kingston, Ontario, March 2–3, 2012.

Maclean, Mavis and John Eekelaar, eds. *Managing Family Justice in Diverse Societies.* Oxford: Hart, 2013.

Maclean, Mavis and John Eekelaar. "The Significance of Marriage: Contrasts between White British and Ethnic Minority Groups in England." *Law and Policy* 27 (2005): 379–98.

Macner, Esther. "Jewish Prenuptial Agreements: The Promises and the Pitfalls." paper delivered at the Seminar on New Approaches to the Agunah Problem, HBI Project on Gender, Culture, Religion and Law, April 15, 2015.

Mair, Jane. "Belief in Marriage." *International Journal of the Jurisprudence of the Family* 5 (2014): 63–88.

Malik, Maleiha. "Family Law in Diverse Societies." In *Routledge Handbook of Family Law and Policy*, edited by John Eekelaar and Rob George, 424–438. Abingdon: Routledge, 2014.

Maltz, Judy. "Shas Mobilizes Seminary Girls to Disrupt Women of the Wall Prayer Service." *Haaretz*, October 4, 2013. www.haaretz.com/news/israel/.premium-1.550540.

Mama, Amina. "Gender Studies for Africa's Transformation." In *African Intellectuals: Rethinking Politics, Language, Gender and Development,* edited by Thandika Mkandawira. London: Zed Press, 2005.

Marty, M.E. and S.R. Appleby, eds. *Accounting for Fundamentalisms: The Dynamic Character of Movements.* Chicago: University of Chicago Press, 1991.

Masci, David and Elizabeth Lawton. *Applying God's Law: Religious Courts and Mediation in the U.S.* Pew Research Center, April 8, 2013. www.pewforum.org/2013/04/08/applying-gods-law-religious-courts-and-mediation-in-the-us/.

Maslin, Simeon J. "Yes There is a Reform Divorce Document, But Don't Call it a Get." www.reformjudaism.org/yes-there-reform-divorce-document.

Masud, M.K. "The Sources of the Maliki Doctrine of Ijbar." *Islamic Studies* 24, no. 2 (1985): 215–253.

Mautner, Menachem. *Law and the Culture of Israel.* Oxford: Oxford University Press, 2010.

Maxwell, David. "Writing the History of African Christianity: Reflections of an Editor." *Journal of Religion in Africa* 36 (2006): 379–399.

Mayer, A. *Islam, Tradition and Politics.* Boulder, CO: Westview, 1999.

Mayer, Ann Elizabeth. *Islam and Human Rights: Tradition and Politics.* 5th ed. Boulder, CO: Westview Press, 2013.

Mbe, Akoko Robert. "New Pentecostalism in the Wake of the Economic Crisis in Cameroon." *Nordic Journal of African Studies* 11, no. 3 (2002): 359–376.

McCarthy Brown, K. "Fundamentalism and the Control of Women." In *Fundamentalism and Gender*, edited by John Stratton Hawley, 175–201. New York: Oxford University Press, 1994.

McGoldrick, D. *Human Rights and Religion: The Islamic Headscarf Debate in Europe.* Oxford: Hart, 2006.

"McGuinty to Ban Religious Tribunals." *Kitchener Record,* September 12, 2005.

McLain, L. and J. Flemming. "Constitutionalism, Judicial Review and Progressive Change." *Texas Law Review* 84, no. 433 (2005).

Melcher, Christopher C. "Evaluating the Enforceabilty of a Premarital Agreement." *Family Law News* 31, no. 1 (2009).

Melissaris, Emmanuel. *Ubiquitous Law: Legal Theory and the Space for Legal Pluralism.* Surrey: Ashgate Publishing Company, 2009.

"Mendel Epstein and Martin Wolmark 'Plotted to Torture Husband'." October 10, 2013, www.bbc.co.uk/news/world-us-canada-24485128.

Mendeni, Elif, Ednan Aslan and Marcia Hermansen, eds. *Muslima Theology: The Voices of Muslim Women Theologians.* Frankfurt am Main: Peter Land Verlag, 2013.

Merry, Sally Engle. *Getting Justice and Getting Even: Legal Consciousness among Working Class Americans.* Chicago: University of Chicago Press, 1990.

Merry, Sally Engle. "Legal Pluralism." *Law and Society Review* 22 (1988): 869–896.

Metzker, Isaac, ed. "Jewish Forward." In *A Bintel Brief: Sixty Years of Letters From The Lower East Side To The Jewish Daily Forward.* New York: Schocken Books, 1971.

Mhango, Mtendeweka Owen. "The Constitutional Protection of Minority Religious Rights in Malawi: The Case of Rastafari Students." *Journal of African Law* 52, no. 2 (2008): 218–244.

Mhango, Mtendeweka Owen. "Upholding the Rastafari Religion in Zimbabwe: *Farai Dzvova v. Minister of Education, Sports and Culture and Others.*" *African Human Rights Law Journal* 8, no. 2 (2008): 221–238.

Miller, Kathleen Portuan. "Who Says Muslim Women Can't Divorce? A Comparison of Divorce under Islamic and Anglo-American Law." *New York International Law Review* 22, no. 1 (2009): 201–248.

Mir-Hosseini, Ziba, ed. *Gender and Equality in Muslim Family Law: Justice and Ethics in the Islamic Legal Tradition.* London: IB Tauris, 2013.

Mir-Hosseini, Ziba, Mulki Al-Sharmani and Jana Rumminger, eds. *Men in Charge? Rethinking Authority in Muslim Legal Tradition.* London: Oneworld, 2015.

Mir-Hosseini, Ziba, Zinah Anwar, Marwa Sharafeldin, Lena Larsen, and Kari Vogt, eds. *Gender and Equality in Muslim Family Law: Justice and Ethics in the Islamic Legal Process.* New York: I. Tauris, 2013.

Moghadam, Valentine M. "Islamic Feminism and its Discontents: Toward a Resolution of the Debate." *Signs: Journal of Women in Culture and Society* 27, no. 4 (2002).

Mohammad, Fadel. "Reinterpreting the Guardian's Role in the Islamic Contract of Marriage: The Case of the Maliki School." *The Journal of Islamic Law* 3, no. 1 (1998).

Moon, Richard J. *Law and Religious Pluralism in Canada.* Vancouver: University of British Columbia Press, 2009.

Moore, Russell D. "After Patriarchy, What? Why Egalitarians Are Winning The Gender Debate." *JETS* 49, no. 3 (2006): 569–576.

Moore, Sally Falk. "Law and Social Change: The Semi-Autonomous Social Field as an Appropriate Subject of Study." *Law & Society Review* 7 (1973): 719–750.

Morsink, Johannes. *The Universal Declaration of Human Rights: Origins, Drafting, and Intent.* Philadelphia: University of Pennsylvania Press, 1999.

Muel-Dreyfus, Francine. *Vichy and the Eternal Feminine.* Translated by Kathleen A. Johnson. Durham: Duke University Press, 2001.

Mukasonga, Scholastique. *Our Lady of the Nile.* Translated by M. Mauthner. New York: Archipelago Books, 2014.

Mulhere, Kaitlin. "Inclusive Dialogues." *Inside Higher Education*, January 21, 2015.

Munta, Makau W. "Savages, Victims, and Saviors: The Metaphor of Human Rights." *Harvard International Law Journal* 42, no. 1 (2001): 201–245.

Murray, Stephen and Will Roscoe. *Boy-Wives and Female Husbands: Studies in African Homosexualities.* New York: St. Martin's Press, 1998.

Muslim Brotherhood. "Muslim Brotherhood Statement Denouncing UN Women Declaration for Violating Sharia Principles." Cairo, March 13, 2013). www.ikhwanweb.com/article.php?id=30731.

Nagel, Thomas. "Public Education and Intelligent Design." *Philosophy and Public Affairs* 36 (2008): 187–205.

Nasir, Jamal J. *The Status of Women Under Islamic Law and Modern Islamic Legislation.* 3rd ed. Leiden; Boston: Brill, 2009.

Ndebele, Njabulo. *The Cry of Winnie Mandela: A Novel.* Oxford: Ayebia-Clarke, 2004.

Nechushtan, Yossi. www.colman.ac.il/research/research_institute/katedra_HumanRights/Psika/Documents/9/9_june_2013_3_Lahav_EN.pdf.

Nemes, Hody. "Postnup Parties Get Happily Married Orthodox Couples To Plan for Divorce." *The Jewish Forward,* February 9, 2014. http://forward.com/articles/192443/postnup-parties-get-happily-married-orthodox-coupl/?p=all#ixzz2swsr8ZDT.

Nethercott, Scott and David Eisenberg, eds. *Islamic Finance: Law and Practice.* Oxford: Oxford University Press, 2012.

New York University's School of Law calendar page. https://its.law.nyu.edu/eventcalendar/index.cfm?fuseaction=main.detail&id=25378.

Newman, Barbara. *Sister of Wisdom, St. Hildegard's Theology of the Feminine.* Berkeley: University of California Press, 1987.

Ngwena, Charles. "Reforming African Abortion Laws and Practice: The Place of Transparency." In *Abortion Law in Transnational Perspective,* edited by Rebecca Crook, Joanna Erdman and Bernard Dickens. Philadelphia: University of Pennsylvania Press, 2014.

Nussbaum, Martha. *Sex and Social Justice.* Oxford: Oxford University Press, 1999.

Nzegwu, Nkiru. "Gender Equality in Dual-Sex System: The Case of Onitsha." *JENdA: A Journal of Culture and African Women Studies* 1, no. 1 (2001).

Oakley, Ann. "Interviewing Women: A Contradiction in Terms?" In *Doing Feminist Research,* edited by Helen Roberts and Paul Kegan, 30–61. London: Routledge, 1988.

Obbo, Christine. "*African Women" Their Struggle for Economic Independence.* London: Zed Press, 1981.

Office of National Statistics. Marriages in England and Wales 2010.

Ogundipe-Leslie, Molara. *Recreating Ourselves: African Women and Critical Transformation.* Trenton: Africa World Press, 1994.

Oinas, Elina and Signe Arnfred. "Introduction: Sex & Politics-Case Africa." *Nordic Journal of Feminist and Gender Research* 17, no. 3 (2009): 149–157.

Oomen, Barbara. *Chiefs in South Africa: Law, Power and Culture in the Post-Apartheid Era.* Oxford: James Currey, 2005.

Othman, Aida. "And Sulh is Best: Amicable Settlement and Dispute Resolution in Islamic Law." *Arab Law Quarterly* 21 (2007): 64–90.

Oulé-Jansen, Yakaré. "Muslim Brides and the Ghost of *Shari'a*: Have the Recent Law Reforms in Egypt, Tunisia, and Morocco Improved Women's Position in Marriage and Divorce and Can Religious Moderates Bring Reform and Make it Stick?" *Northwestern Journal of International Human Rights* 5, no. 2 (2007): 181–212.

Ouzgane, Lahoucine and Robert Morrell, eds. *African Masculinities: Men in Africa from the Late Nineteenth Century to the Present.* Basingstoke: Palgrave MacMillan, 2005.

Oyewumi, Oyeronke. *The Invention of Women: Making an African Sense of Western Gender Discourse.* Minneapolis: University of Minnesota Press, 1997.

Panel discussion on "The Plight of the Agunah in Our Community: Bridging Gaps Between Rabbinate, Academy, & Community," Beth Avraham Yoseph of Toronto Congregation, Thornhill, Ontario, April 29, 2012. http://koshertube.com/videos/index.php?option=com_seyret&task=videodirectlink&Itemid=4&id=11072.

Parsitau, D. and Mwaura, P. "God in the City: Pentecostalism as an Urban Phenomenon in Kenya." *Studia Historiae* 36, no. 2 (2010): 95–112.

Patel, Faiza, Matthew Duss and Amos Toh. *Foreign Law Bans: Legal Uncertainties and Practical Problems*, 1. New York: Brennan Center for Justice/Center for American Progress, May 2013.

Patton, M.Q. *Qualitative Evaluation Research Methods.* Thousand Oaks, CA: Sage Publications, 1990.

Paul VI. "Address of Pope Paul VI to the Participants in the National Congress of the Italian Women's Center." *Libreria Editrice Vaticana*, December 6, 1976. https://w2.vatican.va/content/paul-vi/it/speeches/1976/documents/hf_p-vi_spe_19761206_congresso-nazionale-cif.html.

Petrus, Theodore. "Defining Witchcraft Related Crime in the Eastern Cape Province of South Africa." *International Journal of Sociology and Anthropology* 3, no. 1 (2011): 1–8.

Pew Research. "State Legislation Restricting Use of Foreign or Religious Law." Pew Research Center, Religion and Public Life Project.

Pius XII. "Questa Grande Vostra Adunata." Address of His Holiness Pope Pius XII to Members of Various Catholic Women's Associations, October 21, 1945. http://catholictradition.org/Encyclicals/questa1.htm.

Piven, F.F. and Cloward, R.A. *Poor People's Movements: Why they Succeed, How they Fail.* New York: Pantheon Books, 1977.

Plaskow, Judith. "Blaming the Jews for the Birth of Patriarchy." In *Nice Jewish Girls,* edited by Evelyn T. Beck. Watertown, MA: Persephone, 1982.

Plaut, W. Gunther. *The Torah: A Modern Commentary.* Cincinnati: Union of American Hebrew Congregations, 1981.

Presser, Stephen B. "Marriage and the Law: Time for a Divorce?" In *Marriage and Divorce in a Multicultural Context: Multi-Tiered Marriage and the Boundaries of Civil Law and Religion*, edited by Joel A. Nichols. Cambridge: Cambridge University Press, 2013.

Puglia, Cristina. "Will Parties Take to Takhim? The Use of Islamic Law and Arbitration in the United States." *Chicago-Kent Journal of International and Comparative Law* 13, no. 151 (2013).

Rackman Center. "The Necessity of the Property Component in Halakhic Marriage." Conference hosted by Rackman Center for the Advancement of the Status of Women, Bar-Ilan University, Israel, June 12, 2013.

Radan, Peter. "From Dayton to Dover: the Legacy of the *Scopes Trial.*" In *Law and Religion in Theoretical and Historical Context.*, edited by Peter Cane, Carolyn Evans, and Zoe Robinson. Cambridge: Cambridge University Press, 2008.

Raday, Frances. "Claiming Equal Religious Personhood: Women of the Wall's Constitutional Saga." In *Religion in the Public Sphere, A Comparative Analysis of German, Israeli, American and International Law,* edited by Winfried Brugger and Michael Karayanni, 255. Heidelberg: Max Planck Institute, 2007.

Raday, Frances. "Culture, Religion and CEDAW's Article 5(a)." In *The Circle of Empowerment: Twenty Five Years of the UN Committee on the Elimination of Discrimination against Women,* edited by H.B. Schopp-Schilling and C. Flinterman. New York: Feminist Press, 2007.

Raday, Frances. "Culture, Religion, and Gender." *International Journal of Constitutional Law* 1 (2003): 663.

Raday, Frances. "Decriminalizing Adultery: Eliminating Discrimination and Violence against Women." Oxford Human Rights Hub, November 2, 2012. http://ohrh.law.ox.ac.uk/decriminalizing-adultery-eliminating-discrimination-and-violence-against-women.

Raday, Frances. "Gender and Democratic Citizenship: the Impact of CEDAW." *International Journal of Constitutional Law* 10 (2012): 512–515.

Raday, Frances. "The Family Agenda: Promoting Traditional Values in the Human Rights Council." Oxford Human Rights Hub, January 8, 2015. http://ohrh.law.ox.ac.uk/the-family-agenda-promoting-traditional-values-in-the-human-rights-council/.

Raday, Frances. "The Fight Against Being Silenced." In *Women of the Wall: Claiming Sacred Ground at Judaism's Holy Site*, edited by Phyllis Chesler and Rivka Haut. Woodstock, VT: Jewish Light Publishing, 2003.

Ramadan, Tariq. *Radical Reform: Islamic Ethics and Liberation*. New York: Oxford University Press, 2009.

Rand, Ayn. *Atlas Shrugged*. New York: Random House, 1957.

Rao, Rahul. "Re-membering Mwanga: Same-Sex Intimacy, Memory and Belonging in Postcolonial Uganda." *Journal of Eastern African Studies* 9, no. 1 (2015): 1–19.

Ratzinger, Joseph Cardinal, and Vittorio Messori. *The Ratzinger Report: An Exclusive Interview on the State of the Church*. San Francisco: Ignatius Press, 1985.

Razack, S. *Casting Out: The Eviction of Muslims from Western Law and Politics*. Toronto: University of Toronto Press, 2008.

Razavi, Shahra and Anne Jenichen. "The Unhappy Marriage of Religion and Politics: Problems and Pitfalls for Gender Equality." *Third World Quarterly* 31, no. 6 (2010).

Redress, Letter to Commissioner Maiga. Urgent Appeal in respect of Ms. Meriam Yahiya Ibrahim. London. June 10 2014.

Reform Judaism Magazine. http://reformjudaismmag.org/Articles/index.cfm?id=1414.

Reinharz, Shulamit. *Feminist Methods in Social Research*. Oxford: Oxford University Press, 1992.

Renteln, A. *The Cultural Defense*. Oxford: Oxford University Press, 2004.

Reuters Staff. "Pope says saving heterosexuality like saving the rainforest." *Reuters*, December 22, 2008. http://blogs.reuters.com/faithworld/2008/12/22/pope-says-saving-heterosexuality-like-saving-the-rainforest/.

Rimalt, N. *Legal Feminism From Theory to Practice: The Struggle for Gender Equality in Israel and the United States*. Haifa: Pardes Publishing House & Haifa University Press, 2010.

Riskin, Schlomo. *A Jewish Woman's Right to Divorce: A Halakhic History and a Solution for the Agunah*. Hoboken NJ: Ktav Publishing, 2006.

Robcis, Camille. "French Sexual Politics from Human Rights to the Anthropological Function of the Law." *French Historical Studies* 33, no. 1 (2015): 129–156.

Roberts, Simon. "Three Models of Family Mediation." In *Divorce Mediation and the Legal Process*, edited by Robert Dingwall and John Eekelaar. Oxford: Oxford University Press, 1988.

Ross, T. *Expanding the Palace of Torah, Orthodoxy and Feminism*. Waltham, MA: Brandeis University Press, 2004.

Rumminger, Jana, *et al. Cedaw and Muslim Family Laws: In Search of Common Ground.* Selangor, Malaysia: Musawah, 2011.
Rycroft, C. *A Critical Dictionary of Psychoanalysis.* New York: Penguin Books, 1995.
Saris, Anne, Jean-Mathieu Potvin, Naima Bendriss, Wendy Ayotte and Samia Amor. "Étude de Cas auprès de Canadiennes Musulmanes et d'intervenants Civils et Religieux en Résolution de Conflits Familiaux – une Recherche Exploratoire menée à Montréal en 2005-2007." Montréal, 2007 (final report).
Saris, Anne and Jean-Mathieu Potvin. "Canadian Muslim Women and Resolution of Family Conflicts: an Empirical Qualitative Study (2005–2007)." In *Law and Religion in the 21st Century: Relations between States and Religious Communities*, edited by Silvio Ferrari and Rinaldo Cristofori. Burlington: Ashgate, 2010.
Sarna, Jonathan. *American Judaism.* New Haven: Yale University Press, 2004.
Schacht, Joseph. "Islam in Northern Nigeria." *Studia Islamica* 8 (1957): 123–146.
Scharff, Christina. "Disarticulating Feminism: Individualization, Neoliberalism and the Othering of 'Muslim Women". *European Journal of Women's Studies* 18, no. 2 (2011): 119–134.
Scheppele, Kim Lane. "Telling Stories." *Michigan Law Review* 87 (1988–1989): 2073–2098.
Schmidt, Elizabeth. *Peasants, Traders and Wives: Shona Women in the History of Zimbabwe 1870-1939.* Oxford: James Currey, 1992.
Sered, Susan. *What Makes Women Sick.* Waltham, MA: Brandeis University Press, 2000.
Sered, Susan. "Women and Religious Change in Israel: Rebellion or Revolution." *Sociology of Religion* 58, no. 1 (1997).
Serrano, Ken. "Rabbis in Divorce-Gang Sting Could be Out on Bail Soon." *USA Today*, October 16, 2013. http://www.usatoday.com/story/news/nation/2013/10/16/rabbis-fbi-divorce-sting-hearing/2996211/.
Sezgin, Yuksel. *Human Rights under State Enforced Religious Family Laws in Israel, Egypt and India.* Cambridge: Cambridge University Press, 2013.
Shabana, Ayman. *Custom in Islamic Law and Legal Theory: The Development of the Concepts of `Urf and `Adah in the Islamic Legal Tradition.* New York: Palgrave Macmillan, 2010.
Shachar, Ayelet. *Multicultural Jurisdictions: Cultural Differences and Women's Rights.* Cambridge: Cambridge University Press, 2001.
Shachar, Ayelet. "Privatizing Diversity: A Cautionary Tale from Religious Arbitration in Family Law." *Theoretical Inquiries in Law* 9, no. 2 (2008): 573–607.
Shaer, Matthew. "The Orthodox Hit Squad." *Gentleman's Quarterly,* September 2014. www.gq.com/news-politics/newsmakers/201409/epstein-orthodox-hit-squad?printable=true.
Shaheed, Farida. *Report of the Special Rapporteur in the Field of Cultural Rights.* U.N. Doc. A/67/287. August 10, 2012.
Shaikh, Sa'diyya. "In Search of al-Insān: Sufism, Islamic Law, and Gender." *Journal of the American Academy of Religion* 77, no. 4 (2009): 781–822.
Shakdiel, Leah. "Women of the Wall: Radical Feminism as an Opportunity for a New Discourse in Israel." *Journal of Israeli History* (2002).
Shapira, Medel. "Qeri'at ha-Torah by Women: A Halachic Analysis." In *Women and Men in Communal Prayer,* edited by Chaim Trachtman, MD. New York: JOFA in Association with Ktav Publishing Inc., 2010.
Sheskin, Ira M. and Arnold Dashefsky, eds. "Jewish Population in the United States, 2012." *American Jewish Year Book* (2012):143–211. Dordrecht: Springer.

Shiloh, Magalit. "Feminist Voices regarding Gender Equality in the Struggle for the Right to Vote in the Yishuv." In *One Law for Man and Woman: Women, Rights and Law in Mandatory Palestine*, edited by Katvan *et al.* Tel Aviv: Bar Ilan University Press, 2010.

Shocethman, Eliav. "Aliyyot for Women." In *Women and Men in Communal Prayer: Halakhic Perspectives*, edited by Rabbi Daniel Sperber *et al.* New York: JOFA, 2010.

Shore, Sharon. Panel discussion on The Plight of the Agunah in Our Community: Bridging Gaps Between Rabbinate, Academy, & Community, Beth Avraham Yoseph of Toronto Congregation, Thornhill, Ontario, April 29, 2012.

Sh'til, Y. *A Psychologist in a Breslav Yeshiva*. Tel Aviv: Papyrus Publishing House at Tel Aviv University (Hebrew), 1993.

Sierakowski, Slawomir. "The Polish Church's Gender Problem." *New York Times*, January 26, 2014. www.nytimes.com/2014/01/27/opinion/sierakowski-the-polish-churchs-gender-problem.html.

Sivan. E. "Introduction." In *Israeli Hareidim, Integration without Assimilation*, edited by E. Sivan and K. Caplan, 7–10. Jerusalem: Van Leer Institute (Hebrew), 2003.

Sivan. E. "The Enclave Culture." In *Fundamentalism Comprehended*, edited by M. Marty, 11–68. Chicago: University of Chicago Press, 1995.

Sokolic, William. "Three New Jersey Rabbis Convicted in Forced Divorce Scheme." *Reuters*, April 21, 2015. www.reuters.com/article/2015/04/22/us-usa-new-jersey-rabbis-idUSKBN0NC2LJ20150422.

Sonbol, Amira El Azhary. *Women, the Family, and Divorce Law in Islamic History.* Syracuse, NY: Syracuse University Press, 1996.

Souaiaia, Ahmed E. *Contesting Justice: Women, Islam, Law, and Society.* Albany: State University of New York Press, 2008.

Sousa Santos, Boaventura. "Law: A Map of Misreading. Towards a Postmodern Conception of Law." *Journal of Law and Society* 14 (1987): 279–302.

Southern Poverty Law Centre. "Extremist File: David Yerushalmi." www.splcenter.org/get-informed/intelligence-files/profiles/david-yerushalmi.

Sparado, Antonio S.J. "A Big Heart Open to God: The Exclusive Interview with Pope Francis." *America Magazine*, September 30, 2013. http://americamagazine.org/pope-interview.

Spectorsky, Susan A. *Women in Classical Islamic Law: A Survey of the Sources.* Leiden; Boston: Brill, 2010.

Sperber, Daniel. "Congregational Dignity and Human Dignity." *The Edah Journal* 3, no. 2 (2002).

Sperber, *et al.*, eds. *Women and Men in Communal Prayer.* New York: JOFA Publication, 2010.

Stanton, Elizabeth Cady. *Eighty Years and More: Reminiscences 1815–1897* (1898). Project Gutenberg, 2004. Accessed June 2015. www.gutenberg.org/files/11982/11982-h/11982-h.htm.

Steiner, Ben. "The Lieberman Clause Revisited." Forthcoming, 31 *Nashim: Special Issue on New Historical and Socio-Legal Perspectives on Jewish Divorce*, edited by Lisa Fishbayn Joffe and Haim Sperber.

Steiner, Ben. "Readings of the 'Lieberman Clause': Development, Translation and Interpretation." Newton, MA: Thesis, Jewish Theological Seminary, 2014.

Stone, Suzanne Last. "The Intervention of American Law in Jewish Divorce: A Pluralist Analysis." *Israel Law Review* 34, no. 2 (2000): 170–210.

Stop Islamization of America. www.adl.org/civil-rights/discrimination/c/stop-islamization-of-america.

Sultany, Nimer. "Religion and Constitutionalism: Lessons from American and Islamic Constitutionalism." *Emory International Law Review* 28 (2014): 345–424. http://eprints.soas.ac.uk/18874/.

Sunstein, Cass R. and Richard H. Thaler. "Privatizing Marriage." *The Monist* 91 (2008): 377–87.

Syrtash, John. *Religion and Culture in Family Law*. Toronto: Butterworths Canada Ltd., 1992.

Sztokman, Elana. *The War on Women in Israel: A Story of Religious Radicalism and the Ravaging of Freedom*. Naperville, IL: Sourcebooks, 2014.

Tamale, Sylvia. *African Sexualities*. Oxford: Pambazuka Press, 2011.

Taylor, Charles. *A Secular Age*. Cambridge, MA: Harvard University Press, 2007.

Tighe, Elizabeth, *et al. American Jewish Population Estimates*. Waltham: Brandeis University Press, 2013.

Tirosh, Yofi. "Abnormal normality." *Orech Hadin* (2013) (Hebrew).

Tornielli, Andrea. "Never Be Afraid of Tenderness." *La Stampa Vatican Insider*. www.lastampa.it/2013/12/14/esteri/vatican-insider/en/never-be-afraid-of-tenderness-5BqUfVs9r7W1CJIMuHqNeI/pagina.html.

Torok, Ryan. "Till Get Do Us Part." *The Jewish Journal*, March 27, 2014. www.jewishjournal.com/cover_story/article/till_get_do_us_part_israel_meir_kins_las_vegas_wedding.

Totus Tuus. "Catechesis on the Theology of the Body." *Totus Tuus*. www.totus2us.com/vocation/jpii- catechesis-on-theology-of-the-body/.

Triger, Zvi H. "Gender Segregation as Sexual Harassment." *Tel Aviv University Law Review* 35 (2013): 703–746.

Tucker, Judith E. "'And God Knows Best': The Fatwa as a Source for the History of Gender in the Arab World." In *Beyond the Exotic: Women's Histories in Islamic Societies*, edited by Amira El Azhary Sonbol, 168–179. Syracuse, NY: Syracuse University Press, 2005.

Tucker, Judith E. *Women, Family, and Gender in Islamic Law*. Cambridge, UK and New York: Cambridge University Press, 2008.

Turner, Catherine. "Out of the Shadows: Child Marriage and Slavery." *Anti-Slavery International*, April 2013. www.antislavery.org/includes/documents/cm_docs/2013/c/child_marriage_final.pdf.

Tutu, Desmond. *God is not a Christian and Other Provocations*, edited by John Allen. London: Harper Collins, 2011.

Ungar-Sargon, Batya. "Israel Has a Marriage Problem. One American-Born Lawyer is Trying to Solve it." *Tablet Magazine*, October 9, 2013. www.tabletmag.com/jewish-news-and-politics/148148/susan-weiss-american-agunah-warrior.

UNRISD. "Religion, Politics and Gender Equality." *Research and Policy Brief* 11 (2011).

Van der Vyver, Johan D. and M. Christian Green. "Law, Religion and Human Rights in Africa: Introduction." *African Human Rights Journal* 8, no. 2 (2008): 337–356.

Van Klinken, Adriaan. "God's World is not an Animal Farm. Or is it? The Catachrestic Translation of Gender Equality in African Pentecostalism." *Religion and Gender* 3, no. 2 (2013): 240–258.

Van Klinken, Adriaan. "Homosexuality, Politics and Pentecostal Nationalism in Zambia." *Studies in World Christianity* 20, no. 3 (2014): 259–281.

Van Klinken, Adriaan. "Male Headship as Male Agency: An Alternative Understanding of a 'Patriarchal' African Pentecostal Discourse on Masculinity." *Religion and Gender* 1, no. 1 (2011): 104–124.

Volsky, Igor and Jack Jenkins. "Why Isis is not, in fact, Islamic." *Think Progress,* September 11, 2014.

Warner, Andy. "The Case Against Scott Lively—Illustrated." The Center for Constitutional Rights, February 5, 2014. www.huffingtonpost.com/the-center-for-constitutional-rights/the-case-against-scott-li_b_4732099.html.

Webber, Jeremy. "Understanding the Religion in Freedom of Religion." In *Law and Religion in Theoretical and Historical Context*, edited by Peter Cane, Carolyn Evans, and Zoe Robinson. Cambridge: Cambridge University Press, 2008.

Weil, Shalva. "The Ethiopian Jews: Background." *Jewish Women's Archive.* http://jwa.org/encyclopedia/article/ethiopian-jewish-women.

Weinrib, Lorraine E. "Ontario's Sharia Law Debate: Law and Politics Under the Charter." In *Law and Religious Pluralism in Canada,* edited by Richard Moon, 239–263. Vancouver: University of British Columbia Press, 2008.

Weisbrod, Carol. *Butterfly, The Bride: Essays on Law, Narrative, and the Family.* Ann Arbor: University of Michigan Press, 2004.

Weiss, Bernard G. *The Spirit of Islamic Law.* University of Georgia Press, 1998.

Weiss, Susan. Panel on "Lessons from the Front." The Agunah Summit. Conference by The NYU Tikvah Center for Law and Jewish Civilization and JOFA-Jewish Orthodox Feminist Alliance Lecture, New York University School of Law, New York, June 24, 2013.

Weiss, Susan. "Sign at Your Own Risk: The RCA Prenuptial May Prejudice the Fairness of Your Future Divorce Agreement." *Cardozo Women's Law Journal* 6, no. 49 (1999).

Weiss, Susan M. and Netty C. Gross-Horowitz. *Marriage and Divorce in the Jewish State: Israel's Civil War.* Waltham MA: Brandeis University Press, 2012.

Welchman, Lynn. *Honour: Crimes, Paradigms, and Violence against Women.* London: Zed Press, 2005.

Wikipedia contributors, "Humanist Society Scotland," *Wikipedia, The Free Encyclopedia.* https://en.wikipedia.org/w/index.php?title=Humanist_Society_Scotland&oldid=670911843.

Willheim, E. "Australian Legal Procedures and the Protection of Sacred Aboriginal Spiritual Beliefs: a Fundamental Conflict." In *Law and Religion in Theoretical and Historical Context*, edited by Peter Cane, Carolyn Evans, and Zoe Robinson. Cambridge: Cambridge University Press, 2008.

Willig, Mordechai. "The Prenuptial Agreement: Recent Developments." *Journal of the Beit Din of America* (Spring 2012): 12.

Wilson, B.R. *The Social Dimensions of Sectarianism. Sects and New Religious Movement in Contemporary Society.* Oxford: Clarendon Press, 1990.

Witte, John and Johan van der Vyver, eds. *Religious Human Rights in Global Perspective.* The Hague: Martinus Nijhoff Publishers, 1996.

Woods, Patricia. *Judicial Power and National Politics.* New York: State University of New York Press, 2008.

World Health Organization. "World Report on Violence and Health." Geneva, WHO, 2002.

Yanovsky, R. Women censored from Medical Association. www.ynetnews.com/articles/0,7340,L-4631194,00.html. 2015.

Yoseph, Beth Avraham. Paper presented at panel discussion on The Plight of the Agunah in Our Community: Bridging Gaps Between Rabbinate, Academy, & Community, April 29, 2012. http://koshertube.com/videos/index.php?option=com_seyret&task=videodirectlink&Itemid=4&id=11072.

Yoshino, Kenji. *Covering: The Hidden Assault on our Civil Rights.* New York: Random House, 2006.

Zakheim, Barbara. "Results from a Survey of *Agunot.*" *Research Based Strategy* (October 10, 2011): 1–6. Washington, DC: The Mellman Group Inc..

Zalcberg, Sara. "Characteristics of Harmful Sexual Behavior Among Young Ultra-Orthodox (Haredi) Men." *Israeli Criminology* 4 (2015): 48–70 (Hebrew).

Zalcberg, Sara. "'Nobody Knows but God': Reporting Patterns of Ultra-Orthodox (Haredi) Males Who Had Been Sexually Abused." In *Many Faces of Violence: Men as Victims*, edited by Y. Aviad-Wilchek and Y. Maze, 175–104. Ariel University Press, 2014.

Zalcberg, Sara. The Process of 'Returning in Tshuva' (adopting a Jewish religious lifestyle) Among Criminals Who 'Returned in Tshuva.' A Master Thesis, Bar Ilan University, 1998.

Zalcberg, Sima. "Channels of Knowledge and Information about Menstruation and Sexuality among Hasidic Adolescent Girls." *Nashim: A Journal of Jewish Women's Studies & Gender Issues* 17 (2009a): 60–88.

Zalcberg, Sima. " 'Grace is Deceitful and Beauty is Vain': How Hasidic Women Cope with the Requirement of Shaving One's Head and Wearing a Black Kerchief." *Gender Issues* 24, no. 3, (2007): 13–34.

Zalcberg, Sima. "The Rush to Modesty." *Eretz Acheret: About Israel and Judaism* 51, (2009b): 30–42.

Zalcberg, Sima and Sara Zalcberg. "Body and Sexuality Constructs among Youth of the Ultra-Orthodox Jewish Community." In *Religion, Gender and Sexuality in Everyday Life* , edited by A. Kam-Tuck Yip and P. Nynäs, 124–140. Burlington: Ashgate Publishing Ltd, 2012.

Zalcberg Block, S. "Shouldering the Burden of the Redemption: How the 'Fashion' of Wearing Capes Developed in Ultra-Orthodox Society." *Nashim: A Journal of Jewish Women's Studies & Gender Issues* 22 (2011): 32–55.

Zine, Jasmine. "Between Orientalism and Fundamentalism: The Politics of Muslim Women's Feminist Engagement." *Muslim World Journal of Human Rights* 3, no. 1 (2006): 1–24.

Zlotowitz, Meir, ed. "Ibn Janach, Bereishis/Genesis-A New Translation with Commentary Anthologised from Talmudic, Midrashic and Rabinic Sources." *Artscroll Tanach Series*, 1, 104. New York: Mesorah Publications, 1977.

International instruments

Convention on the Elimination of All Forms of Discrimination against Women. 1249 UNTS 13.

International Covenant on Civil and Political Rights. December 16, 1966. United Nations Treaty Series, vol. 999, 171.

Universal Declaration of Human Rights. General Assembly resolution 217 A (III), December 10, 1948.

Vienna Convention on the Law of Treaties. 1155 U.N.T.S. 331

Regional instruments

Africa

African Charter on Human and People's Rights, 1981. International Legal Materials (1982).
African Charter on the Rights and Welfare of the Child, 1990. OAU Doc. CAB/LEG/TSG/Rev.
Protocol to the African Charter on Human and Peoples' Rights on the Rights of African Women, 2003. OAU AHG/Res.240.

Arab

Arab Charter on Human Rights, May 22, 2004. Reprinted in 12 Int'l Hum. Rts. Rep. 893 (2005).
Cairo Declaration on Human Rights in Islam, 1990. UN GAOR.

Europe

Council of Europe. *European Convention for the Protection of Human Rights and Fundamental Freedoms, as amended by Protocols Nos. 11 and 14.* November 4, 1950, ETS 5.

UN conferences

Beijing Declaration and Platform for Action. Fourth World Conference on Women, September 15, 1995. A/CONF.177/20 (1995).
Commission on the Status of Women, "Elimination and Prevention of all Forms of Violence against Women and Girls: Agreed Conclusions." 57th session, March 2013.
World Conference on Human Rights. 4th Session, Agenda Item 5. UN Doc. A/CONF.157/PC/62/Add.18. 1993.

UN treaty body jurisprudence

CEDAW

General Recommendation No. 28 on the Core Obligations of States Parties under Article 2 of the Convention on the Elimination of All Forms of Discrimination against Women. December 16, 2010, CEDAW/C/GC/28.
General Recommendation 29 on Article 16 of the Convention on the Elimination of All Forms of Discrimination against Women. U.N. Doc. CEDAW/C/GC/29. February 26, 2013.
Joint General Recommendation No. 31 of the Committee on the Elimination of Discrimination against Women/General Comment No. 18 of the Committee on the

Rights of the Child on Harmful Practices. CEDAW/C/GC/31/CRC/C/ GC/18. November 14, 2014.

Human Rights Committee

General Comment 28. Equality of rights between men and women (article 3). UN Doc. CCPR/C/21/Rev 1/Add.10. 2000.

Other UN documents

Human Rights Council

Human Rights Council Advisory Committee. *Preliminary study on promoting human rights and fundamental freedoms through a better understanding of traditional values of humankind.* UN Doc. A/HRC/AC/9/2. August 6–10, 2012.

Human Rights Council. Resolution 16/3. *Promoting human rights and fundamental freedoms through a better understanding of traditional values of humankind.* UN Doc. A/HRC/RES/16/3. April 8, 2011. Available at http://daccess-ods.un.org/TMP/2258836.92502975.html.

Human Rights Council. Resolution 26/11. *Protection of the family.* UN Doc. A/ HRC/26/L.20/Rev.1. June 25, 2014. Available at www.family2014.org/HRC25062014EN.pdf.

Special procedure mandates

Amor, Abdelfattah *Report of the Special Rapporteur on freedom of religion or belief* "Civil and Political Rights, Including the Question of Religious Intolerance." Fifty-eighth Session, April 24, 2009. (E/CN.4/2002/73/Add.2).

Bielefeldt, Heiner *Report of the Special Rapporteur on Freedom of Religion or Belief, on violence committed in the name of religion,* A/HRC/28/66, 29 December 2014

"Statement by the United Nations Working Group on discrimination against women in law and practice." October 18, 2012. www.ohchr.org/EN/NewsEvents/Pages/DisplayNews.aspx?NewsID=12672&LangID=ESee.

Cases

Aflalo v. Aflalo 295 N.J. Super. 527, 525 (1996).

Avitzur v. Avitzur 58 NY 2d 113 (1983).

Awad v. Ziriax 670 F. 3d 1111, 1130 (10th Circ. 2012).

Bruker v. Marcovitz [2007] 3 S.C.R. 607; 2007 SCC 54.

Burns v. Burns 223 N.J. Super. 219 (1987).

Christian Lawyers Association v. Minister of Health 1998 (4) SA 1113.

Communication 236/2000. *Doebbler v. Sudan.*

Communication 89/93. *Amnesty International v. Sudan.*

Communications 25/89, 47/90, 56/91, 100/93. *Free Legal Assistance Group and Others v. Zaire,* (1995). African Commission on Human and Peoples' Rights.

Communication 276/03. *Centre for Minority Rights Development (Kenya) and Minority Rights Group (on behalf of Endorois Welfare Council).*

Communications 48/90, 50/91, 52/91, 89/93. *Amnesty International and Others v. Sudan*, (1999). African Commission on Human and Peoples' Rights.
Director of Prime Minister's Office v. Hoffman 47(3) PD 289.
Farai Dzova v. Minister of Education, Sports and Culture and Others (2007) ZNSC 26.
Giahn v. Giahn, New York Law Journal (April 13, 2000) 25.
Hoffman v. Prime Minister Office Tak-Al 2000(2)846.
Hoffman v. Western Wall Commissioner (the Rabbi of the Wall) (1994) 48(2) PD 265
In re Scholl 621 A.2d 808 (1992) Family Court of Delaware.
Julie Levi v. Zion Levi 8 MFLM Supp 101 (2009).
Kaplinsky v. Kaplinsky 198 A.D.2d 212; 603 N.Y.S.2d 574; 1993 N.Y. App. Div. LEXIS 10208.
Koeppel v. Koeppel 138 N Y S 2d 366 (1954).
Lang v. Levi 16 A. 3d 980 (2011) Court of Special Appeals of Maryland.
Light v. Light [2012] Conn. Superior Ct. 55 Conn. L. Rptr. 145.
Margulies vs. Marguilies 42 A.D.2d 517; 344 N.Y.S.2d 482; 1973 NY App. Div. LEXIS 3798.
Mayer-Kolker v. Kolker 359 N.J. Super. 98; 819 A.2d 17; 2003 N.J. Super. LEXIS 116
Minkin v. Minkin 180 N.J. Super. 260; 434 A.2d 665; 1981 N.J. Super. LEXIS 653.
Multani v. Commission Scolaire Marguerite-Bourgeoys [2006] 1 S.C.R. 256; 2006 SCC 6. "Number of Days" appeal number 23834-04. Unpublished.
Pillay v. MEC for Education, Kwa-Zulu Natal and Others 2006 10 BCLR 1237. Places of Worship Registration Act 1855.
Poraz v. Shlomo Lahat, Mayor of Tel Aviv HC 953/87 42 (2) PD (1988).
Prince v. President, Cape Law Society and Others (2002) 2 SA 794 (CC).
R (on the application of Hodkin and another) (Appellants) v. Registrar General of Births, Deaths and Marriages (Respondent) [2013] UKSC 77.
Rubin v. Rubin 75 Misc. 2d 776 (1973).
Schwartz v. Schwartz 153 Misc 2d 789 (1992).
Shakdiel v. Minister of Religions HC 153/87 42(2) PD (22). 1.
Shapiro v. Shapiro 110 Misc 2d 726 (1981).
Soleimani v. Soleimani Kansas District Court, Johnson City no. 11cv 4668, August 28, 2012).
Steinberg v. Steinberg 1982 Ohio App. LEXIS 12314.
Syndicat Northcrest v. Amselem [2004] 2 S.C.R. 551.
Waxstein v. Waxstein 90 Misc.2d 784 (1976).

Statutes

Alabama's Foreign Laws in Court, Amendment 1, 2014.
Arbitrtion Act of Ontario, 1991. S.O. 1991.
Constitution of the United States. Amendments I, 14.
Divorce Act, 1985. R.S.C.
Domestic Relations Law 253 (First N. Y. Get Law), 1983.
Domestic Relations Law 236 (B) (5) (h), 236 (B) (6) (d) (Second N.Y. Get Law), 1992.
Family Law Act, 1990. R.S.O.
Idaho House Concurrent Resolution 44, 2010.

Louisiana Act no. 886, 2010.
Marriage Act of 1949.
Marriage Act of 1994.
Marriage and Civil Partnership (Scotland) Act 2014.
Marriage (Same Sex Couples) Act 2013.
Marriage (Scotland) Act 1977.
Marriages (Approved Premises) Regulations 1995.
Material Support to Designated Entities Act 2011.
Matrimonial Causes Act 1973 as amended by the Divorce (Religious Marriages Act) 2002, s. 10A.
Oklahoma State Question Number 755 (2010).
South Dakota HB 1253, 2012.
Sudan Memorandum to the Penal Code 1991.274320113665.

Index

abduction, 267–8
abortion, 16, 22–4, 50, 55, 78, 80, 82, 140
Abrahamic religions, 3, 15, 26, 49
abuse, 25, 28, 224–5, 232–3, 237–8, 242–3, 260, 263; domestic, 180, 231–2, 234, 237, 242–3; spousal, 257, 265; verbal, 6, 134, 153
access, 23–4, 32–3, 53–4, 59–60, 132, 223, 228–31, 243–4
accommodation, 26, 125, 227, 258, 266
accredited mediators, 255–6, 263–6, 269, 271
activism, 92, 101–2, 127
activists, 7, 69, 128, 166, 195, 234, 237; anti-Muslim, 182, 184; Islamist, 97–8
Adam and Eve, 16, 28–9
administrative jurisdiction, 208–10; default settings, 210–12; interaction, 212–16; secular courts, 210–11
adulterers, 107
adulteresses, 101, 106–7
adultery, 17, 22–3, 56–7, 92, 100–101, 106–7, 180
Africa, gender, religion and human rights, 4, 45–60
African Charter on Human and Peoples' Rights, 53, 56
African Commission, 5, 53–4, 56–7
African Protocol on Women's Rights, 54–5, 58
age, 25, 33, 40, 96, 98, 102, 108, 268–70
agency, 47, 49, 182, 229
agreements: arbitration, 181, 186–7, 194, 206, 217, 219; prenuptial, 191, 194, 200, 204, 217, 238; separation, 190
Agunah Summit, 233–4
agunot, 180, 200, 203–4, 218, 220, 231, 233–4, 237
alimony, 23, 181, 192, 231, 262, 264, 265–6
American courts, 7, 182–3, 189–91
American Jews, 129, 181, 203
anathamatization of gender, 78
annulments, 231, 234, 237
anti-Muslim activists, 182, 184
apostasy, 56
appellate courts, 183, 188
Aquinas, Thomas, 70–1
Arab League, 55
arbitration, 181, 193, 219–20, 238, 270–1; agreements, 181, 186–7, 194, 206, 217, 219; agreements, binding, 211, 213–14, 216–17; religious, 227, 238
arbitrators, 181–2, 186–7, 215–17, 272
arrests, 53, 55, 123, 126, 134, 139, 227
assets, 181, 191, 209, 218, 231, 262, 264; distribution/division, 203, 206, 218–20; family, 179, 262, 265
asymmetry, 16, 224–7, 230; legal-halakhic, 241, 243
Australia, 36, 145
authorities, religious, 8, 14, 16, 58, 173, 185, 190, 195
authority, 34, 168, 170, 185, 202, 242, 258–9; coercive, 96, 99, 202; halakhic, 202–3; male, 49, 51; rabbinical, 188, 193; statutory, 128, 134
Avitzur case, 187, 190

ba'alei teshuvah, 155, 165–6, 168
balance, 16, 116, 135, 140, 142, 263–4, 268, 271
bargaining chips, 180, 231–2, 265

batei din, 204–9, 211–17, 219–21, 226, 228–31, 233, 235, 243
behavior, 71, 78, 160–1, 163–4, 166–7, 175, 260
Beijing conference, 5, 69–70, 77–9
beit din, *see* rabbinical courts
Beit Shemesh, 1, 152–75; background of haredi population, 154–6; denial of "the other" and his lifestyle, 163–4; development as hotbed of haredi zealots, 166–9; extremists and their perception among local residents, 165–6; law enforcement agencies, 169–72; significance of stringent supervision of modesty, 160–3; vandalism, graffiti and "modesty signs", 156–59
belief organisation, non-religious, 39–40
beliefs, 20, 26, 35–7, 40–1, 58, 192–3, 202, 204; non-religious, 36, 39–41; philosophical, 39, 41; religious, 22, 26, 36, 45, 48, 54, 183, 188
believers, 79, 101, 107, 242, 256
Benedict XVI, Pope (Joseph Ratzinger), 69, 71–3, 78–83
benevolent sexism, 111
Ben-Yehuda, N., 153
best interests of children, 211, 216, 219–20
best practices, 193, 205, 208, 215–16, 219
Bible, 27, 52, 57–8; Old Testament, 16
binding arbitration agreements, 211, 213–14, 216–17
Bintl Brivs, 240, 243
birth control, 77
blackmail, 54, 205, 208
blouses, 157–8
Boston, 1, 203–4, 215; rabbinical court, 204, 207, 212, 213, 219
boys, 22, 56–7, 96, 159, 219, 266
British colonialism, 94–5
buildings, registered, 4, 34, 37
buses, 124–5, 142, 159

Cairo Declaration on Human Rights in Islam, 55
caliphate, 93–5, 102
Canada, 194–6, 227, 239–40, 255, 259, 261, 263–5, 267–9; Montreal, 1, 8, 255–74; Ontario, 194–5, 227, 238–9, 249; Quebec, 1, 8, 194, 255–74; Toronto, 228–30, 242–3
Canadian Muslim women, 255, 258–9, 263–5, 267
canon law, 73, 184, 186
capacity, 2, 21, 47, 69, 205, 216, 224, 226; legal, 47, 51
Catholic Church, 4, 17, 52, 55, 69, 73–4, 77, 79–80; *see also* Vatican
CDF (Congregation for the Doctrine of the Faith), 68–70, 73, 80
CEDAW (Convention on the Elimination of All Forms of Discrimination Against Women), 3, 13, 17–18, 21, 23–4, 54–5, 234, 249; Committee, 13, 23–4
ceremonies, 34, 164, 187, 190, 200, 207, 221; marriage, 4, 40, 188, 192, 206–7; religious, 34, 38, 179, 224
chastisement, 28, 107
Chesler, Phyllis, 128, 130
Chicago Rabbinical Council, 188, 204, 215
child marriage, 6, 22, 91–104; contemporary practice, 97; forces fighting, 97–100; and Islamic law, 95–7
child support, 192, 218, 266, 271
children, 21–5, 59–60, 113, 179–81, 206, 219–21, 256–63, 265–73; best interests, 211, 216, 219–20
China, 14, 78
Christianity, 15–17, 27–8, 48–9, 57–8; *see also* Catholic Church; Vatican
Christians, 28, 49, 53–4, 56, 93, 179, 185, 190
Church of England, 33–4
circumcisions, 54, 202
civil courts, 7–8, 181–2, 184–5, 189, 193–4, 223–4, 238–9, 241; and rabbinical courts, 202–20
civil divorce, 181, 186, 189, 203, 215, 225–6, 261, 263
civil enforcement, 181, 194
civil law, 7, 32–3, 40, 94, 183, 189–90, 195–6, 218
civil marriages, 2, 4, 34, 38–9, 256
civil preliminaries, 34, 39–40
civil remedies, 184–6
civil rights movement, 126, 128, 134
civil society, 22, 33, 130
classical epistemologies, 111, 115
coercion, 112, 188–9, 205–6, 212, 216; religious, 6, 152–4, 156, 163, 166, 172, 174
coercive authority, 96, 99, 202
colonialism, 4, 47–8, 58, 60
commitments, 4, 8, 15, 32, 36, 139, 145, 211

communal prayer, 123, 126–7, 130–3, 138, 145; women's, 123, 131, 138, 145
communal services, 126–7, 243
communities, 32–3, 37–8, 40–2, 154–5, 167–9, 228–30, 232, 239–43; diasporic, 185; Jewish, 6, 8, 28, 194, 203, 206, 228, 231; national-religious, 157–9, 164; political, 202; religious, 1, 17, 26–7, 41, 145, 168
community workers, 256–7, 259–60, 261, 268
compassion, 15, 17, 53, 235
complementarity, 5, 55, 68–75, 77–84; invention, 69–75, 78; theological anthropology, 71–2, 77; Vatican commitments, 5, 68–84
compromise, 125, 136–7, 139, 143, 166, 269
conciliation, 264, 270, 272
confidentiality, 259, 270
conflicts, 3–4, 129, 134–5, 140, 156, 168–9, 184–5, 267; defined, 1–9; direct, 17, 134; family, 256–7, 270
Congregation for the Doctrine of the Faith, *see* CDF
conscience, 15, 36, 39, 50, 53, 162, 219
consensus, 4, 14, 20, 59, 101, 138, 182, 268
consent, 33–4, 40, 99–100, 179–80, 190, 204–6, 221, 225
conservative rabbinic courts, 211
constitutional law, 13, 15, 132, 134, 138
constitutionalism, 129
contempt, 184, 187–8, 194, 205, 211, 213–15, 229; orders, 229
content jurisdiction, 216–20; custody, 219–20; property, 217–19
contraception, 5, 16, 22–4, 69
contracts, 7, 14, 32, 51, 112, 182–3, 187–8, 191–5; marital, 112, 187, 225; marriage, 8, 181, 186–8, 224, 262; prenuptial, 187, 190, 194–5
control, 24, 40, 58–9, 161–3, 167–8, 172, 232, 242
Convention on the Elimination of All Forms of Discrimination Against Women, *see* CEDAW
conversion, 49, 207, 212
corruption, 91, 93, 95, 205, 209
counsellors, 8, 258, 260, 262–4
couples, 40, 188–9, 206–9, 238–9, 241–2, 259–60, 263–4, 266; same-sex, 33–4, 68, 82
courts, 128, 135–40, 181–3, 186–90, 192–4, 210–12, 215–17, 236–8; American, 7, 182–3, 189–91; appellate, 183, 188; civil, 7–8, 181–2, 184–5, 189, 193–4, 209–11, 215–17, 219–20; hasidic, 155, 175; national, 57–8; rabbinic, *see* rabbinical courts; religious, 185, 210, 216; secular, 57, 188, 205, 209–16, 219–20; Soleimani, 195
criminal law, 2, 55–6, 58, 94
cross-pollination, 262, 271
cultural life, 13, 15, 18
cultural norms, 15, 37, 109–10, 231–2, 262
cultural rights, 15, 19, 24, 54, 58
culture, 2–4, 13–29, 50, 52, 54–5, 102–3, 152, 223–4; political, 95; traditionalist, 15, 25–6
custody, 192, 194, 196, 209–10, 219–20, 261, 265–9

damages, 181, 194, 234, 238–9
daughters, 47, 57, 60, 92, 99, 127, 156, 159–60
dead marriages, 206, 211, 232
deference, 15, 17, 54, 135, 141, 209
democracy, 128, 136, 143, 226
demonstrations, 164, 174
Dershowitz, Alan, 234, 237–8
diaspora, 126, 129, 145, 185
dignity, 13–15, 19–20, 23, 75–7, 125, 131, 136, 140; equal, 68, 75
discrimination, 2–3, 13, 15, 18–25, 36, 54, 60, 161; gender-based, 19, 54, 57, 59, 137, 240, 255; religious, 4, 55
dispute resolution, 271; processes, 269–70, 271
distinctive and complementary qualities of the sexes, 75–8
distress, 54, 82, 152, 170
diversity, 15, 22, 42, 80, 223, 227, 236, 243; of remedies, 236–7
division of family assets, 262, 264–5
divorce, 6–8, 179–81, 183–6, 188–92, 194–6, 203–6, 223–8, 258–65; cases, 7, 23, 185, 187, 210, 216, 225; civil, 181, 186, 189, 203, 215, 225–6, 261, 263; Islamic, 195, 260–1; Jewish, 7, 181, 188–9, 203–6, 209,

211, 215–17, 220; process, 202, 211, 220, 268; religious, 180–1, 202, 204, 209, 261, 263, 265, 271; unilateral, 112
Dodelson case, 240–1
domestic abuse, 180, 231–2, 234, 237, 242–3
dowries, 183, 262, 266, 274
dreadlocks, 5, 57–8
duality, 69, 79, 135
Dworkin, Ronald, 36–7

ecology, human, 69, 81, 83
economic justice, 108, 117
education, 22, 24, 49, 53, 57–8, 98–9, 165, 167; religious, 256, 266, 268
effectiveness, 8, 182, 191, 204, 240–1
egalitarianism, 6–7, 16, 71, 80, 132, 145, 179, 195–6
Egypt, 27, 58
El Salvador, 23–4
emancipation, 96, 180, 202
employment, 13, 21, 57, 165, 172, 185, 202
Endorois, 5, 54
enforceability, 8, 186, 204
enforcement, 7, 22, 182, 189–90, 192, 195, 205, 270; civil, 181, 194
England, *see* United Kingdom
epistemologies, classical, 111, 115
Epstein case, 240–1
equal dignity, 68, 75
equal religious personhood, 17, 27
equality, 4–7, 13, 15–18, 20–4, 26–8, 50–2, 134–5, 223–5; transformative, 13, 59; Vatican commitments, 5, 68–84
equity, 55, 212, 214–15; gender, 108–9, 112
Establishment clause, 192, 210
ethics, 40–1, 108, 115
exclusion, 5, 53, 115, 145, 159, 161, 233, 235; of women, 26, 50, 74
expert witnesses, 8, 184, 187, 257
extortion, 7, 180, 203, 207, 225, 234, 238; get-based, 181, 186, 190, 194, 228
extremists, 153–9, 162–70, 172–5, 183

faith, 1, 3, 57, 117, 183, 185, 225–6, 228; communities, 80; religious, 4, 23, 57
family assets, 179, 262, 264–5; division, 262, 265
family conflicts, 255–6, 270
family disputes, 8, 227; resolution in Montreal, 255–74
family law, 111, 179, 181, 257, 259, 261, 263, 265; civil, 4, 7, 181, 195; Islamic, 96, 108–9, 112–13, 115; Jewish, 7, 179, 188; reform, 80, 108–17; reform, rationales, 109–13
family members, 25, 158, 264
family property, 2, 181, 186
fathers, 47, 52, 57, 96, 99–100, 102, 264, 266–8
Federation of Muslim Women's Associations in Nigeria (FOMWAN), 99–100
Female Genital Mutilation, *see* FGM
feminism, 4, 6–7, 68–9, 73–4, 78–81, 115–16, 127–8, 131; radical, 78, 80
FGM (Female Genital Mutilation), 22, 25, 58–60
fieldwork, 91–2, 224, 228, 231, 240, 249
fiqh, 100–101, 116–17
First Amendment, 127, 134, 183, 188, 192, 194
fiscal empowerment, 113–14
flogging, 23, 100–101
Florida, 182, 184, 186, 192
FOMWAN (Federation of Muslim Women's Associations in Nigeria), 99–100
forced marriage, 22, 25
foreign law bans in United States, 7, 179–96; emergence, 182–4
forum shopping, 209, 212, 258
Francis, Pope, 68, 70, 78, 82–4
fraudulent marriages, 231, 237
free exercise of religion, 127–8, 135, 138
free will, 188, 225
freedom, 15–17, 19–20, 22, 26, 53–4, 129, 138–39, 264–5; fundamental, 18, 20; of religion, 18–19, 26, 28, 36–7, 54, 182, 210, 215; reproductive, 24
Friedman, M., 153, 155, 162, 165, 168–9, 173, 175
fundamentalism, 125, 129, 133, 152, 161–2, 168, 173, 183

Galatians 3:28, 71–2
gangs, 159, 166–8
garden of Eden, 16, 28
gay lobby, 53

gay marriage, 32, 34, 82
gay people, 52–3, 68, 78, 82, 164
gender, 2–5, 45–7, 49, 68–70, 77–9, 81–2, 108–11, 115–17; agenda, 77–8, 80–2; anathamatization, 78–82; discrimination, *see* gender-based discrimination; equality, 1–4, 18, 51, 125–31, 135, 141, 145, 150; equality, and recognition of marriage, 32–42; equity, 108–9, 112; flexibility, 47; hierarchies, 9, 15, 47; identities, 2, 80, 117; inequality, 8, 32, 181, 184, 192, 234; relations, 2–3, 50, 60, 109–10, 115; roles, 47, 59, 114, 116; segregation, 123–5, 142, 150; stereotypes, 8, 18, 50, 58–9, 68, 71, 77, 80; within African context, 46–8
gender-based discrimination, 19, 54, 57, 59, 137, 240, 255
gendered remedies, 223–4, 236, 241; socio-legal, 8, 223, 244
gendered rights, 4, 70, 82
gendered rites, 4, 70, 82
gendered storytelling, 223–4, 239–41, 243–4
gender-sensitive imams, 255–74
get al t'nai, 231, 237
get refusal, socio-legal gendered remedies, 8, 223–44
get-based extortion, 181, 186, 190, 194, 228
girls, 6, 22–3, 25, 96, 98–9, 104, 113, 159–60; young, 6, 59–60, 96, 102
government employees, 128, 134
governments, 22, 39–41, 54, 133–6, 138–9, 141–3, 183, 260–1
graffiti, 156, 158–9, 168, 171
grandmothers, 45–6, 60, 130
grassroots, 91–2, 114, 223, 236, 239, 243
Greenberg, Blu, 237–8
group prayer, 133, 139, 142–3
guardians, 96, 100–1, 129, 135, 219

ḥadīth, 96–7, 100, 103, 110
Hadjiatou Mani case, 59
hafka'ot, 231, 237
HaKirya, 154–6, 159
Halacha, 134–6, 140, 179–89, 194–6, 202–7, 209–11, 215–18, 225–6; administrative jurisdiction, *see* administrative jurisdiction; civil remedies for gender inequality, 184–6; custody, 219–20; interaction and injustice, 204–6; need for Jewish divorce, 206–8; prenuptial agreement, 190, 195, 238; property, 217–19; undertakings in separation and divorce agreements, 189–92; in United States, 179–96
halakhic authorities, 202–3
halakhic marriages, 224, 227–8
harassment, 137, 163–4, 171
haredi, 153, 156–7, 159–65, 169, 172; community, 165, 168–9, 172; extremists/zealots, 153, 163–4, 166, 168, 174; moderate, 165–6, 172; neighborhoods, 153–5, 163–4; population, 154, 156, 158, 163–4, 168; rabbis, 164, 169; society, 153, 157, 161–2, 167, 169, 172–3; women, 159–61, 163, 173
Haredim Sephardim, 155
hasidic courts, 155, 175
Hausaland, 92–4, 102
Haut, Rivka, 127
hazmanot, 228–30
health, 6, 13, 16, 22–4, 28, 159, 165
Hebrew, 134, 175, 237
heresy, 73, 123–4, 127
hierarchies, 16, 47, 50, 72–4, 258; gender, 9, 15, 47
High Court, Israel, 126, 128, 134, 140
Hoffman, Anat, 132, 144
Holy See, *see* Vatican
homosexuality, 5, 53, 69, 79–80
honour, 3–4, 25, 55–6, 113, 139, 161, 227
human ecology, 69, 81, 83
human rights, 1, 3–5, 13–15, 17–21, 23, 25–9, 51–3, 59–61; activists, 1, 52; law, international, 14–16, 21; norms, 1, 4, 53; secular, 26–7; treaties, 13–14, 24, 55; universal, 18; women's rights as, 13–27
Human Rights Council, 21–2
Humanae Vitae, 69, 77
Humanist Society, 39, 41
humanity, 13, 16, 53, 74–6, 80
Humanum Conference, 68, 70–1, 80, 83
husbands, 110–13, 179–81, 186–95, 205–8, 213–18, 224–6, 229–32, 258–64; missing, 180–1; recalcitrant, 225, 229, 232, 238

IBD (International Beit Din), 234, 237–8
ICCPR (International Convention on Civil and Political Rights), 18, 21
ICESCR (International Covenant on Economic, Social and Cultural Rights), 24
ICWoW (International Committee for the Women of the Wall), 128–9, 132, 134–5, 137
identities, religious, 57, 185
ideology, 68, 70, 82, 124; Zionist, 124–5, 130–1
IFL, *see* Islamic family law
iggun, 233–4
ijbār, *see* child marriage
imams, 8, 16; gender-sensitive, 255–74
impact, 4–5, 58, 60, 182–4, 223–6, 230–2, 239–41, 243
imprisonment, 23, 59, 188
independence, 94–5
inequality, 22–3, 25–6, 28, 230, 232, 234, 236, 243–4; gender, 8, 32, 181, 184, 192, 234
injustices, 93, 96, 117, 204–5, 210, 240, 267
intentions, Islamic Law, 108–17
Inter Insigniores, 69, 77
International Beit Din (IBD), 234, 237–8
International Committee for the Women of the Wall, *see* ICWoW
International Convention on Civil and Political Rights, *see* ICCPR
International Covenant on Economic, Social and Cultural Rights (ICESCR), 24
international human rights law, 14–16, 21
intimidation, 103
Islam, 3–5, 15–17, 27–8, 48–9, 55–6, 97–9, 114–15, 256–8
Islamic divorce, 195, 260
Islamic family law (IFL), 96, 108–9, 113, 115
Islamic law, 54, 56, 92, 94, 98–102, 111–15, 117, 182–3; and alternative ethical system, 102–4; and child marriage, 95–7; intentions, 108–17; post-modern, 101–2
Islamic penal law, 91–5
Islamic traditions, 16, 93, 102
Islamists, 92, 97–8, 102, 115, 166
Israel, 6–7, 123–36, 139–45, 152–4, 172, 175, 185, 187–90; High Court, 126, 128, 134, 140; secular law, 134, 150

Jerusalem, 6, 27–8, 123–4, 126–30, 140, 142, 154–5, 164–5
Jewish communities, 6, 8, 28, 194, 203, 206, 228, 231
Jewish divorce, 7, 181, 188–9, 203–6, 209, 211, 215–17, 220; need for, 206–8
Jewish law, *see* Halacha
Jewish marriage, 7, 179, 181, 187, 203, 212
Jewish state, 125, 143, 164, 175
Jewish tradition, 28, 124, 160–1
Jewish women, 129, 134, 183, 203, 223, 226, 230, 232
Jewishness, 125, 207, 212
Jews, 71–3, 124–5, 129, 185, 190, 192, 202–3, 208–9; American, 129, 181, 203; liberal, 184, 188; observant, 185, 210, 224
jihad, 93, 95, 173
John Paul II, Pope, 69, 71–3, 78, 82–3
John XXIII, Pope, 73
journalists, 56, 83, 92, 98
Judaism, 4–5, 15–17, 27–8, 127, 131, 145, 223–4, 226–7; Orthodox, 73, 80, 188, 225–6, 237; Progressive, 132, 169; Reform, 189, 226; *see also* Halakha
judges, 7, 195, 209, 212, 255, 258–9, 261–3, 272, 274
judicial review, 186, 194
jurisdiction, 32, 181–2, 185–6, 188–90, 202–3, 205, 210–13, 215–16; administrative, *see* administrative jurisdiction; content, *see* content jurisdiction; primary, 210–11
jurisprudence, 100, 102, 104, 117, 185, 218
jurisprudential tradition, 101–3

Kaduna, 91
Kano, 91, 94
Kansas, 182, 195
Kenya, 5, 54
ketuba, 187–8, 217, 224–5, 238; *see also* marriage, contracts
khalitza, 232, 248
kherem, 229–30

khul, 261
kiddushei ta'ut, 231, 237
kiddushin, 224, 227–8, 243
knowledge, 97, 114, 207, 224, 238–9, 249, 256–7, 264
Koran, *see* Qu'ran

land, 54, 124, 128, 140, 172, 185
language, 13, 15, 18, 71, 74, 81, 93, 99–100
lawyers, 58–9, 72, 215, 255–7, 259, 261, 263, 265–6, 269, 272, 274
leaders, 93, 124, 143–4, 165–6, 191, 229, 242, 258; religious, 5, 34, 49, 53, 55, 58–9, 168, 237
leadership, 50–1, 129, 140, 169
Leadership Conference of Women Religious (LCWR), 80
Lebanon, 256, 261, 268
legal capacity, 47, 51
legal norms, 9, 262, 271
legal pluralism, 223–4, 228, 236–7, 239, 243–4
legal systems, 132, 140, 195, 202–4, 210, 234, 236–7, 257–9; plural, 6, 17, 46, 237
legitimacy, 50, 93, 102, 127, 133, 175, 216, 221
leverage, 136, 220, 225, 231
liberal Jews, 184, 188
lifestyle, 163–4, 168

madhab, 263
mahr, *see* marital gifts
makom, 124, 142
Maliki School, 92, 96, 100–2
mamzerim, 180, 208, 221, 225
maqāṣid al-sharīʿa approaches, 114–17
marital contracts, 112, 187, 225
marital gifts (*mahr*), 111–12, 183, 195, 262, 265–6, 271, 273–4
marriage, 4, 98–101, 108–14, 179–83, 187–91, 206–8, 217–18, 237–8; ceremonies, 4, 40, 188, 192, 206–7; child, 6, 22, 91–104; civil, 2, 4, 34, 38–9, 256; contracts, 8, 181, 186–8, 224, 262; dead, 206, 211, 232; early, 6, 92; forced, 22, 25; fraudulent, 231, 237; gay, 32, 34, 82; halakhic, 224, 227–8; Jewish, 7, 179, 181, 187, 203, 212; mixed, 267–9; Muslim, 37; non-civil, 39–40; recognition, 32–42; religious, 4, 38, 41, 179, 226, 256; same-sex, 68, 70
media, 123, 129, 227
mediation, 255, 270
mediators, 255–6, 258, 266, 269–70, 272; accredited, 255–6, 264–6, 269, 271, 272
mehitza, 128, 133, 141, 143
mercy, 82, 107, 225
mesuravot get, *see get* refusal
metaphor, 6, 123–44
Minkin case, 187–8
minorities, religious, 26, 57, 185
Mishnah, 217–18
missing husbands, 180–1
mixed marriages, 267–9
models, 38, 40, 71, 83, 109, 117, 179
modernity, 1, 130, 153, 167
modesty, 3, 7, 153, 156–7, 159, 161–3, 168–9, 173; norms, 160, 162; significance of stringent supervision, 160–3; signs, 156, 158, 169; stands, 158
money, 98–9, 196, 242, 260, 262, 269, 273
monogamy, 23, 33, 55, 202
monotheisms, 15–17
Montreal, 1, 8, 255–74
morality, 23, 40–1, 55, 93, 102, 125
Morocco, 257
Moses, 27, 187–8
mosques, 59, 93, 256
mothers, 52, 55, 57, 60, 76, 79, 266–8
motives, 160, 162–3, 265
multiculturalism, 227, 236
Muslims, 8, 56–7, 95, 108–11, 114, 173, 182–3, 185–6; *see also* Islam

Namibia, 51
national-religious community, 157–9, 164
negotiation, 136, 181, 206, 209, 231, 263–5, 271–3
neighborhoods, 154–8, 163, 165
Neturei Karta, 165, 175
New York State, 186, 190, 211, 217; "get" laws, 186
Niger, 59
Nigeria, 6, 46, 93–4, 96–8; Kaduna, 91; Kano, 91, 94; Northern, 1, 5–6, 91–107; Sokoto, 91, 93–5, 102; Zamfara State, 92–3; Zaria, 91, 95, 98

Nigerians, 92–4, 97, 103–4; Northern, 91, 93–4, 97, 104, 107
non-civil marriages, 39–40
non-religious beliefs, 36, 39–41
norms, 15, 19, 32, 136–7, 161–2, 172, 267, 271; cultural, 15, 37, 109–10, 231–2, 262; human rights, 1, 4, 53; legal, 9, 261, 271; modesty, 160, 162; religious, 3, 7, 15–16, 21, 52, 258–9, 261–2, 271; traditional, 172–3
Northern Nigeria, 1, 5–6, 91–107; sharī'ah revolution, 92–3
Northern Nigerians, 91, 93–4, 97, 104, 107

observance, 58, 152, 169, 219, 223–4, 228, 230, 232
observant Jews, 185, 210, 224
OIC (Organisation of Islamic Cooperation), 5, 20, 55
Old Testament, 16
Ontario, 194–5, 227, 238–9, 249
openness, 47, 167, 172
ordination, women, 5, 69, 74
Organisation of Islamic Cooperation, *see* OIC
Organization for the Resolution for Agunot, 231
Organization of Islamic Cooperation, 79
Organization of the Islamic Conference, 79–80
Orthodox Judaism, 73, 80, 188, 225–6, 237
Orthodox ketubah, 187–8
orthodoxy, 91, 125, 129, 133, 143, 145, 228
ostracism, 60, 229, 232, 241
other, the, 163–4, 166, 172
Oyewumi, O., 46, 48

parents, 45, 59, 99, 181, 219, 257, 261, 266, 268–70
parity, 73–4
Parks, Rosa, 126, 141
patriarchy, 15–17, 51, 71, 127, 129, 134–5, 141, 145; religious, *see* religious patriarchy
Paul VI, Pope, 69, 73–4, 77
penal law, Islamic, 91–5
Pentecostal churches, 49–50
Persona Humana, 69, 77
philosophical beliefs, 39, 41
physical violence, 6, 28, 153, 159–60, 172
pilgrimage, 127, 133
Pius XI, Pope, 73
Pius XII, Pope, 73–5
plural legal systems, 6, 17, 46, 237
pluralism, 2, 48, 125, 236; legal, 223–4, 228, 236–7, 239, 243–4; religious, 126, 130–1
police, 55–6, 59, 126, 133–4, 139, 141–2, 170–2, 174
polygamy, 22–3, 25
polygyny, 54–5
Popes: Benedict XVI, 69, 71–3, 78–83; Francis, 68, 70, 78, 82–4; John Paul II, 69, 71–3, 78, 82–3; John XXIII, 73; Pius XI, 73; Pius XII, 73–5
positionalities, 223–4
poverty, 91, 95–8
power, 49–51, 137–9, 142, 194, 208–10, 240, 243, 263–4
practices, religious, 2, 18, 22, 34, 37, 131, 137, 145
prayer groups, women's, 123, 127, 132–3, 141–2
pregnancies, 22–4, 55, 60
preliminaries, civil, 34, 39–40
prenup, 191–2, 215
prenuptial agreements, 191, 194, 200, 204, 217, 238; halachic, 190, 194–5, 238; RCA, 192, 194, 220, 239
prenuptial contracts, 187, 190, 194–5
pressure, 130, 140, 143, 157–8, 168–9, 264, 266, 270
priests, 16, 39, 41, 53, 70, 73, 83
primary jurisdiction, 210–11
private sphere, 1, 145, 226, 228
privileges, 2, 50–2, 109, 116–17
Progressive Judaism, 132, 170
prohibition of cultural and religious practices discriminating against women and girls, 22–5
property, 15, 23, 51, 55, 96, 194–5, 213, 217–19; family, 2, 181, 186; *see also* assets
Protestantism, 50, 73
public opinion, 21, 128–30, 139
public sphere, 6, 32, 58, 126, 143–4, 170, 175, 226
punishment, 16, 56–7, 91, 95, 100–101
punishments, stoning, 22–3, 25, 91, 93–5, 100–101, 103

Quebec, 1, 8, 194, 255–74
Qur'an, 16, 28, 91, 95–7, 99–101, 103, 110–11, 113

Rabbinical Council of America, *see* RCA
rabbinical courts, 7–8, 179, 181, 184–94, 209–13, 215, 228–30, 238–9; administrative jurisdiction, 211–12; agreements to arbitrate disputes before, 186–9; American, 8, 185; Boston, 204, 207, 212, 213, 219; and civil courts, 202–20; conservative, 211; interaction and injustice, 204–6; need for Jewish divorce, 206–8; reputable, 209, 213–14; Toronto, 228–30, 242–3
rabbis, 123–8, 134–6, 164, 168, 179–80, 225–35, 238, 241–2; haredi, 164, 169
radical zealots, 154, 163, 165–8
rage, 134, 235
Ramah A, 154–7, 164–5
Ramah B, 154–6, 159–60, 163, 165
rape, 17, 22–3, 25, 55, 112
Rastafarianism, 4–5, 57–8
Ratzinger, Cardinal Joseph, *see* Benedict XVI
Ratzinger Report, 69, 78
RCA (Rabbinical Council of America), 190–1; prenuptial agreement, 192, 194, 220, 239
recalcitrant husbands, 225, 229, 232, 238
recognition of marriage, 32–42
reconciliation, 189, 259–60
reform, 9, 23, 113, 115–16, 127, 129, 131, 136, 143–4; family law, 80, 108–17; movements, 17, 131–2, 145
Reform Judaism, 189, 226
registered building, 4, 34, 37
registration, 34, 38–40
religion: Africa, 48–51; definition, 35–7; free exercise of, 127, 135, 138; freedom of, 18–19, 26, 28, 36–7, 54, 182, 210, 215; monotheistic, 15–16; *see also Introductory Note*
religious arbitration, 227, 238
religious authority, 8, 14, 16, 173, 179, 185, 190, 195; limits, 58–60
religious beliefs, 22, 26, 36, 45, 48, 54, 183, 188
religious ceremonies, 34, 38, 179, 224
religious coercion, 6, 152–75
religious communities, 1, 17, 26–7, 41, 145, 168
religious counsellors, 255–72; consulted by whom and why, 259–61; know-how compared to lay interveners, 263–70; possible overlap with legal system, 262–3
religious courts, 185, 210, 216; *see also* rabbinical courts
religious discrimination, 4, 55
religious divorce, 180–1, 202, 204, 209, 261, 263, 265, 271
religious education, 256, 266–7, 269
religious faith, 4, 23, 57
religious freedom, *see* freedom, of religion
religious leaders, 5, 34, 49, 53, 55, 58–9, 168, 237
religious life, 124, 127, 132, 141
religious lifestyle, 130–1, 135
religious marriages, 4, 38, 41, 179, 226, 256
religious minorities, 26, 57, 185
religious norms, 3, 7, 15–16, 21, 52, 257–8, 261–2, 271
religious observance, 58, 152, 223
religious patriarchy, 15–17, 27; and human rights, 17–22
religious personhood, equal, 17, 27
religious pluralism, 126, 130–1
religious practices, 2, 18, 22, 34, 37, 131, 137, 145
religious premises, 40–1
religious principles, 1, 108, 187, 214–15
religious rights, 53–4, 57
religious rituals, 133, 143, 145, 210
religious social movements, 6, 123–44
religious traditions, 4, 19, 185
religious values, 3, 26, 114
religious weddings, 40–1
religious worship, 34, 126, 129–30, 132, 134, 145; public, 2, 35
religious zealotry, *see* zealotry
religious/secular divide in English marriage law, 33–5; overcoming, 37–40
remarriage, 185, 189, 202–3, 206, 211, 221, 225, 265
remedies, 7–8, 182, 184, 188–9, 223, 227–9, 231–41, 243; diversity of, 236–7; socio-legal, 223, 236, 244; socio-legal gendered, 8, 223, 244
reproductive health services, 24–5
reproductive rights, 24, 78, 80, 99
resources, 6–7, 17, 60, 77, 114, 174, 212
responsibilities, 20–1, 51, 55, 81, 110, 181, 237, 262

rights, 2, 14–16, 18, 51–4, 135–6, 181–2, 192–4, 263–6; cultural, 15, 19, 24, 54, 58; gendered, 4, 70, 82; human, *see* human rights; religious, 53–4, 57; reproductive, 24, 78, 80, 99; sexual, 79–81
rites, 2, 34, 54, 129–30; gendered, 4, 70, 82
rituals, 2, 5, 130, 133, 141, 143, 145, 210
Robinson Arch, 123–5, 136, 140–1, 143
role models, 161, 168
rule of law, 125–6, 135, 139, 142, 226

same-sex couples, 33–4, 68, 82
same-sex marriage, 68, 70
Scientology, 4, 35–7
Scotland, 39–40
secular courts, 57, 188, 205, 209–16, 219–20; administrative jurisdiction, 210–11
secular human rights, 26–7
secular Israeli law, 134–5, 150
secular law, 2, 68–9, 75, 126, 134, 140, 216–17, 220; limits, 58–60; shaping, 78, 81
secular society, 155, 203, 236
secular state, 135, 226
secularism, 13–14
segregation, 125–6, 141, 143, 146, 231, 239; gender, 123–5, 142, 150
seiruvim, 228–30, 241
self-destruction, 81
self-narration, 223, 236, 239–41
sensitivity, 8, 115, 129, 138–9, 272
separation, 125, 132–3, 135, 138–9, 189, 191, 193–4, 259; agreements, 190
separation of church and state, 125, 132, 135, 138–9
services, communal, 126–7, 243
sex stereotypes, *see* gender, stereotypes
sexism, benevolent, 111
sexual rights, 79–81
sexuality, 47–8, 52, 55, 59, 68, 108–9, 116, 161–3
Shabbat, 163
sharī'ah, 5–6, 56–7, 91–8, 100–1, 104, 183–6, 271, 274; history, 93–4
Sharia law, 6, 57, 183–4, 186, 194–5, 227
silence, 21, 100, 161–2, 232, 234–5, 239, 241–2
silencing, 161, 223, 228, 232–5, 241, 243–4
sins, 3, 16, 153, 162
siruv get, *see get* refusal
slavery, 15, 22, 28, 33, 48, 58–60, 71–2, 75
Sobel, Judge Moshe, 140, 142–3, 150
social movements, 124, 128–9
social workers, 255–7, 259, 265, 267
society: African, 46, 48–9, 60; haredi, 153, 157, 161–2, 167, 169, 172–3; Muslim, 28, 113, 115
socio-legal gendered remedies to *get* refusal, 8, 223–44
socio-legal remedies, 223, 236–44
Sokoto, 91, 93–5, 102; Caliphate, 93–5, 102
soldiers, 7, 166, 172
Soleimani case, 195–6
sons, 51, 82, 102, 160, 163
South Africa, 49, 55, 145, 186
Special Rapporteurs, 16, 19–20, 24, 26
spousal relations, 6, 108–17
spouses, 111, 113, 213, 215, 229, 258, 260–5, 271
Stanton, E.C., 16
status quo, 109, 135–7, 141, 240
Stein, Edith, 72–3
stereotypes, 8, 18, 50, 58–9, 68, 71, 77, 80; challenging, 255–74
stoning, 22–3, 25, 91, 93–5, 100–1, 103
storytelling, 224, 240–1, 243; gendered, 223–4, 239–41, 243–4
subordination, 46, 71, 78
Sudan, 53, 55–7, 94
supervision, 161–3, 191, 194; stringent, 161–3
support organizations, 233–4; secondary, 233
symmetry, 26
sympathy, 102, 126, 133
synagogues, 123, 127, 132–3, 136, 200, 230, 239, 241
Syria, 183, 261

tallit, 6, 123, 140, 142
Talmud, 180
Tennessee, 182–3
terrorism, 165, 169, 183
theology, 49, 69, 74–5, 78, 83, 144
Thomas Aquinas, 70–1

Torah, 6, 28, 123, 145, 202, 248; scrolls, 6, 127, 133, 142, 145
Toronto, 1, 223–4, 226, 228–30, 232–3, 235, 237–42, 248
tradition, 7, 9, 18–19, 102, 108, 110, 126–7, 236–7; jurisprudential, 101–3; religious, 4, 19, 185
traditional norms, 173
traditional values, 17, 20–1
traditionalist cultures, 15, 25–6
traditions: Islamic, 16, 93, 102; Jewish, 28, 124, 161
transformative change, 26–7
transformative equality, 13, 59
transparency, 219
transsexuality, 78, 80
trousers, 55–6

UDHR, *see* Universal Declaration of Human Rights
unilateral religious divorce, 260
United Kingdom, 33–4, 37, 39–40, 45, 186
United Nations: Human Rights Council, 21–2; Special Rapporteurs, 16, 19–20, 24, 26
United States, 7, 127–30, 132, 134, 136, 205, 209, 233; agreements to arbitrate disputes before a rabbinical court, 186–9; First Amendment, 127, 134, 183, 188, 192, 194; foreign law bans, 7, 179–96; foreign law bans, emergence, 182–4; Halacha, 179–96
Universal Declaration of Human Rights (UDHR), 14–15, 20–1
universality, 19–21, 48
Uthman Dan Fodio, 93, 102

values: religious, 3, 26, 115; traditional, 17, 20–1
Van Klinken, A., 50
vandalism, 6, 156, 172
Vatican, 53, 57; commitments to complementarity and equality, 5, 68–84
verbal abuse, 6, 134, 153
violence, 1, 6, 20, 22, 24–5, 72, 142, 152–75; physical, 6, 28, 153, 159–60, 172
virginity, 25, 73, 100
von Hildebrand, Dietrich, 69, 72–3

Wall, 123–44
wedding halls, 156–7
widows, 60, 248
wilāyat, 96
witchcraft, 25, 46, 58, 60
witnesses, 34, 92, 107, 112, 173, 207–8, 212, 221
wives, 111–13, 179–81, 186–95, 206–7, 213–15, 217–19, 259–63, 265–6
women, *see Introductory Note*
women cardinals, 83
Women of the Wall, 6, 123–45, 150
workplaces, 57–8, 137

young girls, 6, 59–60, 96, 102

ZABLA, 209, 212, 214
Zamfara State, 92–3
Zaria, 91, 95, 98
zealots, 152–3, 156, 160–1, 163–8, 173–4
Zimbabwe, 47, 50, 52, 60
Zionism, 124, 130–1, 134, 137, 164, 167, 172, 175

For Product Safety Concerns and Information please contact our EU
representative GPSR@taylorandfrancis.com
Taylor & Francis Verlag GmbH, Kaufingerstraße 24, 80331 München, Germany

www.ingramcontent.com/pod-product-compliance
Ingram Content Group UK Ltd.
Pitfield, Milton Keynes, MK11 3LW, UK
UKHW022011180926
475701UK00003B/304
* 9 7 8 0 3 6 7 5 9 7 0 7 8 *